PALAZZO ORSINI

Ingresso al Cassero

The original structure was erected in the 12th century, at the behest of the family of Count Aldobrandeschi di Sovana. In 1313, Romano Orsini received it in the dowry of his future wife, Anastasia, daughter of the Countess Margherita Aldobrandeschi. Thus, the building became the family's residence and a fortress was constructed around it, consisting of three circular towers connected by a revetment. In 1465, the existing Palazzo Orsini was built to celebrate the wedding between Niccolò III Orsini and Elena Conti di Montalcino. Inside, the greatest Sienese, Perugian and Marchigian artists were commissioned to execute the decorations. In 1520, Gianfranco Orsini hired Antonio da Sangallo the Younger to come up with a design for the plans of the new fortress, adapted to the military techniques of the times. In 1604, the Earldom of Pitigliano was handed over to the Medici family by Count Giovanni Antonio Orsini and with this, Palazzo Orsini. In 1737, Palazzo Orsini became the property of the Lorena family of the Grand Duchy of Tuscany. The Lorena family altered the original internal divisions of the rooms and later, in 1793, the family sold the residence to the Bishop of Sovana for his permanent residence. In 1861-65 the original entrance to the fortress was altered with construction of a residential building, in the shelter of the keep.

The visitor reaches Palazzo Orsini from Piazza della Repubblica and taking the flight of steps. From here, another series of steps leads up to the elegant internal courtyard, in the middle of which still stands the hexagonal travertine wellhead decorated with the family crests of the Earldom of Pitigliano and the Count Niccolò III. From here, the visitor enters Palazzo Orsini through a large entrance door in richly carved travertine stone that dates back to 1490. The architrave shows two decorations: above, upturned callipers bearing the inscription TEMPUS ORDO NUMERUS ET MENSURA and below, two hands holding tight to the collar of a mastiff fitted with spikes and a ribbon bearing the message PRIUS MORI QUAM FALLERE extolling the military prowess of Count Niccolò III who was called by the Republic of Venice in 1495 to act as Field Governor of the militias.

Inside, Palazzo Orsini holds an extensive collection of art and objects. Its twenty halls display works by master silversmiths and goldsmiths (from the 14th to the 20th centuries), coins, wooden sculptures (among which, the statue of *Niccolò III in full armour* and *"Madonna with Child"* by **Jacopo della Quercia**), paintings on panel or canvas (including works by **Guiodoccio Cozzarelli, Alessandro Casolani, Francesco Zuccarelli, and Pietro Aldi**), priceless fabrics (from the 15th to the 17th centuries), stone materials, manuscripts and historic books (the museum also holds a historic book library). Palazzo Orsini has retained many of its original ceilings and 15th-century decorations in the original halls (with depiction of the members of the Orsini Family). On the tour of the home, we reach the towers, the keep and the area for production activities (the olive press).

Madonna con Bambino - Jacopo della Quercia

Stemma della Famiglia Orsini di Pitigliano

Relax...

Reminisce...

...Rejoice

Country Resort - Restaurant

BOSCO della SPINA

Your country home in Tuscany

Lupompesi - Murlo - Siena - Tuscany
www.boscodellaspina.com bsturist@boscodellaspina.com
Ph. +39-0577-814605 Fax. +39-0577-814606

Castello di Lamole

Lamole Castle has been overlooking the Chianti hills since the 13th century, in a panoramic spot at 600 m altitude, surrounded by vineyards, chestnut and oak woods. The apartments have been made out of castle rooms with a special attention for the character and charm of the old fabric and they are all furnished with antique furniture and authentic country style tuscan.

In the lovely small restaurant called "Aia dei Canti" you can taste the typical dishes of Tuscan tradition, made as they used to, all the old country recipes with their simple ingredients, accompanied by the most prestigious, select wines from the Chianti area and the whole of Tuscany, including the renowned Castello di Lamole wines, the "Brando della Mole" Sangiovese, made as a pure wine and refined in oak carats and the white "Lauro di Lama" Chardonnay, together with the castle grappas, honey and extra virgin olive oil. Marasco Family and the singer Riccardo Marasco by singing popular music, will be your vacation unforgettable.

50022 Greve in Chianti
(Florence - Italy)
Via di Lamole 80/82, Loc. Lamole
Tel. +39 055 630498, +39 055 8547006
Fax +39 055 630611
E-mail: info@castellodilamole.it
www.castellodilamole.it

AUTHENTIC
Tuscany

TOURING CLUB OF ITALY

Touring Club Italiano
President and Chairman: *Roberto Ruozi*
General Manager: *Guido Venturini*

Touring Editore
Managing Director: *Alfieri Lorenzon*
Editorial Director: *Michele D'Innella*

International Department
Fabio Pittella
fabio.pittella@touringclub.it

Senior Editor: *Gino Cervi*
Editor: *Monica Maraschi*
Writer and Researcher: *Banca Dati Turistica*
Translation: *Elisabeth Poore*
Maps: *Touring Club Italiano*
Design and layout: *Studio Gatelli, Milano*
Cover photo: *G. Sosio*

Advertising Manager: *Claudio Bettinelli*
Local Advertising: *Progetto*
www.progettosrl.it - info@progettosrl.it

Prepress: *Emmegi Multimedia, Milano*
Printing and Binding: *CPM, Casarile*

Distribution
USA/CAN – *Publishers Group West*
UK/Ireland – *Portfolio Books*

Touring Club Italiano, corso Italia 10, 20122 Milano
www.touringclub.it
© 2005 Touring Editore, Milan

Code K7l
ISBN 88 – 365 – 3297 – 7

Printed in February 2005

SUMMARY

WHAT IS THE TOURING CLUB OF ITALY?

Long Tradition, Great Prestige

For over 110 years, the Touring Club of Italy (TCI) has offered travelers the most detailed and comprehensive source of travel information available on Italy. The Touring Club of Italy was founded in 1894 with the aim of developing the social and cultural values of tourism and promoting the conservation and enjoyment of the country's national heritage, landscape and environment.

Advantages of Membership

Today, TCI offers a wide rage of travel services to assist and support members with the highest level of convenience and quality. Now you can discover the unique charms of Italy with a distinct insider's advantage.

Enjoy exclusive money saving offers with a TCI membership. Use your membership card for discounts in thousands of restaurants, hotels, spas, campgrounds, museums, shops and markets.

These Hotel Chains offer preferred rates and discounts to TCI members!

How to Join

It's quick and easy to join.
Apply for your membership online at
www.touringclub.it
Your membership card will arrive within
three weeks and is valid for discounts
across Italy for the entire year.
Get your card before you go and start
saving as soon as you arrive.
Euro 25 Annual Membership fee
includes priority mail postage for
membership card and materials.
Just one use of the card will more than
cover the cost of membership.

Benefits

- Exclusive car rental rates with Hertz
- Discounts at select Esso gas stations
- 20% discount on TCI guidebooks
and maps purchased in TCI bookstores
or directly online at
www.touringclub.com
- Preferred rates and discounts available
at thousands of locations in Italy: Hotels -
B&B's - Villa Rentals - Campgrounds -TCI
Resorts - Spas - Restaurants - Wineries -
Museums - Cinemas - Theaters - Music
Festivals - Shops - Craft Markets - Ferries -
Cruises - Theme Parks - Botanical Gardens

Italy is known throughout the world for the quantity and quality of its art treasures and for its natural beauty, but it is also famous for its inimitable lifestyle and fabulous cuisine and wines. Although it is a relatively small country, Italy boasts an extremely varied culture and multifarious traditions and customs. The information and suggestions in this brief section will help foreign tourists not only to understand certain aspects of Italian life, but also to solve the everyday difficulties and the problems of a practical nature that inevitably crop up during any trip. This practical information is included in brief descriptions of various topics: public transport and how to purchase tickets; suggestions on how to drive in this country; the different types of rooms and accommodation in hotels; hints on how to use mobile phones and communication in general. This is followed by useful advice on how to meet your everyday needs and on shopping, as well as information concerning the cultural differences in the various regions. Lastly, there is a section describing the vast range of restaurants, bars, wine bars and pizza parlors.

TRANSPORTATION

From the airport to the city

Public transportation in major cities is easily accessible and simple to use. Both Malpensa Airport in Milan and Fiumicino Airport in Rome have trains and buses linking them to the city centers. At Malpensa, you can take a bus to the main train station or a train to Cadorna train station and subway stop.

Subways, buses, and trams

Access to the subways, buses, and trams requires a ticket (tickets are not sold on board but can be purchased at most newsstands and tobacco shops). The ticket is good for one ride and sometimes has a time limit (in the case of buses and trams). When you board a bus or tram, you are required to stamp your previously-acquired ticket in the time-stamping machine. Occasionally, a conductor will board the bus or tram and check everyone's ticket. If you haven't got one, or if it has not been time-stamped, you will have to pay a steep fine.

Trains

The Ferrovie dello Stato (Italian Railways) is among the best and most modern railway systems in Europe. Timetables and routes can be consulted and reservations can be made online at www.trenitalia.com. Many travel agents can also dispense tickets and help you plan your journey. Hard-copy schedules can be purchased at all newsstands and most bookstores.

Automated ticket machines, which include easy-to-use instructions in English, are available in nearly all stations. They can be used to check schedules, makes reservations, and purchase tickets.

Many of the express trains need to be reserved in advance. When you reserve a ticket on a Eurostar express train, for example, or the Pendolino, Italy's high-speed train, you will be assigned a seat number. Note that reservations must be made at least one day in advance and that you will not be allowed to board a train where a reservation is required if you haven't got one.

Local trains (classified as "Interregionale", "Diretto" or "Regionale") require a simple ticket, but express Eurocity and Intercity trains require a supplementary ticket ("supplemento"). Almost all of them carry both first- and second-class cars. Only a few ("Locale") usually are second-class only.

All tickets must be time-stamped before boarding: there are numerous time-stamping machines in every station (failure to do so will result in a moderate fine).

Since 1 November 2004 tickes cannot be purchaset on board from the conductor.

Taxis

Taxis are a convenient but expensive way to travel in Italian cities. There are taxi stands scattered throughout major cities. You cannot hail taxis on the street in Italy, but you can reserve taxis, in advance or immediately, by phone: consult the yellow pages for the number or ask your hotel reception desk or maitre d'hotel to call for you.

Taxi drivers have the right to charge you a supplementary fee for every piece of luggage they transport, as well as evening surcharges.

Driving

Especially when staying in the countryside, driving is a safe and convenient way to travel through Italy and its major cities. And while it is best avoided for obvious reasons, driving in the cities is not as difficult as it may seem or may have been reported to be. It is important to be aware of street signs and speed limits, and many cities have zones where only limited traffic is allowed in order to accommodate pedestrians.

Speed limits in Italy are: 50 km/h in built-up areas, 90 km/h on the open road, 110 km/h on expressways (or dual carriageways) and 130 kmph on freeways (or motorways, where tolls are paid). Parklights are compulsory in the daytime on the open road; headlights are compulsory day and night on freeways or motorways.

In case of an accident, you are not allowed to get out of your car unless you are wearing a special, high-visibility, reflective jacket.

The town streets are patrolled by the Polizia Municipale (municipal police). The roads outside cities are patrolled by the Carabinieri (the Italian Military Police): they may set up road blocks where they may ask you to stop by holding out a small red sign. Steep fines are given for not wearing your seatbelt (which is obligatory), for overcrowding a car (most vehicles are allowed to accommodate 4-5 persons maximum), or for using a cellular phone while driving (which is prohibited). Although an international driver's license is not required in Italy, it is advisable. ACI and similar associations provide this service to members.

The fuel distribution network is reasonably distributed all over the territory. All service stations have unleaded gasoline ("benzina verde") and diesel fuel ("gasolio"). Opening time is 7am to12:30pm and 3pm to 7:30pm; on motorways the service is 24 hours a day.

Hotels

In Italy it is common practice for the reception desk to register your passport, and only registered guests are allowed to use the rooms. This is mere routine, done for security reasons, and there is no need for concern.

All hotels use the official star classification system, from 5-star luxury hotel to 1 star accommodation.

Room rates are based on whether they are for single ("camera singola") or double ("camera doppia") occupancy. In every room you will find a list of the hotel rates (generally on the back of the door). While 4- and 5-star hotels have double beds, most hotels have only single beds. Should you want a double bed, you have to ask for a "letto matrimoniale". All hotels have rooms with bathrooms; only 1-star establishments usually have only shared bathrooms.

Most hotel rates include breakfast ("prima colazione"), but you can request to do without it, thus reducing the rate. Breakfast is generally served in a communal room and comprises a buffet with pastries, bread with butter and jam, cold cereals, fruit, yoghurt, coffee, and fruit juice. Some hotels regularly frequented by foreign tourists will also serve other items such as eggs for their American and British guests.

The hotels for families and in tourist localities also offer "mezza pensione", or half board, in which breakfast and dinner are included in the price.

It's always a good idea to check when a hotel's annual closing period is, especially if you are planning a holiday by the sea.

Farm stays

Located only in the countryside, and generally on a farm, "agriturismo" – a network of farm holiday establishments – is part of a growing trend in Italy to honor local gastronomic and wine traditions, as well as countryside traditions. These farms offer meals prepared with ingredients cultivated exclusively on site: garden-grown vegetables, homemade cheese and local recipes. Many of these places also provide lodging, one of the best ways to experience the "genuine" Italian lifestyle.

Bed & Breakfast

This form of accommodation provides bed and breakfast in a private house, and in the last few years has become much more widespread in Italy. There are over 5,000 b&bs, classified in 3 categories, and situated both in historic town centers, as well as in the outskirts and the countryside. Rooms for guests are always well-furnished, but not all of them have en suite bathrooms.

It is well-recommended to check the closing of the open-all-year accommodation services and restaurants, because they could have a short break during the year (usually no longer than a fortnight).

Nearly everyone in Italy owns a cellular phone. Although public phones are still available, they seem to be ever fewer and farther between. If you wish to use public phones, you will find them in subway stops, bars, along the street, and phone centers generally located in the city center. Phone cards and pre-paid phone cards can be purchased at most newsstands and tobacco shops, and can also be acquired at automated tellers.

For European travelers, activating personal cellular coverage is relatively simple, as it is in most cases for American and Australian travelers as well. Contact your mobile service provider for details.

Cellular phones can also be rented in Italy from TIM, the Italian national phone company. For information, visit its website at www.tim.it. When traveling by car through the countryside, a cellular phone can really come in handy.

Note that when dialing in Italy, you must always dial the prefix (e.g., 02 for Milan, 06 for Rome) even when making a local call. For cellular phones, however, the initial zero is always dropped.

Freephone numbers always start with "800". For calls abroad from Italy, it's a good idea to buy a special pre-paid international phone card, which is used with a PIN code.

Internet access

Cyber cafés have sprung up all over Italy and today you can find one on nearly every city block. The Italian national phone company, TIM, has also begun providing internet access at many of its public phone centers.

EATING AND DRINKING

The bar

The Italian "bar" is a multi-faceted, all-purpose establishment for drinking, eating and socializing, where you can order an espresso, have breakfast, and enjoy a quick sandwich for lunch or even a hot meal. You can often buy various items here (sometimes even stamps, cigarettes, phone cards, etc.). Bear in mind that table service ("servizio a tavola") includes a surcharge. At most bars, if you choose to sit, a waiter will take your order. Every bar should have a list of prices posted behind or near the counter; if the bar offers table service, the price list should also include the extra fee for this.

Lunch at bars will include, but is not limited to, "panini," sandwiches with crusty bread, usually with cured meats such as "prosciutto" (salt-cured ham), "prosciutto cotto" (cooked ham), and cheeses such as mozzarella topped with tomato and basil. Then there are "tramezzini" (finger sandwiches) with tuna, cheese, or vegetables, etc. Often the "panini" and other savory sandwiches (like stuffed flatbread or "focaccia") are heated before being served. Naturally, the menu at bars varies according to the region: in Bologna you will find "piadine" (flatbread similar to pita) with Swiss chard; in Palermo there are "arancini" (fried rice balls stuffed with ground meat); in Genoa you will find that even the most unassuming bar serves some of the best "focaccia" in all Italy. Some bars also include a "tavola calda". If you see this sign in a bar window, it means that hot dishes like pasta and even entrées are served.

A brief comment on coffee and cappuccino: Italians never serve coffee with savory dishes or sandwiches, and they seldom drink cappuccino outside of breakfast (although they are happy to serve it at any time).

While English- and Irish-type pubs are frequented by beer lovers and young people in Italy, there are also American bars where long drinks and American cocktails are served.

Breakfast at the bar

Breakfast in Italy generally consists of some type of pastry, most commonly a "brioche" – a croissant either filled with cream or jam, or plain – and a cappuccino or espresso. Although most bars do not offer American coffee, you can ask for a "caffè lungo" or "caffè americano", both of which resemble the American coffee preferred by the British and Americans. Most bars have a juicer to make a "spremuta", freshly squeezed orange or grapefruit juice.

Lunch and Dinner

As with all daily rituals in Italy, food is prepared and meals are served according to local customs (e.g., in the North they prefer rice and butter, in South and Central Italy they favor pasta and olive oil). Wine is generally served at mealtime, and while finer restaurants have excellent wine lists (some including vintage wines), ordering the house table wine generally brings good results (a house Chianti to accompany your Florentine steak in Tuscany, a sparkling Prosecco paired with your creamed stockfish and polenta in Venice, a dry white wine with pasta dressed with sardines and wild fennel fronds in Sicily). Mineral water is also commonly served at meals and can be "gassata" (sparkling) or "naturale" (still).

The most sublime culinary experience in Italy is achieved by matching the local foods with the appropriate local wines: wisdom dictates that a friendly waiter will be flattered by your request for his recommendation on what to eat and drink. Whether at an "osteria" (a tavern), a "trattoria" (a home-style restaurant), or a "ristorante" (a proper restaurant), the service of lunch and dinner generally consists of – but is not limited to – the following: "antipasti" or appetizers; "primo piatto" or first course, i.e., pasta, rice, or soup; "secondo piatto" or main course, i.e., meat or seafood; "contorno" or side-dish, served with the main course, i.e., vegetables or salad; "formaggi", "frutta", and "dolci", i.e., cheeses, fruit, and dessert; caffè or espresso coffee, perhaps spiked with a shot of grappa.

The pizzeria

The pizzeria is in general one of the most economical, democratic, and satisfying culinary experiences in Italy. Everyone eats at the pizzeria: young people,

families, couples, locals and tourists alike. Generally, each person orders her/his own pizza, and while the styles of crust and toppings will vary from region to region (some of the best pizzas are served in Naples and Rome), the acid test of any pizzeria is the Margherita, topped simply with cheese and tomato sauce. Beer, sparkling or still water, and Coca Cola are the beverages commonly served with pizza. Some restaurants include a pizza menu, but most establishments do not serve pizza at lunchtime.

The wine bar (enoteca)

More than one English-speaking tourist in Italy has wondered why the wine bar is called an enoteca in other countries and the English term is used in Italy: the answer lies somewhere in the mutual fondness that Italians and English speakers have for one another. Wine bars have become popular in recent years in the major cities (especially in Rome, where you can find some of the best). The wine bar is a great place to sample different local wines and eat a light, tapas-style dinner.

CULTURAL DIVERSITY

Whenever you travel, not only are you a guest of your host country, but you are also a representative of your home country. As a general rule, courtesy, consideration, and respect are always appreciated by guests and their hosts alike. Italians are famous for their hospitality and experience will verify this felicitous stereotype: perhaps nowhere else in Europe are tourists and visitors received more warmly.

Italy is a relatively "new" country. Its borders, as we know them today, were established only in 1861 when it became a monarchy under the House of Savoy. After WWII, Italy became a Republic and now it is one of the member states of the European Union.

One of the most fascinating aspects of Italian culture is that, even as a unified country, local tradition still prevails over a universally Italian national identity. Some jokingly say that the only time that Venetians, Milanese, Florentines, Neapolitans, and Sicilians feel like Italians is when the national football team plays in international competitions. From their highly localized dialects to the foods they eat, from their religious celebration to their politics, Italians proudly maintain their local heritage. This is one of the reasons why the Piedmontese continue to prefer their beloved Barolo wine and their white truffles, the Umbrians their rich Sagrantino wine and black truffles, the Milanese their risotto and panettone, the Venetians their stockfish and polenta, the Bolognese their lasagne and pumpkin ravioli, the Florentines their bread soups and steaks cooked rare, the Abruzzese their excellent fish broth and seafood, the Neapolitans their mozzarella, basil, pizza, and pasta. As a result of its rich cultural diversity, the country's population also varies greatly in its customs from region to region, city to city, town to town. As you visit different cities and regions throughout Italy, you will see how the local personality and character of the Italians change as rapidly as the landscape does. Having lived for millennia with their great diversity and rich, highly heterogeneous culture, the Italians have taught us many things, foremost among them the age-old expression, "When in Rome, do as the Romans do."

NATIONAL HOLIDAYS

New Year's Day (1st January), Epiphany (6th January), Easter Monday (day after Easter Sunday), Liberation Day (25th April), Labour Day (1st May), Italian Republic Day (2nd June), Assumption (15th August), All Saints' Day (1st November), Immaculate Conception (8th December), Christmas Day and Boxing Day (25th-26th December). In addition to these holidays, each city also has a holiday to celebrate its patron saint's feast day, usually with lively, local celebrations. Shops and services in large cities close on national holidays and for the week of the 15th of August.

State tobacco shops and pharmacies

Tobacco is available in Italy only at state licensed tobacco shops. These vendors ("tabaccheria"), often incorporated in a bar, also sell stamps.
Medicines can be purchased only in pharmacies ("farmacia") in Italy. Pharmacists are very knowledgeable about common ailments and can generally prescribe a treatment for you on the spot. Opening time is 8:30-12:30 a.m. and 3:30-7:30 p.m. but in any case there is always a pharmacy open 24 hours and during holidays.

Shopping

Every locality in Italy offers tourists characteristic shops, markets with good bargains, and even boutiques featuring leading Italian fashion designers. Opening hours vary from region to region and from season to season. In general, shops are open from 9 a.m. to 1 p.m. and from 3/4 to 7/8 p.m., but in large cities they usually have no lunchtime break.

Tax Free

Non-EU citizens can obtain a reimbursement for IVA (goods and services tax) paid on purchases over €155, for goods which are exported within 90 days, in shops which display the relevant sign. IVA is always automatically included in the price of any purchase, and ranges from 20% to 4% depending on the item. The shop issues a reimbursement voucher to present when you leave the country (at a frontier or airport). For purchases in shops affiliated to 'Tax Free Shopping', IVA may be reimbursed directly at international airports.

Banks and post offices

Italian banks are open Monday to Friday, from 8:30 a.m. to 1:30 p.m. and then from 3 to 4 p.m. However, the afternoon business hours may vary.
Post offices are open from Monday to Saturday, from 8:30 a.m. to 1:30 p.m. (12:30 on Saturday). In the larger towns there are also some offices open in the afternoon.

Currency

Effective 1 January 2002, the currency used in many European Union countries is the euro. Coins are in denominations of 1, 2, 5, 10, 20 and 50 cents and 1 and 2 euros; banknotes are in denominations of 5, 10, 20, 50, 100, 200 and 500 euros, each with a different color.

Credit cards

All the main credit cards are generally accepted, but some smaller enterprises (arts and crafts shops, small hotels, bed & breakfasts, or farm stays) do not provide this service. Foreign tourists can obtain cash using credit cards at automatic teller machines.

Time

All Italy is in the same time zone, which is six hours ahead of Eastern Standard Time in the USA. Daylight saving time is used from March to October, when watches and clocks are set an hour ahead of standard time.

Passports and vaccinations

Citizens of EU countries can enter Italy without frontier checks. Citizens of Australia, Canada, New Zealand, and the United States can enter Italy with a valid passport and need not have a visa for a stay of less than 90 days.
No vaccinations are necessary.

Payment and tipping

When you sit down at a restaurant you are generally charged a "coperto" or cover charge ranging from 1.5 to 3 euros, for service and the bread. Tipping is not customary in Italy. Beware of unscrupulous restaurateurs who add a space on their clients' credit card receipt for a tip, while it has already been included in the cover charge.

Foreign Embassies in Italy

Australia
Via A. Bosio, 5 - 00161 Rome
Tel. +39 06 852721
Fax +39 06 85272300
www.italy.embassy.gov.au.
info-rome@dfat.gov.au

Canada
Via G.B. de Rossi, 27 - 00161 Rome
Tel. +39 06 445981
Fax +39 06 445983760
www.canada.it
rome@dfait-maeci.gc.ca

Great Britain
Via XX Settembre, 80/a - 00187
Rome
Tel. +39 06 42200001
Fax +39 06 42202334
www.britian.it
consularenquiries@rome.
mail.fco.gov.uk

Ireland
Piazza di Campitelli, 3 - 00186
Rome
Tel. +39 06 6979121
Fax +39 06 6792354
irish.embassy@esteri.it

New Zealand
Via Zara, 28 - 00198 Rome
Tel. +39 06 4417171
Fax +39 06 4402984
nzemb.rom@flashnet.it

South Africa
Via Tanaro, 14 - 00198 Rome
Tel. +39 06 852541
Fax +39 06 85254300
www.sudafrica.it
sae@flashnet.it

United States of America
Via Vittorio Veneto, 121 - 00187
Rome
Tel. +39 06 46741
Fax +39 06 4882672
www.usis.it

Foreign Consulates in Italy

Australia
2 Via Borgogna
20122 Milan
Tel. +39 02 77704217
Fax +39 02 77704242

Canada
Via Vittor Pisani, 19
20124 Milan
Tel. +39 02 67581
Fax +39 02 67583900
milan@international.gc.ca

Great Britain
via S. Paolo 7
20121 Milan
Tel. +39 02 723001
Fax +39 02 86465081
ConsularMilan@fco.gov.uk

Lungarno Corsini 2
50123 Florence
Tel. +39 055 284133
Consular.Florence@fco.gov.uk

Via dei Mille 40
80121 Naples
Tel. +39 081 4238911

Fax +39 081 422434
Info.Naples@fco.gov.uk

Ireland
Piazza San Pietro in Gessate 2 -
20122 Milan
Tel. +39 02 55187569/02 55187641
Fax +39 02 55187570

New Zealand
Via Guido d'Arezzo 6,
20145 Milan
Tel. +39 02 48012544
Fax +39 02 48012577

South Africa
Vicolo San Giovanni Sul Muro 4
20121 Milan
Tel. +39 02 8858581
Fax +39 02 72011063
saconsulate@iol.it

United States of America
Via Principe Amedeo, 2/10
20121 Milan
Tel. +39 02 290351
Fax +39 02 29001165

Lungarno Vespucci, 38
50123 Florence
Tel. +39 055 266951
Fax +39 055 284088

Piazza della Repubblica
80122 Naples
Tel. +39 081 5838111
Fax +39 081 7611869

Italian Embassies and Consulates Around the World

Australia
12, Grey Street - Deakin, A.C.T.
2600 - Canberra
Tel. 02 62733333, 62733398,
62733198
Fax 02 62734223
www.ambitalia.org.au
embassy@ambitalia.org.au
Consulates at: Brisbane, Glynde,
Melbourne, Perth , Sydney

Canada
275, Slater Street, 21st floor -
Ottawa (Ontario) K1P 5H9
Tel. (613) 232 2401/2/3
Fax (613) 233 1484 234 8424
www.italyincanada.com
ambital@italyincanada.com
Consulates at: Edmonton,
Montreal, Toronto, Vancouver,

Great Britain
14, Three Kings Yard, London
W1K 4EH
Tel. 020 73122200
Fax 020 73122230
www.embitaly.org.uk
ambasciata.londra@esteri.it
Consulates at: London, Bedford,
Edinburgh, Manchester

Ireland
63/65, Northumberland Road -
Dublin 4
Tel. 01 6601744
Fax 01 6682759
www.italianembassy.ie
info@italianembassy.ie

New Zealand
34-38 Grant Road, Thorndon,

(PO Box 463, Wellington)
Tel. 04 473 5339
Fax 04 472 7255
www.italy-embassy.org.nz
ambwell@xtra.co.nz

South Africa
796 George Avenue, 0083 Arcadia
Tel. 012 4305541/2/3
Fax 012 4305547
www.ambital.org.za
ambital@iafrica.com
Consulates at: Johannesburg,
Capetown, Durban

United States of America
3000 Whitehaven Street, NW
Washington DC 20008
Tel. (202) 612-4400
Fax (202) 518-2154
www.italyemb.org
stampa@itwash.org
Consulates at: Boston, MA -
Chicago, IL - Detroit, MI - Houston,
TX - Los Angeles, CA - Miami, FL -
Newark, NJ - New York, NY -
Philadelphia, PA - San Francisco, CA

ENIT (Italian State Tourist Board)

Australia
Level 4, 46 Market Street
NSW 2000 Sidney
PO Box Q802 - QVB NSW 1230
Tel. 00612 92 621666
Fax 00612 92 621677
italia@italiantourism.com.au

Canada
175 Bloor Street E. Suite 907 –
South Tower
M4W3R8 Toronto (Ontario)
Tel. (416) 925 4882
Fax (416) 925 4799
www.italiantourism.com
enit.canada@on.aibn.com

Great Britain
1, Princes Street
W1B 2AY London
Tel. 020 7408 1254
Tel. 800 00482542 FREE from
United Kingdom and Ireland
italy@italiantouristboard.co.uk

United States of America
500, North Michigan Avenue
Suite 2240
60611 Chicago 1, Illinois
Tel. (312) 644 0996 / 644 0990
Fax (312) 644 3019
www.italiantourism.com
enitch@italiantourism.com

12400, Wilshire Blvd. – Suite 550
CA 90025 Los Angeles
Tel. (310) 820 1898 - 820 9807
Fax (310) 820 6357
www.italiantourism.com
enitla@italiantourism.com

630, Fifth Avenue – Suite 1565
NY – 10111 New York
Tel. (212) 245 4822 – 245 5618
Fax (212) 586 9249
www.italiantourism.com
enitny@italiantourism.com

It needs no introduction—a land where history, art and nature collide in the most magnificent ways—light and dark, sweet and savory, gentle sandy coasts and rolling inland hills, ancient walled cities and soaring cypress trees—this is Tuscany. Beginning with the Grand Tour, travelers have come to central Italy to experience first hand the eternal splendors of Tuscany.

As the fast pace of modern life threatens to erase all that we hold sacred, the enduring charm and wonder of Tuscany remains a constant, an oasis of tradition that helps us experience and savor the good life as it was and as it shall be for centuries to come—preserved in the churches, palaces, museum masterpieces, and forever in the hearts of the Tuscan people.

Heritage

Highlights

- The cupola of the Duomo in Florence, a Renaissance masterpiece
- The distinctive Abbey of San Galgano, roofless and open to the sky
- San Gimignano's unique skyline with towers
- Volterra, a treasure house of Etruscan and medieval art
- Lucca's unusual, elliptical Piazza Anfiteatro

Inside

Arezzo lies on the lower western slopes of the Alps of Poti, overlooking the plain between Valdarno, the Casentino and Valdichiana.

The Romanesque Church of San Francesco, the Gothic-Renaissance Palazzo della Fraternità dei Laici, and further up the hill, the Gothic Duomo, are reminders of Arezzo's important past. The town's years of greatness began in the 11th century, when the Commune was founded, and lasted until the 14th century when Arezzo was bought by Florence (1384) for 40,000 florins. During the many years of war with Florence and Siena, the city protected itself with new walls, built along the line of today's Via Garibaldi. In the north-east, the walls merged with the old Etrusco-Roman walls. Much earlier Arezzo had been an important Etruscan town built around the Fortress. Later, under the Romans, the town expanded towards the plain, and the ancient walls were extended.

The old town center is strongly medieval in appearance, a fitting backdrop for the Giostra del Saraceno (Joust of the Saracen), a tournament held every year in Piazza Grande, re-enacting the past. Here, people living in rival neighbourhoods gathered to support teams of knights armed with lances who jousted at a Saracen effigy, Buratto Re delle Indie.

Arezzo's famous citizens include Maecenas, patron of Horace and Virgil, Guido d'Arezzo, the inventor of the musical scale, Petrarca, Vasari, and Pietro Aretino. Arezzo is also associated with Piero della Francesca, who painted one of his greatest works in the Church of San Francesco.

San Francesco ❶

Originally constructed in the 13th century, the church was rebuilt between 1318 and 1377, and much-needed restoration was carried out in the early 20th century. The brick and stone facade is unfinished; the campanile was built in the 15th century.

Inside the church is one of Italy's greatest works of art: the **Leggenda della Vera Croce**** (Legend of the True Cross), the magnificent fresco cycle painted by Piero della Francesca between 1453 and 1466 on the choir walls, drawing inspiration from the 13th-century «Legenda aurea» by Jacopo da Varagine.

The excellent restoration work recently carried out has given new life to the masterpiece, a real showcase of the art of fresco painting.

The church has some other important works: the rose window* in the facade has stained glass by Guillaume de Marcillat, showing St Francis and Honorius III (1524). There are Gothic and Renaissance aedicules on the right wall, some remodeled in the early 19th century, and many frescoes.

**Arezzo:
the church of San Francesco**

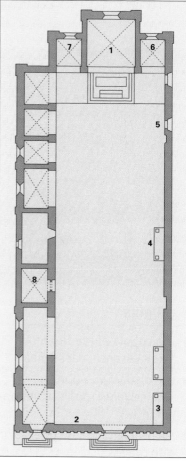

1 Piero della Francesca's fresco cycle
2 Frescoes by Parri di Spinello
3 Carbonati Chapel
4 Madonna and Saints by Parri di Spinello
5 Annunciation by Spinello Aretino
6 Guasconi Chapel
7 Tarlati Chapel
8 Frescoes by Lorentino d'Arezzo

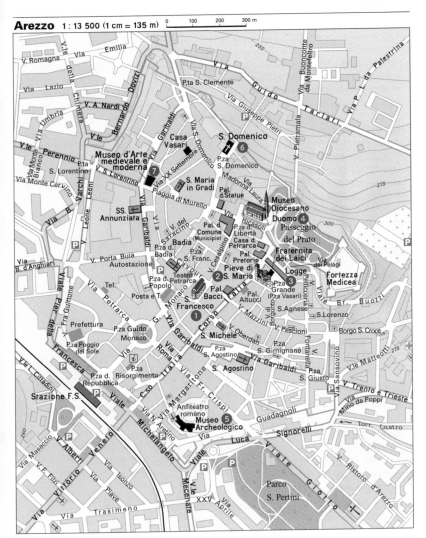

Arezzo   1 : 13 500 (1 cm = 135 m)

Pieve di Santa Maria ❷

This church is one of the most fascinating examples of the Romanesque style in Tuscany. The large sandstone building was started after 1140, replacing an earlier building begun around 1000. Gothic additions were made until the early 1300s, then Vasari intervened in the 16th century; the church was restored in the late 19th century. The Romanesque facade* (13th century) shows Pisan and Luccan influence. It has five blind arcades and a triple row of deeper open galleries, supported by 68 columns with capitals. The central portal architrave and lunette are decorated with reliefs (1216); the Months* are depicted in the archivolt. The impressive bell tower* (1330) on the right side is sometimes called the tower 'of the Hundred Holes' because of its many divided windows. The spacious Romanesque *interior* was restored in the 19th century. The most important artwork is the huge **polyptych**** (Madonna and Child with Saints, Annunciation, Assumption and Saints) by Pietro Lorenzetti (1320-24) at the high altar.

AREZZO IN OTHER COLORS...

■ ITINERARIES: P 98
■ FOOD: P 123, 126, 131
■ SHOPPING: P 162, 166, 168
■ EVENTS: P 174, 178
■ PRACTICAL INFO: P 194

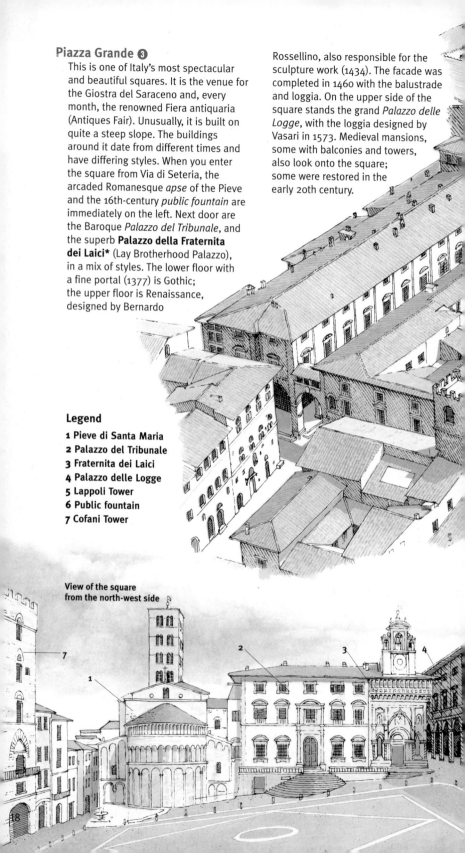

Piazza Grande ❸

This is one of Italy's most spectacular and beautiful squares. It is the venue for the Giostra del Saraceno and, every month, the renowned Fiera antiquaria (Antiques Fair). Unusually, it is built on quite a steep slope. The buildings around it date from different times and have differing styles. When you enter the square from Via di Seteria, the arcaded Romanesque *apse* of the Pieve and the 16th-century *public fountain* are immediately on the left. Next door are the Baroque *Palazzo del Tribunale*, and the superb **Palazzo della Fraternita dei Laici*** (Lay Brotherhood Palazzo), in a mix of styles. The lower floor with a fine portal (1377) is Gothic; the upper floor is Renaissance, designed by Bernardo

Rossellino, also responsible for the sculpture work (1434). The facade was completed in 1460 with the balustrade and loggia. On the upper side of the square stands the grand *Palazzo delle Logge*, with the loggia designed by Vasari in 1573. Medieval mansions, some with balconies and towers, also look onto the square; some were restored in the early 20th century.

Legend

1 Pieve di Santa Maria
2 Palazzo del Tribunale
3 Fraternita dei Laici
4 Palazzo delle Logge
5 Lappoli Tower
6 Public fountain
7 Cofani Tower

View of the square from the north-west side

The irregularly-shaped square is built on a slope following the contour of the hill.

0   50 m

Duomo ❹

This impressive Gothic cathedral, with 16th-century steps in front, was started in the late 13th century, and completed in the early 16th century. The neo-Gothic facade (1901-14) replaces the original, left unfinished in the early 15th century. On the right side is a portal with lunette and terracotta sculptures. The neo-Gothic campanile (1859) stands beside the apse with its high divided windows. The vast *interior* is striking, with soaring pillars, ogival arches and vaults, as well as large stained glass windows (16th century), mostly by Guillaume de Marcillat. Artworks include the fresco of St Mary Magdalen* by Piero della Francesca, the cenotaph* of Bishop Guido Tarlati (1330) and the sarcophagus of San Donato*, in marble with intricate Gothic sculpturework, by various 14th-century Tuscan artists.

Museo Archeologico Nazionale «Gaio Cilnio Mecenate» ❺

The museum occupies the monastery of San Bernardo, rebuilt after destruction in 1943. The building partly covers and partly overlooks what survives of the **Roman amphitheater** built under the Emperor Hadrian; the arena and remains of the ambulatories can still be clearly seen. The museum's twenty rooms house pieces from 18th-century and 19th-century private collections as well as finds from excavations in the town and surrounding area. The exquisite krater* with Herakles and the Amazons, by Euphronius (500 BC), is in the *Etruscan section*, which contains Archaic and Hellenistic finds from Arezzo. The "quincussis", in the coin collection, is one of the best preserved Etruscan coins ever found. The *Roman section* is worth a visit for its excellent collection of **coralline vases****, or Aretine ceramic ware, with bright coral glaze, and reliefs. The ceramics rooms* are particularly interesting, with Villanovan and Etruscan objects. In particular, a cup* with red figures, attributed to Douris (470 BC), and an Attic amphora with black figures.

Other important exhibits are the jewelery and glass collections, and the priceless *Gamurrini collection* of objects found in the area of Arezzo and Lake Bolsena.

Arezzo Cathedral

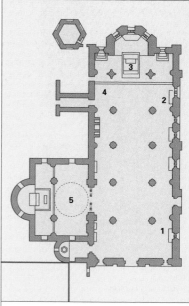

1 Tomb of Gregory X
2 Ciuccio Tarlati Chapel
3 Urn of St. Donatus
4 Mary Magdalen by Piero della Francesca
5 Lady Chapel (Madonna del Conforto)

San Domenico ❻

This 13th-century Gothic church stands in a small tree-lined square, off the main track. The facade has a fine Romanesque portal and small bell gable with 14th-century bells. In the light interior, the wonderful **Crucifix**** painted by Cimabue as a young man (1260-65) hangs in the apse. The walls of the nave and chapels are decorated with 14th-century and 15th-century frescoes and sculptures of the Aretine and Sienese schools.

Museo Statale d'Arte Medievale e Moderna ❼

The museum occupies the Renaissance *Palazzo Bruni-Ciocchi* or *Customs House* (15th century) at the road junction known as *canto alla Croce* (Cross corner), which also has other interesting examples of 14th-century and Renaissance architecture. Don't miss the museum's beautiful 15th-century courtyard, attributed to Bernardo Rossellino. Some of the museum's twenty-odd rooms have Renaissance portals and fireplaces. The painting and sculpture collections provide good coverage of Aretine and

Cortona, the old center

Visconti of Milan. The landscape around here still has the magic of Piero della Francesca's backgrounds. The old walled town is a dense network of narrow lanes, stairs, medieval houses and Renaissance palazzi.

From Piazza Baldaccio, Via Trieste climbs to the church of **Santa Maria delle Grazie**. Inside: Last Supper by Giovanni Antonio Sogliani (1531); Madonna of Mercy, a large glazed terracotta of the Della Robbia school; and Madonna and Child by Tino di Camaino (1316).

In Piazza del Popolo, the heart of the old town, we find the 14th-century Palazzo Pretorio, with stone and glazed terracotta coats-of-arms on the facade. A lane leads down to the ancient **Chiesa della Badia** (Abbey Church), rebuilt in the 14th century. The unusual asymmetrical interior houses a 16th-century stone altar-frontal.

Further on is Piazza Mameli, and the **Museo Statale di Palazzo Taglieschi**. Works here include a wood polychrome Madonna attributed to Jacopo della Quercia, a polychrome terracotta Nativity attributed to Andrea Della Robbia, and a large collection of traditional local objects.

Just outside the town is the small brick church of *San Stefano*, Byzantine in structure, probably 7th-8th century.

Tuscan art from the 14th to 19th centuries. On the ground floor, medieval to early Renaissance sculpture, including some Madonnas from the old gates of the 14th-century town walls. On the *first floor*, looking over the Renaissance garden: works by Tuscan artists, goldsmithery (14th-16th century), and ivories* (11th-15th century); in addition, two panels* by Bartolomeo della Gatta, urns of St Lorentino and St Pergentino* (1498) and a parade helmet* in embossed and gilded copper (mid 15th century). Still on the first floor, as well as Giorgio Vasari's large painting of the Wedding Feast for Esther and Assuer*, there is a wonderful **majolica and porcelain collection****, comprising over 300 pieces (14th-18th century) from the most important Italian producers. On the second floor, paintings ranging from the 16th century (altarpiece of St Jerome* by Luca Signorelli, standard of St Rocco* by Vasari) to the 19th century, with works by Fattori, Cecioni and Signorini.

DAY TRIPS

ANGHIARI [27 km]

Anghiari's name is linked with Leonardo's famous drawing of the battle on 29th June 1440, when the Florentines and the Pope's troops defeated Duke

CORTONA [28 km]

Interesting for its artworks and history, Cortona has breathtaking views over the Valdichiana. It is almost entirely surrounded by massive Etruscan walls, renovated in medieval times. The narrow stone-paved streets are lined by houses with projecting facades and timber supports. Next to the entrance of some medieval palazzi, the "door of the dead" - a local peculiarity - can be seen: narrow and raised above ground level, these doors were presumably used for removing coffins.

The town's heart is Piazza della Repubblica, with the 13th-century **Palazzo Comunale**, and its crenelated tower, and the 12th-century *Palazzo del Capitano del Popolo*, modified in the 16th century. In the neighbouring *Piazza Signorelli*, part of the courtyard of **Palazzo Casali** and the flank of the building, covered with coats-of-arms, remain as they were when the palazzo was built in the 13th century. Palazzo Casali houses the **Museo dell'Accademia Etrusca**, founded in 1727 together with the *Biblioteca (Library)*.

Etruscan antiquities held here include the famous large bronze **oil lamp**** decorated with satyrs and

Cortona, Palazzo Comunale

mermaids (4th century BC). There are also Egyptian works (funerary boat), Roman works, a 12th- to 13th-century mosaic, medieval and modern applied art objects, coins*, gemstones, medals, seals, miniatures and costumes. Paintings include: a 13th-century Pisan school Crucifix on wood; a work by Pinturicchio (Madonna and St John), a Nativity attributed to Luca Signorelli, and a Madonna and Saints* by Pietro da Cortona (1626-28). One room is devoted to the modern Cortona painter Gino Severini. The upper floors house the Library, and objects, including late Archaic jewelery*, excavated from grave II of the Etruscan hypogei known as the 'Meloni' (Melons).

Museo Diocesano. In the former *Chiesa del Gesù* (early 16th century) opposite the Duomo. The first room has works by Pietro Lorenzetti (Ascent to Calvary), Luca Signorelli (Deposition*; Communion of the Apostles*), Sassetta (Madonna and Saints*), Beato Angelico (**Annunciation****, Madonna and Saints*), Bartolomeo della Gatta (Assumption). The former *sacristy* has: Pietro Lorenzetti (Madonna and Angels*), the famous Vagnucci reliquary* by Giusto da Firenze (1457), and Scenes from the Life of St Margaret by the 13th-century Aretine school; the *lower church* (1555) houses 16th-century frescoes partly attributed to Vasari, and furnishings from the same period.

From Piazza della Repubblica, the delightful Via Santucci climbs up to San Francesco, which still has its original Gothic portal and left flank. Inside, a Byzantine ivory reliquary of the Holy Cross (10th century), and the Gothic tomb of Bishop Ubertini (14th century). Via Berrettini leads upwards past a

La Verna Sanctuary

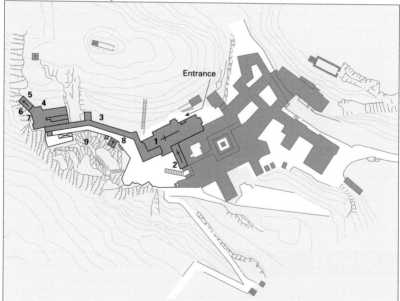

1 Chiesa Maggiore	**4** St Francis' second cell	**7** Chapel of St Anthony of Padua
2 Santa Maria degli Angeli	**5** Chapel of the Stigmata	**8** St Francis' first cell
3 Corridor of the Stigmata	**6** Chapel of St Bonaventura	**9** Sasso Spicco

buttress and charming houses to the little 15th-century church of San Nicolò. The standard of the Company of San Nicolò, painted on both sides by Luca Signorelli (Deposition*; Madonna and Saints) is preserved here. The road then leads on to the sanctuary of St Margaret, on a large square with a breathtaking view over Valdichiana, Monte Amiata and Lake Trasimeno. The neo-Gothic church houses St Margaret's body in a 17th-century urn, the Gothic tomb and the 13th-century wood Crucifix reputed to have spoken to Margaret. From the sanctuary square, **Via Santa Margherita** leads down towards the center, flanked by Gino Severini's mosaic Stations of the Cross.

Madonna 'del Calcinaio'**. Situated about 3 km before the town. This elegant Renaissance church is seen as typical of the period between 1400 and 1500. Designed by Francesco di Giorgio Martini, it was built between 1485-1513 in the shape of a Latin cross, with an octagonal cupola and clean external lines. The stained glass windows by Guillaume de Marcillat (16th century) in the light, Brunelleschi-style interior are beautiful. The high altar (16th century) houses the Madonna del Calcinaio (14th-15th century).

Also outside the town are two Etruscan sites: the Tanella di Pitagora (3 km south-west) and the hypogei known as the Meloni (2 km north-west). Archeological finds from the Meloni are on show in the Museo dell'Accademia Etrusca.

LA VERNA [4 km]

This "bare rock between Tiber and Arno" (Dante) is an unusual rocky outcrop in the Casentino, with sheer cliffs on three sides, wooded with fir and beech. It was given to St Francis of Assisi by Count Orlando Cattani of Chiusi in 1213; the following year he went to live there in rough log shelters with several others. In September 1224, on a later visit, St Francis received the stigmata here ("from Christ took the last seal"). La Verna is still the site of a Franciscan sanctuary.

Convento della Verna.
A passage behind the convent leads to the square and the main buildings: the 14th-15th century **Chiesa Maggiore** or *Basilica*, with Renaissance terracottas by Andrea Della Robbia (Adoration of the Child*, Annunciation*); and the small church of *Santa Maria degli Angeli*, founded in 1216, which preserves a fine altar-frontal*, also by Andrea Della Robbia. A corridor decorated with frescoes leads to the **Cappella delle Stimmate** (Chapel of the Stigmata), built in 1263. Inside: a tondo* of the Della Robbia school (Madonna and Child), a large terracotta (Crucifixion) by Andrea Della Robbia and a 16th-century choir. A glass-shielded stone in the floor marks the spot where St Francis is said to have received the stigmata. Other points of interest are: the chapels of St Bonaventura and St Anthony of Padoa; the first and the second cell of St Francis; and *Sasso Spicco*, the huge jutting rock which St Francis also lived under.

Lucignano, with the Collegiate Church overlooking the town

LUCIGNANO [28 km]

The town, with its 14th-century tower, overlooks the Valdichiana from a hilltop, and is still partly walled. The oval layout of the old center is a fine example of medieval town planning.
Visitors can see a good selection of medieval artworks of the Sienese school. The **Museo Comunale**, houses various paintings, including a Madonna by Luca Signorelli and the Tree of St Francis*, also known as The Golden Tree, a treasured 14th-century reliquary. Opposite, the Church of the *Collegiata*, houses wood sculptures. The old church of **San Francesco** has frescoes by Bartolo di Fredi and other 14th-century and 15th-century Sienese painters.

Sansepolcro 1 : 9 500 (1 cm = 95 m)

SANSEPOLCRO [35 km]

The town is famous for its crafts (embroidery, wrought iron, goldsmithery), and for the Palio della Balestra (a crossbow contest between local archers and archers from Gubbio). But its greatest claim to fame is as the birthplace of Piero della Francesca. The town is still very appealing, with largely Renaissance houses and palazzi in the old center.

Piazza Torre di Berta ❶, on elegant Via XX Settembre, is the heart of the town. Historic palazzi with towers look onto the square; the most noticeable is the Mannerist *Palazzo Pichi*, with its ashlar arches.

Other palazzi and towered houses in Via Matteotti provide a picturesque setting for the **Duomo ❷**, built in the complex Romanesque-Gothic style of the first half of the 11th century, with 14th-century modifications. The Romanesque *interior*, shows Gothic influence. The Duomo houses various medieval and Renaissance artworks and a large 8th- to 9th-century wood Crucifix*, known as the "Volto Santo" (Holy Face), because it is reminiscent of the Crucifix in the Duomo in Lucca.

Museo Civico ❸. Known especially for works by Piero della Francesca, it features in the central hall: a large fresco of the **Resurrection****, a masterpiece painted in the artist's prime; polyptych of the Madonna of Mercy; a saint's bust (perhaps St Julian); and a detached fresco depicting St Ludovic. The other rooms display valuable items, furnishings and vestments belonging to the diocese and cathedral. There are also various paintings by Tuscan artists, in particular the processional standard* painted on both sides by Luca Signorelli, and two terracottas of the Della Robbia school (Madonna and Child and a large Nativity*).

In Piazza San Francesco, the **Casa di Piero della Francesca ❹** is an excellent example of 15th-century civil architecture. The artist himself may have been involved in designing the house, which is now the Research Center for the Piero della Francesca Foundation.

The **Fortezza Medicea ❺** is situated along the town walls, which are open after the medieval Porta Fiorentina. The fort, a good example of 16th-century military architecture, was possibly designed by Giuliano da Sangallo.

FLORENCE

Dante Alighieri and the birth of the Italian language, great artists such as Giotto and Michelangelo, monuments and museums, local wars and civic virtues, Chianti and the great food, the lively character of the people: these are just some of the reasons why the most important Tuscan city, situated on the River Arno at the foot of the Fiesole hills, is associated to such an extent with Italian national identity.

The city first began to distinguish itself in medieval times, as the arts and crafts began to thrive. But as early as Roman times - the Latin name of the city "Florentia" means flourishing - Florence's position on trade routes had benefited it. The city really came into its own in the Renaissance, under the rule of the Medici, great patrons of the arts and founders of the city's museums collections.

For centuries Florence was an obligatory stop on the Grand Tour, the educational travels of young aristocrats from all over Europe. Today it is still a top tourist destination. Florence is truly an open-air museum, because of its unique treasures and architecture. At the same time, it has kept its identity as a modern city, with its economy and local population, despite the impact of crowds of tourists. Indeed tourism is a fundamental part of the economy.

The craft activities so important in the past still flourish: furniture restoration, gold production, lace-making and the famed Florentine straw-plait. Florentine food and cooking has maintained past traditions, and features deliciously good simple country cooking, as well as sophisticated modern adaptions of time-honored recipes. Likewise, 20th-century urban and industrial development has not spoilt the large historic center; here it is possible to wander along loggias and past noble facades, to marvel at squares which look as they did in medieval and Renaissance times, and to rest in centuries-old gardens blending nature and culture.

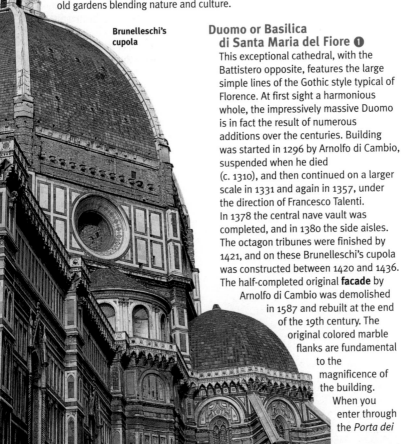

Brunelleschi's cupola

Duomo or Basilica di Santa Maria del Fiore ❶

This exceptional cathedral, with the Battistero opposite, features the large simple lines of the Gothic style typical of Florence. At first sight a harmonious whole, the impressively massive Duomo is in fact the result of numerous additions over the centuries. Building was started in 1296 by Arnolfo di Cambio, suspended when he died (c. 1310), and then continued on a larger scale in 1331 and again in 1357, under the direction of Francesco Talenti. In 1378 the central nave vault was completed, and in 1380 the side aisles. The octagon tribunes were finished by 1421, and on these Brunelleschi's cupola was constructed between 1420 and 1436. The half-completed original **facade** by Arnolfo di Cambio was demolished in 1587 and rebuilt at the end of the 19th century. The original colored marble flanks are fundamental to the magnificence of the building. When you enter through the *Porta dei*

Canonici*, the vast *tribune** opens out, with three large polygonal apses, and smaller intermediate ones. Above rises the lofty octagonal drum supporting the enormous ribbed **Cupola**** by Brunelleschi. On the *left flank* is the early 15th-century richly decorated Gothic-Renaissance *Porta della Mandorla* (Almond Door)*. In the gable, Assumption of the Virgin, a high relief by Nanni di Banco (1414-1421), and in the lunette, Annunciation, a mosaic by Domenico and Davide Ghirlandaio (1491). The simple, harmonious lines of the Latin-cross **interior** create an impression of majesty and austerity, illuminated by stained glass windows by Lorenzo Ghiberti in the apses.

A staircase descends from the 2nd bay of the right aisle to the remains of **St Reparata**, the ancient cathedral demolished in 1375.

The great **Cupola*** by Brunelleschi, soaring to a height of 91m above the octagon, is decorated by a fresco of the Last Judgement by Giorgio Vasari and Federico Zuccari (1572-79); below, eight 16th-century statues of the apostles. To the left of the octagon is the *Sagrestia delle Messe**, or Mass Sacristy; here Lorenzo the Magnificent took refuge from the Pazzi conspiracy, on the day that his brother Giuliano was killed (26 April 1478). The sacristy has a bronze door* and a lunette (Resurrection*) by Luca della Robbia (1444). The climb up to the cupola (*463 steps*) starts from the end of the *left aisle*. It is worth it: the dome structure can be seen more closely, and the view* from the walkway around the lantern (107m) is fantastic. In the 3rd bay, **equestrian memorial to John Hawkwood****, painted by Paolo Uccello (1436); in the 2nd, equestrian memorial to Niccolò da Tolentino*, painted by Andrea del Castagno (1456).

Campanile di Giotto ❶

The campanile, 84.7m high, stands away to the side of the Duomo. It is famed for its Gothic gracefulness, its magnificent colored marbles, and its fine sculpture work. It was started in 1334 by Giotto; Andrea Pisano continued with the base, and Francesco Talenti (1350-59) completed the upper levels with double and triple divided windows, and projecting crowning cornice. The base is decorated with two tiers of 14th-century bas-reliefs (copies: originals in the Museo dell'Opera del Duomo). The first tier reliefs are attributed to Andrea Pisano and completed on the side nearest the Duomo by Luca della Robbia. The second tier reliefs are attributed to Andrea Pisano, to his school and to Alberto Arnoldi. Above, in niches, stand statues of patriarchs, kings, prophets and sibyls by Andrea Pisano, Donatello and Nanni di Bartolo (copies; originals in the Museo dell'Opera del Duomo). A staircase with 414 steps climbs up to the terrace with a great view* over the city.

View of the Duomo and Giotto's Campanile

Basilica di Santa Maria del Fiore

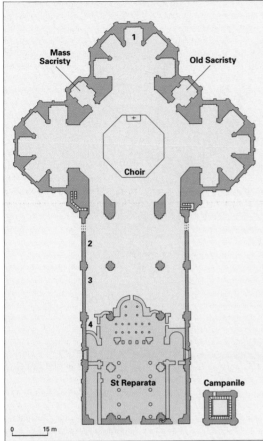

1 Arca of San Zanobi by L. Ghiberti
2 Panel of Dante and his worlds
3 Monument to John Hawkwood, frescoed by Paolo Uccello
4 Monument to Niccolò da Tolentino, frescoed by Andrea del Castagno

Scenes from the Life of John the Baptist. The most famous is the *East Door*, opposite the Duomo, called the **Porta del Paradiso**** (Door of Paradise) by Michelangelo. This Renaissance masterpiece by Lorenzo Ghiberti (1425-52) illustrates scenes from the Old Testament in ten panels. The original panels were restored after being damaged in the 1966 flood, and are now in the Museo dell'Opera del Duomo. The **interior**, below the octagonally segmented cupola, has a marble inlay floor* and marble walls bedecked with pilasters, linteled columns and a gallery with double divided arches. The cupola shimmers with 13th-century Byzantine-style mosaics* (Last Judgement; Stories of Genesis, the Baptist and Christ), by Venetian and Florentine artists, including possibly Cimabue. In the apse, other Byzantine-style mosaics* by Jacopo da Torrita (1225), as well as the tomb of the anti-Pope John XXIII*, attributed to Donatello and Michelozzo (1427).

Battistero di San Giovanni ❷

A religious focal point and one of Florence's oldest buildings, the Battistero was described by Dante as his "bel San Giovanni" (lovely St. John). It was built between the 11th and 13th centuries over Roman buildings. Its octagonal Romanesque structure, with a double tier of pilasters on white and green marble sides, is surmounted by an octagonal pyramidal roof over a cupola. The famous bronze **doors****, placed at the cardinal points of the compass, constitute a kind of large-scale illustrated Bible.
The oldest *South Door** is the work of Andrea Pisano (1330), and depicts

Museo dell'Opera di Santa Maria del Fiore ❸

The museum, founded in 1891, features important 14th- and 15th-century Florentine works of sculpture, including originals from the Battistero, the Duomo and the Campanile. In the former courtyard, the **panels**** from Ghiberti's Door of Paradise. In the *old facade room*, sculptures from the old facade of the Duomo: Madonna and Child*, St Reparata*, Boniface VIII*, and relief with Madonna of the Nativity*, all by Arnolfo di Cambio; St John*, by Donatello; and St Luke*, by Nanni di Banco. There is also a section devoted to Brunelleschi and his cupola, with the artist's death mask, a

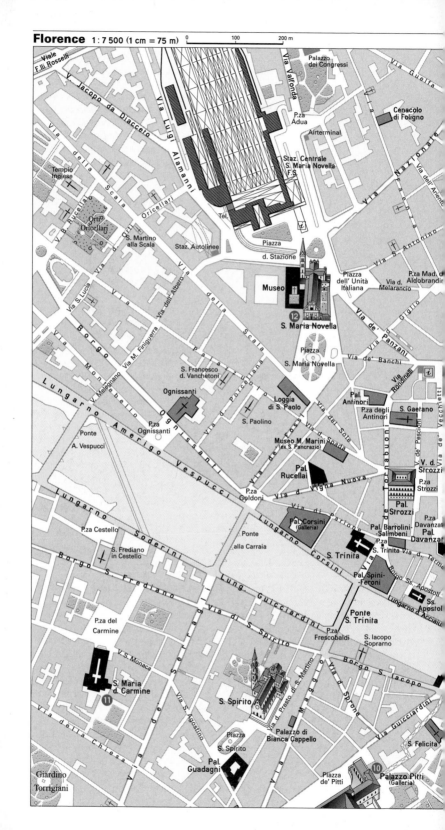

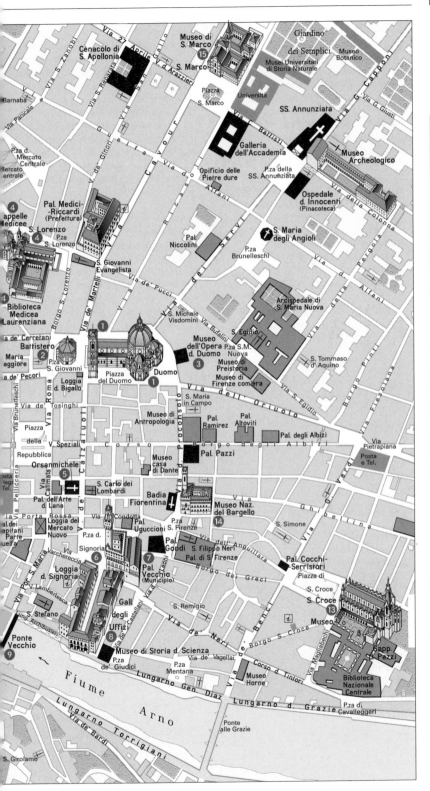

wood model of the cupola and the lantern, and apparatus used in the construction of the cupola.

On the mezzanine floor, the **Pietà****, a dramatic, unfinished group of figures sculpted by Michelangelo (1550-53), formerly in the Duomo interior. On the upper floor, in the *sala delle cantorie*: **cantoria**** (singing gallery) by Donatello (1433-39), with a procession of dancing putti; below, Mary Magdalen*, a disturbing wood statue, one of Donatello's later works (1453-55), formerly in the Battistero; **cantoria**** by Luca Della Robbia (1431-38), with reliefs of children singing and making music; 16 **statues****, formerly in niches in the Campanile, by Andrea Pisano (Sibyls and Prophets), Donatello (Habbakuk*, also referred to as 'Pumpkinhead', because of the statue's baldness ; John the Baptist; three Prophets) and Nanni di Bartolo (Abraham and Isaac*, partly

by Donatello). Next door, in the *sala delle formelle* are the relief **panels**** removed from the Campanile: the lower tier ones are by Andrea Pisano, probably partially to a design by Giotto, although the last five are by Luca Della Robbia (1439); the upper tier panels (Sacraments) are by Andrea Pisano, his school and Alberto Arnoldi. In the *sala dell'Altare*, **altar frontal**** in silver and enamel with Scenes from the Life of the Baptist, by 14th- and 15th-century Florentine goldsmiths, with a richly worked Crucifix in silver above.

San Lorenzo ❹

One of the great masterpieces of early Renaissance church architecture in Florence, the basilica is also inextricably linked to the memory of the Medici family. It was built by Filippo Brunelleschi in 1442-46 and completed in 1461 by Antonio Manetti. Standing on the site of

San Lorenzo Complex

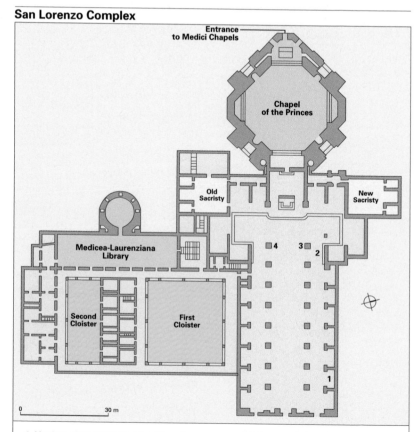

1 Marriage of the Virgin, by Rosso Fiorentino
2 Altar of the Sacrament, by Desiderio da Settignano

3-4 Bronze pulpits by Donatello and assistants

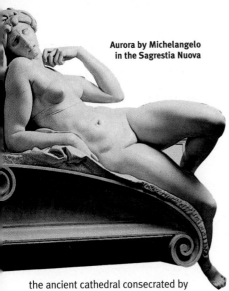
Aurora by Michelangelo
in the Sagrestia Nuova

the ancient cathedral consecrated by St Ambrose in 393, it was reconstructed in Romanesque style in the 11th century. The facade, which Michelangelo presented a design for, remains unfinished in rough stone. The **interior**, with columned central nave and side aisles, is still today extremely harmonious and exceptionally unmodified, a fine display of the great Brunelleschi's genius. At the beginning of the right aisle, Marriage of the Virgin*, by Rosso Fiorentino (1523), and at the end, the marble altar of the Sacrament*, by Desiderio da Settignano (1460). Opposite, one of two bronze pulpits* by Donatello (c. 1460) and pupils. The left transept leads into the 15th-century **Sagrestia Vecchia**** (Old Sacristy), a great Renaissance creation designed by Brunelleschi (1421-26) and decorated by Donatello (1435-43). Square in shape with a hemispherical cupola, the stone ribbing stands out cleanly against the white walls. Donatello designed the colored stucco medallions in the pendentives of the cupola (Life of St John*) and lunettes (Evangelists*), and the frieze of cherubs.To the left of the sacristy entrance, the sarcophagus of Giovanni and Piero de' Medici*, in porphyry and bronze, a masterpiece by Verrocchio (1472).

Cappelle Medicee ➍

The Medici Chapels consist of the Cappella dei Principi (Chapel of the Princes) in the cupola of San Lorenzo, and the Sagrestia Nuova (New Sacristy). The octagonal **Cappella dei Principi*** is

an elaborate, self-celebratory, Medici mausoleum. Planned by Cosimo I, it was built under Ferdinando I and designed by Matteo Nigetti. The Opificio delle Pietre Dure (Semi-precious Stone Factory) was created in 1588, to prepare the stone required for it. The final result has been described as a grandiose funereal mantle, because of the gloomy tones of the porphyry and granite used. The **Sagrestia Nuova**** is a masterpiece by Michelangelo, and prototype of Mannerist architecture. Called "new" to distinguish it from Brunelleschi's "old" sacristy, it is the funeral chapel of Lorenzo the Magnificent's family. It was commissioned from Michelangelo in 1520 by Pope Leo X and his cousin Cardinal Jiulio. The artist worked there until 1534: it was then completed by Vasari and Ammannati (1554-55). The chapel, with frame in pietra serena, holds **works sculptured**** by Michelangelo. The tomb of Lorenzo the Magnificent and his brother Giuliano is formed of a simple base supporting the statue of the Madonna and Child*. The tombs of Giuliano Duke of Nemours and Lorenzo Duke of Urbino are

San Lorenzo: Old Sacristy

◻ Distribution of reliefs by Donatello

opposite each other. Respectively they bear the allegorical figures of Giorno* (Day) and Notte* (Night) on one side, and Aurora* (Dawn) and Crepuscolo* (Dusk) on the other.

Biblioteca Medicea Laurenziana ❹

The library is reached through a Brunelleschi-style *first cloister* (left of the facade of the basilica of San Lorenzo). One of the most interesting 16th-century Florentine buildings, it was designed by Michelangelo, and houses one of Italy's most important manuscript collections.

At the entrance is an extremely original *staircase*: built in 1559 by Ammannati, to a design by Michelangelo, it consists of three flights side by side. The *reading room* is a spacious peaceful place, with large wood benches, also designed by Michelangelo. The superb carved ceiling echoes the pattern of the brickwork floor.

Orsanmichele ❺

This impressive building is one of Florence's most interesting examples of 14th-century architecture. Built as a grain market in 1337, it was then modified. Intricate divided windows were fitted in the arcades on the ground floor; two floors were added on top, with divided windows. In the late 1300s it became a church (*San Michele in Orto*) for the city's guilds. Outside, in the pilasters between the arcades, in niches or **tabernacles***, statues of the patron saints of the various guilds were commissioned from the greatest artists working in the city in the 15th-16th centuries. From left to right along Via dei Calzaiuoli: St John the Baptist by Lorenzo Ghiberti (1412-16); Incredulity of St Thomas* by Andrea del Verrocchio

Piazza della Signoria and the Uffizi

Pal. Guiducci
Pal. Uguccioni
Pal. d. Condotta
Piazza
Palazzo delle Assicurazioni Generali di Venezia
Equestrian Mon. to Cosimo I
Palazzo del Tribunale di Mercatanzia
Neptune Fountain
d. Signoria
Palazzo Vecchio
Via de'Gondi
Loggia d. Signoria
Post Office
Via d. Ninna
Via dei Leoni
Palazzi d. Uffizi
Porta d. Suppliche
Piazzale degli Uffizi
F. Arno
0   45 m

■ Original nucleus (1299-1315)

■ First enlargement, begun in 1343. This part was affected by Vasari's modifications (1558-71)

■ Enlargement onto Via della Ninna (1507-55)

□ "Fabbrica Nuova" (New Building) by Bartolomeo Ammannati (1588-96)

(1483); and St Luke by Giambologna. In Via Orsanmichele: St Peter, attributed to Brunelleschi (1413); St Philip and statues of four martyr saints*, by Nanni di Banco; and St George, and bas-relief with St George and the princess, both by Donatello (copies; originals in the Bargello Museum). In Via dell'Arte della Lana: St Matthew and St Stephen* by Ghiberti; St Eligius by Nanni di Banco; and in Via de' Lamberti: St Mark, copy of an early work by Donatello. In the rectangular **interior**, at the end of the right aisle, is the famous tabernacle* by Andrea Orcagna, in marble bedecked with mosaics and decorated with reliefs, one of the most beautiful works of art created in Gothic Florence (1355-59).

Piazza della Signoria ❻

Just as Piazza del Duomo is the religious focal point of Florence, this square, created in the 13th and 14th centuries, has always been the center of political power and of the city's civic life. Vast and imposing as it is, it is towered over by the massive Palazzo Vecchio; in the background, the three lofty arches of the **Loggia della Signoria*** (also known as the *Loggia dei Lanzi*). The square's original Gothic form (1376-1382) by Benci di Cione and Simone Talenti was designed for the Seigniory's assemblies and public ceremonies. Later it became a workshop for sculptors and then basically an open-air art gallery, featuring two masterpieces: **Perseus*** by Benvenuto Cellini (1554) and **Rape of the Sabine Women***, by Giambologna (1583). In the open space of the square, copies of well-known sculptures stand near the monumental *Fonte di Piazza* or Neptune Fountain, by Bartolomeo Ammannati (1563-75), with Neptune, nicknamed "il Biancone" (or "Big White Man") by Florentines, and graceful, dynamic bronze figures of sea deities and satyrs. In addition to Michelangelo's famous David (original in the Galleria dell'Accademia), there is the Marzocco, or the lion which is the symbol of Florence, by Donatello (original in the Museo del Bargello), and Judith and Holofernes, a bronze sculpture by Donatello (original in Palazzo Vecchio).

Palazzo Vecchio ❼

The main civil building in Florence and one of the most important medieval public palazzi in Italy. It has served many purposes over the centuries, always related to the city's political life. Arnolfo di Cambio designed it in 1299 as *Palazzo dei Priori*. In the 15th century it became *Palazzo della Signoria* and subsequently a residence of the Medici. From 1865 to 1871, when Florence was the capital, it housed the Chamber of Deputies of the Kingdom of Italy, and since 1872 it has been the seat of the Municipality. Many alterations have been made, but the original nucleus is a solid trapezoid mass in austere ashlar-work, with two tiers of elegant divided windows, crowned by a battlemented gallery. The

tower, known as the *Torre d'Arnolfo** (94m) was built in 1310.

Inside*, in the 15th-century *first courtyard*, a 16th-century fountain with a copy of the bronze Putto with Dolphin by Verrocchio (original now on the Juno Terrace). The monumental *great staircase* designed by Vasari ascends to the upper floors; the **Salone dei Cinquecento*** is a vast grandiose room built by Antonio da Sangallo and assistants (1495-96) for meetings of the Consiglio Generale del Popolo. It features paintings by Vasari and his school on the ceiling, and the marble group sculpture **Victory***, by Michelangelo (1533-34). To the right of the entrance is the *Studiolo di Francesco I**, entirely covered with late Mannerist 16th-century Florentine paintings, and decorated with bronze statuettes. Left of the Victory is the entrance to the *quartiere di Leone X*, with the *room of Leo X* (Giovanni de' Medici, son of Lorenzo, the family's first pope) decorated by Vasari and assistants. On the second floor, two rooms decorated by Vasari: the *quartiere degli Elementi* and the *quartiere di Eleonora*. The *cappella di Eleonora** was decorated by Bronzino (1545). Beyond the Cappella dei Priori is the *Sala dell'Udienza**, with gilded lacunar ceilings by

Palazzo Vecchio, one of the most important public medieval buildings

Giuliano da Maiano and frescoes by Francesco Salviati; next, the *sala dei Gigli**, with a magnificent carved and gilded ceiling - again by Giuliano da Maiano (1478) - and a large fresco by Domenico Ghirlandaio (1485). Also here is the restored bronze group by Donatello, **Judith and Holofernes***.

An interactive **Children's Museum** has recently opened in the Palazzo Vecchio, where children can play, dress up and make models.

Botticelli, the Birth of Venus

Galleria degli Uffizi and Corridoio Vasariano ⑧

Possibly the most important art gallery in Italy, the Uffizi houses Italian masterpieces from all ages and a selective representation of foreign artists. It is also the oldest museum in Europe. It was founded at the end of the 16th century, and was then expanded, by the Medici family, to include objects of technical and scientific interest. The collection of paintings once included only 16th-century artists (those defined by Vasari as "modern"). It was later extended with works by Venetian and Flemish painters, and donations. Then the scientific section was separated off, to concentrate on painting and sculpture again. Since the second half of the 19th century, with the acquisition of 14th- and 15th-century paintings, the gallery has formed the most complete collection of great Italian paintings.

At present around 2000 works are displayed; a radical renovation is planned, to enable the public to see the 1800 works currently in storage.

On the **ground floor** is the **cycle**** of Eminent Men (including Petrarch, Boccaccio and Dante) by Andrea del Castagno (c. 1450), and a detached fresco (Annunciation*) by Sandro Botticelli (1481).

First corridor. This area, occupied by the original gallery, houses a large first section on 13th- to 15th-century Tuscan painting: Duccio di Buoninsegna (Madonna Rucellai*, 1285), Cimabue (Maestà* from Santa Trìnita), Giotto (All Saints' Madonna*, c. 1310), Simone Martini and Lippo Memmi (Annunciation*, 1333), Ambrogio and Pietro Lorenzetti, Bernardo Daddi, Taddeo Gaddi, Giottino (Deposition*), Lorenzo Monaco, Gentile da Fabriano (Adoration of the Magi*, 1423), Masaccio and Masolino (Madonna and Child with St Anna*, 1424), Beato Angelico, Paolo Uccello (Battle of San Romano*), Domenico Veneziano (Madonna and Child with Saints*, c. 1445), Piero della Francesca (portraits of the Dukes of Urbino*, c. 1465), Filippo Lippi (Coronation of the Virgin, 1441-47, Madonna and Child with Angels), Hugo van der Goes (**Portinari Triptych****), Sandro Botticelli (**Birth of Venus****, **Spring****, Adoration of the Magi), Leonardo (**Adoration of the Magi****, Annunciation*), Verrocchio (Baptism of Christ*), Perugino, and Luca Signorelli.

The next rooms are the oldest in the Uffizi; room 18 is octagonal, and interesting because it shows the gallery's traditional approach of combining ancient works (statues) with modern works (paintings). It contains classical statues such as the Medici Venus* (1st century BC) and 16th-century Florentine paintings, including portraits by Bronzino and works by Vasari, Pontormo, Rosso Fiorentino, and Andrea del Sarto. The other rooms feature 15th- and 16th-century paintings

Cimabue's Maestà from Santa Trìnita

by other schools (Venetian, Lombard, Emilian, German, Flemish): Luca Signorelli (Madonna and Child*, c. 1490, Holy Family*), Perugino (Monks, Portrait of Francesco delle Opere, 1494), Albrecht Dürer (Portrait of Father, 1490, Adoration of the Magi, 1504), Giovanni Bellini (**Sacred Allegory****, c. 1490), Giorgione (Judgement of Moses, Judgement of Solomon), Andrea Mantegna (Madonna 'delle cave'*, triptych), Vincenzo Foppa, Correggio (Madonna in Adoration*, Rest during the Flight to Egypt).

Second and third corridor. Here the first rooms are given over to Florentine painting of the early 16th century: Michelangelo (**Tondo Doni****, an unconventional representation of the holy family), Raphael (portraits of the Dukes of Urbino and of Francesco Maria della Rovere*, **Madonna 'del Cardellino'*** or 'of the Goldfinch', 1506, portrait of **Pope Leo X****), Andrea del Sarto (Madonna 'delle Arpie'* or 'of the Harpies', 1517), Pontormo (Supper at Emmaus*, 1525), Rosso Fiorentino (Moses Defending the Daughters of Jethro, 1523 c.).
Further rooms are devoted to the Venetian school, the Emilian school, and central Italy: Titian, with a whole room (Flora*, c. 1520, **Venus of Urbino****, Venus and Cupid*, c. 1550), Parmigianino (Madonna 'dal collo lungo'* or 'of the long neck'), Dosso Dossi, Mazzolino, Sebastiano del Piombo (Death of Adonis), Lorenzo Lotto (Susannah and Old Men), Paolo Veronese (Holy Family, c. 1564), Jacopo Bassano, Tintoretto, and Federico Barocci (Madonna 'del popolo'* or 'of the people', 1579).

The next section features 17th- and 18th-century Italian and non-Italian artists: Pieter Paul Rubens (Portrait of Isabella Brant*, 1626); Caravaggio (**Bacchus*,** Medusa, Sacrifice of Isaac), Annibale Carracci (Venus, 1588), Rembrandt (Old Man*, two Self Portraits*, c. 1634 and c. 1664), Canaletto (views of Venice) and Francesco Guardi.

The **Corridoio Vasariano** completes the visit to the gallery. The walkway was built in 1565 by Vasari, and joins the Uffizi to Palazzo Pitti over the Ponte Vecchio. It is hung with some very important 17th- and 18th-century works by both Italian and non-Italian artists, starting with the famed *collection of self-portraits*, and including works by painters from the 16th century up to today (Vasari, Bernini, Rubens, Rembrandt, Velázquez, Canova, and Delacroix).

Ponte Vecchio ❾

The oldest and most famous bridge in Florence, it was built in 1345 by Neri di Fioravante on a previous structure first mentioned in 996. It was also the only bridge in Florence not to be destroyed when the German army retreated in August 1944 (though access to the bridge was heavily mined). Built on three arches, it is lined with shops, in the past wool merchants and greengrocers, today jewelers. Above the shops on the upstream side of the bridge, is the Corridoio Vasariano linking the Uffizi with Palazzo Pitti. There is a great view of the river, the Ponte Santa Trìnita and the embankments of the Arno from the terraces halfway across the bridge.

Ponte Vecchio, Florence's famous old bridge

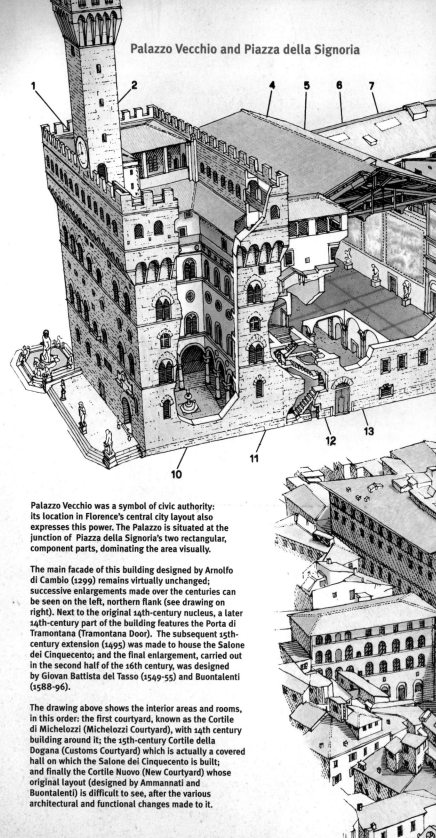

Palazzo Vecchio and Piazza della Signoria

Palazzo Vecchio was a symbol of civic authority: its location in Florence's central city layout also expresses this power. The Palazzo is situated at the junction of Piazza della Signoria's two rectangular, component parts, dominating the area visually.

The main facade of this building designed by Arnolfo di Cambio (1299) remains virtually unchanged; successive enlargements made over the centuries can be seen on the left, northern flank (see drawing on right). Next to the original 14th-century nucleus, a later 14th-century part of the building features the Porta di Tramontana (Tramontana Door). The subsequent 15th-century extension (1495) was made to house the Salone dei Cinquecento; and the final enlargement, carried out in the second half of the 16th century, was designed by Giovan Battista del Tasso (1549-55) and Buontalenti (1588-96).

The drawing above shows the interior areas and rooms, in this order: the first courtyard, known as the Cortile di Michelozzi (Michelozzi Courtyard), with 14th century building around it; the 15th-century Cortile della Dogana (Customs Courtyard) which is actually a covered hall on which the Salone dei Cinquecento is built; and finally the Cortile Nuovo (New Courtyard) whose original layout (designed by Ammannati and Buontalenti) is difficult to see, after the various architectural and functional changes made to it.

Legend

1 Clock
2 Torre di Arnolfo
3 Aedicule supported by columns
4 Patrol walkway
5 Vasari's monumental staircase
6 Salone dei Cinquecento
7 Wood-beamed ceiling in the Salone
8 Sala degli Elementi
9 Terrazzo di Saturno
10 Cortile di Michelozzo
11 Secret staircase known as the Scala del Duca d'Atene
12 Cortile della Dogana
13 Cortile Nuovo
14 Sala di Leone X
15 Sala dei Gigli
16 Sala dell'Udienza
17 Sala dei Dugento
18 Camera dell'Arme

Gli Uffizi

Loggia dei Lanzi

Fontana del Nettuno

Piazza della Signoria

Palazzo Pitti ⑩

This monumental palazzo was built around 1458 by the Pitti, a family of Florentine merchants and bankers, probably to a design by Brunelleschi. Simple but imposing, its three floors are in ashlar-work, with arches. It was enlarged in the 16th century, and the two 'rondòs' were added between 1764 and 1839. Today, together with other buildings in the Bòboli Gardens, the palazzo houses some important Florentine museums: the Galleria Palatina, the Appartamenti Reali, the Galleria d'Arte Moderna, the Museo degli Argenti (Silver Museum), the Museo delle Carrozze (Carriage Museum), the Galleria del Costume and the Museo delle Porcellane. The central doorway leads to the magnificent *courtyard** by Bartolomeo Ammannati (1570): on the side opposite the entrance is the 17th-century Grotto of Moses; the terrace above features the delightful late 16th-century *Fontana del Carciofo* (Artichoke Fountain). A staircase on the right leads from the courtyard to the Galleria Palatina, the Appartamenti Reali and the Galleria d'Arte Moderna.

Masaccio, Payment of the Tribute Money (detail), fresco in the Cappella Brancacci (Brancacci Chapel)

Galleria Palatina ⑩

The collection is displayed in Palazzo Pitti in magnificent rooms with vaults frescoed by Pietro da Cortona (1637-47) and Ciro Ferri (1665). It includes remarkable works, particularly of the 16th and 17th centuries, notably by Raphael, Andrea del Sarto and Titian. The Sala di Venere takes its name from the marble statue of the **Venus Italica**** by Antonio Canova. The room features four masterpieces by Titian (**Concert****, c. 1510, **Portrait of Julius II****, 1545, Portrait of a Lady or 'La Bella'*, **Portrait of Pietro Aretino****), as well as works by Rubens (Landscapes) and Salvator Rosa. In the following rooms, masterpieces by Rosso Fiorentino (Holy Conversation*, 1522), Titian (**Portrait of a Gentleman**** and Mary Magdalen*), Rubens (The Four Philosophers*, Consequences of War*), Antonie Van Dyck (Portrait of Cardinal Bentivoglio*), Tintoretto (Portrait of Luigi Cornaro*), and Veronese (Portrait of a Man*). There are also works by Giorgione (**The Three Ages of Man****, c. 1500), Fra' Bartolomeo (Mourning on the Dead Christ*), Andrea del Sarto (St John the Baptist*, 1523), and Bronzino

Palazzo Pitti and the Bòboli gardens

(Guidobaldo della Rovere*). The Sala di Psiche (Cupid's Room) is given over to works by Salvator Rosa.

There is an important group of masterpieces by Raphael; **La Velata** or Portrait of a Lady (1516), **Madonna 'del granduca'****, c. 1506, Portraits of Agnolo Doni* and of **Maddalena Doni** *, Madonna 'del Baldacchino' ('of the Canopy'), unfinished, Portrait of Tommaso Inghirami*, **Madonna 'della Seggiola'**** ('of the Chair'), and **La Gravida**** (Pregnant Woman).

Santa Maria del Carmine ⓫

This originally medieval church is located in the square of the same name. It is famous for its frescoes by Masaccio and Masolino decorating the *Brancacci Chapel*, at the end of the right transept. The cycle of **frescoes**** was begun by Masolino and Masaccio in 1424 and completed by Filippino Lippi after 1480. The frescoes, illustrating the life of St Peter, were much studied by Renaissance painters and, in the words of Vasari, were considered a true "school of the world". The human figures are depicted with great realism and psychological insight, and the use of perspective is masterly. The neighbouring Gothic *sacristy* houses paintings and frescoes attributed to Lippo d'Andrea (1400) and Agnolo Gaddi.

Santa Maria Novella ⓬

This is one of Florence's most famous churches and a Gothic masterpiece. It was built by architects of the Dominican Order from 1278 and completed in the mid-14th century. The 14th-century marble *facade** was modified in 1458 by Leon Battista Alberti (commissioned by Giovanni Rucellai) who designed the classical doorway and the part above the central cornice with two side volutes. To the right of the facade is the old cemetery, with family tombs of Florentine nobles, lined with arcades. The graceful, harmonious, Gothic **interior** is in the form of a Latin cross; the central nave and two side aisles feature polystyle pilasters, large arches and ogival cross vaults. At the end of the right transept, the Cappella Rucellai features the tomb slab of Fra' Dati*, a bronze bas-relief by Lorenzo Ghiberti (1426), and a marble statue at the altar (Madonna and Child*) by Nino Pisano (14th century). The 1st chapel to the right of the high altar is the Cappella di Filippo Strozzi, with frescoes by Filippino Lippi (Scenes from the Lives of St John and St Philip*, 1502) and the Tomb of Filippo Strozzi*, by Benedetto da Maiano (1491-95). In the *Cappella Maggiore*, the famous **fresco*** cycle (Scenes from the Life of the Madonna, Coronation of Mary, Scenes from the Life of St John the Baptist and Evangelists) by Domenico Ghirlandaio and assistants (1485-90); at the altar, a bronze Crucifix by Giambologna. The Cappella Gondi, designed by Giuliano da Sangallo (1503), features a famous wood **Crucifix**** by Brunelleschi. At the head of the left transept, the Cappella Strozzi* (6) has detached and restored frescoes (Last Judgement, Paradise*, Inferno*) by Nardo di Cione (1350-57). In the nearby *sacristy*, a lavabo in glazed terracotta by Giovanni della Robbia (1498) and **Crucifix ****, a panel by Giotto. *Left aisle*: in the 3rd bay, a remarkable **fresco**** by Masaccio (Trinity with the Madonna, St John, and the Lenzi donors), an important innovative work of the early Renaissance.

The restored Crucifix by Giotto in Santa Maria Novella. The Renaissance facade of Santa Maria Novella

Basilica di Santa Croce ⓭

An important example of Florentine Gothic architecture, the basilica is famous as the resting place of some eminent Italians. It was built to a design by Arnolfo di Cambio between 1295 and 1385, but the marble facade and campanile date from the 19th century. The large, simple **interior**, is divided into a spacious, light central nave and two aisles by ogival arches on large columns, and has an open beamed ceiling. The walls are lined with tombs, monuments and plaques in memory of celebrities. Along the right aisle is the 16th-century tomb of Michelangelo, Dante's cenotaph (1829), the monument to Vittorio Alfieri by Antonio Canova (1810), and the tombs of Niccolò Machiavelli, Gioachino Rossini and Ugo Foscolo. Also found on this side are the magnificent marble pulpit* by Benedetto da Maiano, a high-relief Annunciation* by Donatello (c. 1435) and the **monument to Leonardo Bruni****, a work by Bernardo Rossellino (1444-45), and prototype of Florentine Renaissance tombs. At the end of the *right transept* is the Cappella Baroncelli, frescoed with Scenes from the Life of the Virgin*, a masterpiece by Taddeo Gaddi (1332-38). The apse chapels feature two masterpieces of medieval painting by Giotto: the Cappella Peruzzi houses a fresco cycle with scenes from the life of St John the Baptist* and St John the Evangelist*, painted in the artist's prime (c. 1320-25); in the nearby Cappella Bardi are **scenes from the life of St**

Francis**, again by Giotto. At the end of the left transept, above the altar, is the famous wood Crucifix* by Donatello, criticised by Brunelleschi for its excessive realism. Along the *left aisle*, monuments

The well-known basilica of Santa Croce

Santa Croce Complex

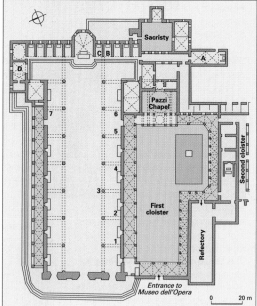

Entrance to
Museo dell'Opera

0   20 m

1 Michelangelo's Tomb
2 Dante's Cenotaph
3 Pulpit by Benedetto da Maiano
4 Machiavelli's Tomb
5 Annunciation by Donatello
6 Monument to L. Bruni, by B. Rossellini
7 Monument to C. Marsuppini, by Desiderio da Settignano
A Medici Chapel, by Michelozzo
B-C Frescoes by Giotto
D Wood Crucifix by Donatello

The vast, solemn interior of the basilica of Santa Croce

The Basilica di Santa Croce and the Bargello

and various art objects, especially for its Tuscan Renaissance sculpture and medieval French ivories.

On the **ground floor**, the *Sala del Trecento* (14th-century Room) houses works originally in Orsanmichele, as well as a Madonna and Child by Tino di Camaino and a sculpture group by Arnolfo di Cambio. The *Sala del Cinquecento* (16th-century Room) features works by Michelangelo and other important 16th-century works including Mercurio Volante* (Winged Mercury) by Giambologna. Other works here by Michelangelo are the Pitti Tondo* (c. 1504), with the Madonna, Child and infant St John, Bacchus* (1496-97), the **David-Apollo**** (1530-32) and the bust of **Brutus**** (1539).

On the **first floor**, the *Salone del Consiglio Generale** features famous works by Donatello: a bust of Niccolò da Uzzano*, in polychrome terracotta; the Marzocco (1418-20), or lion supporting the Florentine lily, symbol of the city; Atys-Amor*, an intriguing bronze of a winged cupid; a marble David* (1408-09) and the famous bronze **David**** (c. 1440); **St George**** (1416) and a bas-relief of St George and the Princess, both once in Orsanmichele. There are also works by Filippo Brunelleschi and Lorenzo Ghiberti (the two **panels**** of the Sacrifice of Isaac made as trials for the famous competition in 1401 for the north door of the Battistero), by Michelozzo (Annunciation), by Luca Della Robbia (Madonna 'della Mela'* and Scenes from the Life of St Peter), and by Desiderio da Settignano (Infant St John*). Next come the *Sala Islamica*, with carpets, fabrics, and other Arabian works; the *Sala Carrand* (paintings, sculptures, and especially applied art objects from the 1888 Carrand donation); the *Chapel of St Mary Magdalen*, frescoed by Giotto's workshop, with carved and inlaid choir stalls (late 15th century); the *Sala degli Avori*, with 265 ivory works (5th to 17th centuries); the *Sala Bruzzichelli*, with

to the musician Luigi Cherubini, to Leon Battista Alberti, Galileo's tomb and the monument to Carlo Marsuppini*, by Desiderio da Settignano, one of the most remarkable tombs of the 15th century.

Museo Nazionale del Bargello ⑭

The museum is housed in the austere *Palazzo del Bargello**, built in various stages between the 13th and 14th centuries. It was the headquarters first of the Podestà (or governing magistrate) and then, from 1574, of the Captain of Justice, or 'Bargello'. It opened in 1865 with support from the Uffizi, the Mint and the State Archives, as well as considerable private bequests. Today the museum is one of the best in the world, for its collections of sculpture

16th-century furniture and a Madonna and Child* by Jacopo Sansovino; and the *Sala delle Maioliche*, with a collection of Italian majolica dating from the 15th century.

On the **second floor**: the Della Robbia rooms, with a collection of glazed terracottas by Giovanni and Andrea; the *Sala dei Bronzetti*, with works by Benvenuto Cellini (Ganymede* and Greyhound), and by Antonio Pollaiolo; the *Sala del Verrocchio*, with the famous bronze David*, the marble Lady holding Flowers* and the terracotta bust of Piero di Lorenzo de' Medici*. The visit ends with the *Medagliere* section, an extremely rich collection with works by Pisanello, Matteo de' Pasti, Michelozzo, Cellini and others.

Museo di San Marco ⑮

The museum occupies the splendid and carefully restored Dominican convent of St Mark. The convent was largely rebuilt by Michelozzo (1439-44), who established an important center of culture and learning here, hosting among others Beato Angelico, St Antonino, Savonarola and Fra' Bartolomeo. The collection of works by Beato Angelico is outstanding: in the *Cloister of St Antonino**, St Dominicus Kneeling before Jesus on the Cross*; the *Sala del Capitolo* is frescoed with the magnificent **Crucifixion****.

Fra' Angelico's most famous frescoes (1442-45) are found in the cells and corridors of the first floor. At the head of the stairs **Annunciation**** and Crucifix with St Dominicus*. In the first corridor: Noli Me Tangere; Deposition; **Annunciation****; Crucifixion; Nativity; **Transfiguration****; Christ Scorned; and Coronation of the Virgin*.

In the *Pilgrim's Hospice*, among frescoes by Beato Angelico, is the famous **Deposition of Christ**** started in 1424 by Lorenzo Monaco; and the **Tabernacle of the Linaiuoli**** with the Virgin and musician angels (1433) in a marble frame designed by Ghiberti. At the end of the second corridor is the *Prior's quarter*, inhabited by Savonarola, and a portrait of him, by Fra' Bartolomeo.

San Miniato al Monte

On a hilltop square with a beautiful view* over the city, this church, like the Battistero, is a superb example of Florentine Romanesque architecture. The *facade* in white and green marble has a geometrical design; below, there are five round blind arcades on Corinthian half-columns, and above, a niche window surmounted by a 13th-century mosaic. The *interior* has a central nave and two side aisles, columned, with beamed roof and raised choir above the crypt. At the

The elegant facade of San Miniato al Monte

The famous vineyards of Chianti

from the mid-sixties, when small family growers began to be replaced by large wine producers and specialised vineyards.

The wine is what has really put Chianti on the map. Casks and bottles of Gallo Nero were first sold outside the area in the 16th century. From the 1960s, Chianti began to attract inhabitants from abroad. Britons (as well as Germans, Dutch and Swiss) have settled in such large numbers in abandoned villas and country houses here that the area is sometimes called Chiantishire.

end of the nave, with its fine marble inlay floor, is the Cappella del Crocifisso* by Michelozzo (1448), with glazed terracotta vault by Luca Della Robbia and painted panels by Agnolo Gaddi (1394-96) at the altar. The presbytery, behind a marble screen*, has a pulpit* dating from 1207. In the beautifully arcaded apse, a magnificent 13th-century mosaic showing Christ between the Virgin and St Minias.The crypt with six rows of slender columns (11th century) has frescoes* by Taddeo Gaddi (1341) in parts of the vault.

EMPOLI [32 km]

A commercial and industrial center that developed in the lower Valdarno on the left bank of the River Arno, on key transport routes. Empoli was involved in the struggle between the Guelphs and Ghibellines. Its 15th-century walls still today surround the old center, with its many museums, monuments and works by Tuscan masters, all testimony to its important past. The town is also famous for glass-making.

The main monuments on the central square (Piazza Farinata degli Uberti) are: the church of the **Collegiata**, dedicated to St Andrew, with a lovely white and green marble Romanesque facade, and the **Museo della Collegiata**. The museum has a good selection of works by Renaissance artists: Masolino da Panicale (Cristo in Pietà*, 1425), Tino Camaino, Mino da Fiesole, Filippo Lippi and Neri di Bicci. Other frescoes by Masolino da Panicale are found in **Santo Stefano**, a 14th-century church that has been heavily modified. In the 1st chapel on the right, Leggenda della Vera Croce (Legend of the True Cross), 1424; in the right transept, lunette and Madonna and Child*.

The *Museo-Casa F. Busoni* is in Piazza della Vittoria, in the house where the composer Ferruccio Busoni was born. It contains documents and objects relating to his life and work.

DAY TRIPS

CHIANTI [40 km]

Chianti lies between Siena and Florence, and has often been fought over by them. The area has not always been clearly defined. «Clante», in Etruscan times, was the name of a tributary of the Arbia river. In the early 13th century, the area around it was seized from Siena by Florence, and organised into the Chianti League. They adopted the symbol of the black cockerel, today used by Chianti winegrowers. From the 18th century, «Chianti» began to refer to an increasingly wide area, as the reputation of the local wine grew. So much so, that by 1932 it became necessary to define the area's borders more precisely. Chianti has been further transformed by changes in agriculture

FLORENCE IN OTHER COLORS...

■ **ITINERARIES:** P 107, 109
■ **FOOD:** P 123, 126, 131
■ **SHOPPING:** P 162, 166, 168
■ **EVENTS:** P 174, 179
■ **PRACTICAL INFO:** P 202

FIÈSOLE [8 km]

In the center of Fiesole there is a large and extremely interesting archeological area, proof of the importance of the town

Map of Fièsole showing streets and landmarks including S.Francesco, Giardini Pubblici, Pal. Vescovile, Teatro Romano, Museo Bandini, Antiquarium Costantini, Campo Sportivo, Tomba Etrusca, S. Alessandro, S. Girolamo, Seminario, Duomo, Museo, Posta e T., V.Gramsci, F.ne Sotterra, Borgunto, Piazza Mino da Fiesole, Pal. Pretorio (Munic.), S.M. Primerana, Via S. Apollinare, Via Vecchia Fiesolana, Via S. Ansano, Via Verdi, Via Montececeri, Via Fra Giovanni Angelico, Badia Fiesolana, Via Badia d. Roccettini, S.Domenico, Via Giuseppe Mantellini, Largo Leonardo da Vinci.

in Etruscan and Roman times. Its commanding hilltop position (with the best view of Florence) overlooking the valleys of the Arno and Mugone meant that it was a favorite location for the Medici from the 1400s. From then on, villas and gardens were built in the surrounding hills as holiday retreats for noble Florentine families. Today Fièsole is an increasingly important cultural center, with many events such as Estate Fiesolana (Fiesole Summer), where plays are performed in the Teatro Antico.

The town's focal point is **Piazza Mino da Fiesole**, ❶ where the Roman forum was. There are some interesting 14th-century palazzi, and the **Duomo** ❷ dedicated to San Romolo. It was built in Romanesque style in the 11th century, enlarged in the 13th and 14th centuries, and the facade was reconstructed in the 19th century. The simple basilica-style *interior* features some important medieval artworks: in the Salutati Chapel*, frescoes by Cosimo Rosselli (15th century) and two sculptures by Mino da Fiesole (altar-frontal with a Madonna in Adoration* and the tomb of Bishop Salutati*).

The **Archeological area** ❸ includes the remains of Roman civic buildings and a small museum. The ancient ruins surrounded by the beautiful hills create a wonderfully romantic scene. The **Roman theater** dates from the beginning of the Empire. With seating capacity for

The Roman baths at Fièsole

3000, it is carved out of the hillside and divided into four sections. There are also ruins of the *baths* (1st century BC), of a *Roman temple*, rebuilt in the 1st century BC, and a section of the *Etruscan walls*, with huge blocks of stone. The **Museo Civico** ❹ contains objects from excavations at Fiesole. Another museum, the Costantini Antiquarium, has a collection of ancient vases from various places. The Museo Bandini has terracottas of the Della Robbia school, and Tuscan school paintings, particularly of the 13th and 14th centuries.

The Fiesole archaeological site

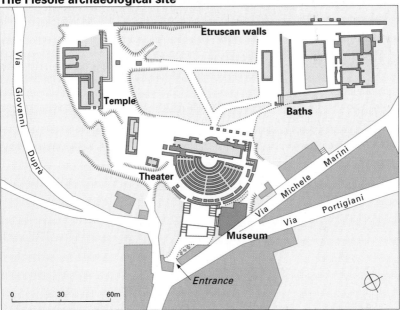

Etruscan walls

Temple

Baths

Theater

Via Giovanni Dupré

Via Michele Marini

Via Portigiani

Museum

Entrance

0   30   60m

IMPRUNETA [15 km]

This largely agricultural town, situated in the hills south of Florence in the Chianti area, is best-known for producing 'cotto' (terracotta). According to legend the town grew up in the 8th-9th century around the Pieve di Santa Maria, where the followers of St Romulus gathered to protect a venerated image of the Madonna. The image still attracts many faithful believers, who come to the basilica of **Santa Maria all'Impruneta*** (the ancient church of the legend) in the town's central square. Renovated in the 15th century, it has a 17th-century portico and crenelated 13th-century bell tower. The Renaissance interior has two fine aedicules* attributed to Michelozzo (1456), decorated with glazed terracottas* by Luca Della Robbia; the one on the left houses the image of the Madonna dell'Impruneta. The adjacent **Museo del Tesoro** features an original marble bas-relief depicting the finding of the Madonna's* image (c. 1430); it is not known who the work is by.

The basilica
of Santa Maria
all'Impruneta

GROSSETO

This market center is the capital of the Maremma region, a flourishing agricultural area, once plagued by malaria, whose marshes have been reclaimed over the centuries. After the ancient Etruscan city of Roselle was abandoned in 1138, Grosseto became a bishopric. The town was subject to Siena and later Florence until its decline between the 18th and 19th centuries.

In modern times the city has expanded beyond its walls and become an important center for the hinterland and coast. The coastal area is one of the most beautiful and unspoiled in the whole of Tuscany, largely because of the Parco della Maremma.

The attractive old town within the fine hexagonal 16th-century town walls can be admired from the walkway along the ramparts.

Grosseto 1 : 12 500 (1 cm = 125 m)

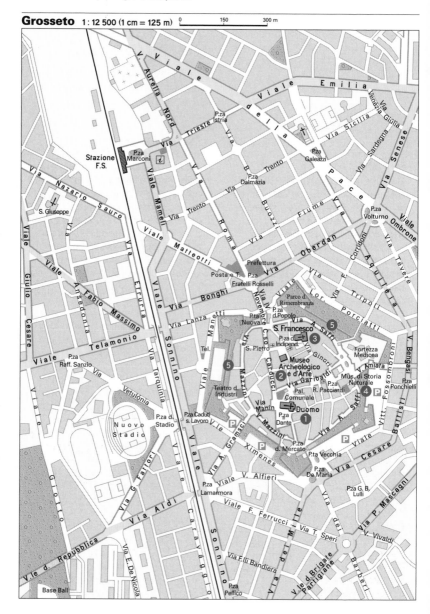

Duomo ❶

The Duomo, built between 1294 and 1302 on the site of the original 12th-century church, has been restored a number of times. The pink and white marble facade was added in the 19th century, but retains the original symbols of the Evangelists above the capitals of the columns, and on the right flank, two divided Gothic windows with 15th-century stained glass. The Latin-cross interior, contains a large font by Antonio Ghini (1470); the richly decorated altar-frontal (1474) at the altar of the Madonna delle Grazie is by the same artist. The right transept features a 15th-century panel (Madonna of the Assumption*) by Matteo di Giovanni.

Flank of the Duomo, in Piazza Dante

Museo Archeologico e d'Arte della Maremma - Museo d'Arte Sacra della Diocesi di Grosseto ❷

The museum, in the former Palazzo del Tribunale (Courthouse), contains Etruscan, Roman and medieval archeological finds, and an Etruscan section which includes the large Chelli collection, a bequest from the museum's founder (1860), with objects largely from the areas around Chiusi and Volterra. It also houses antiquities from the Etruscan and Roman city of Roselle, and archeological finds from the whole Maremma area. The Museo Diocesano, a museum within the museum, contains an equally rich collection of paintings and sculptures from the Duomo and other churches in the diocese, mostly by the Sienese school of the 13th-17th centuries.

San Francesco ❸

The brickwork church, built in the 13th century by the Benedictines, has a simple facade. Only the rebuilt cloister remains of the convent, and a well (1590), known as the Pozzo della Bufala (Buffalo Well). Inside, above the high altar, is a painted Crucifix*, thought to be an early work by Duccio di Buoninsegna.

Museo di Storia Naturale ❹

The museum, founded in 1961, is a fine showcase for the area's natural history. It contains interesting collections of paleontological finds, minerals, coleoptera and mammals.

Mura ❺

The ramparted hexagonal city walls were built by the Medici between 1564 and 1593, replacing the old medieval walls; in 1835 the bastions were turned into walkways and gardens. At the north-east bastion, is the Fortezza Medicea, the rather dilapidated late 16th-century fortress built around a 14th-century Sienese construction.

DAY TRIPS

FOLLONICA [44 km]

Follonica is an important industrial center in the Maremma, and also a lively seaside resort, with its long sandy beach lined with umbrella pines. The Bay of Follonica stretches from Piombino at the western point, to Punta Ala in the south. Opposite lie Elba and the smaller islands of Palmaiola and Cèrboli.

The **Museo del Ferro e della Ghisa** (Museum of Iron and Cast-Iron), is housed in the former ILVA iron works. The unusual church of San Leopoldo (1836-38) is also related to the iron industry. It is a unique example of industrial church architecture, with its cast-iron pronaos, pulpit, altar rail and candelabra.

GROSSETO
IN OTHER COLORS...
■ ITINERARIES: P 106, 109
■ FOOD: P 123, 134, 142
■ SHOPPING: P 163
■ EVENTS: P 175
■ WELLNESS: P 191
■ PRACTICAL INFO: P 213

Massa Marittima

1 : 7 000 (1 cm = 70 m)

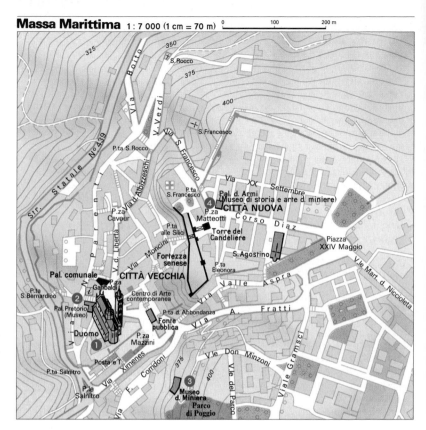

ISOLA DEL GIGLIO [52 km]

This second-largest island in the Tuscan Archipelago (reached by ferry from Porto Santo Stefano) is largely mountainous with cliffs along the coast. Low-growing vegetation, the pleasantly-perfumed maquis, alternates with rocky terrain. There is also an abundance of olive trees, chestnut trees, fig trees, arbutus or strawberry trees and vines producing the strong, prized Ansedonia wine. **Giglio Porto**, on the east coast, is the best place to arrive. The town around the small port comes alive in the summer months. **Giglio Castello** is an old village surrounded by medieval walls, with a 14th-century gate, dominated bv the Pisan *Rocca*. There is a long sandy beach at **Giglio Campese** on the west coast of the island.

MASSA MARITTIMA [50 km]

Massa Marittima divides into the lower medieval *Old Town* with many treasures of art and architecture, and the *New Town*, laid out to a geometric plan, higher up the hill. Silver and copper mining, which made the settlement rich in the Middle Ages, ceased in the late 14th century. Economic decline, largely due to the ravages of malaria (which

Massa Marittima, the Duomo's majestic facade, with the campanile behind

19th-century drainage programs did much to eliminate) paradoxically helped to preserve much of the character of the town.

Piazza Garibaldi is the focal point of the Old Town, where most of the important civil and religious buildings are found: the Duomo, the *Palazzo Vescovile*, the 13th-century **Fonte Pubblica** (Public Fountain) or **Fonte dell'Abbondanza** (Fountain of Plenty), the forbidding Palazzo Pretorio and the **Palazzo Comunale***. This enormous 13th- to 14th-century Romanesque palazzo in travertine has three tiers of divided windows, and later crenelation.

Duomo ❶. A masterpiece of Pisan Gothic-

of-arms in stone (15th-17th century). Today, it is a museum: the archeological section includes flints and Neolithic objects, finds from Etruscan tombs near Lake Accesa (8th-3rd century BC), and remains from a mining village dating from the 7th-6th centuries BC.

There are two museums related to mining in the town: **Museo della Miniera ❸**, in a complex of tunnels below the Old Town, used as shelters during the second world war; and the **Museo di Storia e Arte delle Miniere ❹**, in Piazza Matteotti, containing mining maps, minerals from the district, mining equipment and measuring instruments.

Flamingos near Orbetello

Romanesque architecture, dedicated to San Cerbone. It was started in the 12th century and enlarged in the 13th, with the extension of the choir area and the polygonal apse. The lower part of the facade features arches, and above, two tiers of open galleries supported on small columns with a Gothic coping. The main doorway is sculptured with reliefs (scenes from the life of San Cerbone); the left flank is dominated by the white and green outer wall of the central nave. At the end stands the imposing, partially rebuilt, campanile. In the light *interior*, non-uniform columns with fine sculptured capitals divide the nave and two side aisles. Various 14th-century works of art are housed here, including a Madonna delle Grazie* (1316) attributed to Duccio di Buoninsegna, a polychrome wood Crucifix* by Giovanni Pisano and the **tomb of San Cerbone***, a fine Gothic work sculptured with reliefs.

Palazzo Pretorio ❷, once the residence of the governing magistrate, was built around 1230. It has a solid facade with two tiers of divided windows and coats-

ORBETELLO [44 km]

Two narrow, low strips of sand separate the Tyrrhenian Sea from the Lagoon of Orbetello, which lies between the Maremma and Monte Argentario, with its olive trees, vines, citrus and fruit trees growing amongst the native maquis. The very ancient town of Orbetello lies on a spit reaching into the lagoon, which was artificially extended to reach Monte Argentario in 1842, thus dividing the lagoon into two parts.

The landward side of the town still conserves part of the walls built by the Spanish in the 17th century along the line of previous walls. It's worth visiting the town's medieval **Duomo**, with its graceful little Gothic facade, finely worked main doorway and oeil-de-boeuf. The **Biblioteca Civica** (Municipal Library) has a very interesting section about the Maremma, and an important Etruscan **pediment from the Temple of Talamone***, dating from Hellenistic times.

The Maremma Nature park

PARCO DELLA MAREMMA [15 km]

The Park was established by the Tuscan Regional Authority in 1975. It stretches from Principina a Mare to Talamone, and includes the swampy area around the mouth of the Ombrone River, and the **Monti dell'Uccellina**. These hills, reaching 415m at their highest, fall steeply into the sea towards the south, and in the north gradually slope down to the beach at Paduletto. There are two entrances to the park: *Alberese* (15km) (where the Visitors' Center is located) and *Talamone* (28km). Visitors to the park follow set itineraries: some can be covered on any day, and others only at certain times and on certain days.

The area contains many mini ecosystems: long, deserted, sandy beaches meet with steep cliffs, especially below the Monti dell'Uccellina. The area's natural beauty attracts thousands of visitors every year. The Maremma proudly preserves some of its most unique features, such as the 'butteri' or local version of cowboys, and its reputation as an untamed area of legend and adventure. The work of epic proportions carried out to drain the swamps and reclaim agricultural land is also an integral part of the area's history.

La Tomba della Pietraia in the Etruscan necropolis at Vetulonia

The Trappola Swamp (700 hectares) is one of the largest remaining marsh areas in Tuscany. Maremma cattle are still bred here, and together with the rather wild local breed of horses, are a typical feature of this fascinating area. There is a wide variety of vegetation: woods with elm, ash and white poplar; marsh vegetation extending south of the Ombrone, where it is gradually replaced by native pine; and maquis dominating in the Monti dell'Uccellina. The Park also provides a habitat for fauna such as wild boar, fallow deer and roe deer.

TERME DI ROSELLE [10 km]

Roselle, to the north east, on the spur of a hill, is the site of an ancient Roman and Etruscan city. The *remains** of the 3km-long polygonal city walls (6th-2nd century BC) are striking, in parts reaching a height of 5m. Excavations have brought to light the remains of the Roman city including a small amphitheater and baths; deeper excavations have revealed the layout of the late-Archaic town, with 7th- to 6th-century BC houses and artisans' workshops.

VETULONIA [22 km]

This medieval village in the Maremma, previously called Colonna, lies on a hill overlooking the plain around Grosseto. It was built on the site of the important Etruscan city of Vetulonia, whose location had been forgotten after it was destroyed, probably in the early Middles Ages.

The **Museo Archeologico**, at the entrance to the town houses Villanovan and especially Etruscan antiquities from ancient Vetulonia (from the 8th century BC to Hellenistic times). Between two medieval towers in the upper part of the town you can see the 6th- to 5th-century BC polygonal blocks belonging to the **Mura dell'Arce,** the oldest part of the city walls.

LIVORNO

"I magine a delightful, pocket-sized, brand-new town, that would fit nicely into a snuff-box; that's Livorno". This is how Charles de Brosses (1739) described the new town – a late Renaissance 'ideal city' which was very successful. It was founded in 1577 by the Medici Grand-duke Francesco I, at the southern edge of the Arno flood plain, beside an old Pisan fortified village.

Its prosperity was the result of the seaport and the famous 'constitution' of 1593, which encouraged immigration by protecting the freedom of newcomers, and particularly Jews. It was, as De Brosses noted, inhabited by "all kinds of nations of Europe and Asia". Modern Livorno is a thriving commercial and industrial city. In the old center, the five-pointed Medici fortress can still be seen, with its surrounding moat, and beyond, traces of the enlargement carried out under the Dukes of Lorraine in the early 19th century. In 1881 Livorno was chosen as the location of the Naval Academy.

Venezia Nuova ❶

This colorful district was once inhabited by fishermen and sailors.

It was called New Venice because it was built using Venetian workers and techniques, under the Medici (1629).

It still maintains features of the original layout, with a dense network of canals and bridges, narrow lanes, and shops and houses built over the water. Standing in the central Piazza dei Domenicani is the 18th-century, octagonal church of *Santa Caterina*. The **Bottini dell'Olio** in

The Fosso Reale (Royal Moat) around the Fortezza Nuova

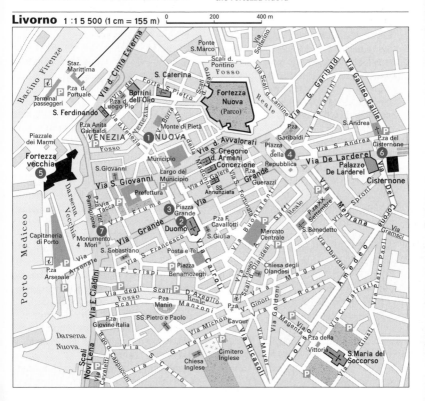

Livorno 1 : 1 5 500 (1 cm = 155 m)

Livorno, the Fortezza Vecchia (Old Fortress)

Viale Caprera were built in 1705 as warehouses for storing oil. These two large spaces, with vaults supported by stone columns, now house a library. Not far away is the church of *San Ferdinando*, built in 1707-14 by G.B. Foggini, with a Baroque interior richly decorated with stucco, marble and statues.

Duomo ❷

This late Gothic building (1594-1606) was rebuilt after being totally detroyed by bombs in 1943. It has a simple facade with marble portico on Doric columns. The *nave* houses tombs and ceiling paintings by Jacopo Ligozzi, by Empoli and by Passignano.

Piazza Grande ❸

This square in the heart of the old Medici town, surrounded by porticoed palazzi, is the city's center. It was completely reconstructed after the second world war. Opposite the Duomo, behind *Palazzo Grande*, is Largo Municipio (Municipal Square). On the right is *Palazzo Comunale*, built in 1720, with a double marble staircase. On the left is the 16th-century *Palazzo della Camera di Commercio*, by the Pistoia architect Annibale Cecchi; the facade has a large loggia.

Piazza della Repubblica ❹

This rectangular-shaped piazza, built between 1844 and 1848, features two classical-style statues: Ferdinand III,

Livorno, the Cisternone (Cistern)

towards the Fortezza Nuova, by Francesco Pozzi (1837); on the opposite side, Leopold II by Emilio Santarelli (1885). The neo-Classical Cisternino is almost on the corner with Via Grande. Designed by Poccianti, it was built as a water cistern between 1837 and 1842. However it was never used for this purpose, and today houses exhibitions, especially of figurative art. On the flanks there are architraved open galleries, and at the back a small apse; in front of this, is a monument to Domenico Guerrazzi by Lorenzo Gori and the facade of the 18th-century Palazzo del Picchetto. Facing onto the square is the late 16th-century **Fortezza Nuova** (New Fortress), surrounded by a moat dug by thousands of slaves and peasants at the beginning of the 17th century.
In the upper part there is a beautiful park with a fine view of the city.

Fortezza Vecchia ❺

This massive fortified complex with three bastions and two entrances was built in 1521-34 to a design by Antonio da Sangallo il Vecchio. It was seriously damaged during the second world war. It incorporates the so-called *Mastio della Contessa Matilde** , a solid 11th-century tower surrounded by a fortress dating from 1377, known as the *Quadratura dei Pisani*, attributed to Puccio di Landuccio.

View of Portoferraio with the 16th-century fortifications above the town

Piazza del Cisternone ❻

The square takes its name from the large cistern, with Doric-columned portico, built here in the first half of the 19th century. It is reached from Piazza della Repubblica along the broad *Via de Larderel*, where the neo-Classical facade of the 19th-century *Palazzo de Larderel* stands out at number 88.

Monumento dei Quattro Mori ❼

This most well-known of Livorno's monuments is in Piazza Micheli, and was built in honor of Grand-duke Ferdinand I in 1595. It is named after the four powerful, realistic, bronze figures of Moorish slaves, by Pietro Tacca, which were added to the base in 1626. The square looks onto the *Darsena Vecchia,* the old dock. Beyond stretches the *Porto Mediceo(B1)*, with above the remains of the fort which guarded the port's entrance. On the right, the 16th-century reddish walls of the Fortezza Vecchia can be seen.

DAY TRIPS

ISOLA D'ELBA [100 km]

Elba is the third largest Italian island, and the largest in the Tuscan Archipelago: 10km from the mainland,
it is about 27km long and 18km wide. The coastline is very indented, and rocky cliffs alternate with sandy beaches.
The interior of the island is very hilly; the highest peak is Monte Capanne (1018m).
Elba has been inhabited since prehistoric times. It was a Greek colony and then was inhabited by Etruscans who were drawn by its mineral resources. The Romans settled the island more extensively; they established the first towns (including Marciana, Portoferraio, Capoliveri) and built villas there.
The history of the island is complex. It was under the dominion of Pisa and Florence in the Middle Ages, and part of the Napoleonic principality in the early 19th century. But the island retained its own identity for centuries, with the local economy based on fishing and agriculture. The iron and steel industry became important at the beginning of the 20th century, but did not survive damage during the second world war. Especially since the 1960s, tourism has boomed, and this has helped to promote the local wine industry.

The main town (and point of entry to the island) is **Portoferraio**, which was originally a military station. Subsequently fishing, mining and salt-mining became important local activities, and finally at the end of the 19th century, iron and steel. The industry never recovered after damage inflicted in the second world war. From the modern port, the road leads up to the first bastion, Palle di Sotto, partially cut directly into the rock, and then to the Fronte d'Attacco*, built on various levels linked by walkways and tunnels. Beyond is Forte Falcone, and then **Napoleon's House** or the Palazzina dei Mulini, the main residence of the Emperor and his entourage. Of note: the

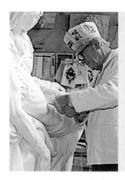

STONE-CARVING

Over 150 types of minerals found on Elba (e.g. quartz, azurite, pyrite, hematite, tourmaline) are used to make beautiful jewelery and other objects; in summer visitors can admire them, browsing round the lively arts and crafts shops in the old town centers.

PIOMBINO [82 km]

This largely new town lies on the southern tip of the promontory of the same name. Piombino was a metal-working center in ancient times. Modern iron and steel production began at the end of the 19th century, and both the town and the port expanded.

Emperor's personal library, the Galleria furniture, the valets' room (with German, French and Italian caricatures of Napoleon), the reception hall, and the apartment of Paolina Borghese.

The road past the 16th-century Duomo and Palazzo Municipale leads through the Porta a Mare to the Medici mole.

Then on to the Fortezza della Linguella, with its octagonal tower, housing the **Museo Civico Archeologico**.

Other towns on Elba are: *Rio Marina*, a small port with the **Museo dei Minerali Elbani** and the **Parco Minerario** which provides an interesting tour of a nearby mine; *Porto Azzurro*, a seaside resort lying below the great Fortezza Stellare*; and *Marciana*, a small village with narrow houses in winding lanes and a great view of the sea. From here you can take the cable car up to the top of **Monte Capanne**.

In the center of the old town is the 14th-century church of **Sant'Antimo**, with a 14th-century and a 13th-century tomb, and a font by Andrea Guardi (1470). There is a Renaissance *cloister* on the right flank of the church. In nearby Corso Vittorio Emanuele II, is the *Palazzo Comunale*, restored in 15th-century style, with a tower built in 1598. *Piazza Verdi* at the end of the Corso, is overlooked by a solid 15th-century section of the ancient walls, containing the *Porta Sant'Antonio*, linked to a tower built in 1213. The *Cittadella* at the top of the town was fortified in 1465-70; in the square here you will find the **Museo Archeologico del Territorio di Populonia**, with prehistoric objects, finds from the Etruscan necropolis at Populonia, and Roman antiquities. From the promontory, a great view* over the Channel of Piombino and the Tuscan Archipelago.

LIVORNO IN OTHER COLORS...

FOOD: P 123, 150
SHOPPING: P 163, 167
EVENTS: P 176
WELLNESS: P 189
PRACTICAL INFO: P 215

The harbour at Piombino

LUCCA

Lucca developed as a city-state in the Middle Ages, and remained independent until 1847. The old town has been kept largely intact over the centuries by the city walls; in the early 1800s they were cleverly changed into a pleasant walking area.

As early as the 14th century, Lucca's flourishing silk industry and enterprising bankers enabled it to develop commercial links with western Europe and to become extremely prosperous. Its independence also meant that it was able to guarantee its citizens peace and tolerance; it is no coincidence that in the darkest years of the Counter-Reformation in Italy, certain books could only be published in Lucca (or in Venice). It can only be hoped that the city walls will continue to preserve the delightful atmosphere of the old center from the ravages of contemporary urban development. Its escape from the hectic confusion of modern life is all the more amazing given that the city is the center of an economically strong and dynamic area.

The main surviving element of the Roman city is the oval shape of the arena in Piazza dell'Anfiteatro, surrounded by medieval houses. The old medieval town features tower-houses and winding lanes, as well as unexpected open spaces with grand Romanesque buildings.

Aerial view of Lucca

Lucca: Duomo

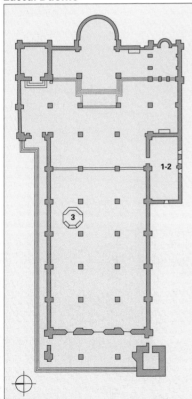

1 Tomb of Ilaria Del Carretto
2 Madonna and Saints by Ghirlandaio
3 Volto Santo Tempietto
(Small Temple with the Volto Santo)

Duomo ❶

Dedicated to St Martin, Lucca's 12th- to 13th-century Romanesque cathedral interior was remodeled in the 14th-15th centuries. The massive Romanesque marble facade* (1204) is largely the work of Guidetto da Como. It features a portico on three wide arches, and three tiers of small delicate open galleries in colored marble with small columns, each different from the others. The 13th-century campanile on the right is crenelated. The late Pisan-style apse* is impressive. Columns divide the graceful Gothic *interior* into a central nave and two side aisles; the transept is divided in two and has high arched galleries. The choir and apse windows are 15th-century. The church contains a number of artworks, including St Martin on Horseback and Beggar*, by a Lombard-Luccan artist (early 13th century). The Sacristy houses the famed funerary monument, **Tomba di Ilaria del Carretto****, of the wife of Paolo Guinigi, medieval lord of Lucca. This masterpiece by Jacopo della Quercia (1408) is one of the greatest Italian 15th-century sculptures.

Piazza San Martino ❷

Together with the adjacent squares, this square creates a spectacular medieval scenario. The Duomo towers over it and other lower buildings surround it. On the left, *Palazzo Bernardi* by Bartolomeo Ammannati (1556), with a walled garden. On the right, backing onto the impressive campanile, the 13th-century *Casa dell'Opera del Duomo*, a typical example of a Luccan medieval house, with arches and divided windows.

The Guinigi Tower

Via Guinigi ❸

One of the city's most attractive streets, with an unspoilt medieval appearance. The street features the **Case dei Guinigi***, a dense complex of 14th-century towers and palazzi in brick. These are perhaps the latest and most impressive examples of Romanesque-Gothic Luccan houses, with columned arcades on the ground floor, and wide windows on the upper floors. Don't miss the large palazzo on the corner

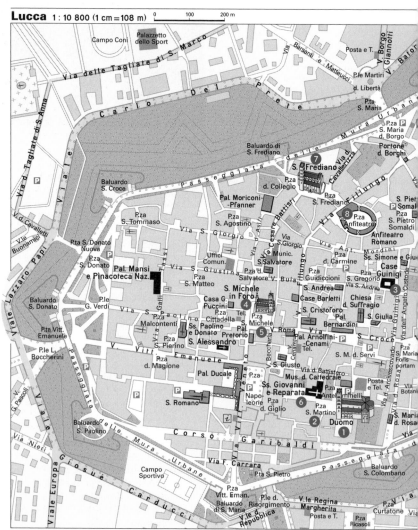

Lucca 1 : 10 800 (1 cm = 108 m)

of Via Sant'Andrea, with its high tower (44m) and oak tree growing on top. The palazzo houses the *Museo Storico della Liberazione* (History Museum of the Liberation, 1943-45).

San Michele in Foro ❹

Construction of the church started in 1070 and continued until the 14th century. It is a fine example of Pisan-Luccan architecture. Four tiers of small open galleries crown the high facade; they are richly decorated* with marble inlay. In the pediment an enormous statue of the archangel St Michael, again Romanesque. Standing below on the right edge is a copy of the statue of the Madonna and Child by Matteo

Lucca, Piazza del Mercato

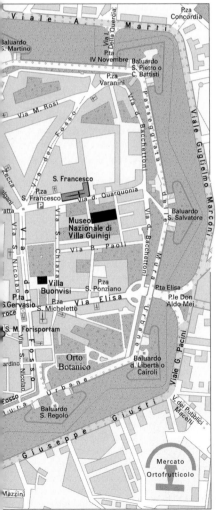

Civitali (1480; original inside). The flank is magnificent, with its dynamic arcading and 14th-century loggia. At the end stands the sturdy arched campanile. The remarkable apse* is in Pisan style.

Columns with Romanesque capitals divide the *interior* into a central nave and two side aisles. Artworks include: on the counter-facade, Madonna and Child, a 14th-century fresco attributed to Giuliano di Simone; in the right aisle, Madonna and Child*, a glazed terracotta by Andrea della Robbia; in the right transept, Four Saints*, a panel by Filippino Lippi.

Piazza San Michele ❺

This lively, colorful center of city life occupies the area of the ancient Roman forum. The marble church of San Michele in Foro looks onto the square with its 13th- and 14th-century houses. On the corner with Via Vittorio Veneto, is the Renaissance *Palazzo del Podestà* or *Palazzo Pretorio*. Building started in 1494 possibly to a design by Matteo Civitali. It was then enlarged in 1588 by Vincenzo Civitali and has a columned portico with large divided windows. The *Casa di Giacomo Puccini* is in nearby Via di Poggio; it houses musical instruments, portraits and mementos of the great composer.

Santi Giovanni e Reparata ❻

The church was built in the 12th century over earlier church buildings, and was partly remodeled in the 17th century. It preserves the original Romanesque main doorway with reliefs (1187). The *interior*, divided into central nave and two side aisles by ancient columns with Romanesque capitals, has a transept and a deep apse. Recent excavations have brought to light the early-Christian and early-medieval floor plans of the basilica, and of the adjacent *Baptistery*, a large square structure with fine Gothic cupola dating from 1393. Roman remains can also be visited, below floor level.

San Frediano ❼

Built in 1112-47 and altered in the 13th century, the church has an extremely fine, simple facade with columned open gallery, surmounted by a Byzantine-style mosaic (Ascension*), restored in the 19th century. The harmonious basilica *interior*, divided into central nave and side aisles by ancient columns, has a vast apse. At the beginning of the *right aisle* is a magnificent Romanesque baptismal font* in the form of a fountain (12th century), sculpted with reliefs. There are many artworks by Matteo Civitali. The series of **reliefs**** decorating the Cappella dei Trenta at the end of the left aisle is by Jacopo della Quercia. Next to the church are the remains of the 13th-century *Cemetery of Santa Caterina*, in the form of a three-sided cloister. The oldest side was changed into the Chapels of Santa Maria del Soccorso and of Santa Zita.

Piazza Anfiteatro ❽

The square, previously known as Piazza del Mercato (Market Square), was created in 1830, when buildings occupying the ancient Roman amphitheater were demolished. Part of the outer ring of the 2nd-century construction and the original oval ground-plan can still be seen. During the Middle Ages buildings and houses continued to be built around the arena. The delightful and architecturally interesting square is most lively on July evenings when it is the venue for concerts of all kinds.

DAY TRIPS

FORTE DEI MARMI [37 km]

This famous bathing resort spreads around the fortress built in 1788 by Leopold I. The Forte still stands, though rather the worse for wear, in the main square (Piazza Garibaldi). The modern-day, fashionable town no longer has the atmosphere of the old port. In the past, marbles were shipped from here, giving the town its name. Only the wharf remains, extending 300m into the sea, and marking the point where blocks of marble from the Apuan Alps were loaded. Today the town's regular grid-like layout features beautiful private villas and once-famous nightspots, such as *La Capannina*, a seafront disco that was all the rage in the fifties and sixties. Forte dei Marmi was discovered in the 19th century by European artists and intellectuals. It has a lively literary tradition: part of this is the «International Festival of Satire», one of the best-known events of the kind in Europe. The Festival led to the opening of the **Museo della Satira e della Caricatura**, with caricatures, a video library and multimedia archives, housed in the Fortezza.

MASSACIUCCOLI [6 km]

The coastal strip separating Pisa from the sea is extremely rich in naturalistic terms. In many places you can clearly see the different types of vegetation ranked in parallel bands back from the coast, protecting the remaining patches of forest behind from the sea winds. The area is at the center of the **Parco Naturale di Migliarino-San Rossore-Massaciùccoli**, extending for 23,000 hectares. The park's plant and animal life (many fallow deer and wild boar) make the park well worth visiting. It provides rest areas and picnic areas, as well as birdwatching points, cycle paths, and walking paths with information about the park and its flora and fauna. **Lago di Massaciùccoli**, a lake in the park, was once a delta lagoon of the Arno. Standing on the lakeside is the house where the great composer Giacomo Puccini

LUCCA IN OTHER COLORS...

■ **ITINERARIES:** P 100
■ **FOOD:** P 127, 131, 143
■ **SHOPPING:** P 164, 167, 171
■ **EVENTS:** P 179
■ **WELLNESS:** P 184
■ **PRACTICAL INFO:** P 216

Viareggio 1 : 19 500 (1 cm = 195 m)

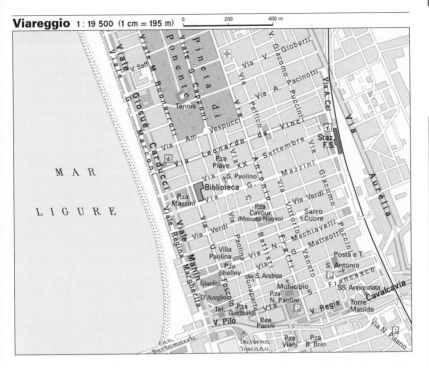

(1858-1924) lived for 33 years, from 1891. Now it is the **Museo Villa Puccini**, and houses the composer's tomb, as well as memorabilia related to his life.

VIAREGGIO [24 km]

Viareggio first developed in the 15th century around an earlier fortification. For centuries the only sea outlet for Lucca, it was a town of sailors and shipbuilders. Until, that is, it discovered the fashion for bathing that swept Europe in the 19th century. Today Viareggio is an extremely well-established seaside resort. But it hasn't forgotten its more traditional past: fishing and especially shipbuilding are still important activities. Its shipyards are renowned for the pleasure boats they produce. The city comes alive in the winter, during the famous Carnevale, with its float procession which arouses interest nationwide. The skilful work of the artisans who build the floats all through the year can be admired in their hangar-workshops in the north of the city.

Viareggio is an appealing place, not so much for individual buildings or monuments, but as a whole, with its elegant avenues, its pinete (pine groves), and the beautiful **seafront** with gardens. It also has many fine examples of Art Deco architecture: the Savoia cinema with a neo-Classical touch; the Art Nouveau Duilio '48 stores; the Galleria del Libro, which began life in 1929 as a fashion atelier; Caffè Margherita with decorations by Galileo Chini; and the Balena baths. The seafront walk leads to the Burlamacca Canal, and continues on along the long mole which starts here.

Viareggio at carnival time

MASSA

The town is in two parts: a small medieval nucleus gathered around the hill where the Rocca Malaspina stands, and the wider-spread 16th-century town centered on Piazza degli Aranci (with orange trees on three sides of the square). It is situated on the banks of the Frigido river, below the Apuan foothills. The town has grown and now reaches almost as far as Marina on the coast. It was the capital of the Malaspina Duchy, before becoming part of the Duchy of Modena. Most of the town's key buildings are connected to the Malaspina family.

Duomo ❶

Dedicated to St Peter and St Francis, the Duomo's original 1389 form has been much modified. It has a modern marble facade (1936) with two tiers of superimposed arches. There is a Riccomanni font on the right of the Baroque *nave* flanked by chapels.

The Cybo Malaspina and Bishops* crypt has the tombs of Lorenzo and Eleonora, respectively by Stagio Stagi and Pietro Aprile. The last chapel (of the Sacrament) on the right features: at the altar, a fresco fragment (Madonna) by Pinturicchio; on the sides, a 15th-century triptych and a Crib in

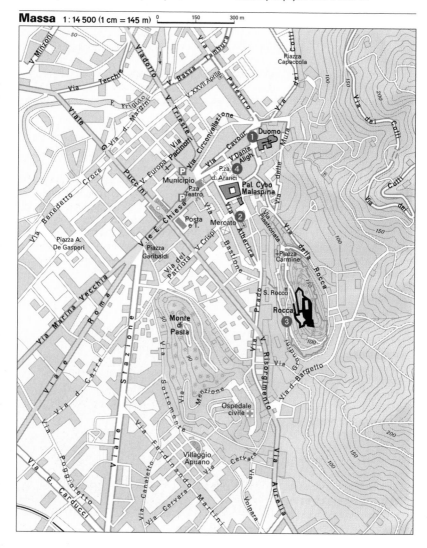

Massa 1 : 14 500 (1 cm = 145 m) 0   150   300 m

polychrome terracotta by Benedetto Buglioni (16th century). In the presbytery, six bronze candelabra by Ferdinando Tacca; on the left, a 14th-century wood Crucifix.

Museo Diocesano ❷

The museum is housed in new premises, in the former Palazzo Vescovile; it contains works representative of the history of art and of the church in the Diocese. These include furnishings, vestments, gold objects and artworks from the cathedral of St Peter and St Francis, and other churches.
Worth noting: a Crucifix by Ferdinando Tacca, the 17th-century collection of chasubles, and a 17th-century silver *Madonna of the Rosary*.

Rocca ❸

On top of a ramparted hill, the Rocca consists of a medieval nucleus connected by a loggia to a 15th- to 16th-century Renaissance palazzo, built by the Malaspina. The fine polychrome facade

with decorated windows can be seen from the 16th-century courtyard. The entrance loggia on the right leads to the 14th-century fortress and walls. From the top of the fort there is a wonderful view over the town and the coast. Inside is the **Museo del Castello Malaspina**, with archeological exhibits.

Piazza degli Aranci ❹

This central square in the old town features a fountain-obelisk (1853) and is overlooked by the long colored facade (1701) of the 16th- to 17th-century **Palazzo Cybo Malaspina**, with its arcaded courtyard.

Museo Etnologico delle Apuane «Luigi Bonacoscia» ❺

The museum is at 85 Via degli Oliveti, towards the sports stadium. It contains one of the most complete ethnological collections in Tuscany, with over 10,000 finds organised in 30 sections. All aspects of everyday life and culture are covered, such as domestic life, work and clothing.

CARRARA

Carrara is set among olive-cloaked hills; the Apuan Alps, blue and bare in the background, are streaked with white debris from the marble quarries there. Half a million tons are extracted every year, 70% from the valley of the River Carrione, which flows down to Carrara. In the past the marble blocks were slid down the slopes on soap-coated timbers, by the "lizzatori" or sled-men, who controlled them with heavy ropes. They were then loaded onto sailing boats at Marina di Carrara; later there was the railway. Today marble is transported by road from the three hundred or more quarries, to *studios*, where it is transformed by skilled marble workers trained at the specialist school of marble.

Duomo ❶

A Romanesque-Gothic building (11th-14th century), all marble, in white and grey stripes. The Pisan-style facade has 12th-century arcading below, a fine sculpted Romanesque main doorway, a columned open gallery and a splendid Gothic rose window in a square lacunar frame. Also worth noting: the Romanesque doorway on the right flank (where there is a 16th-century fountain with a statue of Andrea Doria as Neptune, by Baccio Bandinelli), the apse with columned open gallery and the campanile with

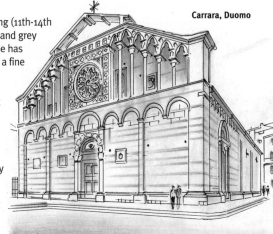

Carrara, Duomo

Carrara
1 : 13 500 (1 cm = 135 m)

[Map of Carrara with labeled streets and locations including Duomo, Chiesa della Madonna d. Grazie Lugnola, Accad di Belle Arti, Municipio, S. Francesco, and various Vie and Piazze]

divided windows. The simple (restored) interior with central nave and side aisles on columns with fine capitals, has various marbles and remains of 13th- to 16th-century frescoes on the walls.

Accademia di Belle Arti ❷
In the courtyard of the 16th-century *Palazzo Cybo Malaspina*, Roman

sculptures and fragments from the Roman colony of Luni and the quarries. The **Edicola dei Fantiscritti*** is interesting; it is a Roman altar found in the Fantiscritti Quarry, and carved with the names of famous visitors, including Giambologna and Canova.

Museo Civico del Marmo. This large municipal museum is at 85 Viale XX Settembre (about 3km from the center). It has five sections: *Roman Archeology and Local History*; *The Marble Collection*, a long gallery with over a thousand samples of marbles from all over the world; *Industrial Archeology*, with both old and modern tools, machinery and marble working methods, some illustrated with old photos; *Technical Applications of Marble*; and *Modern Sculpture*, with about thirty works by contemporary sculptors.

View of Carrara

DAY TRIPS

PARCO NATURALE DELLE ALPI APUANE [2 km]

The Park was established in 1985 by the Tuscan Regional Authority; it covers the mountainous area between the Versilia coast and the Magra-Aulella and Serchio rivers, and includes 16 municipalities in the Massa-Carrara and Lucca Provinces. Michelangelo came here to find marble when commissioned to work on Pope Julius II's never-to-be-completed tomb. Giambologna, Canova and many others worked with marble from these mountains, named after an ancient Ligurian tribe.

The geology of the area (mostly extremely finely crystalised limestone) makes the Apuan Alps pretty rugged, with their precipitous, unforested peaks

MARINA DI MASSA [5 km]

Five kilometers south-west of Massa, this pleasant seaside resort lies beside a pineta (pine grove). The beach is very popular and has lovely fine sand.

PONTREMOLI [56 km]

This is the main city of the Lunigiana region, and today is known especially for hosting the prestigious Bancarella Prize, founded by local booksellers. The simple, original old town lies between the Verde and Magra Rivers. The hills in the surrounding countryside are heavily wooded with chestnut trees. The Castello del Piagnaro, overlooking the town from a hilltop, takes its name from the *piagne*, or slate slabs, common in the area. It houses the **Museo delle Statue-Stele Lunigianesi**, with its enigmatic prehistoric sandstone sculptures, or statue-stelae, found locally.

The Baroque **Cattedrale** has a neo-Classical facade and campanile remodeled from a 14th-century tower. The church of **San Francesco**, on the left bank of the River Verde, has a Romanesque campanile and inside, a fine polychrome bas-relief (Madonna with Child) attributed to Agostino di Duccio (15th-century). Just outside the town, 1.6km along state

MARBLE FORMATION

Marble is a crystaline kind of calcium, formed from calcareous rocks which have undergone a second crystaline process, due to the effect of pressure or heat. Calcium with no impurities produces white marble; calcium containing other minerals apart from calcite has a colored appearance (Photo: green serpentine quarry).

and steep gorges, in curious contrast with the gentler shapes of the Apennines and the green, beach-lined coast. The Alps are one of the world's greatest sources of marble, particularly the exceptional white marble. You can drive up the Alps almost as far as the quarries. The most interesting routes start from Massa and Carrara; another interesting road from the Aurelia Highway goes across the mountains to Castelnuovo di Garfagnana.

The Park's three *Visitor Centers* are at Forno di Massa, Castelnuovo di Garfagnana and Seravezza (Park Headquarters). They organise talks and guided walks.

highway 62 towards Filattiera, you will find the 16th-century **Sant'Annunziata**, an interesting single-nave church with raised presbytery. It contains a polyptych of the Madonna and Child by the Genoese artist Giacomo Serfolio (15th-16th century) and a 16th-century marble octagonal tempietto* (small temple) decorated with statues and a bas-relief (Annunciation). Beside the church is the former *Convent of the Augustinians*, with two 15th-century cloisters. It houses the State Archives, and the Città del Libro Foundation, which organizes the renowned Bancarella Prize.

MASSA - CARRARA
IN OTHER COLORS...

ITINERARIES: P 100
FOOD: P 124, 127, 143
SHOPPING: P 164
EVENTS: P 176
WELLNESS: P 188
PRACTICAL INFO: P 196, 219

PISA

Visitors to Pisa tend to concentrate on the area around the cathedral. The visual impact, harmony of style, and sheer artistic mastery of each of the buildings separately and the effect of them all together will more than satisfy even the most demanding traveller. And that's not all. If you manage to tear yourself away from this magical place, one of Italy's greatest cities of art awaits you, with a rich array of monuments and museums, along with the city itself. Pisa's great beauty is unique, a reminder of its glorious past as a maritime republic, in control of a large part of the Mediterranean until its disastrous defeat by Genoa at the Battle of Meloria in 1284. The Florentines battled for centuries against Pisa; when they finally took the city (1406), they acknowledged its uniqueness by promoting learning and the university. Pisa is still a renowned and very lively university town, with a considerable student population.

Piazza del Duomo ❶

This space known as the *Campo dei Miracoli* (Field of Miracles) is the setting for Europe's greatest and best-known group of Romanesque buildings. Their greatness is heightened by the ideas underlying their construction: the key buildings (Battistero, Duomo, Campanile, Spedale and Camposanto) trace life's path, from birth to death, for medieval man. The sight is more than just the sum of its parts. Of key importance was the construction in the second half of the 13th century of the Camposanto to the north and the Spedale Nuovo to the south: the two long forms were deliberately not placed exactly parallel to the Duomo or to each other, thus making the space relations between the components more interesting. The current appearance of Piazza del Duomo dates from the 19th century when minor buildings were eliminated to make way for the more important ones.

The Piazza was built outside the main city center and protected by the first part of the city walls built in 1155, still perfectly preserved. Its buildings illustrate the Romanesque Pisan style, bringing together classical influence (the basilical design of the Duomo), Lombard influence (galleries and arches on facades), and oriental influence (black and white bands, blind arches with molding).

Camposanto ❷

Started in 1277 (but finished only in 1464), the rectangular Camposanto was for centuries the cemetery for noble and illustrious citizens. The large **portico** was

Campo dei Miracoli with the Battistero, Duomo and Campanile

decorated with a vast number of medieval frescoes, by artists such as Bonamico Buffalmacco, Taddeo Gaddi, Andrea Bonaiuti, Antonio Veneziano, Spinello Aretino, and in the 15th century to a considerable extent by Benozzo Gozzoli. The frescoes were seriously damaged in the second world war; they were detached from the walls and removed for restoration. Thus the walls are now bare. The floor is completely covered with tomb stones, and there are some remarkable funerary monuments. The restored frescoes are now in a spacious room next to the portico. They include **Triumph of Death****, Last Judgement* and Inferno*, probably by Buffalmacco, Scenes from the Life of Jobe by Taddeo Gaddi and Life of the Anchorites in the Hermitage*. In the chapel on the east side are fragments of detached and restored frescoes by, among others, Antonio Veneziano, Taddeo Gaddi, Benozzo Gozzoli, and Buffalmacco.

Duomo ❸

On the facade of this imposing white building, the greatest example of the Romanesque Pisan style, an inscription reads: "From the year Christ was born of the Virgin, One thousand and sixty-three years had passed when the famous gallant powerful citizens of Pisa began to construct this church". It was started by Buscheto and completed in the 12th century with the construction of the facade by Rainaldo. The facade, with blind arches below, has four tiers of columns with open galleries, decorated with sculptures and marble inlay. The three doorways feature bronze panels with bas-reliefs by the Giambologna school (late 16th century). Elegant decoration runs along the flanks and transepts to the beautiful apse with two tiers of columns. To the left of the apse is the Portale San Ranieri, with fine bronze panels* by Bonanno Pisano (1180).

Pisa: Duomo

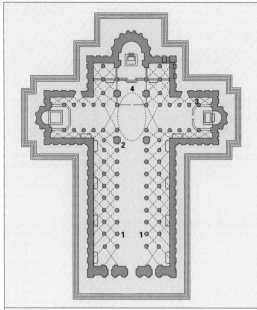

1 Stoup by Felice Palma
2 Pulpit by Giovanni Pisano
3 Tomb of Arrigo VII by Tino di Camaino
4 Presbytery with 15th century inlaid stalls

The walls of the light, awe-inspiring **interior** are in black and white marble bands. Closely-ranked columns divide the nave and side aisles; the interior also features a 16th-century wood ceiling, an ellipsoidal cupola, and a deep apse. At the end of the *nave* stands the magnificent marble **pulpit**** by Giovanni Pisano (1302-11; reassembled in 1926). It is an important and complex masterpiece of Italian Gothic sculpture, resting on columns and statues, with allegories related to changes in the Church at the time. Nearby hangs *Galileo's lamp*, in bronze (1587), named after the Pisan scientist because he was supposed to have understood the principle of the pendulum from the swinging of the lamp. In the *Presbytery* are 15th-century inlaid stalls* reconstructed in the early 17th century. At the sides, paintings by Andrea del Sarto (including St Agnes*, St Margaret and St Catherine*) and by Sogliani. On the altar, a bronze Crucifix by Giambologna. In the apse vault, a large 13th-century mosaic depicting the Redeemer between Mary and St John the Evangelist* (head of the latter by Cimabue).

Pisa 1:10 500 (1 cm = 105 m)

0   100   200 m

Via delle Cascine

Viale delle Cascine

Staz. Pisa-S. Rossore F.S.

P.le Griffi

Via C. Cammeo

Via Niccolini

Via Contessa

Camposan ②

Battistero ④

① P.za Manin

Duomo ③

P.za del Duomo

Campani ⑤

Museo dell'Oper del Duom

P.ta S. Maria

Museo d. Sinopie

ex S. Giorg d. Tedeschi

V. Andrea Pisano

Via Giunta Pisano

Via Diotisalvi

Via Gabba

Via Andrea Pisano

V. Bonanno Pisano

Orto

botanico

Via Savi

Università

Via Risorgimento

Via Pisano

Domus galilaeana

Piscina

V. Rustichello da Pisa

Via Nicola Pisano

V. Enrico Fermi

Via Trieste

V. Trento

S. Nicola

Museo Naz. di Pal. Reale

P.za Solferino

Campo Sportivo d. Abetone

Via Volturno

Lungarno

⑩ S. Maria d. Spina

Lun

Arsenale d. Galee

Simonelli

P.te Solferino

P.za Saffi

Cittadella Vecchia

Lungarno

F. Arno

Lungarno Sonnino

Via S. Paolo

Via S. Antoni

Ponte d. Cittadella

Lungarno Cosimo I°

P.ta a Mare

⑫ S. Paolo a Ripa d'Arno

P.za S. Paolo a Ripa d'Arno

Via F. Niosi

Via Manzo

Strada Statale N° 1

L.go Degazia

V. Zerboglio

V. Lavagna

Via B. da Padule

Via Fazio

Via Pia a Mare

L.go Marinai d'Italia

Via Nino Bixio

S. Anton

Crisp

Ponte dell'Aurelia

Viale D'Annunzio

Via S. Giovanni al Gatano

Via Conte

Via Livornese

Staz. Autolinee

Via Cesare Battisti

Via Vecchia

Via Aurelia

Via Quarantola

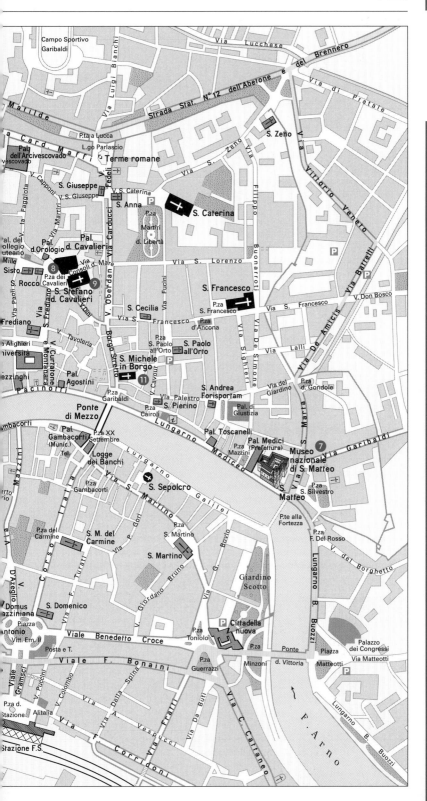

Battistero ❹

A majestic round Romanesque building in white marble, surrounded by arcading and galleried columns with a Gothic cornice. Started in 1152 by Diotisalvi, it was continued in the 13th-century by Nicola and Giovanni Pisano, and completed in the second half of the 14th century, under the direction of Cellino di Nese, with an eight-sided pyramidal cupola. There are four fine portals*: especially noteworthy is the one facing the Duomo, flanked by carved columns and with reliefs in the architrave. In the interior, a circle of columns and pilasters with figured capitals support a gallery beneath the cupola (18m in diameter). In the center, the octagonal font* by Guido da Como (1246), with rosettes and marble inlay. To the left, supported by columns resting on lions, the **pulpit**** by Nicola Pisano (1260), decorated by five reliefs with scenes from the life of Christ, figures of the Prophets and of the Virtues. In front of the altar, a 13th-century pavement of marble, rosette and inlay panels. Along the walls, large statues by Nicola and Giovanni Pisano and school, previously placed outside the building.

Campanile or «Torre di Pisa» ❺

Universally known as the *Leaning Tower*, and undisputed symbol of the city, this is one of the world's most famous towers, partly because of its beauty, and partly because of its tilt. Building started in 1173, but was then stopped when the ground began to subside under the tower, causing it to lean to one side. Building then continued and was completed, possibly by Tommaso Pisano, in the

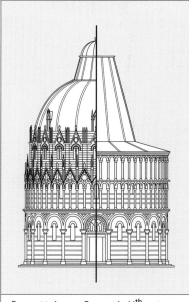

Pisa: Baptistery, elevation

Prospect today   Prospect in 14th century

second half of the 14th century. The cylindrical tower is surrounded below by blind arches, and then by six tiers of columns with open galleries, similar to those of the cathedral apse. In the inside, shaped like a cylindrical well, a spiral staircase with 294 steps climbs to the top of the tower (54m); here Galileo carried out experiments on falling objects.

Museo dell'Opera del Duomo ❻

The museum houses artworks from the Campo dei Miracoli buildings and is situated in a vast complex at the eastern end of Piazza del Duomo, once Palazzo dei Canonici. The enormous collection includes works by Nicola and Giovanni Pisano (busts and statues from the Battistero, *Madonna and Child* in ivory) and by Tino di Camaino (altar-tomb of San Ranieri and monument to Arrigo VII).

Museo Nazionale di San Matteo ❼

Since 1949 housed in the former Benedictine convent of San Matteo, the recently

THE LEANING TOWER'S LEAN

The tower leans around 5° 30' off the vertical, to the south, with an annual increase of about 6". In 1990 consolidation work was begun which took 12 years; today it is again possible to climb to the top of the tower, where Galileo Galilei carried out his famous experiments on falling objects.

reorganized museum shows the development of medieval Christian painting and sculpture in Europe. The ground floor has an excellent collection of *medieval ceramics*, with a series of ceramic tondoes* of Islamic origin (11th century) and of Pisan manufacture (13th century), used to decorate the outer walls of the city's churches. There are also ceramic fragments and objects from excavations in various parts of the city, and 12th- to 15th-century stone sculptures. The first floor is given over to: *12th- to 14th-century Sculpture*, with works by Tino di Camaino and the Pisanos; 14th- and 15th-century *Wood Sculptures* of the Pisan and Sienese schools; *15th-century Sculpture* featuring the **gilded bronze reliquary-bust of St Luxorius****, by Donatello and a Redeemer*, terracotta bust from Verrocchio's workshop. In the

Medici in the city. Many of the 16th-century buildings around the square were to a large extent designed by Giorgio Vasari. The largest is **Palazzo dei Cavalieri***(1562), the remodeled medieval Palazzo degli Anziani (Palazzo of the Elders), and today the premises of the Scuola Normale Superiore, founded in 1810 by Napoleon. It has an impressive curved facade with graffiti decoration, and a double staircase (19th century). In front of the palazzo is the statue of Cosimo I and to the right, the church of Santo Stefano dei Cavalieri. **Palazzo dell'Orologio** (Clock Palazzo), in the northern corner of the square, has its original facade set on two ancient towers joined by a grandiose arcade. Count Ugolino della Gherardesca (1288) was imprisoned in the right tower with his sons and grandsons. Their ghastly death by starvation is recounted by Dante in his Inferno.

The Church of Santa Maria della Spina, on the Gambacorti Arno embankment

rooms devoted to painting: fragments of frescoes and large crosses painted on panels, from Pisan churches; a magnificent **Madonna and Child with Saints****, a polyptych by Simone Martini (1319); and works by Gentile da Fabriano, Masaccio and Beato Angelico.

Piazza dei Cavalieri ❽

This was the center of Pisa when it was a republic, and was then modified in the late 16th century to make room for the seat of the Order of the Knights of St Stephen, founded by Cosimo I de' Medici. The piazza thus came to symbolize the power of the

Santo Stefano dei Cavalieri ❾

The church and campanile were built to a design by Giorgio Vasari (1569). The marble facade dates from 1606. In the *interior*, with a large central nave and two side aisles, three fragments from the knights' galleys in carved wood (17th century), as well as panels, and paintings in the wood ceiling, by Cigoli, Allori, Empoli and Ligozzi.

Santa Maria della Spina ❿

This enchanting little Gothic-Romanesque church was originally a small chapel on the banks of the Arno, and was enlarged in 1323. It takes its name from a thorn preserved in the church, supposedly from Christ's crown (which is now in Santa Chiara). In 1871 it was dismantled and reconstructed further up to protect it from the flood waters of the Arno. It is surrounded by arches enclosing divided windows; higher up it is covered with niches, pinnacles and spires, with statues from the school of Nino Pisano. On the central spire, a Madonna and Child by Nino Pisano (original in the Museo di San Matteo). There are white and dark bands in the light *interior*. At the altar, Madonna and Child, and at the sides, St Peter and St John, statues* by Andrea and Nino Pisano. On the left wall, a small tabernacle by Stagio Stagi (1534) that once contained the thorn.

San Michele in Borgo ⓫

Built in the 11th century, this church was enlarged and modified in the 14th century. It has a sturdy Gothic-Romanesque facade in the Pisan style (14th century), with fine doorways and three tiers of columns with open galleries. The interior has a central nave and two side aisles, with presbytery raised over the crypt. The inner lunette of the left doorway features a 13th-century fresco of St Michael. On the left wall, a marble Crucifix of the Pisan school (second half of 14th century).

San Paolo a Ripa d'Arno ⓬

The facade and left flank of this fine Pisan-Romanesque 11th- to 12th-century church echo the decoration on the Duomo. The interior was badly damaged in the war and heavily restored. It has a central nave and side aisles, with transept, cupola and semicircular apse. The columns with fine capitals support Arab-style pointed arches. In the left transept, Madonna and Four Saints by Turino Vanni (1397); and in the apse a 14th-century stained glass window. Behind the apse of the church, the chapel of **Sant'Agata*** stands apart . This small 12th-century church is octagonal with a pyramidal cupola.

PISA IN OTHER COLORS...

 FOOD: P 124, 154
 SHOPPING: P 164, 167
 EVENTS: P 177, 180
 WELLNESS: P 185, 191
 PRACTICAL INFO: P 225

DAY TRIPS

SAN MINIATO [42 km]

The town, strategically situated on the Via Francigena, looks down over the plain where the Arno flows between Florence and Pisa. The town's layout has remained intact and its medieval appearance is a reminder of the emperors who passed this way (Henry IV, Barbarossa, Federick II).
The church of **San Domenico**, with its unfinished facade, stands in Piazza del Popolo. It contains frescoes and paintings by the 14th- to 18th-century Florentine school. The **Duomo** commands a magnificent view over the Arno valley. It retains the original Romanesque fine brick facade with sculptured marbles, and the campanile, which is the remodeled tower of an old castle, still with its external gallery. Looking onto Piazza del Duomo: the **Museo Diocesano d'Arte Sacra**, with paintings from the Tuscan school and beautiful 13th-century majolica tondoes removed from the facade of the Duomo; the *Palazzo Vescovile* (13th-century) and the medieval *Palazzo Pretura-Miravalle*, where according to legend Countess Matilda of Canossa was born in 1046.
The *tower* at the top of the hill, known as Frederick's tower, was the prison of Pier delle Vigne, one of Frederick II's stewards. He killed himself here, as recounted in Dante's Divine Comedy.

SAN ROSSORE [5 km]

The Estate of San Rossore covers 4,800 hectares in the Park. First it belonged to the Duomo of Pisa; later it was a Medici hunting reserve, and then it belonged to the Savoys. Now it is the summer residence of the Italian President. An area of around 400 hectares, in the southern part, is subject to flooding. Its marshes, well-known by bird-watchers, attract thousands of birds every year. The complex of the *Cascine Vecchie*, renovated in the early 19th century, houses a center which provides information about the Park and organises guided tours.

Volterra, the 13th-century Palazzo dei Priori

VOLTERRA [66 km]

Volterra is perched on cliffs "at the highest point of a high hill", as Stendhal wrote, between the valleys of the Era and the Cècina rivers. The countryside seen from the town's various scenic viewpoints is striking: its rocky abysses produced by centuries of erosion seem to be about to swallow up the eyrie-like town. And in fact houses, churches and Etruscan burial sites have crumbled away over the years. However, Volterra still looks medieval, with its buildings in grey stone, while the collections in the nationally-important archeological museum bear witness to its great Etruscan past. It was the Etruscans who first used alabaster for their cinerary

urns, and still today the town is justly proud of its workmanship of this noble material.

Piazza dei Priori ❶ is one of Italy's most interesting medieval squares. Surrounded by austere palazzi, it was a marketplace as early as 851. It features the 15th-century *Palazzo Vescovile*, the apse of the Duomo and Palazzo dei Priori, a solid 14th-century building with crenelated tower, and magnificent facade with divided windows and glazed terracotta coats-of-arms.

The 12th- to 13th-century Romanesque **Duomo** ❷ has a simple facade, with a geometrically decorated marble portal and a blind arcade in the gable. The *interior*, with central nave and side aisles on marble columns, has an ornate 16th-century lacunar wood ceiling. It features various artworks including a pulpit* on four columns with 13th-century sculptures, a Deposition*, a 13th-century silver and gilded polychrome wood sculpture group, and the elegant ciborium* by Mino da Fiesole (1471). In the *Cappella dell'Addolorata*, there is a

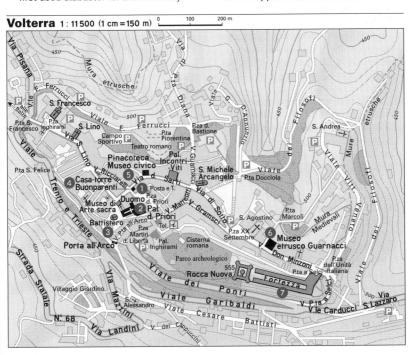

Volterra 1 : 11500 (1 cm = 150 m)

Volterra, the Roman theater

fresco by Benozzo Gozzoli (Arrival of the Magi*). Standing opposite the Duomo is the **Battistero**, ❸ a fine 13th-century octagonal building, with a Romanesque portal in the green and white banded front. Inside, a font* by Andrea Sansovino (1502). The nearby Museo dell'Opera del Duomo di Arte Sacra contains sculptures (St Linus*, by Andrea Della Robbia), goldsmithery (bust of St Octavian* in embossed silver, attributed to Antonio del Pollaiolo), illuminated anthem-books and paintings (Madonna Enthroned and Saints*, by Rosso Fiorentino, 1521).

The **Quadrivio dei Buonparenti** is a charming medieval crossroads in the old town. The lofty **Buonparenti tower-house*** ❹ marks this meeting point of the town's main roads, also overlooked by palazzi, tower-houses, austere churches and craft workshops. Several typical 13th-century tower-houses stand out, including the previously-mentioned Buonparenti tower-house*, linked by a foot-bridge to the *Buonaguidi tower*.

The **Pinacoteca and Museo Civico** ❺ are housed in the *Palazzo Solaini*, attributed to Antonio da Sangallo il Vecchio. It has an elegant courtyard, with loggia on the second floor and halls with beautiful ceilings. Around fifteen rooms on two floors contain works by Florentine, Sienese and Volterran artists from the 14th to the 17th centuries. In addition to works by Domenico Ghirlandaio and Luca Signorelli, there is the exceptional **Deposition from the Cross****, a Mannerist masterpiece by Rosso Fiorentino (1521).

The **Museo Etrusco Guarnacci** ❻ has forty rooms housing an enormous collection of antiquities from prehistoric to imperial Roman times. The most interesting part is the Etruscan section. It contains many cinerary urns in tufa, alabaster and terracotta (4th-1st century BC) from local excavations, including the famous **Urna degli Sposi** (Urn of the Married Couple, 1st century BC). There are also sculptures (the renowned **Ombra della Sera*** or Shadow of the Evening, a 3rd-century BC bronze Etruscan statuette), tablets, ceramics, bronzes and weapons.

Volterra also has a **Roman Theater**, dating from the Augustan age (5-20 AD). It is also worth taking a walk along Viale dei Ponti, which gives great views of the Cècina valley and the **Fortezza** ❼. This is one of Italy's most impressive Renaissance forts; because it is still used today, as a prison, it cannot be visited.

The famous **Balze*** is a deep ravine which can be seen 2 km outside town towards the north-west.

PISTOIA

Pistoia is surrounded by 14th-century walls. In the past it was a place where artistic creativity and civil conflict co-existed. Here an elegant Romanesque style developed, open to outside influences. And here the struggles began between two Guelph factions (the white and the black), leading to years of civil war and forcing the great poet Dante Alighieri into exile from Florence.

Pistoia enjoyed centuries of greatness as a city-state, especially in the 13th century, when Pistoian bankers lent money to French kings and princes, and the city's prosperity allowed it to extend the city walls. Economic and political decline followed in the 14th century. The city was taken by Florence, and financial activity slowed, until the 18th century.

Industrial development in the 19th and 20th centuries led the city to sprawl beyond the old walls. But the old nucleus of the town still stands as a fine example of harmonious urban planning, where Gothic and Renaissance styles mix happily.

Piazza del Duomo ❶

This artistic and historic center of the city is an impressive sight, surrounded by medieval buildings. They include: the Duomo with its tall campanile; the Palazzo Vescovile and the Battistero; and facing each other, the Palazzo del Podestà and the Palazzo del Comune. At the corner of Via Tomba stands the medieval *Torre di Catilina*, named after the Roman patrician who fled to Etruria after his plotting was revealed by Cicero; Catilina was defeated (62BC) and buried near the city walls.

Duomo ❷

Romanesque in the Pisan style, the Duomo was built in the 12th-13th centuries. It has a stone facade, with three tiers of columns with open galleries, and a marble portico added in the second half of the 14th century. The dynamic 67m-high campanile* has Pisan-style columns and a 16th-century cusp. Andrea della Robbia created the glazed terracotta bas-relief in the main doorway lunette (Madonna and Child with Angels*) and the exquisite decoration of the barrel vault. The majestic *interior* with central nave and side aisles, and raised tribune added in the 17th century, features some important artworks. They include: a very old Crucifix on panel by Coppo di Marcovaldo (1275), a magnificent bronze candelabrum by Maso di Bartolomeo (1442), and a fine font* designed by Benedetto da Maiano. The chapel of San Jacopo (St Jacob) preserves the **altar frontal of St Jacob****, an exceptional work by Sienese, Pistoian and Florentine goldsmiths started in 1287 and completed in the mid-15th century. The precious silver three-sided altar-piece is decorated with panels in relief and statues.

Battistero ❸

Octagonal in shape, this graceful Gothic baptistery was started in 1337 by Cellino di Nese, possibly to a design by Andrea Pisano, and completed in 1361. It has white and green marble walls, with blind arcading. Its three doorways are richly decorated with reliefs and statues. Inside, the 14th-century font (for full immersion) was found during restoration carried out in 1960.

Pistoia, Piazza del Duomo

Madonna dell'Umiltà ❹

The basilica is an important example of Renaissance architecture, built in elegant Brunelleschi style (1494-1522) probably to a design by Giuliano da Sangallo. Octagonal in shape, it is surmounted by a large cupola. The *interior* consists of a large rectangular vestibule with a fine barrel vault, and a spacious octagon with large niches, two tiers of divided windows, and a cupola by Giorgio Vasari. At the high altar, a fresco (Madonna of Humility) by Pietro Tacca (late 16th century); the octagon chapels were decorated by Bartolomeo Ammannati.

Museo Civico ❺

The museum occupies the upper floors of the Palazzo del Comune, whose beautiful frescoed rooms have carved ceilings. The collection comprises two hundred 13th- and 14th-century works,

from Romanesque painting to local works showing Giottoesque influence. It features works by Lorenzo di Credi, Ridolfo del Ghirlandaio, Gerino Gerini, Giovanni Battista Naldini, Pompeo Batoni, and Ludovico Cigoli.

Fortezza di Santa Barbara ❻

This is a fine example of 16th-century military architecture, and part of the fortified walls designed by Buontalenti. The square fortress was built on the site of a medieval fortress, and is surrounded by a public park.

Palazzo dei Vescovi ❼

An important example of medieval Pistoian civil architecture, this 14th-century building with divided windows and loggia was modified a number of times. There are two parts to the Palazzo. The **Percorso Archeologico Attrezzato** shows the ancient origins of Pistoia and how the city was laid out. It also has coins and Etruscan tomb remains. The **Museo Capitolare di San Zeno** houses the Tesoro dell'Opera di San Jacopo (Treasury of St Jacob) with silverware and precious objects, featuring a reliquary of St Jacob (1407) from the Ghiberti workshop.

PISTOIA IN OTHER COLORS...

■ ITINERARIES: P 98
■ FOOD: P 124, 128, 132
■ SHOPPING: P 164, 167
■ EVENTS: P 177, 180
■ WELLNESS: P 186, 187
■ PRACTICAL INFO: P 226

Sant' Andrea ⑧

This beautiful 12th-century church with a Romanesque facade has reliefs by Gruamonte and Adeodato (1166) on the central doorway architrave, and figures of animals in the frames of the smaller portals. The *interior*, with narrow nave and side aisles, houses one of the masterpieces of medieval Italian sculpture: the **pulpit**** (1298-1301) by Giovanni Pisano, with its outstandingly dramatic reliefs. The pulpit is supported by seven porphyry columns: two rest on lions, one on a bent human figure denoting Adam crushed by sin, and the central one on a base with a griffin, an eagle and a lion symbolizing Christ's qualities. The Prophets and Prophetesses of the Old Testament rest against the capitals. The body of the pulpit depicts: Annunciation and Birth of Christ, Adoration of the Magi, Joseph's Dream, Massacre of the Innocents, Crucifixion, and Last Judgement. At the corners, figures of the apostles, the evangelists and of Christ. Also by Giovanni Pisano, the wood Crucifix* in an elegant 15th-century tabernacle halfway along the right aisle, and possibly the font with relief at the beginning of the left aisle.

San Giovanni Fuorcivitas ⑨

A wonderful example of the local Romanesque style, the church was built in the 12th century and finished only in the 14th century by Comacine masters. The flank towards Via Crispi, with walls banded in travertine and green marble, was the last part to be built. The main doorway architrave was sculpted by

Gruamonte (1162). The *interior* with single nave and raised presbytery features many artworks. On the right wall, a marble pulpit* by Fra' Guglielmo da Pisa (1270). In the middle of the church, a stoup* with the theological and cardinal Virtues (early work by Giovanni Pisano). In the presbytery on the left of the high altar, a polyptych* by Taddeo Gaddi (1353-55); and at the left altar, Visitation*, a glazed terracotta sculpture attributed to Luca della Robbia (1445).

DAY TRIPS

COLLODI [5 km]

The old center spreads up and along a ridge, in Valdinièvole. Collodi was the pen-name taken by the Florentine Carlo Lorenzini (1826-90), writer of *Pinocchio*. The **Parco di Pinocchio**, for children, includes a monument to Pinocchio with the Fairy by Emilio Greco (1956), a mosaics square, the Paese dei Balocchi, or Toyland, with sculptures by Pietro Consagra, and the *Laboratorio delle Parole e delle Figure* (Workshop of Words and Pictures), with exhibitions of work by illustrators of children's books.

Collodi, Villa Garzoni and the garden

The remains of a fortress and fortifications are found at the top of the town. Lower down, you can visit **Villa Garzoni** and its magnificent 17th-century garden with statues and fountains.

MONSUMMANO TERME [13 km]

Monsummano Terme is a spa town, offering a range of therapeutic thermal treatments. In the early 17th century, the

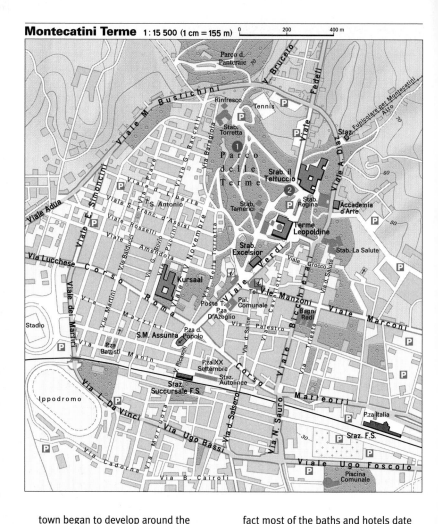

Montecatini Terme 1 : 15 500 (1 cm = 155 m)

town began to develop around the sanctuary of **Santa Maria di Fontenuova**, built in 1605 to celebrate the miracle of a good spring in a swampy valley. Birthplace of the 19th-century poet Giuseppe Giusti, his beautiful house in the town contains objects and documents relating to his life.
From Monsummano Terme, a road of 3.8km leads to **Monsummano Alto** (340m), a pretty medieval hamlet, with a few houses still remaining, ruins of the fortress and walls, and the Romanesque church of San Niccolò; a wonderful view over the Valdinièvole can be enjoyed from the top of the hill.

MONTECATINI TERME [15 km]
One of Europe's most enjoyable and fashionable spa towns. The atmosphere and setting suggest bygone days, and in fact most of the baths and hotels date from the early 1900's. But as early as the 14th century, Ugolino da Montecatini, a doctor, considered the waters here to be a good cure for liver problems. The thermal baths were owned by the Medici and then the Dukes of Lorraine. Montecatini really began to become known in the 18th century when Piero Leopoldo carried out modernisation works.
The main spas or thermal establishments are in the **Parco delle Terme ❶**, a large park area in the center of the city. Many of them are in early 20th-century Art Nouveau buildings; some are more modern structures in concrete and glass, and there is also the famous neo-Renaissance spa, **Terme Tettuccio ❷**, a Montecatini icon.

PRATO

The Romanesque Duomo with Pisan and Luccan influence; the Gothic churches of San Domenico and San Francesco; and the Renaissance basilica designed by Sangallo: the importance of art in Prato is revealed in the different architectural styles found there, relating to the three centuries when Prato was most prosperous and great. However Prato is probably better known for its enterprise in the textile industry, which still today, as in the past, continues to drive the city's economy. Prato grew beyond its 14th-century walls in the 1900s. But the center still remains attractive, and has some wonderful buildings and outstanding works by important Italian artists.

Duomo ❶

The Romanesque facade in white and green bands overlooks the square; on the right of the main doorway is the Pulpit of the Holy Girdle* (1434-38) whose structure was designed by Michelozzo. The original panels of the pulpit by Donatello, depicting dancing putti, are in the Museo dell'Opera del Duomo. The Gothic-Romanesque campanile (12th-14th century) stands beside the right flank of the Duomo.

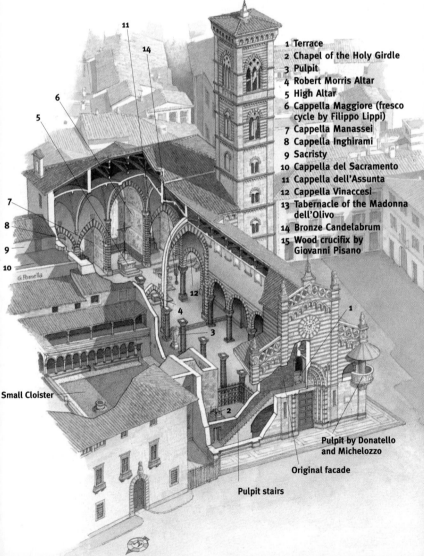

1 Terrace
2 Chapel of the Holy Girdle
3 Pulpit
4 Robert Morris Altar
5 High Altar
6 Cappella Maggiore (fresco cycle by Filippo Lippi)
7 Cappella Manassei
8 Cappella Inghirami
9 Sacristy
10 Cappella del Sacramento
11 Cappella dell'Assunta
12 Cappella Vinaccesi
13 Tabernacle of the Madonna dell'Olivo
14 Bronze Candelabrum
15 Wood crucifix by Giovanni Pisano

G.Pomella

Small Cloister

Pulpit by Donatello and Michelozzo

Original facade

Pulpit stairs

In the long narrow interior, the walls provide the first example ever of two bands of color used in an interior in Italy. The nave houses a pulpit by Mino da Fiesole and Antonio Rossellino (1473); at the high altar is the magnificent cycle of **frescoes**** (Scenes from the life of St John the Baptist and St Stephen) by Filippo Lippi (1452-66), assisted by Fra' Diamante. This exceptional early Renaissance work includes the figure of Salome dancing, perhaps the portrait of Lucrezia Buti; the friar-artist fell in love with her and stole her away from the convent to marry her. There is another

PRATO IN OTHER COLORS...

◼ **Food:** P 124, 128, 155
◼ **Shopping:** P 165, 171
◼ **Events:** P 177
◼ **Practical info:** P 229

cycle of frescoes* (1433) in the 1st chapel on the right of the presbytery, with scenes from the lives of St Stephen and the Virgin, attributed to Paolo Uccello. The *Chapel of the Holy Girdle*, at the beginning of the left aisle, features a *Madonna and Child**, a masterpiece by Giovanni Pisano (c. 1317), at the altar.

Museo dell'Opera del Duomo ❷

Located in the 16th-century Palazzo Vescovile, the museum was founded in 1967 to house works from the cathedral and objects related to the Sacred Girdle, including the reliquary by Maso

Prato 1 : 11 500 (1 cm = 115 m)

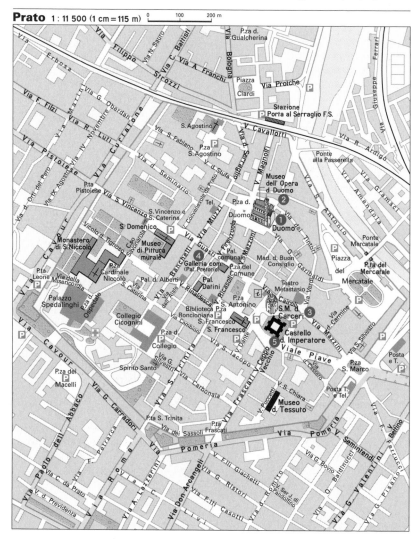

Prato, Church of Santa Maria delle Carceri and the Emperor's Castle

di Bartolomeo (1446). Other works are: the detached fresco with *Madonna and Child with Angels* (13th century), *Madonna and Child with Saints Clement and Just* by the Maestro of the Nativity of Castello, the panel of *Santa Lucia* attributed to Filippino Lippi, the panel of the *Funeral of St Jerome* by Filippo Lippi, and a detached fresco depicting Jacopone da Todi by Paolo Uccello. The highlight of the collection are the seven panels by Donatello, with the delightful **Dance of the Putti****.

Santa Maria delle Carceri ❸

This masterpiece of Renaissance architecture was built in a place where an image of the Virgin had been painted on a pre-existing prison wall. The church was started in 1485 by Giuliano da Maiano, and continued by Giuliano da Sangallo (1486-95). It has a Greek-cross plan; its graceful colored marble exterior remained unfinished. The *interior* has Brunelleschian and classical forms. The glazed white terracotta decoration, on blue background, by Andrea Della Robbia and assistants (c. 1492) stands out against the sandstone frame of the building. The stained glass windows date from the late 15th century, and the high altar from 1515.

Museo Civico ❹

The museum was established in 1788 by Grand-duke Peter Leopold of Lorraine. It was moved to Palazzo Pretorio in 1912, and comprises 14th- and 15th-century masterpieces of painting. These include: a predella from the Duomo (*Stories of the Sacred Girdle*) and an altar-panel (*Madonna and Child with Saints Francis, Bartholomew, Barnabas and Catherine of Alexandria*) by Bernardo Daddi, a polyptych by Giovanni da Milano painted for the Spedale della Misericordia, the *Madonna 'del Ceppo'* by Filippo Lippi, *Madonna and Saints* by Luca Signorelli, *Madonna Enthroned and Child, with Saints Jerome, Francis, Anthony of Padoa and Ludovic of Toulouse* by Francesco Botticini and *Madonna and Child with St Stephen and St John the Baptist* by Filippino Lippi. There are also glazed terracottas by Andrea della Robbia. Works currently not displayed include a frescoed tabernacle by Filippino Lippi, a painting by Battistello and plaster works, sculptures, drawings and cartoons by Lorenzo Bartolini.

Castello dell'imperatore ❺

Also known as the *Fortress of Santa Barbara*, it was remodeled by Frederick II in the 1240s. It has similarities with Swabian castles in Puglia and Sicily. The massive construction on a square plan has powerful crenelated walls and solid outer towers. Inside, spiral staircases lead to the towers and the battlement walkway, which gives a grand view of the city.

DAY TRIPS

POGGIO A CAIANO [8 km]

The **Villa Medicea* (Medici Villa)** is a prototype of Humanist pleasure villas. It was designed in the late 15th century by Giuliano da Sangallo for Lorenzo il Magnifico, on the site of a previous small medieval fort. The main hall features a splendid 16th-century *fresco cycle** celebrating Medici achievements, by Andrea del Sarto, Franciabigio, Pontormo and Alessandro Allori. The bas-relief frieze* in glazed terracotta is attributed to Andrea Sansovino. The large *park* around the villa was created in the 19th century.

SIENA

The most uniform and compact of the Tuscan cities, Siena lies on three hills, high in Tuscan countryside resembling the background of Guidoriccio's famous fresco in Palazzo Pubblico. The city developed around its heart, the shell-shaped Piazza del Campo, and along the three main streets (Banchi di Sopra, Banchi di Sotto, Via di Città). These three streets display an amazing range of 13th- and 14th-century architecture. Siena enjoyed incredible growth and prosperity in its heyday, helped by the wise government of local families. Sienese merchants and bankers traded all over Europe, and the city began its impressive production of architecture and art. Sienese Gothic painting reached its peak with Duccio di Buoninsegna, Simone Martini and the Lorenzetti. Everything changed in the 14th century, when Siena was struck by the plague and famine, and lost its independence. The city's medieval character has survived to an amazing extent: it can be seen in the city's architecture, in the lanes and houses, in the artisans' workshops, in its links with the surrounding countryside, in the food and wine, and finally in the frenzied magic of the Palio. This renowned horse race takes place twice a year, and is all over in a few minutes of intense competition.

Piazza del Campo ❶

The piazza shaped like a scallop-shell - called simply **il Campo** by the Sienese - has always been the focal point of the city's life and is certainly one of Italy's greatest medieval creations. The brick-paved square (1347) is divided into nine sections. The facade of Palazzo Pubblico and the soaring Torre del Mangia lie at the lowest point; the other sides are enclosed by palazzi (not all old), some crenelated and towered, interspersed with lanes and alleys leading to the streets behind. The square was built between the 12th and 14th centuries at the city's fulcrum; as early as 1297, in the earliest known example of controlled town-planning, the republic proclaimed that specific rules had to be respected in buildings on the Campo. Every year on the 2nd and 16th July, the square is the venue for the famous **Palio**.

Fonte Gaia ❷

This rectangular fountain in the high part of the Campo was built in 1419 by Jacopo della Quercia. As early as 1346 water had been brought to the square, and to the whole city, by means of an amazing network of underground waterways and tunnels. The beautiful marble 15th-century panels of the fountain (today in the Museo Civico) were replaced by copies in 1868. To the right of the fountain is the curved front of **Palazzo Sansedoni**, with three tiers of divided windows. It is in reality five separate 13th- to 14th-century constructions that were joined together in the 18th century. On the left, beyond the *Costarella dei Barbieri* leading to Via di Città, **Palazzo d'Elci** looks very medieval with its crenelations, although it was modified in the 16th-17th centuries.

Piazza del Campo with
Palazzo Pubblico

Spectacular view of the town

Palazzo Pubblico ❸

The building is a symbol of the independence and power of the rulers of Siena; it is one of the most important examples of civil Gothic architecture in Tuscany, and marks the transition from the concept of fortress to the concept of palazzo. The higher central core of the building was built by the Council of Nine between 1284 and 1305; the two side wings were completed around 1310. Two tiers of elegant divided windows embellish the upper part in brick, crowned with crenelation and the enormous 'Bernardinian Monogramn' (1425). The greatest Sienese artists were called to decorate the interior. The **Torre del Mangia*** (102m), built in 1338-48, rises from the end of the left wing; above the brick body of the tower is stone bracketing, which provides the base for the stone belfry. The **Cappella di Piazza**, at the foot of the tower, is in the form of a marble loggia. It was built in 1352-76 and the upper part was completed in Renaissance style in the 15th century. The Torre del Mangia has the best view* of the city and the countryside around.

Museo Civico

The museum, in the grand rooms of the Palazzo Pubblico, houses a rich collection of works mostly by Sienese artists of the 16th-18th centuries. The best of the rooms is the *Sala del Mappamondo*, a large hall where the Council of the Republic used to meet. On the back wall is the renowned **Maestà*** (Majesty) fresco by Simone Martini (1315); opposite is the **Seige of Montemassi Castle by Guidoriccio da Fogliano*** (1328), a fresco attributed to Simone Martini although there is some doubt about this now. There are also works by Vecchietta, Sano di Pietro and Sodoma. The *Sala della Pace* or *dei Nove* is just as interesting, with a cycle of frescoes on **Effetti del buono e cattivo governo*** (Effects of good and bad government), commissioned by the Council of Nine from Ambrogio Lorenzetti in 1337-39. The *Sala del Concistoro* preserves a doorway* sculpted by Bernardo Rossellino (1446) and, in the vault, frescoes by Domenico Beccafumi. The *Cappella**, with wrought-iron screen (1437) and inlaid wood **choir*** (1425-36) is frescoed with scenes from the life of the Madonna by Taddeo di Bartolo (1407) and, at the altar, Holy Family with St Leonard*, by Sodoma. On the floor above, the *Loggia dei Nove*, looking onto Piazza del Mercato and the countryside around Siena, features the original marble panels from the Fonte Gaia*, by Jacopo della Quercia, reconstructed in 1904.

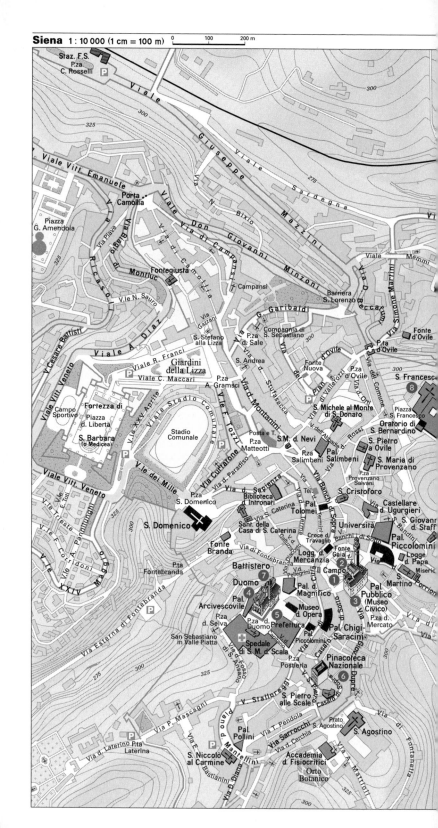

Duomo ❹

Pride and joy of the Sienese for
centuries, this is one of the greatest
creations of medieval Italian
architecture. Although predominantly
Gothic, it has Romanesque features. An
early cathedral dedicated to the
Assumption is believed to have been
built on the site around the 9th century.
But from around 1215-20 the building,
with the exception of the crypt, was
gradually modified and enlarged,
purportedly to a design by Nicola
Pisano. In 1285 the facade was started,
and completed with the apse in the late
14th century. The mosaics on the facade
and the bronze door are modern. The
stunning Gothic-Romanesque *facade**,
largely by Giovanni Pisano, in
polychrome marble, is enlivened by
sculptures also by Giovanni Pisano or his
school; many of the originals are now in
the Museo dell'Opera Metropolitana.
The black and white right flank features
large Gothic windows and the Porta del
Perdono (Door of Forgiveness): in the
lunette, a bas-relief by Donatello
(original in the Museo dell'Opera). The
Romanesque *campanile**, banded in
black and white, was built in the late
13th century: its six tiers of windows
progress from single openings at the
bottom, to six-fold windows at the top.
The Latin-cross **interior** is divided into
vast central nave and side aisles by
polystyle pilasters; the effect of the
black and white bands on the walls and
pilasters is remarkable. The polychrome
marble **pavement**** is absolutely
unique, and can only be seen in its
entirety on certain occasions. Composed
of 56 panels depicting religious and
secular scenes, it was made between
1369 and 1547 by many different artists.
In the **transept**, the hexagon of the
dome is decorated with six large gilded
statues of the saints (Giovanni di
Stefano, 1488) below a blind arcade. To
the right, the round Baroque *Cappella
del Voto* was designed by Gian Lorenzo
Bernini (1661), who also sculpted the
two marble statues* at the entrance.
In the raised *presbytery*, the high altar,
with a 16th-century bronze ciborium, is
by Baldassarre Peruzzi. The *apse* has a
wood choir * (14th-16th century) with
inlay work by Fra' Giovanni da Verona
(1503), from Monte Oliveto Maggiore.

Pulpit by Nicola Pisano inside the Duomo

Above is a stunning round stained glass window* (Scenes from the Life of the Virgin) made in 1288 from cartoons attributed to Duccio di Buoninsegna. In the *left transept*, is the famous marble **pulpit**** by Nicola Pisano (1266-68), a milestone in Italian Gothic sculpture. It was made with the help of his son Giovanni and other pupils including Arnolfo di Cambio. Octagonal in shape, it is supported by nine marble columns; around the base of the central column are eight allegorical figures, and the alternating outer columns rest on lions. The panels contain scenes from the life of Christ, separated by statues of prophets and angels. The beautiful round Renaissance *Chapel of St John the Baptist** (1492) contains paintings by Pinturicchio (1504-06) and a bronze statue of St John the Baptist* by Donatello (1457).

At the end of the left aisle is the entrance to the Renaissance **Libreria Piccolomini**** built in 1492 by Cardinal Francesco Todeschini Piccolomini (later Pope Pius III) to house the library of his uncle, Pope Pius II. The walls of the room are entirely frescoed with **Scenes from the Life of Pius II**** by Pinturicchio (1502-1509). In the middle is a group of statues, the Three Graces*, a 3rd-century Roman copy of the Hellenistic

original. Some precious 15th-century illuminated anthem-books are also displayed. Beside the entrance to the library, is the great Piccolomini Altar*, with four statues of saints, early works by Michelangelo.

Piazza del Duomo ⑤

This asymmetrical space features some of the city's oldest and most important buildings. On the left of the Cathedral, is the *Palazzo Arcivescovile*, built in Gothic style in the 18th century. Opposite, the long facade of the Spedale di Santa Maria della Scala, and on the right of the Duomo, the 16th-century **Palazzo del Governatore dei Medici**, now the Prefettura and Provincial Government building. Still on the right, further back, is *Piazza Jacopo della Quercia*. This is the place where the enormous Duomo Nuovo (New Cathedral) was to have been built, an extension of the cathedral planned in the 14th century. Some completed parts survive: the colonnade and surrounding buildings, and the immense unfinished facade.

Pinacoteca Nazionale ⑥

This enormous collection was started by the scholar Giuseppe Ciaccherio, with his passion for the Sienese 'primitives'; it is housed in the *Palazzo Buonsignori* and the adjacent Gothic *Palazzo Brigidi*. The gallery contains masterpieces by key artists and traces the development of Sienese art from the late 12th century to the first half of the 17th century. Guido da Siena has two altar-frontals: Quaresima* (Lent) and St Peter Enthroned*. The section dedicated to Duccio di Buoninsegna includes the famous tiny panel of the **Madonna 'dei Francescani'****, an early work, and a Madonna and Saints*. There are two masterpieces by Simone Martini (**Madonna and Child****, and **Altarpiece of Beato Agostino Novello****); there are numerous works by Ambrogio Lorenzetti (Madonna and Saints*, Madonna and Child*, **Madonna, Saints and Angels****, **Annunciation****) and by Pietro Lorenzetti, the fine **Altarpiece 'del Carmine'****(1329); the splendid landscape **panels**** (a city by the sea, and a castle on the shore of a lake) are near works by Sassetta, which include a Last Supper* and St Anthony Abbot*.

There are some notable works by Giovanni di Paolo (Last Judgement*, **Madonna of Humility****) and by Sano di Pietro (**Apparition of the Virgin to Pope Callistus III****, Madonna and Saints*). There is a large section with works by Francesco di Giorgio Martini (Annunciation*, Nativity and Saints*, Coronation of the Virgin*).

The section featuring *16th-century Sienese painting* includes works by Domenico Beccafumi (Descent of Christ to Limbo*, Stigmata of St Catherine*, Nativity of the Virgin*, cartoons** for the pavement of the Duomo of Siena), Sodoma (**Christ at the Column****, Deposition*) and by Brescianino (Charity, Hope and Fortitude*).

Battistero ❼

The Baptistery is dedicated to St John the Baptist, and looks onto Piazza San Giovanni. It is beneath part of the cathedral, down a 15th-century flight of stairs, past the **portal*** by Giovanni di Agostino designed for the right flank of the Duomo Nuovo. The baptistery was built in 1316-25, among the large arches supporting the extension of the Duomo apse. The upper part of its Gothic facade (second half of the 14th century) is unfinished. It has three large splayed portals. The rectangular interior with two pilasters was frescoed by various artists, including Vecchietta, in the mid 15th-century.

The hexagonal **font**** (1417-34) is an early 15th-century masterpiece. In the middle of the font stands a marble ciborium, surmounted by a statue of St John the Baptist and decorated with bas-reliefs, by Jacopo della Quercia; the bronze angels are by Donatello and Giovanni di Turino. The font is decorated by six gilded bronze bas-reliefs depicting scenes from the life of the Baptist, interspersed with statuettes of the Virtues (two, Faith* and Hope*, by Donatello). The scenes are the work of: Jacopo della Quercia (**Angel Announcing the Birth of the Baptist to Zacharias****), Turino di

Sano and Giovanni di Turino (Birth of the Baptist), Giovanni di Turino (Baptist Preaching), Lorenzo Ghiberti (Baptism of Christ*, St John in Prison*) and Donatello (**Herod's Feast****).

San Francesco ❽

This large 14th-century Franciscan basilica stands in the vast square of the same name, with the oratory of San Bernardino on its right. It has a great view over the countryside to the hills of Chianti in the background. Completed in 1482, half-destroyed by fire in 1655, it was restored to its supposed original Gothic form in the late 19th century. The interior, with its enormous nave illuminated by divided windows, features splendid works by the Lorenzetti brothers in the transept: in the first chapel, **Crucifixion****, a detached fresco by Pietro Lorenzetti (1331); in the 3rd chapel, **St Ludovic of Angers before Boniface VIII**** and Martyrdom of the Franciscans*, also detached frescoes, by Ambrogio Lorenzetti (c. 1331).

Basilica dei Servi ❾

This large building was begun in the 13th century by the Servites, who settled in Siena in 1234. It was consecrated only in 1533, with its unfinished 15th-century facade. It has a 14th-century campanile. The church is situated on the edge of town, and the flight of stairs at the entrance has a wonderful view* over the walled city. The light Latin-cross *interior* divided by slender marble columns into central nave and side aisles, retains its original Renaissance character, despite 19th-century restoration work. Of particular interest among the 13th- to 16th-century works here are:

The basilica of Santa Maria dei Servi

Madonna 'del Bordone'** (2nd altar right aisle), painted in 1261 by the Florentine Coppo di Marcovaldo to buy his freedom from Siena after the battle of Montaperti; in the apse, Massacre of the Innocents*, a fresco possibly by Niccolò di Segna or his brother Francesco; frescoes by Pietro Lorenzetti; and at the altar, Adoration of the Shepherds by Taddeo di Bartolo (1404).

CHIANCIANO TERME [77 km]

Set amid gentle hills and vales, west of the Valdichiana, between Montepulciano and Chiusi, this is a popular spa town. Therapeutic use of the Sillene spring is recorded as early as 1005, but the Romans and Etruscans also knew about its powers. Prosperity came in the 20th century, with increased consumption of bottled water, and construction of hotels, spas and thermal treatment centers. The medieval town has turned into a real health resort, with its five springs (Fucoli, Santa, Sant'Elena, Santissima and Sillene). The **Thermal Area** has hotels, spas, villas, elegant shops along winding avenues, parks and gardens. Of note: the large *Parco delle Fonti* ❶ and adjacent *Parco dei Fùcoli* ❷ (recreational), the *Stabilimento dell'Acqua Santa*, with its modern water pavilion, and the *Sorgente Santa Elena* in a large park with pines and oaks. Villa Simoneschi houses the *Museo Civico Archeologico delle Acque* with archeological finds and ceramics. In the old center, you can visit the Romanesque church of St John the

Chianciano Terme 1 : 11 500 (1 cm = 115 m)

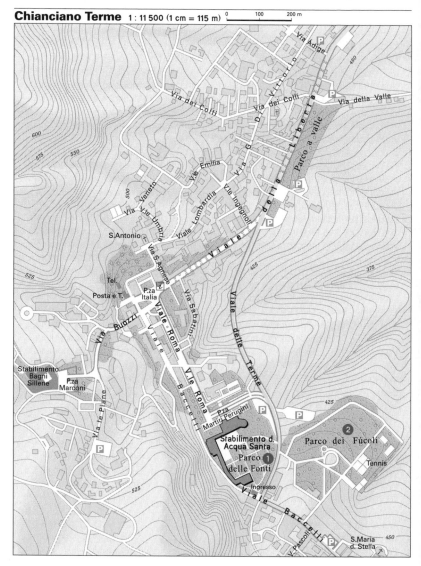

Chiusi 1 : 7 000 (1 cm = 70 m)

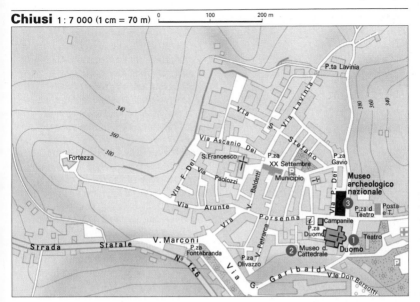

Baptist and the adjacent **Museo della Collegiata** (Collegiate Church Museum) with 14th- and 15th-century works by Sienese and Florentine schools, silverware, 16th-century anthem-books and funerary urns. The 13th-century *Palazzo del Podestà* is decorated with 15th- and 16th-century coats-of-arms.

CHIUSI [77 km]

Chiusi stands on a sandstone hill, among olive groves, in the south of the Valdichiana. Once the important Etruscan city of Chamars, it was renowned as the dominion of the legendary King Porsena, who defeated Rome. It is worth visiting to see the Etruscan tombs in the countryside around, and its museum collections. The old center still reveals the town's Roman layout, of Etruscan origin. There are also many medieval buildings, and buildings dating from the times of the Grand-duchy.

The Romanesque **Duomo** ❶ has a central nave and side aisles divided by ancient Roman columns, and a rare mosaic pavement dating from the 5th century in the presbytery. Beside the Duomo is the **Museo della Cattedrale** ❷, with stone and mosaic fragments (from excavations beneath the church), early-Christian inscriptions, church vestments, two reliquaries in wood and ivory of the 15th century from the Embriaci workshop, and the

marvellous collection of 21 illuminated **codexes and anthem-books*** from the Abbey of Monte Oliveto Maggiore (15th century). Below the museum is the so-called *Labyrinth of Porsena* which can be visited. It is an incredible system of tunnels the Etruscans built, 120m long, leading to a large cistern, probably 1st century BC. From here stairs lead back up to the Duomo.

Still in the area of the Duomo, the **Museo Archeologico Nazionale** ❸ has good collections of Etruscan finds and Greek ceramics from excavations around the city. Particularly arresting are the cinerary urns and polychrome clay and alabaster sarcophagi, including the sarcophagus* of Laris Sentinate Larcna. The **Etruscan Necropolis** is scattered over around twenty points in the area, and includes burial chambers carved out of the rock and used for cremation. Those which can be visited are: the *Tomba Dipinta del Leone (Painted Tomb of the Lion)*, a 6th-century BC burial chamber, and the 4th-century BC *Tomba della Pellegrina*.

MONTE OLIVETO MAGGIORE [9 km]

Monte Oliveto Maggiore stands on a hilltop covered with cypresses overlooking the magical Sienese hills. This famous convent was founded by Bernardo Tolomei in 1313 when he left his wealthy family and went to live there

Abbey of Monte Oliveto Maggiore

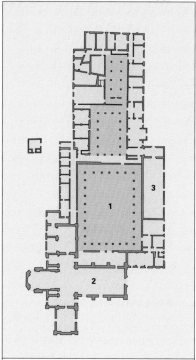

1 Great Cloister with frescoes by Luca Signorelli and Sodoma
2 Church with carved wood choir
3 Refectory with 17th century frescoes

as a monk. The monastery is the mother house of the Olivetan Benedictine order; its abbey is an outstanding artistic and religious monument.

Before reaching the **Abbey** you will see a medieval brick building with crenelated tower, built in 1393 to defend the monastery. A cypress-lined avenue leads to the **monastery**, with the **abbey church** beside. It was built in 1400-17, and modified in the 18th century, but preserves the original Gothic-Romanesque campanile and the Gothic facade with elegant portal. The *Chiostro Grande (Great Cloister)* dating from 1443 features one of the greatest Renaissance works of art: a fresco cycle depicting the **Life of St Benedict****, by Luca Signorelli (1497-98) and Sodoma (from 1505). A landscape frescoed by Sodoma (Christ at the Column, and the wonderful Christ carrying the Cross*), and a vestibule with frescoes from the Siena school lead to the *interior* of the abbey

church which was remodeled in Baroque style in 1772.

The enclosure complex is a part of the monastery that cannot be visited. It includes two other cloisters, the *Refectory* and on the first floor, the 16th-century *Library**, the Chapter House and a **workshop** for the restoration of parchments, old papers and bindings.

MONTEPULCIANO [68 km]

The town lies on a ridge between the Orcia Valley and Valdichiana. Its old center is one of the most beautiful in the region, with excellent examples of Renaissance architecture, created by talents such as Michelozzo, Antonio da Sangallo il Vecchio, Baldassarre Peruzzi, and Vignola. The town is a delight for the eyes, with its lanes, palazzi, arches and loggias, culminating in Piazza Grande. The civic and religious center of the town, this is where both the Duomo and the Palazzo Comunale are located. The Teatro Poliziano is not far away, named after the great Renaissance poet, Angelo Ambrosini, born in Montepulciano, who wrote under the name of Poliziano.

Porta al Prato is the main way into the city. It is part of the 13th-century city walls, and was reconstructed in the early 16th century as part of the fortification system designed by Antonio da Sangallo il Vecchio.

The **Corso** was the main road through the town in the 16th century, and today is lined with many 16th-century palazzi and mansions.

It divides into three sections. Via di Gracciano nel Corso is the main thoroughfare of the 'borgo' of Gracciano. Here stands the brick **Torre di Pulcinella** (1524), and at the top the metal-coated wood figure of Punch which strikes the hour.

Via di Voltaia nel Corso forms the second section of the Corso. It passes 16th-century palazzi in the southern part of the old center. These include: **Palazzo Cervini***, possibly designed by Antonio da Sangallo il Giovane, and *Palazzo Bruschi* with the 19th-century much-frequented *Caffè Poliziano*. Via dell'Opio nel Corso is the last section, and here you will find what is presumed to be the **House of Poliziano** and, in Via del Teatro, the magnificent 18th-century **Teatro Poliziano ❶**.

THE 'CRETE'

These beautiful, bare hills near Siena have something very special. Visit when spring flowers are blooming, or in summer when the area takes on a desert-like appearance. The Crete near San Giovanni d'Asso are known for their truffles. A large market-fair is held here after the harvest in autumn.

Sant'Agostino ❷ is a 15th-century church with a late-Gothic and Renaissance facade* partly by Michelozzo. Its richly decorated festooned portal has a terracotta relief in the lunette, again by Michelozzi. The single nave features a wood Crucifix

painted by Antonio da Sangallo il Vecchio. It also contains the choir of the original church, decorated with frescoes depicting religious and knightly orders, by a pupil of Pomarancio.

Piazza Grande ❸ at the top of the hill, is slightly sloping, and was created in the 15th century by Michelozzi. In addition to the Duomo and the Palazzo Comunale, there are some other important palazzi. These include the **Palazzo Nobili-Tarugi*** by Antonio Sangallo il Vecchio, featuring half-columns and a deep ground-floor loggia, and the Renaissance **Palazzo Contucci** perhaps completed by Baldassarre Peruzzi.

Montepulciano 1 : 9 500 (1 cm = 95 m)

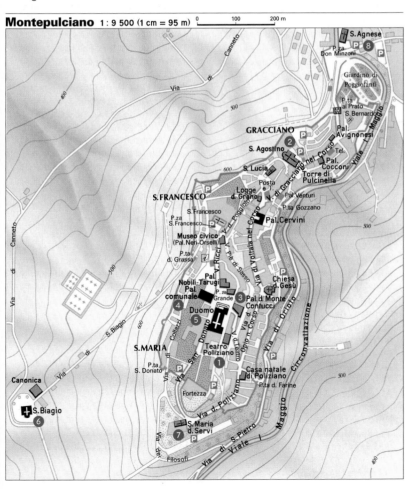

Montepulciano, Piazza Grande and Palazzo Comunale

The **Palazzo Comunale** ❹ was constructed in a number of stages between the late 14th century and the first half of the 15th century. Its facade, entirely in stone, is almost certainly by Michelozzi and is reminiscent of the general structure of the Palazzo Vecchio in Florence. The crenelated tower with niches provides a great view of the town, the Valdichiana and the Orcia Valley. The 14th-century courtyard is splendid, with a cistern and two loggias opposite each other. It was restored in the 1960s.

Duomo. ❺ The facade of this Mannerist building by Ippolito Scalza (1592-1630) is incomplete. The 15th-century campanile was built with the original church. The grand Latin-cross *interior* features a barrel-vaulted central aisle, and high transept and cupola. It houses the reclining statue of Bartolomeo Aragazzi*, secretary to Pope Martin V, previously part of a funeral monument sculpted by Michelozzo (15th century). On the high altar, there is an Assumption*, a large triptych by Taddeo di Bartolo (1401).

San Biagio. ❻ From Via del Poggiolo there's a lovely view of the church, surrounded by medieval and Renaissance mansions. The church is well-positioned south-west of the old center, on a kind of natural terrace looking over the surrounding hills. It is an extremely important Renaissance building, and a masterpiece by Antonio da Sangallo il Vecchio (1518-45). Sober and harmonious, it is built in travertine to a Greek-cross plan, with a cupola and two bell-towers. Its majestic *interior* has four large arches which support the cupola with its high drum and niches. The large marble altar-frontal at the high altar has a revered fresco of the Madonna and Child with St Francis (14th century).

There are two other 14th-century churches which are worth a visit. **Santa Maria dei Servi** ❼ was built at the foot of the 'rock' which formed the end-point of the first city walls. The simple portal in the plain Gothic facade leads into the

Monteriggioni, the charming turreted walls

interior which features a Madonna and Child* attributed to Duccio di Buoninsegna. **Sant'Agnese** ❽ has been modified a number of times, but you can still see the simple Gothic portal of the original building. Inside, a fresco attributed to Simone Martini and a Madonna del Latte (Madonna of the Milk) by the 14th-century Sienese school.

MONTERIGGIONI [15 km]

The old town, surrounded by its **walls**, looks over the gentle Sienese hills, a superbly typical Tuscan panorama. It was a Sienese fortified outpost against the Florentines, and was considered to be impregnable. Its legendary walls (1212-1270) are crowned by 14 square towers. In the center of the town, in the small square on the only street linking the two city gates, is the church of *St John the Baptist*, an example of the transition from Romanesque to Gothic.

PIENZA [53 km]

This quiet little town, standing on a hilltop, looks over a great expanse of countryside. It was founded by Pius II Piccolomini and designed in the mid-15th century by Bernardo Rossellino, according to the humanist criteria of Leon Battista Alberti's theory of the "ideal city".

Both the Pope and the architect died in 1464 before the project was finished. But the cultured Pius II, who was born here in 1405, nevertheless left his humanist mark on the town.

Piazza Pio II, at the highest point of the hill, is Rossellino's greatest success in all the reconstruction carried out between 1459 and 1462. Much demolition work was done to enable the Florentine architect to create a trapezoid shape, in line with rigorous principles of perspective laid down in *De re aedificatoria* by Leon Battista Alberti and in other Renaissance texts which dictated

Pienza: Town Layout by Bernardo Rossellino

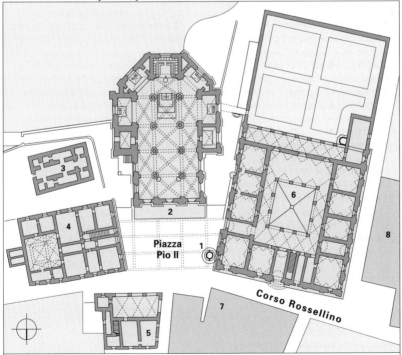

Piazza Pio II

Corso Rossellino

1 Well (1462)
2 Cathedral (1459-62)
3 Palazzo dei Canonici (pre 1459)
4 Palazzo Vescovile-Museum (15th century)
5 Palazzo Comunale (15th century)
6 Palazzo Piccolomini (1459-62)
7 Palazzo Ammannati (15th century)
8 San Francesco (13th century)

The 14th-century Palazzo Comunale in Piazza Pio II

rationality, proportion and symmetry in architecture. The 'back wall' of the ideal 'open-air room' (the square) is the facade of the Cathedral; at the sides, Palazzo Piccolomini, with in front a **well***, and the austere **Palazzo Vescovile**, with its beautiful main doorway and two tiers of windows. The palazzo now houses the **Museo Diocesano** which contains church vestments, including the **cope of Pius II****, exquisite 14th-century English embroidery, and precious goldsmithery; it also contains 15th-century illuminated anthem-books, Flemish tapestries and Sienese school panel paintings, notably a Madonna of Humility*, attributed to the Maestro dell'Osservanza, and a Madonna and Child* by Pietro Lorenzetti.

The **Cathedral** is dedicated to the Virgin of the Assumption. It was built in 1459-62 on the site of the old Romanesque church, to a design by Rossellino, who was clearly inspired by Alberti's Renaissance principles. The facade is divided into three parts by columned arches, in travertine, and the gable above bears the Piccolomini crest. Above the three portals are a central oeil-de-boeuf and two tabernacle niches. The octagonal campanile on the left flank is decorated with spires. The light Latin-cross Gothic-style *interior* has central nave and side aisles all of the same height. The polygonal apse has five chapels around it. Artworks here, all commissioned by Pius II between 1461 and 1463, include: Madonna Enthroned and Child with Saints*, altarpiece by Matteo di Giovanni, inlaid wood choir* in Gothic style (1462), and **Assumption****, an exceptional altar painting by Vecchietta.

Palazzo Piccolomini. Rossellino demolished the buildings on the right side of the square to build this immense palazzo. The building's perfect placing in perspective shows off its precise Renaissance lines, inspired by Palazzo Rucellai in Florence. After centuries of neglect, it was returned to its original appearance by restoration work completed in the thirties. It encloses an elegant courtyard with portico on the ground floor. The courtyard leads to a terrace garden* overlooked by a grand three-level loggia on the south side, with a great view* over the Orcia valley.

Corso Rossellino. The borgo's main thoroughfare, again by Rossellino, is lined with Renaissance palazzi and mansions. Also here is the church of **San Francesco**, the only medieval building within the Gothic-style city walls, dating from the late 13th century. Near the *Porta al Ciglio*, an arch leads to *Via del Castello*, a pedestrian walkway leading back towards Piazza Pio II, again with lovely views* over Valle d'Orcia.

SAN GALGANO [9 km]

The abbey, outstanding example of the Gothic-Cistercian style in Italy, was built between 1224 and 1288, and modeled on French Cistercian churches. Today it is open to the sky on top, after the vault and campanile collapsed in the late 18th century.

The nobleman Galgano Guidotti retreated here in penitence and was canonised in 1185; a small church was built here in his honor in the late 12th century, and a Cistercian monastery was founded. There are still remains of the chapter house and part of the cloister.

The ancient **small church*** is not far away, on the hill of Montesiepi; it features an interesting vault with concentric bands in terracotta and travertine. The nearby 14th-century chapel is decorated with frescoes* by Ambrogio Lorenzetti (Madonna Enthroned and Annunciation).

SIENA IN OTHER COLORS...

ITINERARIES: P 101
FOOD: P 128, 132, 135
SHOPPING: P 165, 167, 171
EVENTS: P 177, 181
WELLNESS: P 185, 186, 188, 189, 190
PRACTICAL INFO: P 234

SAN GIMIGNANO [38 km]

In the 13th century, at its peak of prosperity, the town boasted 72 towers, symbols of pride for the local families, and nine *hospitatores* (lodges) for the merchants who came here in large numbers. Today 15 towers stand out on the skyline of this wonderful place - protected by Unesco as a World Heritage site - which stands on a hill overlooking the Valdelsa. It is extremely popular as a tourist destination, but its squares and lanes, art, good food and its sheer uniqueness still make it well worth a visit. The 13th-century **Porta San Giovanni** is a typical Sienese depressed arch, in the **walls*** (1261-63) which still surround the town. The Gate marks the southern entry to the town of the ancient Via Francigena, which runs through San Gimignano, and is lined with old palazzi, tower-houses and turrets. An archway in the inner walls leads to the splendid Piazza della Cisterna. Beyond the square, **Via San Matteo** leads to Porta San Matteo, another ancient point of entry to the town.

Piazza della Cisterna ❶ and Piazza del Duomo (late 13th century) form the lively and harmonious center of the town; its most important monuments are built around these two squares. The *cistern*, in the center of the large square with elegant medieval palazzi, dates from 1287 and was enlarged in 1346. Between the two squares stand the twin 13th-century (slightly diverging) *Torri degli Ardinghelli*, with the loggia of Palazzo del Popolo behind.

The abbey church of San Galgano

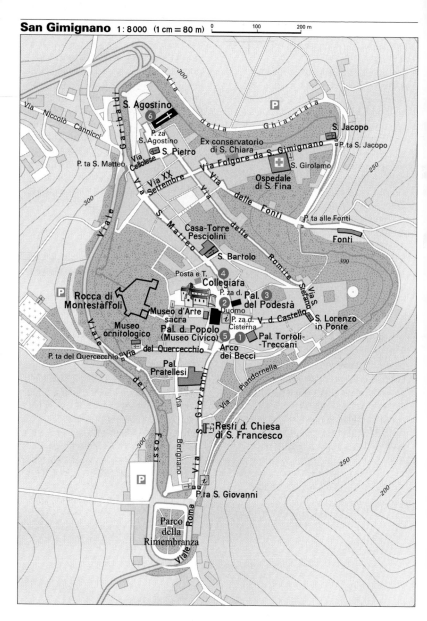

San Gimignano 1 : 8000 (1 cm = 80 m)

0   100   200 m

Piazza del Duomo. ❷ Like the adjoining Piazza della Cisterna it is also brick-paved and surrounded by medieval palazzi and towers. Up a flight of stairs from here is the church of the Collegiata, with on its left the facade of the Palazzo del Popolo. The old **Palazzo del Podestà*** ❸, with its partly stone and partly brick facade and large ground-floor vault (the *loggia*), is overlooked by the imposing tower, known as *la Rognosa** (51m), at the beginning of Via San Matteo. The twin *torri dei Salvucci* mark the other end of the street.

Collegiata. ❹ This 12th-century Romanesque building, with its simple 13th-century facade, has been modified and restored a number of times.
The interior preserves the Romanesque columned central nave and side aisles, with 14th-century ribbed vault. Fresco cycles line the aisle walls: on the right, Scenes from the New Testament*, by Lippo and Federico Memmi (mid-14th century); on the left, Scenes from the Old Testament* by Bartolo di Fredi (c. 1367). Towards the presbytery in the

San Gimignano, Piazza della Cisterna

great view* of the town. The Palazzo houses the **Museo Civico**. The first room, the grand Sala di Dante is frescoed with a Maestà* by Lippo Memmi (1317). On the second floor is the Camera del Podestà, frescoed by Memmo di Filippuccio with scenes of conjugal life, and three *Pinacoteca* rooms with Tuscan school paintings of the 13th-15th centuries by Coppo di Marcovaldo (Crucifix*), Benozzo Gozzoli, Filippino Lippi (Annunciation**), Pinturicchio (Madonna of the Assumption and Saints*).

Sant'Agostino ❻ The irregular-shaped square has stairs leading up to the church. It is an imposing Romanesque-Gothic construction built in 1280-98 with a plain brick facade and four high Gothic windows in the right flank. The single-nave interior, with three Gothic-style apse chapels, has many artworks: in the chapel of San Bartolo, a marble altar* by Benedetto da Maiano (1494); on the high altar, **Coronation of Mary***, masterpiece by Piero del Pollaiolo (1483); on the choir walls, **Life of St Augustine****, a magnificent fresco cycle by Benozzo Gozzoli; on the left wall, a large fresco of St Sebastian*, by the same artist.

right aisle, is the **Cappella di Santa Fina***, a Renaissance milestone, by Giuliano and Benedetto da Maiano (1468). In the altar area, the altar-frontal* and marble ciborium* are by Benedetto da Maiano (1475); the frescoes* are by Domenico Ghirlandaio (1475) and assistants.
Palazzo del Popolo. ❺ It was built in 1288 and enlarged in the 14th century. The facade is decorated with crests and flanked by two large loggia arches* and the *Torre Grossa** (54m), which gives a

The medieval towers of San Gimignano

By car, foot or bike Tuscany offers a plethora of intriguing tours for all interests and modes of travel. A bike tour along the ancient wine roads can offer a close and personal perspective to the land that will lend greater appreciation to that evening glass of wine. Or perhaps a walking tour of scenic hill town markets to enhance your search for the

perfect local handicraft.
From hidden architectural gems
to historical sites of major
importance the following
section offers detailed routes
and suggestions to fill your
days with unexpected pleasures
and traditional favorites
of the land, culture and people.

Itineraries & special interest

Highlights

- Via Francigena, the most traveled pilgrim route to Rome in medieval times
- The Tuscan Archipelago, the largest protected area of sea in Europe
- The WWF Oasis, Lake Burano
- Monte Amiata Animal Park
- Industry Museums

THE ETRUSCAN TRAIL

Mommsen wrote in his History of Rome (1854) that it is not known where the Etruscans came from, but this is relatively unimportant; it is their civilisation which is interesting. This developed more or less in the arc formed by the Arno and the Tiber, between the Apennines and the Tyrrhenian Sea. The nucleus of this ancient civilisation and some of its finest creations were in Tuscany. The literary myth of Etruria emerged in the Romantic age when the surviving lonely remains of the Etruscan civilisation inspired many to give free reign to imagining what it had been like. In 1848 the English consul in Rome, George Denis, wrote one of the finest books about this people: Cities and Cemeteries of Etruria. Still today it is a fascinating guide to the Etruscan ruins scattered around the Maremma, or buried in the bare splendor of the rocky Volterra landscape. The Etruscans left no written records, and what we know of them today comes from objects related to their death rites and burial practices. Their approach to death reveals a powerful love for life, depicted in frescoed burial chambers. Their necropolises and frescoed tombs were often richly and nobly decorated. As Lawrence wrote: "The Etruscan cities vanished completely, like flowers. Only their tombs, like bulbs, remained below ground".

The most important necropolises in Tuscany are: in Vetulonia (Tumulo del Diavolino, Tumulo della Pietrera, and Tumulo del Duce); in Populonia (the Bronzetto di Offerente tomb in the Casone necropolis, the Flabelli tomb in the Porcareccia necropolis, and the Carri tomb in the San Cerbone necropolis); in Volterra (three necropolises, with ancient tombs and more recent burial chambers); and in Chiusi (Tomba della Scimmia, Tomba della Pellegrina, and Tomba del Deposito de' Dei). Gold objects, bronzes, vases, weapons and ornaments which furnished the tombs, sarcophagi and rare surviving temple statues, can be seen in numerous museums.

At least thirty towns in Tuscany have Etruscan museums: for example, Arezzo (the museum is named after a famous Etrurian, Caius Cilnius Maecenas), San Gimignano, and Certaldo. There are also Etruscan museums in Fiesole, in Volterra and in Pistoia, where a fascinating underground tour shows the remains of the Etruscan settlement. But Florence is the best place to start a journey into the Etruscan world. The museum features objects related to everyday life, and to the divinatory arts of haruspicy (prophecy through inspection of animal entrails) which the Etruscans were famous for. It also contains masterpieces such as the bronze statues of the Arringatore or Orator (early 1st century BC, so more Roman) and the Chimera (4th century BC), the Francois Vase (570 BC), the Mater Matuta (460-450 BC) and the Sarcophagus of the Amazons (4th century BC), painted and decorated with scenes from Greek mythology.

The Roman theater in Volterra, built in the Augustinian age

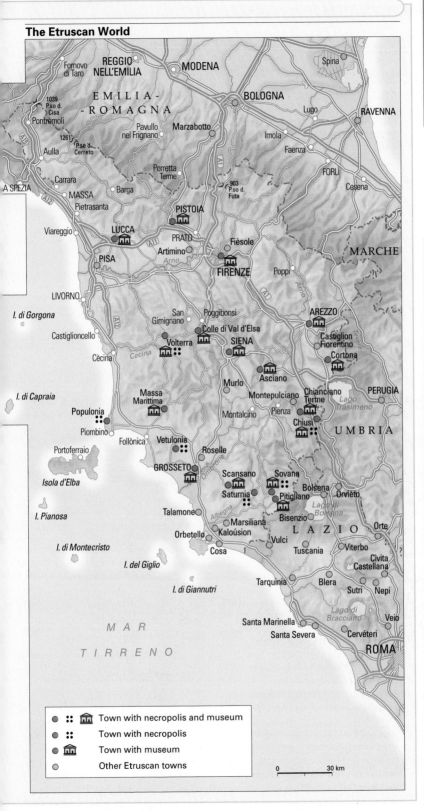

The Etruscan World

Fornovo
di Taro
REGGIO
NELL'EMILIA
MODENA
Spina

1039
P.so d.
Cisa
Pontremoli
EMILIA-
-ROMAGNA
BOLOGNA
RAVENNA

1261
P.so d.
Cerreto
Pavullo
nel Frignano
Marzabotto
Lugo
Aulla
Imola
Faenza

Carrara
Porretta
Terme
FORLÌ

A SPEZIA
MASSA
Barga
903
P.so d.
Futa
Cesena

Pietrasanta

Viareggio
LUCCA
PISTOIA
Fièsole
MARCHE

PISA
PRATO
Artimino
FIRENZE
Poppi

Arno

LIVORNO
San
Gimignano
Poggibonsi
AREZZO

I. di Gorgona
Colle di Val d'Elsa
Castiglion
Fiorentino
Cortona

Castiglioncello
Volterra
SIENA
Cècina
Cecina

Asciano
PERUGIA

I. di Capraia
Murlo
Montepulciano
Chianciano
Terme
Lago
Trasimeno

Massa
Marittima
Montalcino
Pienza

Populonia
Chiusi
UMBRIA

Piombino
Follònica
Vetulonia
Roselle

Portoferraio
GROSSETO

Isola d'Elba
Scansano
Sovana

Saturnia
Pitigliano
Bolsena
Orvieto

I. Pianosa
Talamone
Bisenzio
Lago di
Bolsena

Marsiliana
LAZIO
Orte

I. di Montecristo
Orbetello
Kaloúsion
Vulci

Cosa
Tuscania
Viterbo

I. del Giglio
Civita
Castellana

I. di Giannutri
Tarquinia
Blera
Sutri
Nepi

Lago di
Bracciano
Veio

MAR
Santa Marinella

TIRRENO
Santa Severa
Cervéteri

ROMA

		Town with necropolis and museum
		Town with necropolis
		Town with museum
		Other Etruscan towns

0   30 km

99

VIA FRANCIGENA: MEMORY, MYTH AND REALITY

The Via Francigena was the most traveled of the «Romee», the medieval roads that pilgrims followed to Rome. From the 8th century, it was the route through France (hence the name) that linked Canterbury Cathedral and Rome, the heart of Christianity. It was also widely used by soldiers, travelers and merchants.

We know about the ancient route mostly from the churches and castles built along it that still survive today, and partly from the writings of medieval travelers. Perhaps the best-known is the diary written by Archbishop Sigericus of Canterbury, on his journey to Rome in 990.

The itinerary is 340 kilometers long. It passes through many towns, both small and large, whose fame and prosperity depended on the Via Francigena in the Middle Ages.

From the Lunigiana to Versilia

In Pontrèmoli, high in the Lunigiana, the village and castle of Piagnaro date from the 9th and 10th centuries. Lower down, in Filattiera, the small Romanesque church of San Giorgio preserves an unusual inscription. Also of interest, in the Lunigiana plains, are Sarzana, with two important medieval churches, and the remains of the Roman town Luni, which the region takes its name from. Carrara (4 km from the Aurelia Highway) with a fine Romanesque-Gothic Duomo, and Massa, which developed as a result of the Via Francigena between the 11th and 12th centuries, are situated before Versilia, an area featuring the high Apuan Alps. Pietrasanta was founded in 1255, and the Francigena was the main road through the town. Camaiore has the ancient abbey of San Pietro and a Longobard church.

From Lucca to San Gimignano

From Lucca, with its splendid Romanesque architecture, the road moves on towards other towns in interesting landscapes: Altopascio, which developed as a hopitaller center in the 11th century; Fucecchio, with an abbey founded in the 10th century; and San Miniato, where the Francigena met with the Florence-Pisa road.

The Via Francigena in Tuscany

Via Francigena
Detour
● LUCCA — Main stopping points on the itinerary
○ Camaiore — Other stopping points
⌂ Religious building
▣ Medieval village
♜ Castle
∴ Excavations
🏛 Civic building

Scenic view of San Gimignano

The route begins to climb in Valdelsa; it first passes through Castelfiorentino, with a church dating from 1195, and then turns towards Gambassi Terme, with the Romanesque church of Santa Maria a Chianni. It then reaches Certaldo, which features a 12th-century Palazzo Pretorio. Towards the south, standing out on the horizon are the unique towers of San Gimignano, another wonderful town. It was a center of international fame which developed between the 9th and 12th centuries because of its position on the route.

Landscapes and colors around Siena

The Sienese 13th-century architectural style can be seen in the Fonte delle Fate (Fountain of Fairies) at Poggibonsi, in the tower-house of Arnolfo di Cambio, in Colle di Val d'Elsa, in the monastery of Abbadia Isola, and in the splendid town walls of Monteriggioni. Siena, a superb city with a strongly medieval flavor, was described as «daughter of the road» because its fortunes were so closely linked with the Via Francigena. Continuing past Siena, the medieval past can be seen in the fortress-farm of Cuna, the walls of Buonconvento, in San Quìrico d'Orcia with its delightful Collegiata (Collegiate Church), and in the turreted and battlemented castle complex of Spedaletto. It's worth doing a detour to see the abbey of Sant'Àntimo, which did not lie on the Via Francigena but is the most beautiful Romanesque church in the province of Siena. The road then climbs through the magnificent countryside around Mont'Amiata, to Radicòfani with its fortified castle.

PARCO NAZIONALE DELL'ARCIPELAGO TOSCANO

AREA
17,694 HECTARES (LAND), 61,474 HECTARES (SEA).

HEADQUARTERS
VIA F.D. GUERRAZZI 1 – 57037 PORTOFERRAIO
(LI), TEL. 0565919411, FAX 0565919428,
E-MAIL: PARCO@ISLEPARK.IT

VISITORS' CENTERS
CASE DEL PARCO AT RIO NELL'ELBA AND
MARCIANA (ISOLA D'ELBA), TEL. 0565901030.

WEB SITE
WWW.ISLEPARK.IT

ACCESS
PORTOFERRAIO - FERRY OR HYDROFOIL FROM

PIOMBINO OR LIVORNO: POINT OF ENTRY FOR
ELBA, AND DEPARTURE POINT FOR GIGLIO,
CAPRAIA AND GIANNUTRI ISLANDS.
CAPRAIA - FERRY FROM LIVORNO OR
PORTOFERRAIO.
GIGLIO PORTO - FERRY FROM PORTO SANTO
STEFANO

According to legend, a necklace of
precious pearls adorned Venus's
delicate neck. When the necklace
broke, the pearls fell into the Tyrrhenian
Sea, and formed seven beautiful
islands, the Tuscan Archipelago. Today
the islands are part of a National Park
which also includes Europe's largest
protected sea area.
The islands are very diverse: Capraia is

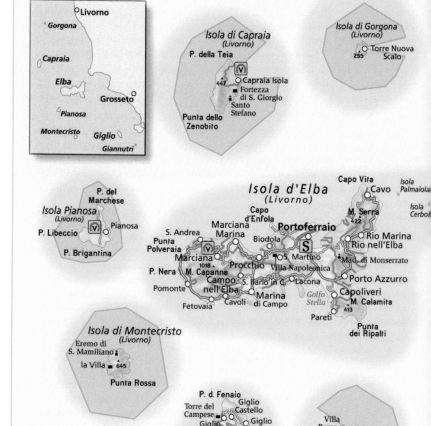

Punta del Capel Rosso, the southernmost part of the island of Giglio. In spring, this stretch of coast hosts the largest colony of herring gulls on the island

volcanic, Montecristo and Gorgona are granitic, and Giglio and Elba are both granitic and calcareous. The island group is a stopping point on sailing routes, and some unusual ecosystems also survive there. Elba is rich in minerals; mining has been carried out there since Etruscan and Roman times. Historically and culturally it is the most interesting of all the islands: its Romanesque churches, the city-fortress of Cosmopolis (today Portoferraio), the sanctuary of Monserrato, and places related to Napoleon's exile on the island.

Montecristo

A number of islands in the Archipelago have been used as prisons; this has protected them from tourism, and flora and fauna have been able to remain as they were. This is especially the case on Montecristo, an island mountain peaking at 645m above sea level, and a safe habitat for the Montecristo goat, and the rare Sardinian discoglossus, a tailless amphibian like a green frog. Like many of the islands, it was once inhabited only by monks and hermits, and is one of the most protected islands of the Mediterranean. Only a guardian and Park Rangers live on this marine and land reserve, and only researchers are permitted to visit. A primordial place, in many ways, as it was for Edmond

Dantès, Alexandre Dumas's hero in "The Count of Montecristo".

Mediterranean flora and more

The islands rise to considerable heights, and the cooler temperatures provide a suitable environment for mesophyll species. Ferns are found on Monte Capanna, Elba's highest peak (1018m), and the Elba cornflower grows on its slopes. Oak trees, including turkey oak and durmast oak, grow on Giglio. Capraia's flora is totally Mediterranean, with expanses of low-growing maquis, and native Sardinian and Corsican vegetation, such as the Sardinian marine lily (Pancratium illyricum) and a local saffron (Romulea revelieri).

Rich resource for biodiversity

Endemism is a term used to indicate animal or plant species found only in a limited area. Many animals are endemic to the Tuscan Archipelago National Park. They include gastropod molluscs, insects, butterflies, and lizards, and all guarantee the preservation of biodiversity in the Mediterranean, an area which is at risk from this point of view. Peregrine falcons, woodpeckers, gulls, swallows and swifts, all fly the skies above the Archipelago. The rarest is the Corsican gull, which is also the Park's emblem.

WWF OASI LAGO DI BURANO

VISITOR CENTER TEL. 0564898829
WWW.WWFTOSCANA.IT/BURANO.ASP
OASIBURANO@INWIND.IT

OPEN FROM 1ST SEPTEMBER TO 30TH APRIL
BOOKING REQUIRED MONDAY TO SATURDAY;
NOT REQUIRED SUNDAY AND HOLIDAYS.

GETTING THERE
BY CAR: STATE HIGHWAY 1 FOR GROSSETO,
EXIT LAGO DI BURANO.
BY TRAIN: TO CAPALBIO SCALO.

From the very beginning the oasis has given priority to making its paths highly accessible, also for wheelchairs. The area has the advantage of having no natural land barriers; in addition, the oasis provides aids for the sightless.

Description

The oasis covers an area of 400 hectares, and forms an interesting and complete mini eco-system of the Maremma. Lake Burano is a saline lake separated from the sea by a virtually intact sand dune, with prickly juniper and other vegetation typical of the Mediterranean maquis (sea-lily, lentisk, myrtle, phyllirea, Mediterranean buckthorn, juniper, rosemary). The lake is edged with reed-beds and pools of water, and the water-sodden meadows around are subject to seasonal flooding. Various species that grow in sand are established on the sandy shore areas. Around 20,000 birds are found there, including coot, pochard and grey heron, depending on the season. Winter and spring are the best times for bird-watching, while summer is the best time to enjoy the oasis's unspoilt natural beauty.

Accessibility

The oasis provides barrier-free access for wheelchairs, with metal netting laid over the sand on the paths.
The track around the lake is 1 km long, and is provided with lowered observation points, some of which are equipped with telescopes. All information boards are the right height to enable easy reading. A Braille map of the area (30 x 40 cm) can be consulted, and information brochures are provided. The visitor center has a restroom for the disabled.

CLUB CAVALGIOCARE

PRESSO AIT LA CASELLA
PODERE CASELLA 264
SOVICILLE (SI)

TEL. 0577314323
FOR COURSE INFORMATION:
CELL. 3337919781

WWW.CAVALGIOCARE.IT
INFO@CAVALGIOCARE.IT

GETTING THERE
THE MAIN CENTER IS SITUATED ABOUT 10 KM FROM SIENA. FROM THE SIENA RING-ROAD, TAKE STATE HIGHWAY 73, AND THEN THE TURNING FOR SOVICILLE.

The club is more than just a club; it is synonymous with a method, which has become a trademark. The "Cavalgiocare" method teaches all children, including disabled children, to get to know the world of horses, in an active, positive and enjoyable way.

Description

Cavalgiocare enables children to have fun as they learn about horses and riding. The method puts emphasis on becoming familiar with horses and learning how to relate to them. Unlike more traditional riding courses, the priority is to establish communication with the horse through touch, rather than getting on the horse at all costs. The school uses the "Brain Gym" pedagogical method: an active and enjoyable approach, free of stress, dedicating respect and attention to each learner. The association's main center is at the Podere Casella. There are other centers too, in particular La Balzana farm at Pratovecchio, near Arezzo. During the year, holiday weeks are organised, for various age-groups, as well as farm days and courses for school children of all ages.

Accessibility

The Cavalgiocare method is open to everyone: individuals, groups and families. It is suited to

learners of any age, from children as young as 2 or 3, to adults.
Cavalgiocare's approach to horses and riding involves and inspires everybody, including people with motor, intellectual or sensory disabilities.

ASSOCIAZIONE SPORTIVA BARONI ROTTI

Loc. Manciano 225
Castiglion Fiorentino (AR)
TEL. 0575653260
CELL. 3386703248
WWW.BARONIROTTI.NET
FRANCOBNT@INTERFREE.IT

GETTING THERE
A1 motorway, exit Monte San Savino; follow the signs for Castiglion Fiorentino (around 9 km).

A flying school, where learners can "take off", past all obstacles. The school offers courses for the disabled to obtain their licences and fly without any problem.

Description
The Baroni Rotti Association was founded by a group of people who were passionate about flying; in addition it was also the first school to offer courses for disabled people. The course which leads to an ultralight aircraft pilot's licence is tailored to meet trainees' needs, and lasts around six months, with attendance once a week. Obtaining a licence requires at least 23 hours of theory and 12 hours flying. A preliminary test evaluates the needs and difficulties of applicants. There are two levels: the first leads to the pilot's licence, and the second qualifies the pilot to transport passengers.

Accessibility
The course is open to all flying enthusiasts, including those with motor disabilities or with slight sensory disabilities. Before lessons start, applicants have a test flight, and a check-up by a sports doctor to evaluate their suitability for the course. The minimum age required is 16 (with parents' authorisation). Both the school and the runway are barrier-free. Accomodation is available, at the Residence Conte Serristori, next to the school. It has 15 apartments (2 modified for the disabled),

with bathrooms, 8 of which are barrier-free. The Residence also has a restaurant and swimming pool (tel. 0575653260, fax 0575653415, www.centroserristori.it).

VELAINSIEME

SEA BASE: Castiglione della Pescaia (LI)

HEADQUARTERS: Piazza S. Lucia 6
Montepulciano (SI)
TEL. 0578756053
WWW.VELAINSIEME.IT
VELAINSIEME@TIN.IT

GETTING THERE
State Highway 1, exit Grosseto; continue towards Castiglione della Pescaia (21 km from Grosseto).

Velainsieme is a highly interesting initiative: as well as providing sailing holidays for those with motor disabilities, it also organises courses for wheelchair-users who wish to obtain their sea pilot's licence. The aim of the association is to form mixed crews, where sailing enthusiasts, disabled and not, fully participate together in life on board.

Description
The association was founded in 1997. In summer it organises holidays on its boats in the Tyrrhenian Sea; in spring and autumn the boats are used to teach enthusiasts how to sail. Particular attention is given to environmental protection, seen as one of the association's priorities. Velainsieme has installed tanks for collecting black water on its new boats, in line with European regulations aimed at reducing marine pollution.

Accessibility
The association is particularly attentive to the needs of the disabled. Working and living together, on boats which have not been specifically modified for the disabled, helps the crew to know each other and work as a group. The difficulties and obstacles of life on board become an opportunity for communication and interaction between people who share a love of sailing. Holidays, courses and various activities are also specifically organised for wheelchair-users. One boat, Bavaria 44, has particularly good accessibility.

Children

PARCO FAUNISTICO MONTE AMIATA

(Monte Amiata Animal Park)

Località Podere dei Nobili - Arcidosso (Grosseto) Tel. 0564966867

E-MAIL: INFO@PARCOFAUNISTICO.IT

WEB: WWW.PARCOFAUNISTICO.IT

OPEN: ALL YEAR, EXCEPT MONDAYS WHICH ARE ON, BEFORE OR AFTER NATIONAL HOLIDAYS

OPENING TIMES: 7.15-DUSK

ADMISSION: FULL-PRICE € 3.50, CHILDREN (AGED 6-11) € 2.20

GETTING THERE

BY CAR: A1 MOTORWAY, FROM NORTH, EXIT CHIANCIANO-CHIUSI, FROM SOUTH, EXIT ORVIETO; CASSIA STATE ROAD BETWEEN SIENA AND VITERBO; SIENA-GROSSETO HIGHWAY

BY TRAIN: GROSSETO OR CHIUSI STATIONS; SECONDARY STATIONS MONTE AMIATA AND SANT'ANGELO DI MONTALCINO

The park is in a nature reserve of over 700 hectares, and has various fauna areas, with paths which visitors can observe wild animals from. In one special large area, there are Apennine wolves - normally very difficult to see. The other fauna areas have Apennine animal species, such as fallow deer, roe deer, chamois, and mouflon. There are also some domesticated species such as the very rare Sorcino donkey, a Mont'Amiata breed. The park also organises talks, and conducts research and conservation projects. Special projects focus on the Egyptian vulture and the grey-partridge, and numerous other bird and mammal species. There is also a botanical garden, a butterfly garden, and an observatory. The park is reached by car, but is visited on foot, and is not suitable for children aged under four. Visitors are not allowed to leave the paths, which have many rest and observation areas. Comfortable clothing is recommended; don't forget binoculars and cameras. Pets are not admitted.

Amenities

Restaurant-bar, picnic areas with running water, free parking, parking area for camper vans, stalls for horses. The park center has information brochures, maps, books and souvenirs.

CAVALLINO MATTO

Via Po 1, Marina di Castagneto Carducci (Livorno) Tel. 0565745720

WEB: WWW.CAVALLINOMATTO.IT

OPEN

MARCH AND OCTOBER: ONLY SUNDAY; APRIL AND 10TH-30TH SEPTEMBER: SATURDAY, SUNDAY AND HOLIDAYS; 1ST MAY-9TH SEPTEMBER: EVERY DAY.

OPENING TIMES: 10AM -7PM; IN JULY UNTIL 9PM; IN AUGUST UNTIL MIDNIGHT.

ADMISSION: FULL-PRICE € 12; CHILDREN (AGED 3-10) € 10

GETTING THERE

BY CAR: A12 MOTORWAY GENOVA-ROSIGNANO, EXIT ROSIGNANO, THEN CIVITAVECCHIA-LIVORNO HIGHWAY SOUTHWARDS, EXIT DONORATICO (1KM); FROM EAST, SIENA-GROSSETO HIGHWAY, THEN CIVITAVECCHIA-LIVORNO HIGHWAY EXIT DONORATICO.

A fun park especially suited for children, set in luxuriant Mediterranean vegetation a stone's throw from the sea; the perfect place to visit if you are on holiday on the Tuscan coast and want a change from the beach. Cavallino Matto was opened in 1989; covering an area of 60,000 square meters, it's a favorite for families with children aged under 13. Visitors can enjoy the many attractions, wandering along the tree-lined avenues, or riding on the little train or the funicular: the ancient Egypt area, African Safari, *Colorado Boat* river rides, the roller coaster, *Luna Loop, Comet Game*, the centrifuge ride, canoes, *Camel Trophy*, the Greek temple, and the fantasy trail tunnel. There are also more traditional rides like the carousel, the ferris wheel, the *Mini-caterpillar*, and bumper cars. For very young children: inflatable toys. For all ages: trampolines, target-shooting, go-carting, mini-golf, amusement arcade, and the Aquarium Continente Mare with Mediterranean fauna.

Amenities

Restaurant, self-service, bar, pizzeria-sandwich bar, ice-cream stalls, popcorn and cotton candy stalls, picnic area, souvenir shop, fast photo service, and pay car park.

ABOCA MUSEUM

GENERAL INFORMATION

PALAZZO BOURBON DEL MONTE - VIA NICCOLÒ AGGIUNTI 75 - 52037 SANSEPOLCRO (AREZZO) - 0575733589 - 0575744724 - MUSEUM@ABOCA.IT - WWW.ABOCA.IT/ABOCAMUSEUM

HOW TO GET THERE

A1 MILAN-ROME MOTORWAY, EXIT AT AREZZO, THEN TAKE THE SS 73 TO SANSEPOLCRO. E45 EXPRESSWAY (SS 3 BIS TIBERINA) TO BAGNO DI ROMAGNA-TERNI, EXIT AT SANSEPOLCRO.

OPENING HOURS

AUTUMN AND WINTER, TUESDAYS TO SUNDAYS, 10AM-1PM AND 2.30-6PM; SPRING AND SUMMER, EVERY DAY 10AM-1PM AND 3-7PM. ENTRANCE FEE.

How the museum began

With this museum, Aboca offers a permanent, accessible display of various historical implements and tools connected with the theme of health and the properties of medicinal plants.

What's inside

The Aboca Museum explores medicinal herbs through a collection of historical material. The visit begins with the Mortars Room. The cabinets display ancient books from the Bibliotheca Antiqua. The History Room presents the use of medicinal herbs down the ages by tracing the evolution of medicine from prehistoric times to the present day. This leads on to the Ceramics Room, with its collection of majolica apothecary jars, jugs and bottles, vessels which have taken on considerable artistic and symbolic significance over the centuries. The next rooms display 18th-century pharmacy glassware; explanatory panels describe how herbs were preserved in the previous centuries. The herbal shop and phyto-chemical laboratory reproduce 17th- and 19th-century rooms and illustrate the passage from ancient to modern methods of processing herbs and spices. One intriguing room in the museum keeps under lock and key a collection of poisonous plants and the different kinds of toxic products that only experts were once able to use safely. The 19th-century medical pharmacy displays materials of the day; the Planisphere room presents the geographical origin and spread of ancient and modern spices.

Aims

The museum is a major cultural undertaking by Aboca, a leading grower and processor of medicinal plants, aimed at reviving the use of popular herbal remedies and at providing information on the subject to the general public.

Activities

The study center carries out historical and bibliographical research work and disseminates cultural knowledge regarding the world of medicinal herbs. The museum's activities include symposia and temporary and travelling exhibitions on related themes.

FRATELLI ALINARI MUSEUM OF THE HISTORY OF PHOTOGRAPHY

GENERAL INFORMATION

LARGO FRATELLI ALINARI 15 - 50123 FIRENZE - 05523951 - 0552395217 - 0552382857 - MUSEUM@ALINARI.IT - WWW.ALINARI.IT

HOW TO GET THERE

AUTOBUS 37. BUS 37.

OPENING HOURS

VISITS BY PRIOR ARRANGEMENT UNTIL THE NEW EXHIBITION CENTER OPENS; THE ONLY ROOMS OPEN FOR CONSULTATION ARE THE PLATE LIBRARY, THE VINTAGE ROOM, THE ARTISTIC PRINTS ROOM, THE LIBRARY AND PHOTO LIBRARY, AND THE ARCHIVE. ENTRANCE FEE.

How the museum began

The museum opened in 1985 with the collections hitherto kept in the company headquarters in Largo Alinari. The new exhibition spaces will be situated in the former Leopoldine convent, in Piazza S. Maria Novella, near Florence's main railway station.

What's inside

The museum is divided into eight sections. The Historic Plate Library: 250,000 glass plates (1852-1940) from the Alinari, Brogi, Anderson, Chauffourier, Mannelli and Fiorentini archives. The Vintage Print Collection: 800,000 period photographs and contemporary prints from Italy and abroad. The Negatives Collection: some 2 million negatives from photographic studios and ateliers or from amateur 19th- and 20th-century Italian and foreign photographers, on plates and photographic film. The Photo Library: around 450,000 photographic prints, ektac hromes and slides mainly of artistic subjects and landscapes, taken during the last two centuries. Camera Collection: around 1,000 pieces of studio and laboratory equipment from earliest times to the mid-20th century. The Library: specialising in the history of photography, open on request for consultation, contains over 16,000 volumes on photography, from the earliest reports to well-known 19th-century technical manuals. The Restoration Department: concerned not only with restoring the museum's own holdings, but also with providing a workshop offering training courses for outside restorers. The Documents Archive: containing the company's historical archive and documentation on various significant photographic studios in the 19th and 20th centuries.

Aims

The museum sets out to document the history and development of photography from earliest times to the present day, as well as preserving the historical collection of Fratelli Alinari, the world's oldest company still in operation in the photography and communications sector, and which in 2002 celebrated its 150th anniversary.

The laboratory founded in 1852 by Leopoldo Giuseppe and Romualdo Alinari in Via Cornina, Florence, which later grew to the size of an industrial plant, has operated continuously since 1863. The innovative activity was carried on by Vittorio Alinari from 1890 and throughout the first two decades of the 20th century, taking the archive's holdings to 150,000 negative plates. In 1920 Alinari became a joint-stock company, and added the letters IDEA (Istituto di Edizioni Artistiche) to its name. In the decades that followed some of Italy's most important photographic archives were bought and preserved by Alinari, and attempts were made in later years to add further to the collection by buying up the Villani Archive in Bologna (550,000 negatives) and other similarly important collections. The museum has always striven to acquire original material in Italy and abroad, through painstaking research work in collaboration with leading collectors, and by keeping abreast of material available by studying auction catalogues throughout the world.

Activities

Since its foundation, the museum has always carried out an important exhibition activity, producing many shows in Italy and abroad on internationally-acclaimed photographers. Around five exhibitions are held every year in Florence, and approximately 20 in the rest of Italy and abroad. It has also collaborated on the production of catalogues to its exhibitions and published exquisite books on the history of photography.

SALVATORE FERRAGAMO MUSEUM

GENERAL INFORMATION
PALAZZO SPINI FERONI - VIA DE' TORNABUONI 2 - 50123 FIRENZE - 0553360456-455 - 0553360475 - STEFANIA.RICCI@FERRAGAMO.COM - WWW.FERRAGAMO.COM -

HOW TO GET THERE
AUTOBUS 6 E 37. BUSES 6 AND 37.

OPENING HOURS
OPEN MONDAYS TO FRIDAYS, 9AM-1PM AND 2-6PM; CLOSED SATURDAYS AND SUNDAYS, 1 TO 31 AUGUST AND 23 DECEMBER TO 6 JANUARY. GUIDED TOURS IN ITALIAN AND ENGLISH MUST BE BOOKED IN ADVANCE. NO ENTRANCE FEE.

How the museum began
The museum opened in May 1995, following the success of a travelling exhibition on the history of the company. The aim of the Ferragamo family is to raise public awareness of the artistic talents, imaginative flair and inventiveness of the company's founder, Salvatore Ferragamo, justly ranked as one of the 20th century's most influential designers. The life of Salvatore Ferragamo – which he himself recounts in his autobiography, The Shoemaker of Dreams – reads like the screenplay of a film, its main character embodying a world of values and qualities that made a lifetime dream come true.

What's inside
The museum boasts a collection of 10,000 models of shoes kept by Salvatore

Ferragamo. After his death in 1960 his wife and children enhanced the collection with major new acquisitions, including the pair of shoes designed for Marilyn Monroe, bought at Christie's in New York in 1999. The collection covers not only the shoes crafted by Salvatore himself from the 1920s to the late 1950s, but includes all the later creations right up to the current collections, the aim being to present the creative developments that have made the company what it is today. There is also an archive of documents, films, photographs, press cuttings, advertising materials, clothes and accessories, from the 1950s through to the present day, illustrating the entire history of Salvatore Ferragamo's business from its earliest days. The permanent exhibition space displays a selection of between 140 and 150 items ranging from prototypes to finished shoes, as well as presenting documents and film footage. The models, presented on a biennial rotation, are chosen each time according to specific themes on new issues and open up new fields of inquiry into the history of Ferragamo footwear, how the shoes are made and the materials used.

Aims
The museum serves as an effective communication tool for the company, which over the years has learned to interact with the city and the local area, taking up its own special place on the city museum scene.

Activities
Through its archive, the museum acts as a research and information center for the company's different divisions and is responsible for all cultural and institutional initiatives. It also runs outside events, lending items from its collection for design and fashion exhibitions around the world; it organises travelling exhibitions to some of the world's most prestigious museums, as well as taking part in symposia and giving lectures and courses on the subject of footwear, and publishing its own six-monthly magazine with updates on its activities, the catalogues to its exhibitions and books on the history of the firm and its products. Since 1996 the museum has

been housed in a larger building which also has space for temporary exhibitions on various cultural and fashion-related themes.

Shoes for the stars

In the post-war years Salvatore Ferragamo shoes were one of the symbols of Italian recovery, of a country eager to resume creative productivity. Some of his most memorable inventions date back to this period: the high-heeled shoes with metal reinforcements made famous by Marilyn Monroe, the gold sandals, the invisible sandal with nylon thread upper (with which Ferragamo won the coveted Neiman Marcus Award in 1947, the so-called 'Oscar of the fashion industry', awarded for the first time to a creator of footwear). Once again he was enjoying international success: the Via de' Tornabuoni attracted such personalities as Greta Garbo, Sophia Loren the Duchess of Windsor and Audrey Hepburn.

RICHARD GINORI MUSEUM

GENERAL INFORMATION
VIALE PRATESE 31 - 50019 SESTO FIORENTINO (FIRENZE) - 0554207767 - 0554205655 - MUSEO@RICHARDGINORI1735.COM - WWW.MUSEODIDOCCIA.IT

HOW TO GET THERE
A1 MILAN-ROME MOTORWAY, EXIT AT PRATO-CALENZANO.

OPENING HOURS
OPEN WEDNESDAYS TO SATURDAYS, 10AM-1PM AND 2-6PM; CLOSED SUNDAYS AND HOLIDAYS. ENTRANCE FEE.

How the museum began

The museum was opened in 1965 in a building designed by Fabio Rossi and Pier Nicolò Berardi (Berardi worked with Michelucci on Florence's Santa Maria Novella railway station). The new museum took the place of the previous exhibition area on the ground floor of Villa Buondelmonti di Doccia, the home of the original manufactory. Anyone wishing to visit the

"Doccia Museums", as they were then known, had to collect a special pass from the historic shop in Via Rondinelli, Florence. The new museum inherited the collection which Marquis Carlo Ginori had begun to put together beginning in 1737. The first items in the founder's collection were a series of life-size white porcelain statues, 18th-century models of wax bas-reliefs and statues and sulphur moulds for cameos made of semi-precious stones. In addition, Carlo Ginori had in those early days also established the so-called Earths Museum (a part of which is displayed on the ground-floor of the present-day museum), consisting of a series of blown glass jars with white and blue majolica lids, containing mineral and clays used to make the porcelain paste. As time went by the collection grew, with a selection of the most representative items produced by Ginori, and in the general climate of interest in the decorative and industrial arts that prevailed in the second half of the 19th century, it was decided to open the museum to the public. In 1896, when Ginori merged with Richard, the museum was bequeathed by the Ginori family to the new company, upon condition that it would never be removed from the site where manufacturing took place. In 1958 the old Doccia factory finally closed down, but a new one had already been opened in 1949, a few kilometers away in Sesto Fiorentino, close to which today's museum was eventually built.

What's inside

The collection comprises 8,000 Ginori and Richard-Ginori ceramic items from 1737 to the present day; wax,

terracotta and plaster models, including an extremely rare collection of works by M. Soldani Benzi and G. B. Foggini from the late 17th and early 18th centuries; sulphur moulds for cameos made of semi-precious stones; a Historic Archive of the activities of the manifattura, from the early 1800s to the 1930s; and a Library with printed texts from the mid-18th century to the present day.

Aims

As well as preserving artistic legacy, the museum promotes study programmes, as part of an effort to make information about ceramic culture available to the general public. It still has very close links with the manufacturing activity, which draws on its past to produce re-runs of old items and as a source of inspiration for new designs.

Activities

Course, exhibitions, lectures, guided tours.

PIAGGIO 'GIOVANNI ALBERTO AGNELLI' MUSEUM

GENERAL INFORMATION
VIALE RINALDO PIAGGIO 7 - 56025 PONTEDERA (PISA) -058727171 - 0587290057 - MUSEO@MUSEOPIAGGIO.IT - WWW.MUSEOPIAGGIO.IT

HOW TO GET THERE
FLORENCE-PISA EXPRESSWAY, EXIT AT PONTEDERA, THEN FOLLOW SIGNS TO THE TOWN.

OPENING HOURS
THE MUSEUM IS OPEN FROM WEDNESDAYS TO SATURDAYS, 10AM-6PM; CLOSED FROM SUNDAYS TO TUESDAYS. THE HISTORIC ARCHIVE IS OPENED BY PRIOR ARRANGEMENT (AUTHORISATION REQUIRED).

How the museum began

The Piaggio Foundation was created in 1994 by Giovanni Alberto Agnelli to enhance relations between the world of culture, business and the local environment, as part of an effort to set up a cultural 'arm' to the firm that could interact with the corporation and local and regional bodies. The museum was officially opened in March 2000 and dedicated to the young Giovanni Alberto Agnelli, who died when the project was still at the design stage.

What's inside

The museum exhibits around 80 historic vehicles, that trace the history of Piaggio, and of Gilera in Arcore, which Piaggio took over in 1969.

Aims

The world-famous scooter manufacturer has been on the market since 1884, when the young Rinaldo Piaggio founded a ship fittings company at Sestri Ponente, near Genoa: it was the beginning of a creative adventure marked by major advances in the construction of virtually all forms of transport. The museum is not intended as a mere 'repository' of models or a place that simply recounts the history of a company: it is a space in which to find out about and reflect on the history of industrialisation and Italian society from the last years of the 19th century to the present day. Located in a huge redeveloped industrial area once occupied by Piaggio's 'mechanical equipment' division, the museum is a living space in the working environment itself, since it adjoins the production plant. Andrea Bruno's redevelopment project has respected the building's industrial architecture features.

Activities

The museum is a center for the promotion of art exhibitions and debates on a whole range of different and significant aspects of Italian society. Each year artists, scientists and ordinary citizens flock to the museum's exhibition space and auditorium to attend the various events. The archive is a study and research workshop.

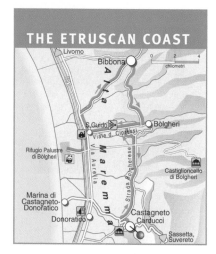

THE ETRUSCAN COAST

ROUTE 37KM: CASTAGNETO CARDUCCI -
SAN GUIDO - BIBBONA - BOLGHERI -
CASTAGNETO CARDUCCI.
ON SEALED ROADS, WITH LITTLE TRAFFIC,
EXCEPT FOR A BRIEF STRETCH ON THE OLD
AURELIA HIGHWAY.

DIFFICULTY EASY; 5 SHORT UPHILL-DOWNHILL
STRETCHES; THE BIBBONA-BOLGHERI (6KM)
SECTION IS A LITTLE MORE DEMANDING.

BIKE + TRAIN THE RAILWAY STATIONS FOR
CASTAGNETO CARDUCCI (DONORATICO AND
BOLGHERI) ARE ON THE ROME – GENOA LINE.

BIKE SERVICE AND INFORMATION CICLOSPORT,
VIA AURELIA 25, DONORATICO (LI);
TEL. 0565777149; WWW.CICLOSPORT.IT
CENTER SPECIALISING IN BIKE SALES, RENTAL,
GUIDES AND TECHNICAL INFORMATION.

TOURIST INFORMATION TOURIST **INFORMATION**
OFFICE, VIA DELLA MARINA 8;
TEL. 0565744276 AND 0565778218;
CASTAGNETO.TURISMO@INFOL.IT
APT LIVORNO, PIAZZA CAVOUR
6, 57125 LIVORNO;
TEL. 0586204611.
CONSORZIO STRADA DEL VINO
COSTA DEGLI ETRUSCHI
(ETRUSCAN WINE TRAIL
CONSORTIUM), LOCALITÀ SAN
GUIDO 45; TEL. 0565749705.

Wines and Cypresses

The Etruscan Coast is ideal
for cycling enthusiasts,
including families with
children.
The route starts from near
the Zì Martino hotel-
restaurant in San Giusto,
below Castagneto Carducci.
Take Via Bolgherese for

Bolgheri. After almost 1km, turn right at
the signpost for Le Pianacce camping-
ground. Soon you reach a cross-roads,
where you turn left. Here there is a short
uphill stretch along the Lamentino road,
among lovely old farms and olive groves.
After about 2km and three cross-roads,
turn left downhill and continue to Via
Bolgherese, where you turn right. Cross
the small Bolgheri stream; the road
continues gently rising and falling
between great oak trees which form a
beautiful green tunnel. This is an
important wine-growing area. After a
double downhill curve, you come
to the famous Sassicaia vineyards.
After the vineyards, Via Bolgherese
meets, in a T-junction, the famous
avenue of cypresses which Carducci
wrote a poem about. Turn left, and it's all
downhill to San Guido and the old
Aurelia highway. From here, it's easy to
get to the Rifugio Palustre di Bolgheri, a
WWF nature park, open from November
to April. Many migrating birds stop here,
and it's a nesting area for red egret, wild
duck and coot. Continue along the old
Aurelia highway northwards for around
2km, to the fork (bear right) for Bibbona,
where you continue on along some uphill
and downhill stretches. After the famous
Ornellaia vineyards, you are back at the
cypress avenue, where you turn left for
Bolgheri. After visiting the town, take the
road downhill to the turning on the left
for Castagneto Carducci. Take Via
Bolgherese again, and continue on back
to your point of departure.

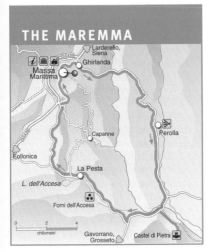

stays fairly high, and then drops (3km) towards the old farm village of Perolla, on the left. A short unsealed road leads to the village, which provides fantastic views over the Grosseto Maremma. The road continues on, still descending, to a T-junction. Turn left towards Gavorrano. After exactly 1.1km, there is a small road on the left, with a yellow signpost marked Castel di Pietra. This short detour to the castle is well worth doing (3 + 3 km). The first 2.3km is gentle, unsealed road, flanked by cypresses; then there's a turning on the right for the 0.7 km climb up to the medieval fortress. Leave your bike at the beginning of the path and walk up to the castle ruins on the hilltop. After returning back to the turn-off point and the sealed road, continue on for 2.5km, until you reach a fork, where you bear right following the sign for Lago dell'Accesa. After 2km, the road climbs steadily to a

ROUTE 41.5KM: MASSA MARITTIMA - PEROLLA - LAGO DELL'ACCESA - MASSA MARITTIMA.

DIFFICULTY THE ROUTE FOLLOWS SEALED ROADS (WITH THE EXCEPTION OF THE DETOUR FOR CASTEL DI PIETRA). IT IS FAIRLY EASY RIDING; THE ONLY SLIGHTLY DEMANDING STRETCHES ARE NEAR LAGO DELL'ACCESA AND THE FINAL CLIMB IN MASSA MARITTIMA (2.5KM).

BIKE SERVICE SUMIN BICICLETTE, VIA FERRINANTI 31, LOCALITÀ VALPIANA, MASSA MARITTIMA; TEL. 0566919111.

ORGANISED BIKE TOURS MASSA VECCHIA, STATE HIGHWAY 439, MASSA MARITTIMA; TEL. 0566903385, FAX 0565901838. A SERIOUS BIKE CENTER, PROVIDING ACCOMODATION, RENTAL BIKES, AND GUIDED TRIPS ON MOUNTAIN OR ROAD BIKES AROUND THE MAREMMA.

TOURIST INFORMATION MUNICIPAL TOURIST OFFICE AND CIVIC MUSEUMS, PIAZZA GARIBALDI, MASSA MARITTIMA; TEL. 0566902289.

The roofs and cathedral in Massa Marittima

Around Massa Marittima

This superb cycle-ride starts from one of Tuscany's most beautiful squares and leads into a corner of Maremma which cyclists are particularly fond of, with its quiet roads winding over hills covered with olive-trees.
The route leaves Massa Marittima in the direction of Siena-Larderello. Just before reaching Provincial Road 439 for Larderello, turn right towards Ghirlanda and Ribolla; for around 6.5 km the road

place called La Pesta, beside the lake. Back on the main road again, at the next fork bear right for Massa Marittima. From here it's 5km downhill to the road leading to the lower slopes of the Massa Marittima hill. From here, the last stretch climbs up to the cathedral square in Massa.

Alternative

The route climbs less (by about 100m) if you leave from the Esso gas station below Massa on the road to Follonica. In this case, you start by following the wide ring-road in the direction of Siena for around 5km as far as the turning for Massa. Then turn right towards the town center, and almost immediately, take the side road on the left for Ghirlanda-Ribolla.

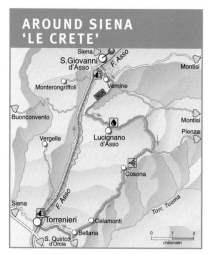

AROUND SIENA 'LE CRETE'

ROUTE 27KM: SAN GIOVANNI D'ASSO - LUCIGNANO D'ASSO - COSONA - TORRENIERI.

DIFFICULTY EASY TO CYCLE, WITH TWO UPHILL STRETCHES: FROM SAN GIOVANNI D'ASSO (1.7KM) AND TOWARDS LUCIGNANO D'ASSO (1.6KM). MAINLY ON UNSEALED ROADS, SO MOUNTAIN BIKES ARE RECOMMENDED.

BIKE + TRAIN ONLY POSSIBLE WITH TRENO NATURA, A TRAIN LINE OPERATING ONLY ON CERTAIN DAYS.

BIKE SERVICE REAL, VIA ROMA 46/50, ASCIANO; TEL. 0577719138

TOURIST INFORMATION APT SIENA, VIA DI CITTÀ 43, SIENA; TEL. 0577280551. WWW.TERRESIENA.IT
MUNICIPAL INFORMATION OFFICE, SAN GIOVANNI D'ASSO, VIA XX SETTEMBRE 15; TEL 0577803101.

NB DETAILED INFORMATION AND MAPS ON WWW.TERRESIENA.IT

A cycling route over the rolling hills ('Crete') and unsealed roads typical of the area south of Siena, between San

Giovanni and Torrenieri around Val d'Asso. From the San Giovanni d'Asso railway station, after 400m you come to an intersection. Turn left towards Montisi, over the level crossing. Cross the bridge over the Asso stream and after 200m turn right up an unsealed road (signposted Agriturismo Trove). The road climbs for 0.8km to a fork. Turn right following the road marked 560A (straight ahead leads steeply down to the Trove Agriturismo or Farm Stay). At the next fork (200m), bear right. You then reach a hamlet where the road continues downhill. Past a sheep gate (don't forget to close it behind you) and a farm, you come to a wide unsealed road. Turn left uphill for Lucignano d'Asso (1.6km). This is the start of a superb ride over the hills. Follow the signs for Montisi-Pienza, to a T-junction, where you turn right (left for Pienza). Follow the lovely, wide, unsealed road, gently rising and falling over the hills (known as the 'Crete') typical of this area, with rolling pastures and isolated farmhouses in the open countryside. When you reach the hamlet of Consona, continue on along the main road, which leads to the sealed road (6.5km from the intersection). Continue downhill towards Torrenieri (2km).

Alternative route

From here you can also return to San Giovanni d'Asso, cycling 9km over mainly flat terrain.

This itinerary can be combined with the Treno Natura route, a 140km circuit which starts and finishes at Siena. The first part, Siena-Asciano-Monte Antico (84km), follows railway tracks that are no longer used. The second part, Monte Antico-Buonconvento-Siena (56km), follows the Grosseto-Siena line which is in regular use. It's possible to do the whole circuit only at certain times, generally on Sundays, when there are three trains: morning, midday, afternoon. This means you can get off at any station, walk or cycle, and then catch the next train at the same station or another one, to complete the circuit.

The characteristic 'Crete' countryside, near Siena

Rows of wine in Chianti

San Polo and the Ema valley

Chianti is generally fairly hilly and difficult for cyclists, but this easy route in the San Polo area is perfect for cycling, even if you are not particularly fit. San Polo in Chianti was a castle, situated strategically on the road between Ponte a Ema and Figline. Nothing remains of it today; only a few important documents and records survive, dating from just after 1000, and held in the archives of the Montescalari and Passignano monasteries.

The route starts from San Polo in Chianti, from the square in front of the town church. Exit from the town on Provincial Road 56 for Florence, ignoring side roads off the main road. Cycle for 4.5km, passing through Quarate, where, near a turning on the right, there is a fountain if you need water. Also, if you look up to the right towards the center of Quarate, you can see an olive tree which, amazingly, grows on top of a tower. The road to Capannuccia presents no difficulty, and is mainly downhill. Once you reach the town, take the second road on the left, by a bar and a fountain. This road leads to Castel Ruggero, which you reach after a 3km ride along the right bank of the Ema stream. The castle is easily recognisable: it is Renaissance in style, and has a tower and large Italian-style garden. From Castel Ruggero the road continues, with Lake Castel Ruggero and the Castel Ruggero farm estate appearing on the left. After a short uphill stretch, take a left fork. After about another 1.7km, there is another fork, with a shrine; bear right. The road continues for about another 700 meters, flanked by cypresses, to a junction with the main sealed road. Continue straight ahead up the Ema valley, towards San Polo, about 3km away.

FLORENTINE CHIANTI

Firenze, Autostr. A1
Capannuccia
S. Andrea a Morgiano
Oggio Ugolino
Quarate
M. Masso ▲ 467
Torr. Ema
S. Stefano a Tizzano
Castel Ruggero
S. Polo in Chianti
Strada in Chianti
Figline Valdarno
Torr. Ema
Greve in Chianti, Siena
0   1   2
chilometri

ROUTE 15.6KM: SAN POLO IN CHIANTI - QUARATE - CAPANNUCCIA - CASTEL RUGGERO - SAN POLO IN CHIANTI.

DIFFICULTY A ROUTE WHICH IS EASILY HANDLED BY FAMILIES WITH CHILDREN; IT FOLLOWS SEALED ROADS, AS WELL AS WIDE, WELL-MAINTAINED, UNSEALED ROADS.

MOUNTAIN BIKE SERVICE AND RENTAL MARCO RAMUZZI, VIA I. STECCHI 23, GREVE IN CHIANTI; TEL. 055853037.

TOURIST INFORMATION MUNICIPAL INFORMATION OFFICE, VIA LUCA CINI 1, GREVE IN CHIANTI; TEL. 0558545243. WWW.GREVE-IN-CHIANTI.COM

ELBA

ROUTE 23KM: RIO MARINA - CAVO - RIO NELL'ELBA - RIO MARINA.
THROUGH THE LEAST INHABITED AND LEAST VISITED PART OF THE ISLAND.

DIFFICULTY ITINERARY OF AVERAGE DIFFICULTY, WITH SOME UPHILL AND DOWNHILL STRETCHES AND THE 7KM PARATA CLIMB BETWEEN CAVO AND RIO NELL'ELBA.

BIKE + BOAT DAILY HYDROFOIL AND BOAT CONNECTIONS LINK PORTOFERRAIO AND CAVO, ON ELBA, WITH THE MAINLAND PORTS OF PIOMBINO AND LIVORNO.

BIKE SERVICE
CALAMITA BIKE, VIA PIETRO GORI 8, CAPOLIVERI; TEL. AND FAX 0565967024. ALSO GUIDE AND BIKE-RENTAL SERVICE.
CICLO SPORT, VIA CARDUCCI 146, PORTOFERRAIO; TEL. 0565914346.

TOURIST INFORMATION
APT DELL'ARCIPELAGO TOSCANO, CALATA ITALIA 26, PORTOFERRAIO; TEL. 0565914671, FAX 0565916350.

From Rio Marina to Cavo

Elba is a wonderful place for cyclists and mountain bikers, but the roads require strong legs. This route, in the north-eastern corner of the island, is of average difficulty. It crosses the iron-mining part of the island, with its red-colored rocks and surviving remains of the old mines that were concentrated in the coastal stretch between Rio Marina and Cavo. From Rio Marina, take the coast road in the direction of Cavo. After a short while, the road turns inland, and climbs gently. After 1.5km, it descends towards the Rio Albano riverbed, and then continues up a short climb (0.6km) and along a flat stretch of around 1km to Cala del Telegrafo.

Here the road starts a pleasant and gradual descent along the coastline, ending at the Cavo beachfront. This is an ideal place to take a short rest, have an energy snack and refill water bottles, before tackling the next part of the route which is largely uphill. It's also worth taking time to make a short detour, before going on towards Rio nell'Elba. A short ride from the seafront through a residential area leads to Capo Castello (Castle Point). There is a great view from here of Isola dei Topi and Capo Vita, the island's northern tip. To pick up the route again, return to the Cavo beachfront, where the road for Rio nell'Elba begins. This most challenging part of the route is known as the Parata road. The 7km climb through maquis (native Mediterranean vegetation) reaches a height of 242m at the Parata Pass, between Monte Serra (on the right) and Torre di Giove (on the left). The road rises gradually, and is easily cycled without excessive effort, but it is fairly long and should be taken carefully. After the pass, you can relax and enjoy the spectacular road which descends down towards Rio nell'Elba and Rio Marina.

The coast near Cavo

ORBETELLO LAGOON

ROUTE 24.7KM (SEALED AND UNSEALED):
ORBETELLO - TERRAROSSA - TOMBOLO DELLA
FENIGLIA - TAGLIATA ETRUSCA - COSA -
TOMBOLO DELLA FENIGLIA - SPIAGGIA DELLA
FENIGLIA - TERRAROSSA - ORBETELLO.
MAINLY ON ROADS WHERE MOTORISED TRAFFIC
IS NOT PERMITTED.

DIFFICULTY EASY TRAIL, SUITABLE FOR FAMILIES
WITH CHILDREN, GOOD FOR BIRD-WATCHING.

BIKE SERVICE
ATALA POINT, VIA VITTORIO VENETO,
ORBETELLO; TEL. 0564867790.
SALES AND REPAIRS; RENTAL ON REQUEST.

TOURIST INFORMATION
PRO LOCO ORBETELLO, PIAZZA DELLA
REPUBBLICA; TEL. 0564860447.
APT GROSSETO, VIALE MONTEROSA 206;
TEL. 0564462611.
MUSEO ARCHEOLOGICO NAZIONALE DI COSA,
VIA DELLE GINESTRE 35, ORBETELLO; TEL.
0564881421. OPEN EVERY DAY EXCEPT
MONDAY, FROM 9AM TO 7PM.

The Feniglia Tombolo

A very easy route in the fascinating
Natural Reserve lying between the
Maremma coast and Mont'Argentario,
on the thin strip of land ('tombolo')
which separates the lagoon from
the sea.

From Orbetello in the direction of
Porto Santo Stefano. Take the road
along the strip of land between the
east and west lagoon, where there is a
cycle track. Once past the dam, after
1.9km, at Terrarossa, turn left towards
Porto Ercole, and continue to a fork
(1.4km) where you turn left. After the
large car park, continue for 300m and
turn left again, taking an unsealed
road which ends near a large gate.
Cross the pathway and follow a tree-
lined avenue (around 300m), which
ends near the Forest Rangers' complex
of buildings.
Here turn left, and follow the unsealed
road which leads into the heart of the
Feniglia Tombolo. After exactly 300m, turn
left towards the lagoon. After another
300m, you reach a T-junction, and turn
right along the sandy shore of the lagoon.
Here you will pass two walkways which
lead towards bird-watching shelters.
Keep cycling along the main way; after
around 5km the road turns into the pine
forest and a wide clearing where deer
and wild boar can be seen. When you
reach the main road, turn left and go
past more Forest Rangers buildings. Just
outside the gate, the road is sealed
again, and you turn left. Past the
Tagliata Etrusca (a regulatory canal) and
La Lampara restaurant, turn right along
the road that climbs to the promontory
with the ruins and museum of Cosa
(around 1km). After visiting this
interesting archeological area, you
return by the same way. When you reach
the entrance to the Riserva Naturale
Duna di Feniglia, follow the unsealed
road through the wood.
After around 3.5 km, it's worth doing
a detour (250m) to the beautiful
beach of Feniglia on the left. Once
back at the main road, it's easy to
return to the other Forest Rangers'
complex again. You then pick up the
road you took on the outward journey.
To return to Orbetello, go through the
gateway and continue to the sealed
road. Here turn right and after 1.4km,
right again, and continue to where
you started from.

PASTA

HAMS AND SALAMI

CHEESE

OIL

WHITE WINE

CAKES

In Italy there are many obsessions but none more pervasive than the obsession with food. The flavors and aromas of Tuscany can at times be overwhelming, but the end result is always delicious. The food of Tuscany is often deceptively simple in its preparation yet complex in the range of possibilities. From a rustic country trattoria, to a traditional osteria or a big city ristorante, the cuisine of Tuscany offers something for every palette along with an exceptional wine to complement any type of meal. The strongest sense memories are those of scent and taste, so go ahead and indulge in the simple seasonal delights of Tuscan food, and don't be surprised if they linger in your subconscious forever.

Food

Highlights

- Pecorino and caciotta are produced all over Tuscany
- Lardo di Colonnata and finocchiona, specialties from the Provinces of Florence and Siena
- Coarse-grained Tuscan pasta goes perfectly with game and mushroom sauces
- Tuscany is a region of great wines: Brunello di Montalcino, Chianti Classico, Vernaccia di San Gimignano

Inside

Fagioli al fiasco - **Tuscan dish made with beans**

'Trattorias' are, by definition, Tuscan, and the best steak is 'alla fiorentina'; this is indicative of the role this region plays in the imaginations (gastronomic and not) of travelers from all countries. Writers doing the Grand Tour have spent rivers of ink to recreate the emotions, the colors and the scents of the sought-after room with a view over the Tuscan countryside: cypresses and broom feature in the landscapes described, wild boar prosciutto and great wines in gastronomic descriptions.

The wide horizon of the Tuscan hills

Tuscany covers a large area, and has an even wider variety of landscapes. There are, however, two elements which are found all over the region: its Mediterranean light, new to travelers crossing the Apennine Mountains for the first time; and its amazing natural beauty, sometimes harsh, but rich in new aromas and flavors. Tuscany is mostly hilly. Of course, there are the Apennines, with the forests and pastures of the Casentino; there are the Apuan Alps; there are the low-lying areas like Valdarno and Versilia, lush with fruit, vegetables and flowers; and Valdichiana and the Maremma, with their cornfields and herds of cattle. But Tuscany is first and foremost hills. Hills in a wide variety of forms: the hills of Chianti, the best-known and seen as most typically Tuscan, both cultivated and uncultivated, with many hilltop towns and small, isolated country churches; the hills of the Garfagnana, cloaked in chestnut woods and fields of spelt (an ancient cereal grown here); the Colline Metallifere (Metalliferous Hills) between Grosseto and Pisa, brooding and lonely; and the 'Crete' near Siena, rolling hills like a motionless sea, perfumed with the scent of thyme and mint.

Great wines, great oil...

Everywhere on the hills, and so almost everywhere in Tuscany, grapevines and olive trees flourish. They are planted together on traditional farms, olive trees and grapevines side by side; on modern estates they are grown separately, and stretch for miles over the hills. The wineries are among the best in the world in terms of production, variety and quality. Sangiovese and Trebbiano grapes do extremely well here. There are forty protected wines, six with the highest quality DOCG label. The red DOCG wines are "Chianti" (Chianti Classico is classified separately), "Brunello di Montalcino", "Vino Nobile di Montepulciano" and "Carmignano". There is also the white DOCG wine, "Vernaccia di San Gimignano". Winemaking has also given a strong impetus to tourism: the region has a well-developed network of Wine Trails (Strade del Vino), with hundreds of producers and restaurants providing warm welcomes to connoisseurs. The olive-growing industry also produces high quality olive oil, under the one all-inclusive "Toscano" quality label. Lucca has for centuries been considered as the top olive-oil area. Traditional methods involved stripping the olives from the tree and then immediately crushing them in stone oil-mills, an admirable but arduous procedure in the past. New technologies have gone way beyond those times. Completing the array of Tuscany's top-quality produce are three animal products: meat, hams and salamis, and cheese. Here again the region excels itself: the Chianina and Maremmana cattle breeds are exceptional, but every district has something special. There are other special local breeds such as the Pisana, the Garfagnina, the Caldana and the Pontremolese; and there has been a revival of the old Cinta Senese pig breed, depicted in frescoes painted in centuries past.

The "Toscana" label for integrated agriculture

Food quality is a complex matter, closely interconnected with the health and quality of the environment. It would be exaggerating to say that Tuscany is a totally unspoilt area, but it is a fact that a large part of the region enjoys extremely high environmental quality. This is due to its geography, but also to the types of agriculture practised there. In order to protect this valuable asset of the environment, the region is taking steps to promote the development of two types of agriculture. Firstly, integrated agriculture, which has low environmental impact because it adopts practices which limit the use of chemical fertilisers, herbicides and pesticides; and secondly, organic agriculture, which prohibits their use entirely, particularly for cereals, cattle, and oil and wine production. A quality label has been established for integrated agricultural products, so that consumers can recognise them easily. In addition, support is being provided for local specialty products; this should help to meet the requirements of a region which has such varied land forms, as well as a production system consisting of a large number of small and medium enterprises. The "Toscano" label already protects regional products such as "Pecorino" (sheep's cheese), "Prosciutto" (ham), and "Olio extravergine di oliva" (extravirgin olive oil). For wine, there is a plan to introduce an over-arching "Toscana" DOC label. Various other products, such as "Farro della Garfagnana" (Garfagnana spelt) and "Marrone del Mugello" (Mugello chestnuts), have achieved the IGP (Protected Geographic Indication) label.

Simple flavors with no nonsense

Tuscans are straightforward people, with a strong sense of irony, as full-blooded as their wine. Their food mirrors their spirit, admitting no compromise or half-measures: "Guelphs and Ghibellines", but also further subdivision into "white Guelphs and black Guelphs, big Ghibellines and small Ghibellines". Individualism features large everywhere, in the big cities, in the villages and in the countryside. The food is simple, but sophisticated in the quality of the ingredients, and the skill with which they are used and combined brilliantly with local country flavors. Fire is a fundamental: cooking is often done over

aromatic wood which as it burns adds flavor to the food. Tuscans will cook anything on a grill or spit, ranging from steak "alla fiorentina", mushroom caps, and birds with lard, to eels from the Arno. And with everything, another fundamental ingredient, Tuscan oil. Oil is used with many dishes that are cooked slowly in terracotta pots, with the patience of country folk, such as minestroni, soups, vegetables and beans stewed with sausage. It is used, uncooked, on bread, which is the third fundamental in Tuscan cooking, to create the humble 'fettunta', the founding father of the great 'bruschetta' family. This is country food, but in the cities things are much the same. The dishes are more sophisticated, descended from more aristocratic traditions, but the spirit is the same. It's said that Tuscans are hard to please at table. This is easy to believe when you realise the standards they are used to.

The tradition of good food

Florence offers the most when it come to food and eating in Tuscany. The capital keeps alive the Medici gastronomic tradition, which was influenced to a certain extent by French cooking. And it is also a stronghold for traditions, such as the local tripe-sellers who fill the squares with the savory smells of their wares, and the 'vinaini', or wine bars opening onto the streets. In Florence, the "Enoteca Pinchiorri" is exceptional, one of the best in Italy, admired even by the most critical connoisseurs. "La Tenda Rossa" in San Casciano, on the Chianti border, is also exceptional, as is "Romano" in Versilia. There is also a long list of superb restaurants which specialise in regional cooking. It's very reassuring to see the fierce determination with which Tuscans defend their gastronomic identity. You don't have to go to a top-class restaurant in order to eat an excellent "ribollita" (bean-and-vegetable soup). It is largely the quality of the ingredients that counts. The covers of some of the Italian Touring Club's most important publications are given in this section.

Today we think of Tuscan food as country food, with strong, plain flavors, never too complicated. Tuscan pasta also has these qualities. There is not a great range of shapes and sizes, but it is always made with care and combined artfully with sauces. These are often made with game, like the famous "pappardelle sulla lepre", or with mushrooms, or with oil and pecorino, the region's two star products. Often coarse-grained, pasta is also sometimes made with chestnut flour as well as normal flour, like for example the "lasagne matte" made in the Lunigiana. Tuscan pasta excels itself with "pici", which according to tradition originated with the Etruscans. They were normally accompanied with "briciolata" (fried bread crumbs); today they are eaten with many other sauces, usually strong in taste and texture. Pasta with fillings, especially "tortelli" with spinach and ricotta, is found everywhere. Sometimes the ricotta is combined with other ingredients, such as potatoes (in the Casentino), or herbs, or even chestnuts, in hill areas, like the Casentino and Lunigiana.

Gnudi

(nude ravioli) A specialty of Monte Amiata (Siena), like a kind of "gnocchi" made out of ravioli filling: the ingredients are spinach, ricotta, egg, grated Tuscan pecorino, flour, nutmeg, salt and pepper. They are eaten with ragù (meat sauce) or with butter and sage, with a sprinkling of grated pecorino on top.

Lasagne bastarde or lasagne matte

(crazy lasagne) This specialty of the Lunigiana (Massa and Carrara) is a type of pasta made with chestnut flour, as well as normal flour, giving it a dark color and sweetish taste. In both fresh and dried forms, it is traditionally eaten with a sauce made of lard, leeks and tomato.

Pannicelli

A local specialty from Valdichiana (between Arezzo and Siena); the pasta mixture, made with egg, is rolled out and cut into quite large rectangles, which are then filled with a mixture of green vegetables (chard or spinach), ricotta, grated pecorino and egg, flavored with nutmeg, salt and pepper. When cooked, they are covered with a little butter and a sprinkling of cheese, and then put back into the oven for a few minutes.

Pappardelle

This type of pasta is basically a large version of "tagliatelle", and it is very unusual not to find it on Tuscan trattoria menus. It is usually eaten with sauces made from game: a well-known dish is *pappardelle sulla lepre* (pappardelle on hare) from the province of Arezzo; "pappardelle" are also really good with wild boar or the more usual rabbit.

Pici

A very large type of spaghetti, made by hand, and a specialty from the Siena area. Pici are made with flour and water, with no egg. Traditionally they were eaten with *briciolata*, or old bread broken up into crumbs and fried in olive oil. Tradition has it that "pici" originated in Etruscan times.

Strapponi

This egg-pasta is a kind of "pappardelle", made by tearing the pasta by hand into irregular strips. Like pici, it is traditionally eaten with *briciolata*. Also very good with meat and mushroom sauces.

Testaroli

A specialty from the Lunigiana. Batter is cooked on a griddle to make a kind of pancake, which is then cut into quarters. They're eaten with "pesto" (basil sauce), or extravirgin oil and pecorino.

FOOD

Tortelli

In Tuscany there are many versions, with different shapes and fillings, of this type of pasta made with eggs. In Versilia and Lunigiana, tortelli are generally round and filled with ricotta, spinach or other green vegetables, mint, pecorino and egg. In the Maremma, tortelli have spinach and ricotta filling and are eaten with meat sauce made without chicken livers. In the Mugello (north of Florence), they are filled with a mixture of potatoes and sausage, and eaten with meat sauce. And in the high areas (Mugello and Lunigiana), there are tortelli filled with chestnuts, eaten with melted butter and parmesan cheese.

AREZZO

Pastificio Poggiolini

Via F.lli Lumière 90, tel. 0575380122, www.poggiolini.it
This pasta shop makes fresh egg pasta with durum semolina. There are numerous different shapes, some quite unusual, such as pici, cappelli d'alpino, spaghetti alla chitarra, and tortelli with Pienza pecorino, with orange, with citron or with chestnuts. Other products: ostrich egg pasta, wholemeal pasta, in various shapes, and colored pasta.

FLORENCE

Pastificio Pecchioli

Piazza Bernardo Tanucci 6/r, tel. 055488897
Only fresh artisan pasta, made with egg, and durum and soft wheat semolina. Many different shapes: tortelli with potatoes, cannelloni, crespelle, ravioli, various fillings for filled pasta, lasagne sheets, and the full range of hand-made cut pasta. The pappardelle are particularly good.

Tanini & C.

Borgo la Croce 20, tel. 0552343782
Tanini is a wholesale fresh pasta outlet; the pasta is made by hand, in a variety of shapes and cuts (tagliatelle, tagliolini, fettucine and pappardelle); also filled pasta, in a range of shapes and fillings.

GROSSETO

La Tagliatella

Via Repubblica Domenicana 20, tel. 0564450940
The fresh pasta made by La Tagliatella contains durum wheat flour and some semolina, which makes it coarser and grainier, so that it holds sauces better. The most popular types are: tortelli with fillings to order, traditional lasagne, and lasagne made with creative variations. The shop also makes special yellow "bigoli", a Kind of big spaghetti, and large grooved tagliatelle, not found in any other pasta shops.

LIVORNO

Pasta Matta

Via Borgo Cappuccini 37, tel. 0586882528
Production of fresh artisan pasta made exclusively with durum wheat and eggs. Filled pasta comes in a wide variety of shapes and fillings; unfilled pasta types include tagliatelle and pappardelle. Sauces also made.

LUCCA

FORTE DEI MARMI
Pastificio L'Angolo

Via Padre Ignazio da Carrara 31/A, tel. 0584881528
This artisan pasta shop produces a wide range of pasta and gastronomy products. The fresh egg pasta is made with 'oo' durum wheat flour (a very high quality Italian flour) in a multitude of shapes. The delicatessen section makes cannelloni, lasagne, gnocchi alla romana, and crespelle with various fillings. Their baked products, both sweet and savory, are excellent.

VIAREGGIO
Pastificio Bergamini & C.

Via Ottorino Ciabattini 93, tel. 058448804
Small artisan pasta producer specialised in fresh pasta and ready-made pasta dishes. Varieties and shapes include: potato gnocchi, gnocchi alla sorrentina and colored gnocchi,

tagliatelle, pappardelle and other traditional types.

Pastificio Franceschi
Via Francesco Baracca 77,
tel. 0584387641,
www.pastafranceschi.com
This artisan pasta producer makes exclusively fresh pasta, with eggs and 'oo' flour. The range of varieties is not enormous, but everything made here is truly excellent. Favorites are the hand-made tortelli with meat and various cheese fillings, fish ravioli, eggplant ravioli and pumpkin ravioli.

MASSA-CARRARA

MASSA
Pastificio Massese
Via Giovanni Pascoli 13,
tel. 058543786
Artisan pasta shop which makes fresh pasta: egg pasta, pasta without egg, with 'oo' flour, granite and durum semolina. They make the usual traditional Italian pasta shapes, as well as local pasta specialties, such as "stringoni", a special type of tagliatelle. The shop also makes wholemeal pasta in all shapes, and colored pasta.

CARRARA
Pastificio Moderno
Piazza delle Erbe 1, tel. 058570433
Small artisan pasta shop producing fresh pasta, and egg pasta, with 'oo' flour, and granite and durum semolina. Pride of the house are the individually hand-made cappelletti, like the ravioli filled with ricotta and spinach, potatoes or fish.

MARINA DI MASSA
Il Buongustaio
Piazza Menconi 4/D, tel. 0585787555
This pasta shop makes fresh pasta both with and without egg, using durum wheat or 'oo' flour; some particularly good products are: tortelli filled with meat and ricotta, cappelletti, potato gnocchi, taglierini and tagliolini.

PISA

La Bottega della Pasta
Piazza Vettovaglie 28, tel. 050542633,

Signor Falciani, the owner, believes in creativity and innovation. Pasta types made here are constantly modified and reinvented. Filled pasta is very popular, with fillings including rocket and scamorza cheese, strawberries, seaweed, chestnuts, veal and truffles; another favorite are the ravioli with pasta dough made with dark chocolate, and lobster and orange filling.

PISTOIA

Pastificio Palandri
Via Bonellina 154, tel. 0573380430
This shop specialises in organic pasta, extruded through bronze dies. It also makes a large range of egg pasta, to a secret recipe, which gives the pasta a special rough, grainy finish (helping the sauce to stick). The range of shapes includes some local specialties such as cappellotti (round pasta) and cinesine (wavy tagliatelle).

See also
Restaurants p. 219

MONSUMMANO TERME
Silvy
Via Mazzini 49, tel. 0572952311
The Silvy pasta shop produces around 18 pasta shapes, both filled and unfilled; it's outstanding for its great range of fillings (around seventy), with, for example, pecorino cheese, kiwifruit, cured ham and truffles.

PRATO

Pastificio Ferraboschi
Via Tintori 81, tel. 057421638
Specialised in fresh egg pasta and fresh filled pasta, made with durum and soft semolina. Types include: panzerotti with ricotta and spinach filling, potato tortelli, filled mezzelune (half-moons). Black pasta colored with cuttlefish ink is also made.

Pastificio Moderno Boeri
Piazza San Marco 33, tel. 0574400959
Fresh artisan pasta, and egg pasta, made with durum and soft wheat flours. The most popular are: ravioli with ricotta or potatoes, tortellini, and oven-ready lasagne and cannelloni.

HAMS AND SALAMI

With its wide variety of land forms and vegetation, producing a wide range of tastes and aromas, Tuscany is proud of its ancient traditions. Chianti, with its hilltop villages and isolated country churches, is where "finocchiona" and "tonno" are made, both excellent with the local wines. The Gargagnana, with its chestnut woods and fields of spelt, where "biroldo", the tasty pork black pudding (blood sausage) is made. Many salamis and hams are made from animals that roam free and graze on acorns and berries, like wild boar and the special Cinta Senese breed. The "campanilismo" of Tuscans (local pride for the village, town or city they come from) has been renowned since the time of Dante; this local pride is also revealed in all the many different local ham and salami specialties. For example, Sienese sausages with ginger, "salamini" from the Valdarno, Sienese "soppressata" or brawn, and "lardo di Colonnata", delicious thinly sliced on hot, toasted bread (bruschetta).

Buristo
Pork sausage from the Sienese Chianti, with a strong spicey flavor. It's sliced, and eaten within, at most, ten days of being made.

Finocchiona
Large, pure pork salami sausage found all over Tuscany, especially in Chianti. It's made with an equal quantity of shoulder meat and hard cheek fat. After being ground, it is seasoned with salt, pepper, fennel seed, garlic and wine.

Lardo di Colonnata
This delicious lard is made from the layer of fat on the pig's back, and is a specialty of the area of Colonnata (Massa Carrara). It is matured in marble vessels, and treated with herbs and spices.

Mallegato
Black pudding (blood sausage) made in the Volterra area, with fresh pig's blood, flavored with spices, pine nuts, currants and lard. It's eaten either sliced or cooked in a little olive oil.

Mondiola della Garfagnana
Pure pork salami, U-shaped, medium-ground; it's pinky-red in color, soft, and strongly spiced.

Mortadella
Pure pork sausage made from various parts of the animal, with pieces of hard fat added. It can be eaten hot or cold. It's produced especially in Versilia (Mortadella di Camaiore) and in the province of Prato.

Prosciutto di cinghiale
This wild boar ham is a specialty of San Gimignano; the flesh is especially firm, and is flavored with salt, pepper and garlic.

Prosciutto di Cinta Senese
Made from pigs of the Cinta Senese breed. The hams are hand-treated with salt and pepper for around 3 weeks.

Prosciutto Toscano DOP
Cured prosciutto crudo; pigs must be at least 9 months old for this ham. Quite salty, when sliced it is a bright red, sometimes pale red.

Rigatino
Also known as "ventresca"; this bacon is quite lean, and is flat and rectangular in shape, and produced all over Tuscany.

FOOD

125

Salame toscano

Made with lean pork cuts and small cubes of hard fat. The meat is cured with spices and garlic soaked in wine; it has a strong taste and dense texture.

Salsiccia di cinghiale (wild boar sausage)

A Sienese specialty; the meat is ground with pork fat, and seasoned.

Soppressata toscana (Tuscan brawn)

Highly flavored pure pork sausage made all over Tuscany, using head, skin and tongue, which are boiled and then spiced and flavored. It's eaten fresh.

Tonno del Chianti (Chianti tuna)

A ham-based specialty from Panzano del Chianti. The hams are first cooked in brine with white wine and bay leaves for around 5 hours, and then transferred to special containers, covered with seed oil and flavored with bay leaves.

Wild boar fillet

The meat is treated dry with salt, pepper, and garlic, and left for 10 days. Then it is transferred to curing rooms.

Zia

A salame which is a specialty from the northern Maremma, made using lean cuts and pork fat. It is cured for two weeks in rooms where berries and aromatic plants are burned.

AREZZO

Macelleria Gastronomia Aligi Barelli

Via della Chimera 22, tel. 0575357754
An old, renovated butcher's shop, with sausages, brawn and 'sanbudella'
made on the premises. Other pork products, selected from the best butchers in the Arezzo province, are stocked here until ready for consumption, and fill the shop.

FLORENCE

Azienda Agricola Massanera

Chiesanuova, via di Faltignano 74/76, tel. 0558242360, www.massanera.com
The Cinta Senese Company has its headquarters at the Massanera Farm. The association was founded to save this local pig species from extinction and to monitor its strict farming and breeding regulations. It brings together the top producers of Cinta Senese hams and salamis.

Baroni Alimentari

Via Galluzzo, tel. 055289576, www.baronialimentari.it
In the heart of the city's market, a vast assortment of artisan salamis from Tuscany and the rest of Italy, special foie gras and gastronomic specialties from all over the world.

Cantinetta dei Verrazzano

Via dei Tavolini 18/20/r, tel. 055268590, www.verrazzano.com
Charming wine-bar situated right in the city's historic center, offering a selection of fine Tuscan hams and salamis, and local cheeses, which can be enjoyed with regional wines. Hot dishes are also available, like wine bread with finocchiona salami and egg.

Procacci

Via Tornabuoni 64/r, tel. 055211656
One of Florence's historic delicatessens, specialising in truffle-based products, and recently acquired by the Antinori family. Don't miss the chicken galantine, flavored with the prized delicacy.

TIPS FOR BUYING AND KEEPING HAMS AND SALAMIS

Buy products guaranteed by the following labels: DOP (Protected Origin Denomination), IGP (Protected Geographic Indication), or STG (Guaranteed Traditional Specialty). Another tip is to buy whole hams or salamis (especially if vacuum-packed), to slice as needed. This prevents oxidation. 'Nostrani' (non-industrial) products should be kept at temperatures between 15°C and 20° C, in conditions where moisture is controlled. Hang whole hams and salamis, to expose them to the air. Industrial products may be kept in the fridge, in sealed containers or wrapped in wax paper covered by tin foil.

Salumificio Senese

Via Ugnano 10, tel. 055751611
This shop has a growing reputation in Florence; here you will find excellent traditional pork and salami products from the Siena area, as well as an interesting Florentine sausage, flavored with Indian spices.

GREVE IN CHIANTI
Antica Macelleria Cecchini

Panzano, via XX Luglio 11, tel. 055852020
Long-forgotten recipes, rediscovered, and now very trendy: pork in oil, like tuna, and brawn made to a Renaissance recipe. Ham is rarely sold here, because only artisan products are made on the premises, and slowly cured in the back workshop, watched over by Cecchini, a wonderfully charismatic man, and his staff.

Antica Macelleria Falorni

Piazza Matteotti 69/71, tel. 055853029, www.falorni.it
A real institution, preserving and representing the best in Italian salamis and hams. For eight generations the Falorni family has worked to promote local breeds (Chianina, local wild boar, and Cinta Senese - which the family farms, free-range, on the largest estate to breed this type of pig). They also work to uphold local traditions, such as processing techniques, and local flavors used in pork products, such as wild fennel, rosemary, sage and juniper. Some recipes seem to come from a time buried way back in the past: for example salami preserved under wheat grains, or ham under ashes. Salamis and hams can be tasted on the premises, with - it goes without saying - a glass of Chianti.

Parco naturale Alpi Apuane p. 63

Castello di Verrazzano

Verrazzano, tel. 055854243, www.verrazzano.com
Situated in the heart of Chianti, this unique winery also breeds wild boar. Their pork products are made by top artisans in this town which is famed for its sausage, ham and salami production; along with other dishes on the restaurant menu, they go well with the winery's robust Chiantis.

LUCCA

Norcineria Artigiana Coturri

Farneta, via Sarzanese, tel. 058359606
Very centrally placed, this is where 'biroldo' (blood sausage) was created. The shop stocks every possible type of ham, sausage or salami from the Garfagnina, made to recipes (some secret) handed down through the generations. A tradition still continuing today, creating products that are difficult to compete with.

MASSA-CARRARA

CARRARA
Larderia Colonnata di Fausto Guadagni

Colonnata, via Comunale 4, tel. 0585768069
Don't miss this opportunity to taste the famed 'lardo di Colonnata', as well as 'vergazzata', a special bacon cured in vats. Lardo di Colonnata is also a key feature on the menu of the family restaurant, Locanda Apuana, where it appears in almost all dishes, often used very creatively.

Macelleria Giannarelli

Codena, piazza Fratelli Rosselli 11, tel. 0585777329
The biggest producer of lardo di Colonnata, making almost half of the region's total production of this delicacy, and always maintaining excellent quality.

Ristorante Venanzio Vannucci

Colonnata, piazza Palestro 3, tel. 0585758062
In the 70s, Vannucci was the first to introduce his artisan lardo di Colonnata to Italy's best-informed gourmets. His lardo is also served in his restaurant, conveniently located in the town's main square; used in some delicious dishes, for example, rabbit stuffed with lard and fillet steak with lard.

PONTREMOLI
Salumeria Angella di Tiziana Bertocchi

Via Garibaldi 11, tel. 0187830161
A fascinating place, with Art Nouveau shelving, a charming reminder of the past; ask to visit their curing rooms, with rows of hanging hams, sausages and salamis being treated according to natural, time-honored, traditional processes.

SAN MINIATO
Macelleria Norcineria Sergio Falaschi
Via Augusto Conti 18/20, tel. 057143190,
www.sergiofalaschi.it
A member of the Cinta Senese
protection consortium, this pork
butcher's shop produces natural
salamis cured in tufa cellars. Some
specialties: wine salami, 'mallegato'
(blood sausage), liver and pork loin
with Vin Santo.

Trattoria La Taverna dell'Ozio
Corazzano, via Zara 85,
tel. 0571462862
This small trattoria, with beamed ceiling
and terracotta floor, transmits great
reverence for the pig, "that noble,
unjustly mistreated animal which has
sustained the poor for generations", as
the owner says. For years he has
conducted a personal campaign to save
local, unique Tuscan products, which are
sometimes threatened by strict health
regulations. His salamis, carefully
selected from the best makers in the
area, are superb, whether eaten on their
own, or as appetisers with unsalted
Tuscan bread.

VOLTERRA
Macelleria Franco e Luciana Bruci
Via dei Sarti 43, tel. 058886265
In front of the Volterra theater, a
medieval building houses the shop, the
processing plant, and the curing cellar
of this pork butcher shop which
produces traditional Tuscan salamis.
The pigs are bred locally, and carefully
selected from small local farmers.

PISTOIA

Norcineria Anzuini di Di. Ma.
Via Carratica 82/84, tel. 057321397
In the historic center, a pork-butcher's
shop that sells its own artisan products
(and also does the butchering), as well
as other products.

PRATO

Fratelli Conti
Via San Giusto 9, tel. 0574630192,
www.salumificio-conti.com
Very central sales outlet for the pork
products factory of the same name; the
shop sells local specialties, such as
Prato mortadella, finocchiona salami,
and pigs' heads.

SIENA

Antica Salumeria Salvini
Costafabbri, State Road 73 Ponente
nr. 46, tel. 0577394399,
www.anticasalumeriasalvini.com
The Salvini describe themselves as the
last pork butcher's in Siena, and not
only because they work in the outer
chic suburbs of this beautiful Tuscan
city. Famous, local, traditional pork
products are made without using any
industrial processing techniques. The
selection of organic salamis is
impressive; excellent Cinta Senese
products.

Azienda Agricola Belsedere
Via Camollia 25, tel. 057747090
In the center of Siena, this shop
sells products from a farm where
everything is done correctly and
carefully. Pigs are bred and
butchered on the farm, the meat is
dry-salted, and cured naturally.
The farm's organic cheeses are also
excellent.

Consorzio Agrario di Siena
Via Pianigiani 9, tel. 0577222368,
www.capsi.it
A sales outlet for the region's best food
specialties: salamis, cheeses, oils,
wines, preserves...

RADDA IN CHIANTI
Casa Porciatti
Piazza IV Novembre 1,
tel. 0577738055,
www.casaporciatti.it
Two pigs are butchered and processed
here weekly, with great care and
attention to detail. The house
specialties are buristo (blood sausage),
Radda tuna (pork fillet which is
seasoned, dried and preserved under
oil, but not cooked like the Chianti
version), and 'lardone', a highly
flavored lard paste. Try them in the
family wine bar, situated in a charming
medieval alley, in Via Chiasso dei
Portici 3.

CHEESE

The central part of Italy is, in terms of cheese production, the area where 'pecorino' begins to be found. Pecorino is made from either sheep's milk or cow's milk, or a mixture of both. Pecorino has been around for a long time: more than other cheeses, it has maintained and passed down through the centuries the practices, habits and craftsmanship associated with its production, and even the creativity of shepherds in various areas as they honed their skills. Grasses, pastures, rennet, molds, manual skill and tradition, all contribute to the final taste, in a time-honored balancing act. Tuscan pecorino, either for eating or for grating, expresses this heritage.

Apuan Coast Pecorino

[Massa] With an intense aroma, and light, salty taste. It can be fresh or mature, and is traditionally eaten with broad beans and pears.

Brusco

[Pistoia] Mature 'caciotta' made with cow's milk. Eaten with polenta, and as a salad with ceps (funghi porcini) and apples, or pears.

Caciotta Toscana

This is Tuscany's most widely-found cow's cheese. Less caciotta is produced than pecorino, as sheep-farming is more widespread in Tuscany, but production of caciotta is still considerable. It is made in round molds with a mixture of cow's milk (60-90%) and sheep's milk (40-10%). Ripening takes place in cool temperatures over a period of time that can vary from 15 to 40 days. In texture it is uniform and firm, and it has a milk white color, with a sweet taste. Today it is produced all over the region and throughout the year; top quality caciotta is made when spring flowers bloom. The best caciottas come from the Apuan Alps, the Casentino, La Verna, Pienza, San Gimignano, Chianti, the hills around Siena, the Val d'Orcia, Mont'Amiata and the Maremma.

Formaggi Caprini della Maremma

Fresh, creamy, soft cheeses made from goat's milk; they may be flavored with pepper, chilli, mint, or chopped almonds.

Il grande vecchio di Montefollonico

[Siena] Pecorino made from the milk of cows who have been at pasture; the texture is smooth, and the taste slightly sharp.

Montanello

[Pistoia] Fresh cheese made from cow's milk, with a sweet taste. Excellent grilled.

Pastorella del Cerreto di Sorano

[Grosseto] Made from both sheep's and cow's milk, with a smooth buttery texture, and an intense, sweetish flavor.

Pecorino del Casentino

[Arezzo] In two versions: fresh or mature. It has a strong taste, with a slightly sharp flavor.

Pecorino della Garfagnana e delle Colline Lucchesi

With a salty and slightly sharp taste. Traditionally this cheese is eaten with fresh bean pods.

Pecorino della Lunigiana

[Massa] Eaten, fresh or mature, with broad beans, pears or fried polenta.

Pecorino della Montagna Pistoiese

[Pistoia] With a smooth texture and salty taste, made from untreated milk. It goes well with honey, pears and Tuscan prosciutto.

FOOD

Pecorino delle Balze Volterrane

[Pisa] Very particular taste, because ripened for a long time under ashes, freshly-harvested wheat, or fresh grass.

Pecorino delle Colline Senesi

[Siena] Soft and sweet in the fresh version, crumbly and sharp in the mature version.

Pecorino di Pienza ripened in barriques

[Siena] This cheese is ripened in small barriques (oak barrels) for 90 days, giving it a specially pungent after-taste.

Pecorino from the Parco di Migliarino-SanRossore

Made only with sheep's milk; it can be quite soft or semi-hard, and has a markedly sweet taste.

Pecorino ripened in walnut leaves

[Siena] With a slight hint of tannin, from being ripened in terracotta jars covered with walnut leaves.

Pecorino Toscano Dop

This is the cheese most typical of the region, and the result of a sheep-breeding tradition that dates from the time of the Etruscans. Known as 'March cheese' (cacio marzolino) because it was generally made in the spring, it was a popular trade item as early as Roman times, and later was found on the tables of Popes and princes. Modern Pecorino Toscano is made in a round mold, is soft or semi-hard, and can be used as a table cheese or a grating cheese. It is made from pure sheep's milk in the period from September to June. The ripening process lasts from 20 to 40 days for soft Pecorino, and not less than 4 months for semi-hard Pecorino. Sweet-smelling, it has a pronounced taste, tending towards the slightly sharp. It is produced all over Tuscany.

Pratolina

[Grosseto] Pure goat's milk cheese, creamy, with a strong taste. Traditionally eaten with white wine.

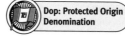 Dop: Protected Origin Denomination

Raveggiolo

Fresh, soft, sheep's cheese; it has a sourish taste with a definite trace of milk. A Pistoian and Sienese specialty.

Ricotta

Produced, from sheep's milk, in the area around Pistoia, the Lunigiana, the Garfagnana and in the Maremma around Grosseto; it has a spongy texture and a creamy taste. Eaten fresh, on its own, or used to make both savory and sweet dishes.

Stracchino

[Grosseto] Soft, cow's milk cheese, with a delicate flavor, slightly sweet.

ENJOYING CHEESE

Generally cheese is eaten before the dessert or the fruit course. But it can also be eaten as an alternative to dessert, or even as an alternative to the main course.

Ideally cheese servings shouldn't be more than a hundred grams, and should be served at a temperature of 18-20° C. If there are a number of different cheeses, it's better to start with the blander, softer cheeses, and to finish with the more mature, stronger ones.

The best accompaniments to cheese are other typical local products, which are part of the same gastronomic culture, and this applies to both wines and bread. Unsalted Tuscan bread, for example, is excellent with pecorino cheese. There are some general guidelines to follow when choosing wines: fresh, soft cheeses go well with dry or smooth white wines; semi-mature cheeses are good with young, red wines; and mature cheeses go well with mature, red wines. Fruit, vegetables, honey and jam provide other interesting accompaniments to cheese. Fresh fruit and vegetables bring freshness to very strong cheeses, and dried fruit is good with soft cheeses. The sweetness of honey and jam means they go well with strong, mature cheeses or cheeses with herbs.

AREZZO

Gastronomia Dario & Anna
Via Vittorio Veneto 14,
tel. 0575902473
In the family since 1963, the shop sells 280 types of Italian, French, Portughese Spanish and Irish cheeses. Also traditional rotisserie take-away foods.

FLORENCE

Antica Gastronomia Palmieri
Via D.M. Manni 46/48/r, tel. 055602081
Next to the shop, a recently-opened osteria where products can be tasted; wide range of Italian, French, English, and Spanish cheeses; local Tuscan salami specialties.

Baroni Alimentari
Via Galluzzo, tel. 055289576,
www.baronialimentari.it
In the heart of the city's market, an excellent range of Tuscan and foreign cheeses, natural cheeses, cheeses matured in oak casks, and goat's milk cheese; Iranian caviar, French and Italian foie gras, and fresh truffles (in season); selection of wines too.

Cantinetta dei Verrazzano
Via dei Tavolini 18/20/r, tel. 055268590,
www.verrazzano.com
This wine bar, situated between Piazza del Duomo and Piazza della Signoria, offers visitors pecorino and goat's cheese to taste along with its wines.

Pegna
Via dello Studio 26/r, tel. 055282701,
www.pegna.it
Since 1860, the shop has stocked every possible kind of regional delicacy (over 7000 products); renovated in 1985, it has superb original mahogany shelving.

GREVE IN CHIANTI
Antica Macelleria Falorni
Piazza Matteotti 69/71, tel. 055853029,
www.falorni.it
Historic butcher's shop run by the same family for 300 years; in addition to its famous salamis and meats, selected cheeses are matured in the 'dungeon', a vaulted underground cellar, dating from 1300.

GROSSETO

FOLLONICA
Caseificio Follonica di Spadi Francesco & C.
Via del Fonditore, tel. 056658409
Goat's and sheep's milk cheeses, ricotta, pecorino with chilli or truffles: these are some of the super-fresh products created here with superb craftsmanship.

Caseificio Maremma di Spadi Fortunato & C.
Via del Commercio 3/5, tel. 056651349,
www.caseificiomaremma.com
Cheese from the Grosseto Maremma, in various sizes.

The Maremmana breed is excellent for meat and milk

LIVORNO

PIOMBINO
Romeo Formaggi
Salivoli, via dei Cavalleggeri 5,
tel. 056544455, www.romeoformaggi.it
500 meters from the tourist port, a shop with a wide range of Italian, French and German cheeses; top-quality Italian salamis and local wines.

LUCCA

Le Delicatezze
Via S. Giorgio 5/7, tel. 0583492633
In the center of Lucca, true to its name for 70 years, this shop sells a range of

delicacies, including over 150 Italian and foreign cheeses; also salamis and local wines.

FORTE DEI MARMI
Salumeria dai Parmigiani
Via Mazzini 1, tel. 058489496
In the center, run by the same family for 50 years, with top-quality Italian cheeses (especially from Tuscany, Piedmont and the Veneto region) and some French cheeses.

MASSA-CARRARA

PONTREMOLI
Salumeria Angella di Tiziana Bertocchi
Via Garibaldi 11, tel. 0187830161
A stone's throw from the Duomo, artisan salamis, such as Pontremoli salami and mortadella, brawn, spallacotta (cooked shoulder ham) and culatello (a choice ham made from loin of pork); range of excellent local cow's milk and mixed milk cheeses.

PISA

VOLTERRA
Caseificio Artigiano di Volterra
Via Pallesse at km 37, tel. 058881516,
www.caciodiruggero.it
Sheep's milk cheese, made by hand and ripened on pinewood slabs. Group visits and tastings.
Da Pina
Via Gramsci 64, tel. 058887394,
www.dapina.it
In a historic palazzo, many rooms with lovely brick vaults where a wide range of local cheeses, salamis, oils, truffles and wines can be tasted. Grappa tasting, and a range of gift and fancy goods for sale.

PISTOIA

Gastronomia Capecchi
Capostrada, via Dalmazia 445,
tel. 0573400208
Next to the bread shop (with special breads, foccaccia and cakes), the delicatessen stocks a good range of local and Piedmont cheeses, buffalo mozzarella and Altamura 'burrata', as well as a range of French cheeses.

SIENA

Gastronomia Morbidi
Via Banchi di Sopra 73/75,
tel. 0577280268
Right in the center of Siena, artisan cheeses and salamis made by the owners, as well as a wide range of fresh and matured cheeses, selected from the top cheese producers.

CASTELNUOVO BERARDENGA
Bottega del Brogi
San Gusmè, via della Porta 7,
tel. 0577359023
Historic shop, in business for 85 years. Next door, pork and wild boar products are made on the premises: brawn, salamis, cured ham. Fresh, semi-mature and mature pecorino cheeses are sold, and there's a well-stocked wine cellar.
Podere Monteapertaccio
dei F.lli Corbeddu
Colle della Battaglia di Montaperti,
tel. 0577369044
In a historically important area, the farm buildings date from 1400; direct sale of cheese made on the farm. Visits can be arranged.

MONTEPULCIANO
Caseificio Cugusi
State Road for Pienza,
via della Boccia 8,
tel. 0578757558
A late 19th-century dairy farm, selling pecorino cheese at all stages of maturity, some flavored with spices. Another sales point in Via di Gracciano del Corso 36.

PIENZA
Caseificio Az. Agr. San Polo
Podere S. Polo 13, tel. 0577665321
In the hills, around 3km from Pienza, cheese factory in a renovated farm complex built in the 1940s-1950s; booking required for visits and tastings.
Caseificio Pienza Solp
Poggio Colombo, tel. 0578748695,
www.pienzasolp.it
Here real Pienza 'cacio' cheese is made to ancient recipes, but with modern techniques and equipment; visits and tasting can be arranged.

OIL

Olive trees have always been a defining feature of the lovely Tuscan countryside, along with grapevines and fields, cypresses and woods. Over 100,000 hectares are planted with olives, and over 17 million kilos of olive oil are produced annually. Tuscany only contributes 4% of Italy's total production, but in terms of the image of Italian olive-oil, its contribution is enormous. It is also a leader in the sale of "labeled" oils.

Since 1998 Tuscan oil has been certified by the IGP (indicazione geografica protetta) label – IGP Toscano – which applies to the whole region. Recently Terre di Siena and Chianti Classico have achieved DOP (denominazione di origine protetta) labels, and it is likely that other products will follow.

Tuscan oils are generally recognisable by their deep green color, their intense aroma and their noticeably pungent flavor which is the result of the growers' picking the olives before they ripen fully naturally. Their fruity aroma is accompanied by a hint of almond, artichoke, and ripe fruit. The flavor is fruity and bitter. The oil must be produced from whole olives harvested at a time established by the IGP Consortium; and the oil must be extracted using only mechanical processes to guarantee the quality of the oil.

The most widespread varieties are Leccino, Frantoio, Moraiolo and Maurino with Pendolino.

Areas suited to olives

Oil is produced all over the whole region, but varies according to differing climate, soil and exposure. The oil produced around Lucca is famed for its special lightness and delicacy. In the Pisan hills, around the Era valley, the oil is soft and fruity. Along the Maremma coast between Pisa and Livorno the oil has a special quality because of the sea nearby, while further south in the Maremma, towards Grosseto, the oil may be more robust. Inland, we find the fruity oils from the slopes of Mt Albano and from Chianti, which are strong and sweet at the same time. The land around Siena is very suited to oil, producing oils rich in color and taste, but always very balanced.

From convents to farms

The Etruscans grew olives in Tuscany on the hills which their towns were built on: the oil was use for lamps, for cosmetics, and for religious rites. It began to be used with food at the time of the Romans, who were perhaps influenced by the Greeks.

In the Middle Ages, the convents and monasteries ensured the continuation of olive growing, and later, the city-states began to become involved in olive oil production. By the 14th century it was already a primary economic resource in great demand. Florence, without a port, regulated production and commerce fairly strictly. The 1428 Municipal Statute of Siena states: «... it is important that the city and the country be plentiful and abundant with oil. Which is one of the things most necessary in the life of man». Meanwhile, in the countryside, the system of tenant farming was developing, with its typical combined growing of different crops and plants (the Medici themselves encouraged the planting of olives and vines together). This system did much to shape the appearance of the Tuscan countryside as it largely is still today.

Tuscany at table

Tuscan oils are perfect for Tuscan cooking, and its strong flavors: whether with soup, "pappa col pomodoro" (a combination of bread and tomatoes), "cacciucco" (fish soup) or game, oil is used both during cooking, and then, after cooking, to give that extra palate-pleasing flavor. It is also used a great deal with uncooked food, such as "fettunte" (bruschetta) and "pinzimonio" (raw vegetables). The traditional dishes originate in the countryside, like the extremely tasty "ribollita", a kind of soup made of leftovers, which is delicious if made as it should be with black cabbage, beans and green vegetables. Another classic favorite is "cannellini" beans, with a little oil and a taste of rosemary. On the coast, fish is the main dish. The delicious "cacciucco" (fish soup) is red from tomatoes, hot from chilli pepper, and flavored with garlic (and according to tradition extra taste is added by putting in a stone taken from the sea).

AREZZO

Fattoria di San Fabiano
San Fabiano 33, tel. 057524566,
www.fattoriasanfabiano.it
Frantoio Oleario Cacioli
Policiano Sud 48/A, tel. 057597002

CORTONA
Tenimenti Luigi d'Alessandro
Camucia, via Manzano 15,
tel. 0575618667

FLORENCE

Marchesi de' Frescobaldi
Via S. Spirito 11, tel. 05527141,
www.frescobaldi.it

BARBERINO VAL D'ELSA
Fattoria Le Filigare
San Donato in Poggio, via
Sicelle 39, tel. 0558072796

FIESOLE
Fattoria di Maiano
Maiano, tel. 055599600,
www.fattoriadimaiano.com

GREVE IN CHIANTI
Tenute di Nozzole
Via di Nozzole 12, tel. 055859811,
www.tenutefolonari.com

IMPRUNETA
Azienda Agrituristica L'Erta di Quintole
Via di Quintole per le Rose 43,
tel. 0552011423, www.ertadiquintole.it

SAN CASCIANO IN VAL DI PESA
Fattoria Le Corti Corsini
Via Piero Di Sotto 5, tel. 055829301,
www.principecorsini.com
Frantorio del Grevepesa
Via Provinciale Chiantigiana 6,
tel. 055821353,
www.principecorsini.com

GROSSETO

Parco della Maremma p. 50

Azienda Regionale Agricola Alberese
Spergolaia Alberese,
tel. 0564407180
Frantoio Maremma
Via Provinciale di Montiano 50,
tel. 0564405249,
www.frantoiomaremma.com

OIL IN ANCIENT TIMES

The cultivation of olive trees spread along the shores of the Mediterranean from the Middle East, reaching a peak at the time of classical Greece. The Romans began to use olives much later, only after the 4th century BC; they very quickly became part of daily life, and one of the key pilasters of the Roman economy. Olives and olive oil were used in food and cooking; the oil was also important in the making of medicinal and cosmetic products, and was also used as fuel for lamps.
In the dark centuries after the fall of the Roman Empire, the cultivation of olives was continued only inside the Benedictine monasteries, where, in their daily life consisting of 'hora et labora' (work and prayer), the monks grew wheat for bread, grapes for wine and olives for oil. Their pharmacies produced, among other

things, the famous Samaritan's Balsam, a wonder cure for cuts, grazes, burns and swellings, made with oil, wine and egg yolk.

Flourishing Tuscan olive trees

MASSA MARITTIMA
Frantoio Sociale
*Citenne, via dei Chiodaioli 17,
tel. 0566919211, www.frantoiosociale.it*
Moris Farms
*Curanuova, tel. 0566919135,
www.morisfarms.it*

LIVORNO

PORTOFERRAIO
Azienda Agricola La Chiusa
Magazzini 93, tel. 0565933046

PISA

VOLTERRA
Azienda Agricola Agrituristica San Michele
*Ulignano, podere S. Michele, tel.
058842062, www.agriturismosanmichele.it*

PISTOIA

Azienda Agricola Il Gabbiano
*Spazzavento, via della Ficaia 8,
tel. 0573570218*

MONTECATINI TERME
Olivicoltori Valdinievole
*Montecatini Alto, via delle Vigne 8/B,
tel. 057267196*

SIENA

Azienda Agrituristica La Torre alle Tolfe
*Strada delle Tolfe 14, tel. 0577255111,
www.letolfe.it*

Azienda Agrituristica Montechiaro
*Strada di Montechiaro 3,
tel. 0577363018*

CASTELLINA IN CHIANTI
Concadoro
*Concadoro, tel. 0577741285,
www.aziendaconcadoro.it*

CASTELNUOVO BERARDENGA
Poggio Bonelli
*Poggio Bonelli, tel. 0577355382,
www.poggiobonelli.it*

GAIOLE IN CHIANTI
Tenuta di Coltibuono
*Badia a Coltibuono, tel. 057774481,
www.coltibuono.com*

MONTEPULCIANO
Il Frantoio di Montepulciano
Via di Martiena 2, tel. 0578716305

PIENZA
Azienda Agritutistica Cretaiole
*Via S. Gregorio 14, tel. 0578748083,
www.cretaiole.it*

POGGIBONSI
Fattorie Melini
*Gaggiano, tel. 0577998511,
www.giv.it*

RADDA IN CHIANTI
Caparsa
Caparsino 48, tel. 0577738174

SAN GIMIGNANO
La Rampa di Fugnano
*Fugnano 55, tel. 0577941655,
www.rampadifugnano.it*

The Tuscan artist, Lorenzetti, is famed for his fresco of Good Government, in the Palazzo Comunale of Siena, where he depicts the perfectly cultivated countryside and the busy, industrious city. Much of the countryside and many of the towns in Tuscany today seem still to belong to that time; here the grapevine, the olive and other local products, together create a festive Renaissance of good eating.

Most vineyards are planted on hills (67%), but there are also many on the plains. Chianti is the main wine, and is produced in the district of the same name. This area between Siena and Florence forms Italy's largest wine-growing district, with over 100 towns and villages. Tuscany also boasts quite a number of other more local wines.

Sangiovese and Trebbiano, a great Tuscan combination

Chianti and Brunello di Montalcino are the top wines. Generally Tuscany is a region of great reds, and noteworthy whites. The main grapes grown are Sangiovese and Tuscan Trebbiano; these both go into the Chianti grape mix, perfected by Baron Ricasoli in the 1800s. Next in importance comes Brunello, which is in fact a local variety of Sangiovese, followed by Ciliegiolo. Other well-known wines are Vernaccia, Fermentino, Ansonica and Malvasia. The vines are grown in a number of ways; most commonly on overhead open arch trellising systems, both single and double, with cordon supports; vines are almost never grown horizontally, a clear indication that wine production is concentrated on quality.

A region at the forefront of quality

For the last few vintages there has been a decrease in overall quantity of wine produced, and an increase in DOC production. The industry's aim is to achieve 'total quality', by creating new DOC wines in the newer areas of production, and by modifying the specifications of established wines to introduce new typologies closer to the market, especially in the reds. There is also a plan to create the Tuscan "DOC Toscana" label; this would embrace all the other denominations, and identify the region's wines with a name known all over the world and synonymous with art, nature and good eating.

Tuscany was one of Italy's first regions to pioneer farm stays for tourists, and has been very successful in this: hamlets, farms and even castles now offer excellent hospitality and country food. The new frontier in rural tourism now is wine cellars and wineries, in the past only rarely open to the public. It was here in Tuscany that the Wine Tourism Movement started in 1993, with the first experiment in Cantine Aperte (Open Wine Cellars). Today this enjoyable springtime festival has been extended to hundreds of places in Italy. Wine Trails (Strade del Vino) are also beginning to appear. Tuscany is the first region in Italy to have passed a law regulating the establishment and operation of these tourist routes.

There are now 14 wine trails, not such a large number, given that some important wines like Chianti Classico and Brunello di Montalcino have not yet been included. But, given how complex it is to establish the trails, and to select farms, restaurants, wineries and places of historic and cultural interest, so that the tourist is guaranteed a really complete experience, the results are more than satisfactory.

Bolgheri Sassicaia DOC

The results achieved with using newer grape varieties in Tuscany have been particularly interesting. This is especially the case for Cabernet Sauvignon, which has improved numerous red wine mixes, and is considered one of the best grapes to use with Sangiovese. It's the main grape used in Bolgheri Rosso, and the only grape used in Bolgheri Sassicaia, the best-known of the so-called "super Tuscans".

Carmignano DOCG

A favorite of the Medici long ago, Carmignano has always been an outstanding wine; now, with its DOCG label, it has achieved even greater visibility. The DOCQ specifications limit production to the Carmignano area and the grape mix to a Sangiovese base (45%-70%). Colored a strong, bright red, it becomes burgundy with ageing. Vinous, with a hint of violets and distinctively subtle aroma when aged;

Brunello di Montalcino DOCG

Brunello was created in the mid 19th-century by an oenologist, Ferruccio Biondi Santi, who decided to make wine with Sangiovese grapes alone, without the traditional mix using other grape varieties as well. Maceration and ageing in oak casks produces a strong, velvety wine, of exceptional character. Today Brunello is known worldwide as one of Italy's top wines, its legendary reputation based on its outstanding quality. The wine is ruby red tending towards burgundy in color. Distinctive, intense, ethereal aroma, with hints of underbrush, scented wood and berry fruits; dry, warm, slightly tannic, robust, smooth, and persistent taste. Minimum alcohol content 12.5°. Brunello is aged for five years, and Brunello Riserva for six. The classic choice of wine for red meat, roast meat and game.

dry, soft and velvety, with a smooth, defined taste. Minimum alcohol content 12.5°. The Riserva label applies for wine aged for three years in casks. A special wine, to accompany meat and quality cheeses.

Chianti Classico DOCG

Chianti Classico, the oldest area of origin of Chianti wine, covers nine municipal districts, between Florence and Siena. Its production, under the symbol of the Black Cockerel, is strictly regulated: only certain vines, Sangiovese grapes (75%-100%), Canaiolo Nero (maximum 10%), and other specified grapes, may be used. The wine is a bright ruby red in color, becoming burgundy red with time. Vinous, with a hint of violets and distinctively subtle aroma when aged; smooth, dry, palatable, slightly tannic taste, that becomes velvety with ageing. Minimum alcohol content 12°. The Riserva version (12.5°) is aged in casks and further aged in bottles. As a young wine, it goes well with grilled red meat; when aged, excellent with game and robust flavors.

Vernaccia di San Gimignano DOCG

The first mention of Vernaccia in vineyards around San Gimignano dates from 1276. Today, Vernaccia wine may be produced only in the San Gimignano area, and only using grapes from San Gimignano Vernaccia vines, sometimes supplemented with other specified varieties. Its pale color becomes golden when aged. It has a specially delicate and penetrating aroma, and smooth, dry taste, with characteristic slightly bitter aftertaste. Minimum alcohol content 11° (11.5° for Vernaccia Riserva). Recommended with Italian-style antipasti (hors d'oeuvres), pasta dishes, soups, fish, white meat, and sweet cheeses such as Pecorino delle Crete Senesi.

Vin Santo

This wine made from dried grapes is one of Tuscany's most typical local products. It is produced largely with Trebbiano grapes, which probably originally came from the eastern Mediteranean and were much appreciated as early as Roman times. The wine produced from this grape is straw-colored, with a slight aroma, fairly strong alcohol content, and neutral in taste; it gains character when combined with Malvasia, Canaiolo Bianco or Vernaccia di San Gimignano. The grapes are dried and the wine is aged for a long time in casks, to produce this dessert wine, which may be dry or sweet. There is also a Vin Santo made from black grapes, called Occhio di Pernice.

Vino Nobile di Montepulciano DOCG

It's hard to say whether the word "Nobile" (noble), which has described this wine since the 18th century, refers to the quality of the wine or social rank of its admirers. The name may refer to the vine of noble lineage, Prugnolo Gentile, which is the basis of the wine's grape mix today, according to its DOCG specifications. The excellent quality of this wine derives from the vines, which are cultivated to produce low yields. After two years of compulsory ageing, the wine is ruby red tending to burgundy, with an intense, ethereal aroma; a dry, balanced and persistent taste, sometimes with wood overtones. Minimum alcohol content 12.5° (13° for Riserva wines). It goes well with everything: pasta dishes, and all kinds of meat.

AREZZO

Fattoria di Gratena
Pieve a Maiano, tel. 0575368664, www.gratena.it
● Chianti Gratena - Docg
● Rapozzo da Maiano Rosso Toscana - Igt
● Siro Toscana Rosso - Igt

Villa Cilnia
Bagnoro, tel. 0575365017, www.villacilnia.com
● Chianti Colli Aretini - Docg
● Chianti Colli Aretini Riserva - Docg
● Cign'Oro - Igt

CORTONA
Tenimenti Luigi d'Alessandro
Camucia, via Manzano 15, tel. 0575618667, www.tenimenti.dalessandro.it
● Cortona Syrah Il Bosco - Doc
● Cortona Syrah - Doc
○ Cortona Fontarca - Igt
◑ Vin Santo - Doc

FLORENCE

Marchesi Antinori
Piazza degli Antinori 3, tel. 05523595, www.antinori.it
● Chianti Classico Pèppoli - Docg
● Chianti Classico Riserva Badia a Passignano - Docg
● Chianti Classico Riserva Tenute Marchese Antinori - Docg

- Santa Cristina Rosso Toscana - Igt
- Solaia Rosso Toscana - Igt
- Tignanello Rosso Toscana - Igt
- ◑ Fattoria Aldobrandesca Aleatico di Toscana - Igt

Marchesi de' Frescobaldi
Via Santo Spirito 11, tel. 05527141, www.frescobaldi.it
- Chianti Rufina Montesodi - Docg
- Chianti Rufina Riserva Nipozzano - Docg
- Pomino Rosso Castello di Pomino - Doc
- Mormoreto Toscana Rosso - Igt
- ○ Pomino Bianco Il Benefizio - Doc

BARBERINO VAL D'ELSA
Casa Emma
Cortine, tel. 0558072239, www.casaemma.com
- Chianti Classico - Docg
- Chianti Classico Riserva - Docg
- Soloio - Igt

Casa Sola
Strada di Cortine 5, tel. 0558075028, www.fattoriacasasola.com
- Chianti Classico Casa Sola - Docg
- Chianti Classico Riserva Casa Sola - Docg
- Montarsiccio Rosso Toscana - Igt

Castello della Paneretta
Strada della Paneretta 35, tel. 0558059003
- Chianti Classico Riserva - Docg
- Chianti Classico Riserva Vigneto Torre a Destra - Docg
- Quattrocentenario Rosso di Toscana - Igt
- Terrine Rosso di Toscana - Igt
- ◑ Vinsanto del Chianti Classico - Doc

Castello di Monsanto
Via Monsanto 8, tel. 0558059000, www.castellodimonsanto.it
- Chianti Classico Riserva il Poggio - Docg

Fattoria Isole e Olena
Isole 1, tel. 0558072763
- Chianti Classico - Docg
- Cabernet Sauvignon Collezione De Marchi Toscana - Igt
- Cepparello Toscana - Igt
- Syrah Collezione De Marchi Toscana - Igt
- ○ Chardonnay Collezione De Marchi Toscana - Igt
- ◑ Vin Santo del Chianti Classico - Doc

Fattoria Le Filigare
San Donato in Poggio, via Sicella 37, tel. 0558072796, www.lefiligare.it
- Chianti Classico - Docg
- Chianti Classico Riserva - Docg
- Germoglio - Igt
- Podere Le Rocce - Igt
- Pietro - Igt

Fattoria Pasolini dall'Onda
Piazza Mazzini 10, tel. 0558075019, www.pasolinidallonda.com
- Chianti Classico Badia a Sicelle - Docg
- Chianti Riserva Montoli - Docg
- San Zanobi Rosso Toscana - Igt
- ○ Le Macchie Chardonnay di Toscana - Igt
- ○ Montepetri Chardonnay-Pinot Grigio Toscana - Igt
- ○ Le Macchie - Igt

GREVE IN CHIANTI
Carobbio
Panzano, via S. Martino in Cecione 26, tel. 0558560133

FOOD

WINE TRAILS

Chianti has three wine trails: *Monstespertoli*, *Colline Fiorentine*, and *Rufina e Pomino*. Around Prato, the *Strada Medicea dei vini di Carmignano* winds past vineyards and Renaissance villas; further south, the *Strada del Vino delle Colline Pisane* boasts the new, successful, red - Montescudaio. Livorno's *Costa degli Etruschi* Trail includes top wines: Sassicaia from Bolgheri, and the fascinating Aleatico, from Elba. In the province of Siena, the big attraction is *Brunello di Montalcino*: there is no trail here, but Montalcino is geared for tourists. Exquisite Moscadello can be tried at Sant'Antimo Abbey, nearby. San Gimignano has the *Vernaccia* Trail; both town and wine need no introduction. Siena province also has the *Strada del Vino Nobile di Montepulciano*, with great basement wine-bars in Montepulciano. Not far away is the *Terre di Arezzo* trail, with Cortona, an exceptional wine center. In Grosseto Province, the *Colli di Maremma* trail stretches from the Argentario, with its white Ansonica, to Scansano, with its Morellino.
For all Tuscan Wine Trails, visit: www.terreditoscana.regione.toscana.it.

- Chianti Classico - Docg
- Leone - Igt
- Pietraforte - Igt

Castello di Querceto
Dudda 61, tel. 05585921,
www.castellodiquerceto.it
- Chianti Classico Castello di Querceto - Docg
- Chianti Classico Riserva Il Picchio - Docg
- Il Querciolaia - Igt

Castello Vicchiomaggio
Via Vicchiomaggio 4, tel. 055854079,
www.vicchiomaggio.it
- Chianti Classico Riserva Petri - Docg
- Chianti Classico Riserva La Prima - Docg
- Chianti Classico San Jacopo - Docg
- Ripa delle Mandorle - Igt
- Ripa delle More - Igt
- Chianti Classico Riserva Petri - Docg

Cennatoio
Panzano, via S. Leolino 35, tel. 0558963230,
www.cennatoio.it
- Chianti Classico Cennatoio - Docg
- Chianti Classico Riserva O'Leandro - Docg
- Arcibaldo Rosso Toscana - Igt
- Etrusco Sangiovese di Toscana - Igt
- Chianti Classico Cennatoio Riserva Oro - Docg
- ◑ Vin Santo del Chianti Classico Occhio di Pernice - Doc

Fattoria Casaloste
Panzano, via Montagliari 32, tel. 055852725, www.casaloste.it
- Chianti Classico - Docg
- Chianti Classico Riserva - Docg
- Chianti Classico Riserva Don Vincenzo - Docg

Fattoria Castello di Verrazzano
Castello di Verrazzano, tel. 055854243, www.verrazzano.com
- Chianti Classico - Docg
- Sassello - Igt
- ◑ Vin Santo del Chianti Classico - Doc

Fattoria Le Bocce
Panzano, via Case Sparse 77, tel. 055852153
- Chianti Classico - Docg
- Chianti Classico Riserva - Docg
- Vigna del Paladino - Igt

Fattoria Le Fonti
Panzano, via Le Fonti, tel. 055852194, www.fattorialefonti.it

- Chianti Classico Riserva - Docg
- Fontissimo Alta Valle della Greve - Igt

Fattoria Villa Cafaggio
Panzano, via S. Martino in Cecione 5, tel. 0558549094, www.villacafaggio.it
- Chianti Classico - Docg
- Cortaccio Toscana Rosso - Igt
- San Martino Toscana Rosso - Igt

Fattoria Viticcio
Via S. Cresci 12/A, tel. 055854210, www.fattoriaviticcio.com
- Chianti Classico Riserva Viticcio - Docg
- Chianti Classico Riserva Beatrice - Docg
- Chianti Classico Viticcio - Docg
- Monile Rosso Toscana - Igt
- Prunaio Rosso Toscana - Igt

Fontodi
Panzano, via S. Leolino 89, tel. 055852005
- Chianti Classico - Docg
- Chianti Classico Riserva Vigna del Sorbo - Docg
- Flaccianello della Pieve Colli della Toscana Centrale - Igt
- Pinot Nero Case Via Colli della Toscana Centrale - Igt
- Syrah Case Via Colli della Toscana Centrale - Igt

La Massa
Panzano, via Case Sparse 9, tel. 055852722
- Chianti Classico - Docg
- Chianti Classico Giorgio Primo - Docg
- La Massa - Igt

La Torraccia di Presura
Via della Montagnola 130, tel. 0558588656, www.torracciadipresura.it
- Chianti Classico Il Tarrocco - Docg
- Chianti Classico Torraccia di Presura - Docg
- Lucciolaio Rosso Toscano - Igt

Panzanello
Panzano, via Case Sparse 86, tel. 055852470, www.panzanello.it
- Chianti Classico - Docg
- Chianti Classico Riserva - Docg
- Il Mastio Rosso Toscana - Igt

Poggio Scalette
Ruffoli, via di Barbiano 7, tel. 0558546108
- Il Carbonaione Alta Valle della Greve - Igt
- Piantonaia Alta Valle della Greve - Igt

S. Lucia in Faulle - Castello dei Rampolla
Panzano, via Case Sparse 22,
tel. 055852001
- Chianti Classico - Docg
- La Vigna di Alceo - Igt
- San Marco - Igt
- ○ Tre Bianco Vendemmia Tardiva
  Toscana - Igt
- ◑ Tre Bianco Vendemmia Tardiva
  Toscana - Igt

San Cresci
Via S. Cresci 4, tel. 055853255,
www.podere-san-cresci.com
- Chianti Classico San Cresci - Docg
- San Cresci Alta Valle della Greve - Igt

Tenuta di Nozzole
Passo dei Pecorai, via Nozzole 12,
tel. 055859811, www.tenutefolonari.com
- Chianti Classico Nozzole - Docg
- Chianti Classico Riserva La Forra - Docg
- Il Pareto Rosso Toscana - Igt
- ○ Le Bruniche Chardonnay - Igt

Tenuta di Riseccoli
Via Convertoie 9, tel. 055853598,
www.riseccoli.com
- Chianti Classico Tenuta di Riseccoli -
  Docg
- Saeculum di Riseccoli Toscana - Igt
- ◑ Vin Santo del Chianti Classico - Doc

Tenuta di Vignole
Panzano, via Case Sparse 12,
tel. 0574592025
- Chianti Classico - Docg
- Chianti Classico Riserva - Docg
- Congius - Igt

Tenuta Montecalvi
Via Citille 85, tel. 0558544665
- Montecalvi Rosso Alta
  Valle della Greve - Igt
- Chianti Classico - Docg

Tenute del Cabreo
S. Cresci, via di Zano 8, tel. 055859811
- Cabreo Il Borgo Rosso Toscana - Igt
- ○ Cabreo La Pietra Bianco Toscana - Igt

Vecchie Terre di Montefili
Via S. Cresci 45, tel. 055853739
- Chianti Classico Vecchie Terre
  di Montefili - Docg
- Anfiteatro Colli della Toscana
  Centrale - Igt
- Bruno di Rocca Colli della Toscana
  Centrale - Igt
- VignaRegis - Igt

Villa Calcinaia
Via di Citille 84, tel. 055854008,
www.villacalcinaia.it
- Chianti Classico Riserva Villa
  Calcinaia - Docg
- Chianti Classico Villa Calcinaia - Docg
- Casarsa Villa Calcinaia Rosso
  Toscana - Igt

Villa Vignamaggio
Via Petriolo 5, tel. 055854661,
www.vignamaggio.com
- Chianti Classico Riserva Castello
  di Monna Lisa - Docg
- Chianti Classico Terre di Prenzano -
  Docg
- Chianti Classico Vignamaggio - Docg
- Wine Obsession Toscana - Igt
- Vignamaggio Cabernet Toscana - Igt
- Levante Salento - Igt
- Chianti Classico Seicento - Docg
- ◑ Vinsanto del Chianti Classico - Doc

IMPRUNETA

Fattoria di Bagnolo
Via Imprunetana per Tavarnuzze 48,
tel. 0552313403,
www.bartolinibaldelli.it
- Chianti dei Colli Fiorentini - Docg
- Chianti dei Colli Fiorentini Riserva - Docg
- Capro Rosso Colli della Toscana
  Centrale - Igt
- ◑ Vin santo del Chianti - Doc

Fattoria Montanine
Tavarnuzze, via Volterrana 45,
tel. 0552373055, www.lemontanine.it
- Chianti - Docg
- Chianti Classico Riserva - Docg
- Casanovarosso - Igt

La Querce
Via Imprunetana per Tavarnuzze 41,
tel. 0552011380, www.laquerce.com
- Chianti dei Colli Fiorentini La Torretta
  - Docg
- Chianti Sorrettole - Docg
- La Querce Toscana - Igt

Festa dell'uva
p. 157

Lanciola
Via Imprunetana per Pozzolatico 210,
tel. 055208324
- Chianti Classico Le Masse di Greve
  - Docg
- Chianti dei Colli Fiorentini - Docg
- Riccionero Toscana - Igt
- Terricci Rosso Toscana - Igt
- ◑ Vin Santo del Chianti Classico - Doc

SAN CASCIANO IN VAL DI PESA

Castello Il Palagio
Mercatale, via Campoli 104,
tel. 055821630, www.castelloilpalagio.it
- Chianti Classico - Docg
- Apotheosis - Igt
- Curtifreda Cabernet Sauvignon
  di Toscana - Igt

FOOD

- Montefolchi Merlot di Toscana - Igt
- ☾ Vin Santo del Chianti Classico
  Amabile - Doc

Fattoria Cigliano
Via Cigliano 17, tel. 055820033
- Chianti Classico - Docg
- Chianti Classico Riserva - Docg
- Suganella - Igt
- Nettuno Cabernet - Igt

Fattoria Corzano e Paterno
Via Paterno 10, tel. 0558249114
- Chianti Riserva I Tre Borri Terre
  di Corzano - Docg
- Chianti Terre di Corzano - Docg
- Il Corzano - Igt

Fattoria Le Corti Corsini
*Via S. Piero di Sotto 1, tel. 055829301,
www.principecorsini.com*
- Chianti Classico Don Tommaso - Docg
- Chianti Classico Le Corti - Docg

Poggiopiano
Via di Pisignano 29, tel. 0558229629
- Chianti Classico Poggiopiano - Docg
- Rosso di Sera Toscana - Igt

**Produttori Associati Castelli
del Grevepesa**
*Ponte di Gabbiano, via Grevigiana 34,
tel. 055821911, ww.castellidelgrevepesa.it*
- Chianti Classico Panzano - Docg
- Chianti Classico Vigna Elisa - Docg
- Coltifredi Rosso Toscana - Igt
- Gualdo al Luco Rosso Toscana - Igt
- Syrah di Toscana - Igt

TAVARNELLE VAL DI PESA
Il Poggiolino
*Sambuca, via Chiantigiana 32,
tel. 0558071635,
www.ilpoggiolino.com*
- Chianti Classico - Docg
- Chianti Classico Riserva - Docg
- Le Balze del Poggiolino Toscana - Igt

Montecchio
*San Donato in Poggio, via Montecchio
4, tel. 0558072907*
- Chianti Classico - Docg
- Chianti Classico Riserva - Docg
- Pietracupa Colli della Toscana
  Centrale - Igt

Podere La Cappella
*San Donato in Poggio, via Cerbaia 10 A,
tel. 0558072727*
- Chianti Classico Riserva Querciolo -
  Docg
- Cantico - Igt
- Chianti Classico - Docg

GROSSETO

Fattoria Le Pupille
*Istia d'Ombrone, piagge del Maiano
92/A, tel. 0564409517,
www.elisabettageppetti.com*
- Morellino di Scansano - Doc
- Morellino di Scansano Poggio Valente
  - Doc
- Saffredi - Igt
- ☾ Solalto - Igt

Val delle Rose
*Poggio la Mozza, tel. 0564409062
Fax 577743057, www.valdellerose.it*
- Morellino di Scansano Riserva Val
  delle Rose - Doc
- Morellino di Scansano Val delle Rose
  - Doc

MASSA MARITTIMA
Moris Farms
*Curanuova, tel. 0566919135,
www.morisfarms.it*
- Morellino di Scansano Riserva -
  Doc
- Avvoltore Maremma Toscana - Igt
- ○ Monteregio di Massa Marittima
  Bianco Santa Chiara - Doc

ORBETELLO
Santa Lucia
*Fonteblanda, via Aurelia Nord 66,
tel. 0564885474, www.azsantalucia.it*
- Capalbio Rosso Losco - Doc
- Morellino di Scansano Tore del Moro
  - Doc
- ○ Capalbio Vermentino Brigante - Doc
- ○ Ansonica Costa dell'Argentario - Doc

Tenuta La Parrina
*La Parrina, tel. 0564862636,
www.parrina.it*
- Parrina Rosso Muraccio - Doc
- Radaia Maremma Toscana - Igt
- ○ Costa dell'Argentario Ansonica - Doc

LIVORNO

PIOMBINO
San Giusto
Salivoli 16, tel. 056541198
- Bontesco Rosso Toscana - Igt
- Rosso degli Appiani - Igt
- ○ Val di Cornia Bianco - Doc

Tenuta di Vignale
Vignale, tel. 056520812
- Val di Cornia Rosso Vinivo - Doc

MASSA

Podere Scurtarola
Via dell'Uva 3, tel. 0585833523,
www.scurtarola.com
- ● Scurtarola Vermentino Nero
  Toscana - Igt
- ○ Scurtarola Vermentino Toscana - Igt

SIENA

Castel di Pugna
Strada Val di Pugna 12/14,
tel. 057746547,
www.castelpugna.com
- ● Chianti Colline Senesi Ellera - Docg
- ● Chianti Superiore Poderina - Docg
- ● Castelpugna Toscana Rosso - Igt

San Giorgio a Lapi
Strada Colle Pinzuto 30,
tel. 0577356836,
www.sangiorgioalapi.it
- ● Chianti Classico - Docg
- ● L'Eremo Toscana Rosso - Igt

CASTELLINA IN CHIANTI
Castellare di Castellina
Castellare, tel. 0577740490,
www.castellare.it
- ● Chianti Classico - Docg
- ● Chianti Classico Riserva Vigna
  Poggiale - Docg
- ● Coniale di Castellare Toscana Rosso
  - Igt
- ● I Sodi di San Niccolò Toscana - Igt
- ● Poggio ai Merli di Castellare
  Toscana - Igt

Castello di Fonterutoli
Fonterutoli, tel. 057773571,
www.fonterutoli.it
- ● Chianti Classico Fonterutoli - Docg
- ● Chianti Classico Castello
  di Fonterutoli - Docg
- ● Siepi Toscana - Igt
- ● Poggio Alla Badiola - Igt

Cecchi
Casina dei Ponti 56, tel. 057754311,
www.cecchi.net
- ● Chianti Classico - Docg
- ● Chianti Classico Messer Pietro
  di Teuzzo - Docg
- ● La Gavina Cabernet Sauvignon
  di Toscana - Igt
- ● Spargolo Sangiovese di Toscana - Igt
- ○ Sagrato di San Lorenzo a Montauto
  Chardonnay di Toscana - Igt

- ● Val di Cornia Rosso Villa del Mosaico -
  Doc
- ○ Val di Cornia Bianco Proda ai
  Mandorli - Doc
- ○ Val di Cornia Vermentino Campo
  degli Albicocchi - Doc

LUCCA

Eredi Bini Dora
Mulerna, tel. 058340521
- ● Solgirato - Igt
- ● Mulerna - Doc
- ○ Mulerna Chardonnay di Toscana - Igt
- ○ Mulerna - Igt

Tenuta di Forci
Via per Pieve S. Stefano 7165,
tel. 0583349007, www.tenutadiforci.com
- ● Cardinal Buonvisi Rosso Toscano - Igt
- ● Forciano Rosso Toscano - Igt
- ● Sangiovese Paganello - Doc
- ○ Colline Lucchesi Bianco Panterino
  - Doc

Terre del Sillabo
Cappella, via per Camaiore,
tel. 0583394487
- ● Niffo Toscana Rosso - Igt
- ○ Colline Lucchesi Sauvignon - Doc
- ○ Chardonnay Toscana - Igt
- ○ Gana Toscana - Igt
- ○ Spante Toscana - Igt

Concadoro
Concadoro 67, tel. 0577741285,
www.aziendaconcadoro.it
- Chianti Classico Concadoro - Docg
- Chianti Classico Vigna di Gaversa - Docg
- Chianti Classico Riserva - Docg
- ◖ Vinsanto del Chianti Classico
  Cerasi - Doc

Fattoria Nittardi
Nittardi, tel. 0577740269,
www.chianticlassico.com
- Chianti Classico Casanuova di Nittardi
  - Docg
- Chianti Classico Riserva Nittardi - Docg
- Maremma - Igt

Fattoria San Leonino
I Cipressi, tel. 0577743108,
www.tenimentiangelini.it
- Chianti Classico San Leonino - Docg
- Chianti Classico Selezione
  Monsenese - Docg
- Chianti Classico Riserva - Docg
- Salivolpe - Igt
- Tuttobene - Igt

Gagliole
Gagliole 42, tel. 0577740369,
www.gagliole.com
- Gagliole Rosso Colli della Toscana
  Centrale - Igt
- Pecchia Rosso Colli della Toscana
  Centrale - Igt
- Chianti Classico - Docg

Podere Collelungo
Collelungo, tel. 0577740489,
www.collelungo.com
- Chianti Classico - Docg
- Chianti Classico Riserva - Docg
- Chianti Classico Campo Cerchi - Docg

Querceto di Castellina
Via Chiantigiana, tel. 0577733590,
www.querceto.com
- Chianti Classico L'Aura - Docg
- Podalirio Toscana Rosso - Igt

Rocca delle Macìe
Le Macie, tel. 05777321

- Chianti Classico Riserva di Fizzano -
  Docg
- Chianti Classico Tenuta Sant'Alfonso -
  Docg
- Roccato Toscana - Igt

San Fabiano Calcinaia
Cellole, tel. 0577979232,
www.sanfabianocalcinaia.com
- Chianti Classico - Docg
- Cerviolo Rosso - Igt
- ○ Cerviolo Bianco - Igt

Tenuta di Bibbiano
Via Bibbiano 76, tel. 0577743065,
www.tenutadibibbiano.com
- Chianti Classico Montornello - Docg
- Chianti Classico Riserva Vigna
  del Capannino - Docg

Tenuta di Lilliano
Lilliano, tel. 0577743070,
www.lilliano.com
- Chianti Classico - Docg
- Anagallis Colli della Toscana
  Centrale - Igt
- Vignacatena Colli della Toscana
  Centrale - Igt
- Chianti Classico Riserva - Docg

Villa Cerna
Cerna, tel. 057754311, www.villacerna.it
- Chianti Classico - Docg
- ○ Chianti Classico Riserva - Docg

CASTELNUOVO BERARDENGA
Antico Podere Colle ai Lecci
San Gusmè, State Road 484,
tel. 0577359084, www.colleailecci.com
- Chianti Classico Riserva San Cosma
  Girasole - Docg
- Chianti Classico Marlena - Docg

Castell'in Villa
Castell'in Villa, tel. 0577359074,
www.castellinvilla.com
- Chianti Classico Riserva Poggio
  delle Rose - Docg
- Santacroce Toscana - Igt
- Chianti Classico Riserva - Docg
- ◖ Vin Santo del Chianti
  Classico - Doc

Castello di Monastero
Monastero d'Ombrone 19,
tel. 0577355789,
- Chianti Classico
  - Docg
- Chianti Superiore
  Montetondo - Docg
- Infinito Rosso di
  Toscana - Igt
- Sangiovese di
  Toscana - Igt

WINE CATEGORIES

Three labels define Italian wines according to quality. IGT (Typical Geographic Indication) guarantees vine cultivation according to certain regulations. DOC (Controlled Origin Denomination) indicates conformity to regulations on area of origin, and production and maturation procedures. The top label is DOCG (Guaranteed and Controlled Origin Denomination); there are around 20 DOCG wines in Italy, 6 in Tuscany.

○ Solo - Igt

◐ Vin Santo del Chianti Lunanuova - Doc

Fattoria Carpineto Fontalpina

Carpineta Montaperti, tel. 0577369219,
www.carpinetafontalpino.it

● Chianti Colli Senesi Gioia - Docg

● Montaperto - Igt

Fattoria della Aiola

Vagliagli, tel. 0577322615,
www.aiola.net

● Chianti Classico Aiola - Docg

● Chianti Classico Riserva Aiola - Docg

● Chianti Classico Riserva Cancello
  Rosso - Docg

● Logaiolo Colli della Toscana Centrale
  Rosso - Igt

● Rosso del Senatore Colli
  della Toscana Centrale Rosso - Igt

Fattoria di Felsina

Via del Chianti 101, tel. 0577355117

● Chianti Classico Berardenga - Docg

● Chianti Classico Riserva Rancia
  Berardenga - Docg

● Vin Santo del Chianti Classico - Doc

● Fontalloro Sangiovese di Toscana - Igt

● Maestro Raro Toscana - Igt

○ Chardonnay I Sistri - Igt

Fattoria Dievole

Dievole, tel. 0577322613, www.dievole.it

● Chianti Classico - Docg

● Chianti Classico Duemila Dievole -
  Docg

● Chianti Classico Riserva Novecento -
  Docg

● Broccato Toscana - Igt

● Rinascimento Toscana - Igt

**Fattorie Chigi Saracini - Agricola Poggio
Bonelli**

Via dell'Arbia 2, tel. 0577355113

● Chianti - Docg

● Chianti Superiore - Docg

● Il Poggiassai Rosso Toscano - Igt

La Casaccia

San Gusmè, tel. 0577222436,
www.casaccia.com

● Chianti Classico - Docg

● Chianti Classico Riserva - Docg

◐ Vin Santo del Chianti Classico - Doc

Poggio Bonelli

Via dell'Arbia 2,
tel. 0577355113/0577355382,
www.poggiobonelli.it

● Chianti Classico - Docg

● Chianti Classico - Docg

● Tramonto d'Oca Toscana Rosso - Igt

Querciavalle - Losi

Pontignano, tel. 0577356842,
www.aziendagricolalosi.it

● Chianti Classico Pontignanello - Docg

● Chianti Classico Riserva Millennium -
  Docg

● Chianti Classico Riserva
  Pontignanello - Docg

● Chianti Classico Riserva Querciavalle -
  Docg

● Armonia Colli della Toscana Centrale
  Rosso - Igt

CHIANCIANO TERME

Gavioli

Maglianella, State Road 146,
tel. 057863995, www.cantinegavioli.it

● Chianti Superiore Brandesco - Docg

● Vino Nobile di Montepulciano - Docg

● Vino Nobile di Montepulciano Riserva
  - Docg

● Rosso di Montepulciano - Doc

● Sergavio Toscana Rosso - Igt

GAIOLE IN CHIANTI

Agricoltori del Chianti Geografico

Via Mulinaccio 10, tel. 0577749489,
www.chiantigeografico.it

● Chianti Classico - Docg

● Chianti Classico Contessa di Radda -
  Docg

● Chianti Colline Senesi - Docg

● Ferraiolo Toscana - Igt

● Pulleraia Toscana - Igt

● Chianti Classico Montegiachi
  Riserva - Docg

● Brunello di Montalcino - Docg

● Nobile di Montepulciano - Docg

○ Vernaccia di San Gimignano - Docg

◐ Vin Santo del Chianti - Igt

Badia di Coltibuono

Badia a Coltibuono, tel. 057774481,
www.coltibuono.com

● Chianti Cetamura - Docg

● Chianti Classico Badia a
  Coltibuono - Docg

● Chianti Classico RS - Docg

● Sangioveto Toscana Rosso - Igt

● Chianti Classico Riserva - Docg

● Chianti Classico Cultus Bonae - Docg

○ Rs Trappoline - Igt

○ Cetamura - Igt

◐ Vin Santo del Chianti Classico - Doc

Barone Ricasoli - Castello di Brolio

Brolio, tel. 05777301, www.ricasoli.it

● Chianti Classico Castello di Brolio -
  Docg

● Chianti Classico Riserva Rocca
  Guicciarda - Docg

● Casalferro Toscana - Igt

● Chianti Classico Brolio - Docg

○ Torricella Toscana Chardonnay - Igt
◐ Vin Santo del Chianti Classico
Brolio - Doc

Capannelle

Capannelle, tel. 057774511,
www.capannelle.com

● Chianti Classico Riserva - Docg
● Capannelle - Idt
● Solare - Igt
● 50 & 50 - Igt
○ Capannelle Chardonnay - Igt

Castello di Ama

Lecchi in Chianti,
tel. 0577746031,
www.castellodiama.com

● Chianti Classico
  Castello di Ama Vigneto
  Bellavista - Docg
● Chianti Classico
  Castello di Ama Vigneto
  La Casuccia - Docg
● Il Chiuso - Igt
● L'Apparita - Igt
● Chianti Classico Castello
  di Ama - Docg
◉ Rosato - Igt
○ Al Poggio - Igt

Castello di Lucignano

Lucignano 1, tel. 0577747810,
www.castellodilucignano.com

● Chianti Classico - Docg
● Chianti Classico Riserva - Docg
● Il Solissimo Toscana - Igt

Castello di Meleto

Meleto, tel. 0577749217,
www.castellomeleto.it

● Chianti Classico Castello di Meleto - Docg
● Chianti Classico Pieve di Spaltenna -
  Docg
● Fiore di Meleto Sangiovese Toscana - Igt
● Rainero Toscana Rosso - Igt
◐ Vin Santo del Chianti Classico - Doc

Colombaio di Cencio

Cornia, tel. 0577747178

● Chianti Classico I Massi
  del Colombaio - Docg
● Chianti Classico Riserva I Massi
  del Colombaio - Docg
● Il Futuro Toscana Rosso - Igt
○ Sassobianco - Igt

Fattoria San Giusto a Rentennano

San Giusto 20, tel. 0577747121,
www.fattoriasangiusto.it

● Chianti Classico - Docg
● Chianti Classico Riserva - Docg

Fattoria Valtellina

Rietine, tel. 0577731005, www.fattoria-
valtellina.com

● Chianti Classico - Docg
● Convivio Rosso Toscana - Igt
● Il Duca di Montechioccioli Rosso
  Toscana - Igt
● Chianti Classico Riserva - Docg
● Brioso - Igt

Riecine

Riecine, tel. 0577749098,
www.riecine.com

● Chianti Classico - Docg
● Chianti Classico Riserva - Docg
● La Gioia di Riecine Rosso Toscana - Igt

Rietine

Rietine 27, tel. 0577731110,
www.rietine.com

● Chianti Classico - Docg
● Chianti Classico Riserva
  - Docg
● Tiziano - Igt
◐ Vin Santo del Chianti
  Classico - Doc

Rocca di Castagnoli

Castagnoli,
tel. 0577731004,
www.roccadicastagnoli.com

● Chianti Classico - Docg
● Chianti Classico Riserva Capraia -
  Docg
● Chianti Classico Riserva Poggio
  a'Frati - Docg
● Stielle Toscana Rosso - Igt
● Buriano Cabernet Toscana - Igt
● Le Pratola Merlot Toscana - Igt
◐ Vin Santo del Chianti Classico - Doc

Rocca di Montegrossi

Monti in Chianti, tel. 0577747977

● Chianti Classico Riserva San
  Marcellino - Docg
● Geremia Toscana Rosso - Idt
● Chianti Classico Rocca di Montegrossi
  - Docg
◐ Vin Santo del Chianti Classico Rocca
  di Montegrossi - Doc

MONTEPULCIANO

Avignonesi

Via Gracciano del Corso 91,
tel. 0578724304, www.avignonesi.it

● Vino Nobile di Montepulciano - Docg
● Vino Nobile di Montepulciano Riserva
  Grandi Annate - Docg
● Rosso di Montepulciano - Doc
● Desiderio Rosso di Toscana - Doc
○ Chardonnay Il Marzocco - Doc

Fassati - Fazi Battaglia

Gracciano, via di Graccianello 3/A,
tel. 0578708708

● Chianti Gaggiole - Docg

- ● Vino Nobile di Montepulciano Gersemi - Docg
- ● Vino Nobile di Montepulciano Riserva Salarco - Docg
- ● Rosso di Montepulciano Selciaia - Doc

Fattoria del Cerro - Saiagricola
Acquaviva, via Grazianella 5,
tel. 0578767722, www.saiagricola.it
- ● Vino Nobile di Montepulciano - Docg
- ● Vino Nobile di Montepulciano Vigneto Antica Chiusina - Docg
- ● Rosso di Montepulciano - Doc
- ● Manero Sangiovese - Igt
- ● Poggio Golo Merlot Toscana - Igt
- ◖ Vin Santo di Montepulciano Antonio da Sangallo - Doc

Fattoria di Palazzo Vecchio
Valiano, tel. 0578724170,
www.vinonobile.it
- ● Vino Nobile di Montepulciano - Docg
- ● Vino Nobile di Montepulciano Riserva - Docg
- ● Rosso dell'Abate Chiarini - Igt
- ● Rosso di Montepulciano - Doc

La Calonica
Capezzine, via della Stella 27,
tel. 0578724119
- ● Vino Nobile di Montepulciano - Docg
- ● Cortona Rosso Girifalco - Doc
- ● Rosso di Montepulciano - Doc
- ● Il Signorelli Toscana Merlot - Igt
- ◖ Vin Santo Toscana - Doc

Nottola
Gracciano 15, State Road 326,
tel. 0577684711/
078707060,
www.cantinanottola.it
- ● Vino Nobile di Montepulciano - Docg
- ● Vino Nobile di Montepulciano Vigna Fattore - Docg
- ● Rosso di Montepulciano - Doc

Podere Corte alla Flora
Via di Cervognano 23,
tel. 0578766003,
www.corteallaflora.it
- ● Vino Nobile di Montepulciano - Docg
- ● Rosso di Montepulciano - Doc

Poderi Boscarelli
Cervognano, via di
Montenero 28,
tel. 0578767277,
www.poderiboscarelli.com
- ● Vino Nobile di

Montepulciano Vigna del Nocio - Docg
- ● Boscarelli - 35° - Rosso Toscana - Igt
- ● De Ferrari Toscana Rosso - Igt

Poliziano
Montepulciano Stazione, via Fontago 1,
tel. 0578738171,
www.carlettipoliziano.com
- ● Vino Nobile di Montepulciano - Docg
- ● Vino Nobile di Montepulciano Asinone - Docg
- ● Rosso di Montepulciano - Doc
- ● Le Stanze del Poliziano - Igt

Romeo
State Road 326, tel. 0578708599,
www.massimoromeo.it
- ● Vino Nobile di Montepulciano - Docg
- ● Vino Nobile di Montepulciano Riserva - Docg
- ● Rosso di Montepulciano - Doc
- ◖ Vin santo di Montepulciano - Doc

Tenuta di Gracciano - Della Seta
Gracciano, via Umbria 59/61,
tel. 0578708340/0552335313
- ● Vino Nobile di Montepulciano - Docg
- ● Rosso di Montepulciano - Doc

Tenuta di Gracciano Svetoni
Gracciano, via Umbria 63,
tel. 0578707097
- ● Vino Nobile di Montepulciano TorCalvano - Docg
- ● Vino Nobile di Montepulciano Riserva TorCalcano - Docg
- ● Le Pancole Rosso di Montepulciano - Doc

Tenuta Valdipiatta
Gracciano, via della Ciarliana 25/A,
tel. 0578757930
- Vino Nobile di Montepulciano - Docg
- Rosso di Montepulciano - Doc
- Trefonti Toscana - Igt
- Trincerone Rosso Toscana - Igt
○ Nibbiano Toscana Bianco - Igt

POGGIBONSI
Fattoria Le Fonti
San Giorgio le Fonti, tel. 0577935690
- Chianti Classico Fattoria Le Fonti - Docg
- Chianti Classico Riserva Fattoria
  Le Fonti - Docg
- Vito Arturo Toscana - Igt
Fattorie Melini
Gaggiano, www.giv.it
- Chianti Classico Riserva
  Massovecchio - Docg
- Chianti Classico Riserva Vigneti
  La Selvanella - Docg
○ Vernaccia di San Gimignano
  Le Grillaie - Docg

RADDA IN CHIANTI
Castello di Volpaia
Volpaia, tel. 0577738066
- Chianti Classico - Docg
- Chianti Classico Riserva Coltassala - Docg
- aToscana - Igt
◐ Vinsanto del Chianti Classico - Doc
Fattoria di Montemaggio
Montemaggio 58, tel. 0577738323,
www.montemaggio.it

- Chianti Classico - Docg
- Chianti Classico Riserva - Docg
La Brancaia
Poppi 42/B, tel. 0577742007,
www.brancaia.com
- Chianti Classico Brancaia - Docg
- Brancaia Il Blu Toscana - Igt
- Brancaia Tre Toscana - Igt
Livernano
Livernano, tel. 0577738353
- Livernano Toscana Rosso - Igt
- Purosangue Toscana Rosso - Igt
○ Anima Toscana Bianco - Igt
Montevertine
Montevertine, tel. 0577738009
- Il Sodaccio di Montevertine Toscana - Igt
- Montevertine Toscana - Igt
- Le Pergole Torte Toscana - Igt
Podere Capaccia
Capaccia, tel. 0574582426,
www.poderecapaccia.com
- Chianti Classico Riserva - Docg
- Querciagrande - Igt

SAN GIMIGNANO
Cà del Vispo
Via di Fugnano 31, tel. 0577943053
- Chianti Colline Senesi - Docg
- Poggio Solivo Rosso di Toscana - Igt
○ Vernaccia di San Gimignano Vigna
  in Fiore - Docg
Fattoria di Pietrafitta
Cortennano 54, tel. 0577943200,
www.pietrafitta.com
- Chianti dei Colli Senesi - Docg
○ Vernaccia di San Gimignano
  Borghetto - Docg
○ Vernaccia di San Gimignano Riserva
  La Costa - Docg
Panizzi
Santa Margherita 34, tel. 0577941576,
www.panizzi.it
- Chianti dei Colli Senesi Vertunno - Docg
- Ceraso Rosso Toscana - Igt
○ Vernaccia di San Gimignano - Docg
Tenuta Le Calcinaie
Santa Lucia 36, tel. 0577943007
- Chianti dei Colli Senesi - Docg
- Teodoro - Igt
○ Vernaccia di San Gimignano Vigna
  ai Sassi - Doc
**Teruzzi E. & Puthod C. - Ponte
a Rondolino**
Casale 19, tel. 0577940143,
www.teruzzieputhod.com
○ Vernaccia di San Gimignano - Docg
○ Carmen Puthod Bianco di Toscana - Igt
○ Terre di Tufi Bianco di Toscana - Igt

LIQUEURS

Tuscany is well-known as a wine-producing region. It also produces a number of local spirits and liqueurs which can be defined as regional specialties: they are produced only in Tuscany, they are high-quality products, and they are made using traditional production methods. Some were "invented" by famous old pharmacies which still continue to make them today; some are liqueurs that were traditionally made on farms in the country; others are special creations like Livorno Punch (Ponce alla livornese).

Grappa is not really local to Tuscany; it is a type of spirit, which has been made for thousands of years in Italy, using marc (grape skins). It is traditionally produced in the north of Italy, but recently, grappa production in Tuscany has begun to attract the attention of connoisseurs and tourists. This is largely because the grapes used are top quality (Tignanello, Ornellaia, Brunello), and because the wineries where the grappas are made are fascinating places to visit.

Alkermes

A sweet liqueur, bright red in color, with a spicy taste, used both as a "tonic", and to color and flavor cakes and biscuits.
Today its red color is still obtained from dried and crushed cochineal ("kermes", hence the product's name).
It can only be made in the Officina di Santa Maria Novella in Florence, one of

Processing white grapes, to make White Vermouth

the oldest pharmacies in the world. The original recipe for Alkermes was created here in 1743, but many believe it was already being made as early as the 13th century. The Officina is well worth a visit, for its high-quality products, as well as for its fascinating premises, with period furnishings and pharmacy equipment.

Amaro Clementi Elixir di Fivizzano

A specialty of Fivizzano (Massa-Carrara), this is a bitter liqueur, or 'amaro', made with chinaroot and other medicinal herbs blended according to an ancient recipe, with no additives or colorants. Ochre in color, with a sharp aroma, it's made to the original recipe created in 1884 by the chemist and pharmacist, Giuseppe Clementi.

Biadina

A dark-colored liqueur, aromatic, delicate, slightly bitter in taste, with a strong herb flavor, and low alcohol content. It's made only in Lucca, to an ancient recipe, and traditionally pine nuts are eaten with it.
The liqueur is linked to the city's old cattle

market: the name "biadina" derives from "biada" (fodder) for horses, both bought in the same shop, a sort of general store selling just about everything. The owner, Tista, would say: "a little 'biada' for the horse and a little 'biadina' for you" as he poured his liqueur for customers.

China Massagli

A liqueur obtained from steeping Chincona Officianalis with a variety of herbs. Dark in color, but clear, and slightly bitter; its unique aroma is a smooth blend of flavors. Made in Lucca to an 1885 recipe invented by the Massagli Pharmacy, which still produces it. Sold abroad as a liqueur; also used for its health and medicinal properties.

Ponce alla Livornese (Livorno Punch)

This tonic has been made for over a century, using coffee, rum and other ingredients which have never been revealed. Civili, a famous old café in Livorno, is named after the tonic's inventor; having a 'ponce' there after lunch or dinner is still a popular traditional ritual in Livorno.

Vermouth di vino bianco (White Vermouth)

This low-alcohol drink is obtained by fermenting the must of white grapes together with spices and aromatic herbs. Amber in color, with a sweetish taste, and a strong spicy, fruity aroma.

It is made in the area around Prato, but today is increasingly difficult to find on sale. Traditionally made in the country by farmers' wives, with unripe white grapes, and herbs gathered in the fields; served as an aperitif or digestive liqueur during Christmas festivities.

FLORENCE

Antinori
Piazza degli Antinori 3, tel. 05523595, www.antinori.it
Grappa di Tignanello, Brandy

Marchesi de' Frescobaldi
Via S. Spirito 11, tel. 05527141, www.frescobaldi.it
Grappa Luce

Officina Farmaceutica di Santa Maria Novella
Via della Scala 16, tel. 055216276, www.smnovella.it
Alkermes

GREVE IN CHIANTI

Castello di Verrazzano
Verrazzano, tel. 055854243, www.verrazzano.com
Grappa di Chianti Classico, Grappa Clara, Grappa Riserva, Grappa di Vin Santo

Castello di Vicchiomaggio
Via Vicchiomaggio 4, tel. 055854079, www.vicchiomaggio.it
Grappa di Vicchiomaggio

LIVORNO

Bar Civili
Via del Vigna 55, tel. 0586408170, www.barcivili.it
Ponce alla livornese

CASTAGNETO CARDUCCI

Marchesi Incisa della Rocchetta
Le Capanne 27, Tenuta San Guido, tel. 0565762003, www.sassicaia.it
Grappa di Sassicaia

Tenuta dell'Ornellaia
Ornellaia-Bolgheri, via Bolgherese 191, tel. 056571811, www.ornellaia.it
Grappa di Merlot

LUCCA

Farmacia Massagli
Piazza S. Michele 36, tel. 0583496067
China Massagli

SIENA

CASTELNUOVO BERARDENGA

Dievole
Dievole 6, tel. 0577322613, www.dievole.it
Grappa di Chianti Classico

Fattoria dell'Aiola
Vagliagli, tel. 0577322615, www.aiola.net
Grappa l'Aiola

GAIOLE IN CHIANTI

Tenuta di Coltibuono
Badia a Coltibuono, tel. 057774481, www.coltibuono.com
Grappa della Badia

Gran Caffè Giubbe Rosse p.153

MONTALCINO

Altesino
Altesino 54, tel. 0577806208, www.altesino.it
Grappa di Brunello

Banfi
Sant'Angelo Scalo, Castello di Poggio alle Mura, tel. 0577840111, www.castellobanfi.com
Grappa di Brunello, Grappa di Moscadello

Caparzo
Caparzo, tel. 0577848390
Grappa di Brunello, Grappa di Chardonnay, Grappa di Chianti

Fattoria dei Barbi
Podernovi, tel. 0577841111, www.fattoriadeibarbi.it
Grappa dei Barbi, Grappa di Brunello, Grappa Riserva

MONTEPULCIANO

Avignonesi
Valiano, via Colonica 1, tel. 0578724304, www.avignonesi.it
Grappa di Vino Nobile, Grappa di Vin Santo

CAKES

Tuscan cooking shows influences from two periods in history: the Middle Ages, when the Via Francigena trade route connected the region with Rome and the Mediterranean; and then the Renaissance, under the Medici, who had links with the courts of Europe. Two very typically Tuscan cakes, Sienese 'panforte' and 'ricciarelli', are medieval in origin. Their main ingredients are honey (the medieval sweetener), dried fruit and oriental spices. Other cakes and biscuits, such as 'cantucci' (a type of biscuit), date from the time of the Renaissance; chocolate reached Italy from the Spanish court at this time too. There are also typical Tuscan cakes and biscuits which are more popular in origin, often with figs, raisins or apples; and in the hills and mountains, 'castagnaccio' (chestnut cake) is made with chestnut flour and flavored with rosemary. The ever-present accompaniment for anything sweet is Vin Santo, a sweet white dessert wine. There is also a version made from black grapes, known as 'occhio di pernice'. Other special local versions of Vin Santo not to miss are Moscadello di Montalcino and Aleatico from Elba.

Soft ricciarelli cakes, from Siena

Cantucci

These hard, golden biscuits are made with flour, eggs and sugar, with whole almonds and pine nuts added, and beaten egg brushed on top. The recipe dates from the time of the Medici, who were given it by pastry-cooks in the entourage of Isabella d'Este, when passing through Florence on the way to Rome. Today they are made all over the region. The version made in Massa Marittima, in the Grosseto area, is lemon-flavored. Cantucci keep very well because they are very dry; this also means that they are perfect for dipping into Vin Santo.

Panforte di Siena

Panforte evolved from flat honey cakes that were eaten in the late Middle Ages. The extra added ingredient of fruit dried over a slow fire – figs, grapes, plums, apples – added a sharp taste, hence the name 'pan forte' (strong cake). The modern version is a round, flat, and very dense cake. Beneath is a paper-thin layer of wafer; the rough surface is sprinkled with icing sugar. Panforte is slightly chewy, and has a strong taste of spices and candied fruit. It is delicious if eaten with Vin Santo or Moscatello di Montalcino. There are two types: white panforte, also known as Panforte Margherita in honor of the Queen of Italy who went to the Palio in Siena in 1879; and dark panforte, where candied melon is used instead of citron, and cocoa and chillies are also added. Panforte is made mostly between October and December, and principally in Siena, but also in Massa Marittima, in the province of Grosseto.

Ricciarelli di Siena

These little cakes, long and oval, are slightly cracked on the surface, and covered with icing sugar. The egg whites used in making them give them a soft, spongy texture, and they taste of almonds and honey. According to legend, the recipe was brought back after the Crusades by Ricciardetto della Gherardesca. The word 'ricciarelli' may possibly be related to him, although they have only relatively recently been called by this name. There is also an explanation for the two winged horses printed on the blue tissue-paper the cakes are traditionally wrapped in. They are the same as the winged horses in the Etruscan Archeological Museum in Volterra, where a branch of the della Gherardesca family comes from. The 'rough' ricciarelli, covered in dark chocolate, are also delicious. Ricciarelli are usually eaten with Vin Santo.

AREZZO

Magi
Via Vittorio Veneto 65, tel. 0575902654, www.festagrande.com
Classic café and cake shop; local cake specialties, tea biscuits and pastries, artisan praline products, ice creams and 'semifreddi', all made on the premises.

CORTONA
Banchelli
Via Nazionale 64, tel. 0575601052, www.giovannibanchelli.com
Traditional cake shop, in the old town center, with a small tea room and a wide choice of cakes and pastries; vast assortment of chocolates in winter and of ice-cream in summer. Other shops: in Cortona, Vicolo della Scala 16; and in Camucia, Viale Matteotti 19

FLORENCE

Biscotteria Castaldini
Viale dei Mille 47/r, tel. 055579684
A great cake shop, partly because the décor has remained unchanged since 1956. Large, attractive cabinets filled with tins of English sweets and glass jars full of colored jellied sweets. The Fernanda cake and superb, crumbly Marengo meringues are house specialties.

Caffè Giacosa
Via della Spada 10/r, tel. 0552776328, www.caffeciacosa.com
Established in 1815, this is a real Florentine institution; it was resuscitated thanks to the designer Roberto Cavalli, and today combines tradition and modernity very successfully. Artisan pralines, and excellent biscuits, tea cakes and pastries.

Caffè Paszkowski
Piazza della Repubblica 6/r, tel. 055210236, www.paszkowski.it
This historical café, opened over 150 years old, is a symbol of Florence when the city was Italy's capital; today, you can still feel its Risorgimento, literary past. Excellent cakes and pastries, to match the café's reputation.

Caffè Rivoire
Piazza della Signoria 5/r, tel. 055214412
A famous café, partly because of its superb position in Piazza della Signoria. In summer it's difficult to find a table; in winter it's difficult to even get inside. The interior retains its historic charm. A varied range of specialties, but everyone comes here for the café's famous hot chocolate.

Dolci e Dolcezze
Piazza Beccaria 8/r, tel. 0552345458
A small but very well known coffee shop. Its fame is due to its elegant décor, the superb quality of its cake selection (initially small, now the range has grown) and, especially, its chocolate cake. It also sells excellent coffee, exquisitely packaged.

Gilli
Piazza della Repubblica 39/r, tel. 055213896, www.gilli.it
Situated in a piazza with four famous shops, this is perhaps the most famous, especially for its cakes and biscuits. It's worth a visit just to look at the premises: a beautiful display counter and shop

CAKES FOR FESTIVALS AND FEAST DAYS

There are many cakes in Tuscany which are eaten on certain feast days and festivals, especially religious festivals which have their origins way back in the past, in folk traditions.
The traditional Easter cake is *Pan Ramerino*. This soft cake, made with zibibbo (a sweet wine) and rosemary, was already known in the Middle Ages. There are some interesting cakes eaten over the Christmas period: these include *Copata* and *Cavallucci*. *Copata* is Arabian in origin, and is made with honey, almonds and walnuts; *Cavalucci* are small biscuits which in Siena are given as gifts to wish friends and family well during the festive season.
Ossi di Morto are tradition-ally eaten around All Saints' Day in November. They are hard biscuits made with almonds. *Pan dei Santi* (Saints' Cake) is a country cake made with an almond, raisin and pine-nut filling. The same ingredients are used to make *Torta co' Bischeri*, which dates from the year 1000, and which is eaten on the Feast of the Ascension (15th August).

window with a great range of products on show. They can be enjoyed standing by the counter, or sitting at the elegant café tables so that you can enjoy the special, lively atmosphere of the square.

Giurovich

Viale Don Minzoni 26, tel. 055574752
Traditional cake shop, making products on the premises: specialties are millefeuille, zuccotto, "canz" ,and princess cake, made with soft meringue.

Gran Caffè Giubbe Rosse

Piazza della Repubblica 13/14 r, tel. 055212280
This cafe was popular with Florentine Futurists, and today is still a favorite with writers and poets. Excellent service, fascinating surroundings, and delectable products of exceptional quality.

Mr Jimmy's

Via S. Niccolò 47, tel. 0552480999, www.mrjimmy.com
Small, décor in perfect American style, in the colors of the American flag: a meeting place for Americans passing through Florence. The cakes are American too: chocolate, carrot, apple, pumpkin; also muffins, cheesecake, cherry pie, cookies and brownies.

Robiglio

Via dei Servi 112/r, tel. 055212784, www.robiglio.it
A famous confectioner's, with a number of shops in the city: Via dei Tosinghi, Viale Lavagnini 18/r, Viale dei Mille 12/r. In this one, in Via dei Servi, an old "historic" oven is still used. All products of extremely high quality, especially Florentine specialties like cantucci, pastries and biscuits, a sweet made with must, and wafers. Don't miss the delicious 'torta campagnola' (country cake).

Scudieri

Piazza S. Giovanni 19/r, tel. 055210733
Café with tables in Piazza Duomo, an enviable position; cakes and pastries produced fresh on the premises daily.

SAN CASCIANO IN VAL DI PESA

Antica Dolce Forneria

Via Macchiavelli 26, tel. 055820321
'Welcome to all good things' is the motto which welcomes visitors here. The shop specialises in making artisan cakes and pastries, as well as bread, pizza, foccaccia.... Excellent 'semifreddi' too.

GROSSETO

Caffè Liberty

Via Manin 14/16, tel. 056427015, www.cittadigrosseto.it/liberty
An elegant central café, ideal for having breakfast, with a wide range of artisan cakes and pastries.

MASSA MARITTIMA

Schillaci

Piazza Garibaldi 11, tel. 0566901827
In the center under a splendid loggia, this café and cake shop is one of the city's meeting places. Two reasons for its success: its delightful, elegant ambience, and its excellent products: superb cantucci and 'cavallucci' (made with dried fruit, chocolate, must and liqueur) are two specialties.

LUCCA

L'Angolo Dolce

Via Borgo Giannotti 391, tel. 0583342462
Just outside the city walls, a warm, intimate atmosphere, with a wide range of American cakes and biscuits: brownies, cheese cakes, apple pies, as well as pastries and small bite-sized savories. Don't miss the delicious chocolate and pear cake.

FORTE DEI MARMI

Caffetteria Il Giardino

Via IV Novembre 10, tel. 058481462
A small, charming cake shop, in the center. Inside, two large counters displaying delicious treats and delicacies, including: pastries, plain and chocolate rice puddings, and croissants.

VIAREGGIO

Caffè Gianni

Viale Marconi 1, tel. 0584962582
One of the most famous cafés and cake shops in Versilia; excellent croissants and brioches for breakfast, as well as fresh pastries and cakes, biscuits and chocolate. Now also a restaurant.

Nilo's

Via Fratti 662, tel. 058454845
In the pine grove area, very popular in

the summer, and providing everything you could possibly wish for: from breakfast in the morning, cakes and quiches, to evening aperitifs.

MASSA

Ariani
Via Cervara 131, tel. 058542621
Since 1955, excellent artisan cakes and delicious assorted biscuits made on the premises; don't miss the rice cake, a local Massa specialty.

MARINA DI MASSA
Ronchi
Via Ronchi 48, tel. 0585240920
Near the sea, small but welcoming; famous for its superb rice cake, a local specialty.

PONTREMOLI
Antica Pasticceria degli Svizzeri
Piazza della Repubblica 21/22, tel. 0187830160, www.aichta.com
Historic, central cake shop, cosy and welcoming: a place which visitors find difficult to resist, and even more difficult to forget, thanks to delicacies such as torrone, Swiss sponge, exquisite little 'amors', and excellent custard creams.

PISA

Cioccolateria De Bondt
Via Turati 22, tel. 050501896, www.debondt.it
A chocolate shop which, as the name promises, sells all types of products made with chocolate and cocoa: pralines and fresh ganache, original creative products, bars of chocolate, chocolate eggs, and dragées. At Christmas, small trees made of candied fruit covered with a light sprinkling of icing sugar.

Wellness pp. 186-187

Salza
Via Borgo Stretto 46, tel. 050580244, www.salza.it
Historic cake shop in the center, with a full range of cakes and pastries, and more besides. Savory products are also made and the shop's catering business is well-known.

SAN MINIATO
Il Cantuccio
Via P. Maioli 67, tel. 0571418344
This artisan cake shop features an enormous variety of cakes, tarts, biscuits and pralines. They also make pandoro, panettone, torrone, and local specialties such as panforte, cavallucci and cantucci.

PISTOIA

Gastronomia Capecchi
Capostrada, via Dalmazia 445, tel. 0573400208
A great range of local cakes and pastries, including 'berlingozzi' and 'befanotti', made on the premises; the shop also sells wine and gastronomy products, and an incredible 60 different types of bread.

Valiani
Via Cavour 55, tel. 057323034
This historic coffee shop occupies the 14th-century rooms of the Oratory of Sant'Antonio Abate, a beautiful place, and a favorite with artists and intellectuals last century. Today, as then, there is a great selection of exquisite cakes and pastries, in traditional style: dry biscuits, and small pastries made on the premises.

MONSUMMANO TERME
Slitti Caffè e Cioccolato
Cintolese, via Francesca Sud 1268, tel. 0572640240, www.slitti.it
Here in the privacy of his workshop, Andrea Slitti creates his chocolate sculptures which have won him several world prizes. In the shop, the old coffee containers hint at the origins of the place, initially a coffee shop. Large assortment of wines and spirits to accompany chocolate.

MONTECATINI TERME
Cialde di Montecatini
Viale Grocco 2, tel. 057279459
The traditional 'cialde' or wafers, which the shop is named after, are truly exceptional, and perfect with ice cream, or a glass of Vin Santo; there are also superb 'brigidini' (aniseed

cakes). The Barfilli family has run the two shops in the city (the second in Viale Verdi 92), and the artisan production premises, in Masas e Cozzile, for two generations.

PRATO

Caffè Pasticceria Nuovo Mondo
Piazza Garibaldi 23, tel. 057427765
When Paolo Sacchetti opened this delightful place in the old town center, it was really innovatory: a top quality cake shop, with an impressive range of modern cakes. Excellent puff pastries with warm custard cream; the caramel millefeuille with whipped cream and forest fruits is a specialty.

F & G
Via di Maliseti 10/A, tel. 0574812560
Awarded a silver medal for the 2001 world championships, this cake shop is renowned for its fine cakes, pastries and pralines.

Luca Mannori
Via Lazzerini 2, tel. 057421628, www.mannoriluca.com
One of Italy's best cake shops, with an excellent professional pastry cook, a master at making both sweet and savory products, who really excels himself at pralines and chocolate cakes. After recent renovations, these can now all be admired in the chocolate counter. Don't miss the biscuit section and decorated mini-portions.

Pasticceria Jolly
Via Volturno 12, tel. 0574465702
Large, open-to-view production premises next to the shop: a vast range of traditional pastries and cakes, including local Prato cantucci, exquisite 'berlingozzi' cakes, and at the beginning of the year, the unique 'panini di Sant'Antonio', special buns made in honor of the patron saint of animals whose festival is on 17th January.

SIENA

Bini
Via Stalloreggi 91/93, tel. 0577280207
Here you can enjoy excellent cantucci, ricciarelli, and panforte, made according to time-tested traditional recipes, as well as many other typical cakes, pastries and biscuits made on the premises.

Gusti Continentali
Via Rossi 107, tel. 0577236640
A new approach, both traditional and innovative at the same time. A range of selected teas, coffees and wines to accompany chocolate. Also luxury products: Domori, Mannori, Slitti, Rovira, Valrhona, Baixas, and fresh pastries and cakes by Luca Mannori.

Nannini - La Conca d'Oro
Via Banchi di Sopra 24, tel. 0577236009, www.grupponannini.it
A classic cake shop, with a beautiful counter in dark wood; the shop includes a café and cocktail bar; traditional products such as panforte, panpepato (spice cake), cavallucci, ricciarelli and cantucci.

CASTELNUOVO BERARDENGA
Lodi Pasini
Via Fiorita 6, tel. 0577355638, www.pasticcerialodipasini.it
This centrally-situated, typically Tuscan cake shop has all the traditional Sienese pastries and cakes, all excellent: delicious chocolate cake, special sorbet made with Vin Santo, sorbets, cantucci, ricciarelli and 'brutti ma buoni' (nut cookies).

FOOD

Cantucci are a delicious way to end a meal; Prato is famous for its cantucci.

JANUARY

Last week of January
CIOCCOLOSITÀ
Monsummano Terme (PT)
> Comune tel. 0572954412
> For chocolate lovers, an artisan chocolate fest: tasting sessions, chocolate-tasting workshops, workshops for school children, and more.

FEBRUARY

February and March
SETTIMANA NAZIONALE DELL'OLIO
Siena
> Enoteca Italiana tel. 0577228811
> An olive oil festival at the Enoteca Italiana, in the Medici Fortress.

MARCH

25th
CAPODANNO FIORENTINO
Florence
> Apt Florence tel. 055233209
> Until 1750, March 25th was the beginning of the new year in Florence. Today, in the piazza of the Chiesa di Santa Annunziata, stalls selling sweets, cakes, flowers and much more.

APRIL

From April to May
SAGRA DEL CARCIOFO
Piombino (LI)
> This gastronomic festival, held in the Pineta di Riotorto, celebrates the purple artichoke grown in this area; other local products as well.

MAY

May
UN MARE DI SAPORI
Marciana Marina (LI)
> Comune tel. 0565904321
> Gastronomy festival with wine-tasting; top Italian wine producers and chefs.

Last Sunday in May
CANTINE APERTE
Montepulciano (SI)
> Movimento del Turismo del Vino (Udine) tel. 043226339
> Wine tasting in wine bars and historic palazzi.

Last Sunday in May
CANTINE APERTE
Radda in Chianti (SI)
> Pro Loco tel. 0577738494
> Series of events, all related to wine; typical local dishes to accompany wine.

Last Sunday in May, first two Sundays in June
SAGRA DEL RANOCCHIO
Émpoli (FI)
> Circolo Arci tel. 0571581071
> In Marcignana, an opportunity to taste fresh frogs, and local gastronomic products and wines, along with dancing and music.

From May to June
SAGRA DEL MACCHERONE
Arezzo
> Apt Arezzo tel. 0575377678
> In Battifolle, food stalls and stands, dancing with band.

May and June
SETTIMANA NAZIONALE DEL VINO
Siena
> Enoteca Italiana tel. 0577228811
> Local wine-tasting at the Enoteca Italiana in the Medici Fortress.

JUNE

First weekend in June
I PROFUMI DI LAMOLE
Greve in Chianti (FI)
> Ufficio Turistico Comunale tel. 0558546299/0558545227
> In Lamole, exhibition and tasting of local wines and products.

First weekend in June
PRENDI UN BICCHIERE
Radda in Chianti (SI)
> Pro Loco tel. 0577738494
> Wine-tasting with Radda wine producers.

JULY

Last week in July
SAGRA DEL PESCE
Piombino (LI)
> A festival in Piazza Bovio, started thirty years ago, to celebrate the importance of the sea for Piombino; Sunday is the best day, with fish fresh from the fishing boats, fried in the large burnished iron pan, especially manufactured for the festival, placed in the center of the piazza.

July and August
SAGRA DEL TORTELLO DELLA CUCINA LOCALE
Vetulonia (GR)
> Pro Loco tel. 0564948116
> An opportunity to enjoy tortelli, and local gastronomic specialties.

AUGUST

10th
CALICI DI STELLE
Greve in Chianti (FI)
> Ufficio Turistico Comunale tel.0558546299/0558545227
> On St Lawrence's Night, people traditionally watch for shooting stars. The real star here, though, is the wine, to enjoy with local products.

10th
CALICI SOTTO LE STELLE
San Gimignano (SI)
> Ufficio Informazioni Turistiche tel. 0577940008
> On St Lawrence's Night, wine-tasting in the town piazza, along with the spectacle of shooting stars.

15th
SAGRA DELLA BISTECCA
Cortona (AR)
> Apt Arezzo tel. 0575377678
> In the park; an opportunity to sample choice cuts of Chianina beef, steaks "alla fiorentina", and lots more.

August
A TAVOLA SULLA SPIAGGIA
Forte dei Marmi (LU)
> Ufficio Informazioni Turistiche tel. 058480091
> A gastronomic event not to be missed: tasting of local Versilia dishes and wines.

August
SAGRA DEL FUNGO PORCINO
Cortona (AR)
> Apt Arezzo tel. 0575377678
> In the Parterre park, local dishes made with locally picked cep mushrooms, and the excellent local wine.

August
SAGRA DEL LARDO DI COLONNATA
Carrara (MS)
> Ufficio Cultura e Turismo del Comune tel. 0585641422
> This Lardo di Colonnata festival has been a favorite with gourmets since it started in 1979.

August
SAGRA DEL TORTELLO ALLA LASTRA E DEL RAVIOLO
Arezzo, loc. Corezzo
Apt Arezzo tel. 0575377678
Tortelli and ravioli tasting

August
SAGRA DELL'ANGUILLA
Orbetello (GR)
Eel-based pasta dishes and main courses

August and September
SAGRA DEL BUONGUSTAIO
San Gimignano (SI)
Ufficio Informazioni Turistiche tel. 0577940008
Two weeks dedicated to the pleasures of food and wine.

SEPTEMBER

September
SAGRA DELLE MORE DI ROVO E DEI PRODOTTI NATURALI
Tavarnelle Val di Pesa (FI)
Pro Loco tel. 0558072338
A blackberry festival in a village near Tavernelle, Sambuca Val di Pesa. Gastronomic stalls and tasting of other natural products like cheese, wine, Vin Santo, honey and medicinal herbs.

September
MOSTRA DEI PRODOTTI TIPICI LUCCHESI
Lucca
Ufficio Turistico Comunale tel. 0583442106/0583442008
In the Palazzo Pretorio loggia, display and tasting of typical local products.

September
IL GUSTO DEL MARE
Follònica (GR)
Pro Loco tel. 0566263332
In Casello Idraulico park, grilled fish and wine tasting.

September
FESTA DELL'UVA E DEL VINO
Chiusi (SI)
Pro Loco tel. 0578227667
In the old center, traditional grape and grape-harvest festival.

September
FESTA DELL'UVA
Capoliveri (LI)
Comune tel. 0565967611
Wine-tasting, and grape

harvest decorations in traditional rural style created by the inhabitants of the four town quarters. A prize awarded to the best.

September
FIERA DEL CACIO
Pienza (SI)
Ufficio Informazioni Turistiche tel. 057874749071
In the historic center of the capital of pecorino. A chance to taste and buy Pienza's famous cheeses. On Sunday evening, open-air music.

September
SAGRA DELL'ANATRA MUTA
Empoli (FI)
Circolo Arci tel. 0571581071
In Marcignana, at the start of the hunting season, wild duck and dancing at the Circolo Arci.

September
SAGRA DELLA BRUSCHETTA
Gaiole in Chianti (SI)
Ufficio Turistico tel. 0577749411
Tasting and stalls with local gastronomic products.

September
SEPTEMBERFEST
Carrara (MS)
Ufficio Cultura e Turismo Comunale tel. 0585641422
Since 1976, the biggest German-style beer festival outside Germany; Carrara is twinned with Ingolstadt. Rivers of Bavarian beer, local food specialties, live music and much more besides.

Second week of September
FESTA DEL VINO
Greve in Chianti (FI)
Ufficio Turistico Comunale tel. 0558546299/0558545227
In the town piazza, Chianti Classico tasting, dancing and singing.

Second weekend in September
SAGRA DELL'UVA
Livorno
Ufficio Turistico tel. 0586895320
A grape festival in Collinaia; other products too.

Last Sunday in September
FESTA DELL'UVA
Impruneta (FI)
Pro Loco tel. 0552313729
Inhabitants of the city's four quarters work all year round to make huge floats, as high

as 12 meters, decorated with grapes. They parade through the town, competing for the prize. Local specialties too.

OCTOBER

October
SAGRA DELLA CASTAGNA
Marciana (LI)
Comune tel. 0565901215
In Poggio, food stalls, with traditional local dishes.

Second to last Sunday in October
SAGRA DELLE CASTAGNE
Greve in Chianti (FI)
Ufficio Turistico Comunale tel. 0558546299/0558545227
In Lucolena, chestnuts to buy; polenta and pasta to eat.

NOVEMBER

Last three weeks of November
MOSTRA MERCATO DEL TARTUFO BIANCO
San Miniato (PI)
C&G Maxicom (Florence) tel. 0552335369
Truffle fair in the town center, with many events promoting the prized delicacy; guided tasting, displays in wine and gastronomy shops, stalls with local products, theme dinners in local restaurants, shows and entertainments.

30th
UN TRENO DI DOLCEZZE
Pisa
Toscana Slow tel. 0577983534
A special train from Pisa, stopping at Lucca, Pistoia and Prato: travellers can taste and try chocolate products, traditional products and Toscano cigars.

DECEMBER

December
MOSTRA MERCATO DEL TARTUFO BIANCO DELLA VAL DI CECINA
Volterra (SI)
Consorzio Turistico di Volterra e dell'Alta Val di Cecina tel. 058887257
Stalls with gastronomic products, talks and discussions on the prized white truffle, and a variety of shows.

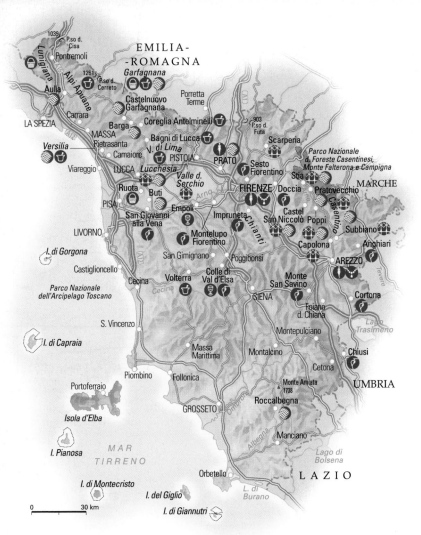

EMILIA-
-ROMAGNA

Garfagnana

1039
P.so d.
Cisa

Pontremoli

Lunigiana

Alpi Apuane

1261
P.so d.
Cerreto

Castelnuovo
Garfagnana

Porretta
Terme

Aulla

Carrara

LA SPEZIA

Barga

Coreglia Antelminelli

903
P.so d.
Futa

Scarperia

MASSA

Pietrasanta

Versilia

Camaiore

Bagni di Lucca

Parco Nazionale
d. Foreste Casentinesi,
Monte Falterona e Campigna

Viareggio

V. di Lima

PISTOIA

PRATO

Sesto
Fiorentino

LUCCA

Lucchesia

Valle d.
Serchio

FIRENZE

Doccia

Stia

MARCHE

Pratovecchio

Ruota

Buti

Arno

PISA

San Giovanni
alla Vena

Empoli

LIVORNO

Imbruneta

Castel
San Niccolò

Poppi

Subbiano

Casentino

Montelupo
Fiorentino

Chianti

Capolona

Anghiari

I. di Gorgona

San Gimignano

Poggibonsi

AREZZO

Castiglioncello

Cecina

Volterra

Colle di
Val d'Elsa

Monte
San Savino

Cortona

Parco Nazionale
dell'Arcipelago Toscano

Cecina

SIENA

Tevere

S. Vincenzo

I. di Capraia

Foiano
d. Chiana

Lago
Trasimeno

Massa
Marittima

Montalcino

Chiusi

Portoferraio

Piombino

Follonica

Cetona

UMBRIA

Monte Amiata
1738

Isola d'Elba

Montepulciano

I. Pianosa

MAR
TIRRENO

GROSSETO

Roccalbegna

Manciano

I. di Montecristo

Orbetello

L. di
Burano

Lago di
Bolsena

LAZIO

I. del Giglio

I. di Giannutri

0   30 km

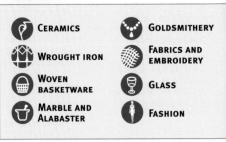

	CERAMICS		GOLDSMITHERY
	WROUGHT IRON		FABRICS AND EMBROIDERY
	WOVEN BASKETWARE		GLASS
	MARBLE AND ALABASTER		FASHION

Quality, style and enduring beauty are the hallmarks of products "Made in Italy" from local handicrafts to famous brand names. Fashion, leather, knitwear, home design items and house wares, ceramics, gastronomic specialties from wine to coffee and chocolate, glassware, jewelry, lace, linens, engravings, handmade paper and books, antique reproductions and the real antiques themselves are just waiting for you and your wallet. Small family owned specialty stores and the ubiquitous regional street markets offer the best opportunities for finding bargains and the source of soon-to-be favorite Tuscan treasures.

Highlights

- Montelupo Fiorentino and Sesto Fiorentino are famous for their art ceramics
- Between Carrara and Versilia, numerous workshops make creative marble products
- Colle di Val d'Elsa and Empoli are glass- and crystal-working centers
- Tuscan cities provide outstanding quality and variety for shoppers

Tuscany has an enormous artistic heritage. There are works of both "high" art (painting, sculpture and architecture), as well as less renowned but just as impressive arts and crafts, such as ceramics, wood carving, goldsmithery, metal-working and textiles. For centuries these arts and crafts were practised by large numbers of artisans. Their numbers diminished when the enlightened patronage especially typical of the Renaissance began to disappear. Artisan know-how took two separate paths, and Tuscan artisanship diversified into two distinct typologies. On the one side, technical skills were applied to the production of less sophisticated but very profitable products. Industrialisation led to the establishment of prosperous districts specialising in particular activities, such as goldsmithery in Arezzo, textiles in Prato, furniture in Poggibonsi, Cascina and Quarrata, and marble-working in Carrara. On the other side, technical and manual skills were directed to maintaining and reviving the existing artistic heritage. In more marginal areas, far from the main roads and routes, arts and crafts developed which were popular in origin; they were concentrated on creating traditional articles, such as tools, furnishings, and decorative objects, in communities using these objects in everyday life. These arts and crafts, fortunately, still survive in Tuscany and provide one of the strongest reasons for exploring the region's hidden corners: a journey of discovery that is always rewarding.

Ceramics

Two types of ceramics industry exist in the region: the production of pottery for everyday use, and the production of more sophisticated articles, ranging from majolica to art ceramics.

The great Tuscan tradition of terracotta production creates objects for everyday use. Since the early Renaissance, Impruneta has been the major terracotta center. The main products are terracotta floor tiles, terracotta vases and pots, and the traditional earthenware cooking pots, ideal for beans and soups.

Production of art ceramics is much more complex and varied, and is particularly strong in the provinces of Arezzo and Florence.

Montelupo Fiorentino has been an important art ceramics center since the 16th century. About 90 industrial manufacturers and craft producers operate here today.

Production in Sesto Fiorentino began in 1737, with the establishment of Manifattura Ginori, a producer of refined majolica ware and china ware, which became known all over Europe. In the 19th and 20th centuries other craft producers also set up here, many still operating today.

Fabrics and Embroidery

The great success of the textile industry in Prato has its roots way back in the past, with specialised craft activities that have been handed down through the generations, and have withstood industrialisation. Local textile products include woolen blankets, rugs and carpets, coarse cloth, and the so-called "truciolone", a modest, coarse fabric, obtained by weaving strips of rag cloth and hemp thread.

In the Casentino there has been a revival of the traditional "panno lana" (wool cloth), a strong, impermeable cloth which is also both soft and light. From the 14th century, the clergy, the nobility and the upper-middle classes took up the custom of embellishing clothing with rich embroidery.

Tuscan embroidery became extremely well-known in the 18th century, when convents began to function also as boarding schools where girls were taught arts and crafts, especially weaving and embroidery. In the first years of the 20th century, when trade opened up across Europe, Tuscan embroidery became even better known. Pistoia is the traditional embroidery capital; embroidery is still a strong tradition in many areas of the region, especially between Florence and Pistoia, and in Chianti.

Glass

Two Tuscan cities are leaders in the glass sector: Colle di Val d'Elsa (Siena), and Empoli (Florence). Initially flasks and demi-johns were produced in Colle di Val d'Elsa; subsequently, more sophisticated forms were made, with blown crystal and skilful engraving. The main products are glasses, sometimes hand-blown, and painstakingly engraved by hand. Empoli is also one of Italy's biggest producers of glasses; today most are manufactured in factories, but there are many successful small craft workshops which create original glass-ware.

Goldsmithery

The Etruscans developed the goldworking technique of microfusion, involving a process known as "granulation", which has been handed down through the centuries. This technique enabled Tuscan goldsmiths to create a wide variety of works of art using gold: jewelery; vestments, altar cloths and holy vessels; and precious

objects for the nobility.
Today many processes have been industrialised, but there are still many artisans working in the sector whose manual skill and creativity are essential.

Marble and Alabaster

The exceptional quality of marble from the Apuan Alps and alabaster from Volterra led to the establishment of exceptional local arts and crafts, using these materials. Sadly, over time, they have been in part eclipsed by the advantages of industrialisation and mass production. In the marble sector, machines have replaced stone-cutters only in the first stages of processing; the finished product still very much

depends on the manual skill and sensitivity of artisans.
The production of objects and ornaments in alabaster has inevitably been affected by industrialisation. Today the better-quality products are created by artisans who are interested in seeking innovatory forms.

Woven basketware

Outside the large centers, this ancient and humble craft still survives. In the towns of the Garfagnana, various types of woven basketware are made, including the large, shell-shaped "valletto", once used for the grape harvest. In the mountains of the Lunigiana, the "vaglio" is produced, used for riddling or sifting pulses and cereals. There are also the painted "zane", elegant baskets used in churches to hold linen for celebrating mass.
In the Brancolerai area, near Lucca, the tradition continues of weaving the "canestra brancolino", a type of decorated wicker basket with no handles.

Wrought iron

Many iron-works were established in the Casentino, because of the many streams there. From processing crude iron, they advanced to producing tools, and more recently, to more sophisticated objects worked by artisans.
In the Garfagnana wrought iron "testi" are made; these are a kind of iron griddle used for cooking "necci" (a local pancake made of chestnut flour). They are widely sold in Lucca.
Scarperia is specialised in the production of knives. Scarperia knives have been renowned, nationally and internationally, since the middle of the 19th century. In addition to standard knives, a wide range of exclusive and unusual knives are produced, such as the famous "palmerino" (a small, light knife), which has almost become a symbol of Scarperia.
The covers of some of the Italian Touring Club's most important publications are given in this section.

AREZZO

✳ **GOLDSMITHERY**
Carniani
   Via del Gavardello 62, tel. 0575381847

CORTONA
✳ **WOOD**
Arte in Legno
   *Montalla-Ponte Ossaia 763,
   tel. 0575601336, www.longoarte.com*
   Furniture

LUCIGNANO
✳ **CERAMICS**
La Bottega
   Via G. Matteotti 47, tel. 0575819039
   Gifts and fancy goods

SANSEPOLCRO
✳ **GLASS**
Vetreria Biturgense
   *Fiumicello industrial area,
   tel. 0575742322,
   www.vetreriabiturgense.it*
   Art glass doors and windows

FLORENCE

✳ **CERAMICS**
Franco Pecchioli Ceramica
   Via Belfiore 30/r, tel. 055332831
   Art ceramics
✳ **DECORATIONS**
Ida Calzolari
   Via Guicciardini 16, tel. 055292376
   Paintings

✳ **GLASS**
Locchi Moleria Vetro
   Via D. Burchiello 10, tel. 0552298371
   Glass objects
✳ **GOLDSMITHERY**
Oreria
   Borgo Pinti 87/A, tel. 055244708
✳ **LEATHER AND SKINS**
Calzature Mannina
   Via Guicciardini 16/r, tel. 055282895
   Leather goods
✳ **METALS**
Antonio Ciulli e Figlio
   Via Bibbiena 24/26, tel. 0557322301
   Metal working
✳ **PAPER AND PRINTING**
Balsimelli
   Vicolo del Canneto 1/r, tel. 055283900
   Bookbinding
✳ **WOOD**
Christophe Quarena
   Borgo S. Frediano 132/r, tel. 055700548
   Furniture

EMPOLI
✳ **GLASS**
Decorazione Emmebi
   Via Pacinotti 23, tel. 0571920005
   Crystal objects
Nuova Cooperativa Empolese Vetrai
   *Ponte a Elsa, via Val d'Elsa 47,
   tel. 0571931593*
   Crystal objects
Società Vetraria Empolese
   Via Livornese 158, tel. 057180346
   Crystal objects
Vetreria in Toscana Co.
   Via Ponzano 88, tel. 0571922414
   Crystal objects

Vetreria S.A.V.E.
Via Tosco-Romagnola 128, tel. 0571590569
Blown glass

FIÈSOLE
✳ **LEATHER AND SKINS**
Andrea Baroni Piccola Pelletteria
Via Pontanico 5, tel. 0556594365
Leather goods

GREVE IN CHIANTI
✳ **LEATHER AND SKINS**
Gino Ferruzzi Pelletterie
Via Giovanni Pastore 3, tel. 055854219,
www.paginegialle.it/ferruzzi
Leather goods

IMPRUNETA
✳ **CERAMICS**
Cotto Chiti
Via Chiantigiana 169, tel. 055207030
Terracotta flooring
Fratelli Masini
Via delle Fornaci 57, tel. 0552011683
Terracotta flooring

SAN CASCIANO IN VAL DI PESA
✳ **PAPER AND PRINTING**
Legatoria Cecchi Vanna
Borgo Sarchiani 132, tel. 0558229953,
www.paginegialle.it/cecchivanna
Bookbinding

TAVARNELLE VAL DI PESA
✳ **WOOD**
Bottega d'Arte
Via Borghetto 20, tel. 0558077904,
www.bottegadartesnc.it
Furniture

GROSSETO

✳ **CERAMICS**
Montis Pescali Ceramiche
Montepescali, via Garibaldi 35,
tel. 0564329673
✳ **GOLDSMITHERY**
Oropamà
Viale Giusti 60, tel. 0564494796
✳ **LEATHER AND SKINS**
Il Riccio
Via Damiano Chiesa 36, tel. 0564417593
Leather goods

FOLLÒNICA
✳ **CERAMICS**
Ceramica L'Idea

Via del Fonditore 43, tel. 056656245
Gifts and fancy goods

ISOLA DEL GIGLIO
✳ **CERAMICS**
Il Giglio
Via Umberto I 14, tel. 0564809229
Art ceramics

MASSA MARITTIMA
✳ **GOLDSMITHERY**
Lorenzo Mattafirri
Vicolo Porte 2/A, tel. 0566901980

ORBETELLO
✳ **GOLDSMITHERY**
Laboratorio Orafo De Robert
Corso Italia 156,
tel. 0564867407

Sagra dell'anguilla
p. 157

ROSELLE
✳ **METALS**
Arte del Ferro Etrusca
Via Batignanese 139, tel. 0564402727
Wrought iron working

VETULONIA
✳ **GIFTS AND FANCY GOODS**
Il Girasole
Via G. Garibaldi 4, tel. 0564949599,
www.dunia2.it/ilgirasole
Gifts and fancy goods

LIVORNO

✳ **GLASS**
Paolo Braschi
Via S. matteo 9/11, tel. 0586402470
Lamps
✳ **WOOD**
L'Albero dell'Olivo
Via del Seminario 18, tel. 0586219277
Furniture

CAPOLIVERI
✳ **DECORATIONS**
Non Ti Scordar
Vicolo Fiume 1, tel. 0565936439
✳ **GOLDSMITHERY**
Giorgio Borghi
Via Cavour 6, tel. 0565968690

PIOMBINO
✳ **METALS**
Bottega del Ferro
Corso Italia 195, tel. 056531311
Gifts and fancy goods

LUCCA

※ **DECORATIONS**
Massimo Bonino
Via Fatinelli 7, tel. 0583494388
※ **FABRICS AND EMBROIDERY**
Giulia Mariti
Via Caserma 5, tel. 0583952296
Piero Ricci
Via Burlamacchi 32, tel. 0583587810
Dressmaking
Piquet
Piazza dell'Arancio 22, tel. 0583955272
Linen and linen sets
※ **MUSICAL INSTRUMENTS**
Michel Alain Eggimann
Via Anfiteatro 23, tel. 0583955813
Stringed instruments
※ **PAPER AND PRINTING**
Litografia Angeli
Via della Zecca 55, tel. 0583467337
Art prints
※ **WOOD**
Giannecchini Ranieri
Via S. Giorgio 27, tel. 0583491247
Frames
Ilaria Borelli Boccasso
Vico Pelago, via di Vico Pelago 879,
tel. 0583957297
Restoration

FORTE DEI MARMI
※ **GOLDSMITHERY**
Orocolato
Via Ponchielli 4, tel. 058489602,
www.studio-casa.com/orocolato

VIAREGGIO
※ **PAPER AND PRINTING**
Legatoria Artistica Arrighini
Via V. Veneto, tel. 0584960395
Bookbinding

MASSA-CARRARA

MASSA
※ **STONE AND MARBLE**
Evangelisti Michele Eredi
Via Poggioletto 73, tel. 0585791331
Marble working

MARINA DI MASSA
※ **FABRICS AND EMBROIDERY**
Riccarda Maria Orsini
Piazza Francesco Betti 28, tel. 0585240736
Linen and linen sets

PONTRÈMOLI
※ **PAPER AND PRINTING**
Legatoria Artigiana
Via Garibaldi 8, tel. 0187831436
Bookbinding

PISA

※ **PAPER AND PRINTING**
Legatoria Artigiana Gianna Tellini
Via San Michele degli Scalzi 106/108,
tel. 050578647, www.giannatellini.it
Bookbinding

SAN MINIATO
※ **LEATHER AND SKINS**
Pelletteria Artistica
Via P. Balducci 30, tel. 0571401456
Leather goods

VOLTERRA
※ **STONE AND MARBLE**
Romano Bianchi
S.S. 68 al km 37,2, tel. 058887237
Alabaster working
Salvatore Scali
Campiano, S.S. 68, tel. 058887737
Alabaster working
Società Cooperativa Artieri
dell'Alabastro
Via Pisana 28, tel. 058886135
Alabaster working

PISTOIA

※ **STONE AND MARBLE**
Salvadori Arte
Sant'Agostino industrial area, via
Salvatore di Giacomo 89, tel. 0573935022
Marble working

MONSUMMANO TERME
※ **CERAMICS**
Studio Chironi
Via Buozzi 34, tel. 0572952222
Art ceramics
※ **LEATHER AND SKINS**
Nuova T4
Via Cesare Battisti 989/C, tel. 057282609
Leather goods

MONTECATINI TERME
※ **PAPER AND PRINTING**
Legatoria del Bino
Via Puglie 24, tel. 057274538
Bookbinding

PRATO

❋ **GLASS**
Vetrate artistiche Mariotti
Via Yuri Gagarin 2, tel. 0574636722
Art glass doors and windows
❋ **METALS**
I Ferri di Enzo
Vergaio, via Reggiana 147/B,
tel. 0574660022
Wrought iron working

POGGIO A CAIANO
❋ **STONE AND MARBLE**
Fratelli Cintolesi
Piazza IV Novembre 19, tel. 055877254
Marble working

SIENA

❋ **CERAMICS**
Ceramiche Santa Caterina
Via P. Mattioli 12, tel. 057745006
Art ceramics
❋ **FABRICS AND EMBROIDERY**
L'Arcolaio
Via Bandini Mario 2, tel. 057743077

CASTELLINA IN CHIANTI
❋ **CERAMICS**
Urbano Fontana
La Fornace, tel. 0577740340
Gifts and fancy goods

CASTELNUOVO BERARDENGA
❋ **STONE AND MARBLE**
Marcello Regoli
Pianella, tel. 0577363305

CHIANCIANO TERME
❋ **PAPER AND PRINTING**
Koinè
Via dei Forni 3, tel. 057831397,
www.legatoriakoine.it
Bookbinding

CHIUSI
❋ **CERAMICS**
Ceramiche Barbetti
Querce al Pino, tel. 0578274404,
www.ceramichebarbetti.it
Terracotta flooring

COLLE DI VAL D'ELSA
❋ **GLASS**
Cristalleria Artistica La Piana

Catarelli, tel. 0577910111, www.calp.com
Crystal objects

MONTEPULCIANO
❋ **CERAMICS**
Biancucci Tosca
Via San Donato 18, tel. 0578757049,
www.creazionidarte.com
Art ceramics
❋ **METALS**
Bottega del Rame
Via dell'Opio nel Corso 64,
tel. 0578758753, www.rameria.com
Copper working

MONTERIGGIONI
❋ **GLASS**
Vetreria artistica La Diana
Via delle Vigne 6, tel. 0577318423
Art glass doors and windows

PIENZA
❋ **CERAMICS**
Ceramiche d'Arte
Via Gozzante 33, tel. 0578749507
Art ceramics

Goldsmithery shops on Ponte Vecchio

POGGIBONSI
❋ **WOOD**
Calattini Giovanni
Via Montenero 68, tel. 0577936422,
www.calattini.com
Decorated furniture

RADDA IN CHIANTI
❋ **GOLDSMITHERY**
Laboratorio Orafo Roberto
Via Roma 9, tel. 0577738545

SAN GIMIGNANO
❋ **DECORATIONS**
La Stamperia
Via San Matteo 88, tel. 0577943230
Art prints

SHOPPING

MARKETS

In Tuscany there is a close connection between antiques, and arts and crafts: they are really two sides of the same coin, something unique to this region. In antique markets, you often unexpectedly run into arts and crafts stalls that you won't find anywhere else. And often, at arts and crafts markets, even specialist ones, you'll find treasures that you've tried for ages and failed to find in antique shops.

AREZZO

Fiera antiquaria
First weekend of every month
One of the best-known antique fairs, with hundreds of stands from all over Italy. Also popular because of its great location: the streets and piazze of Arezzo's historic center, with all types of antique objects, especially ceramics, watches, clocks, and furniture.
For further information: tel. 057523952.

STIA

Biennale europea di arte fabbrile
Beginning of September (in years ending in odd numbers)
This international wrought-iron market is one of the most important in the sector: exhibitions, forging contests, talks and shows.
For further information: tel. 0575504106.

FLORENCE

Arti e mestieri d'Oltrarno
Second Sunday of every month
In the area where most craft shops are located, between Piazza Santo Spirito and Borgo Tegolaio, the best of local arts and crafts.
For further information: tel. 055290832.

**Mercatino dell'artigianato
e del piccolo antiquariato**
Third Sunday of every month (except August and December)
One of the city's regular antique markets; over 70 stalls in Piazza Santo Spirito with furniture, wooden sculptures, clocks and watches, marble objects, jewelery, kitchenware and tableware.
For further information: tel. 055290832.

**Mercatino delle Pulci
o del piccolo antiquariato**
Weekdays (except Mondays from November to February) and the last Sunday of the every month (except July)

In Piazza dei Ciompi, in front of Vasari's loggia, a lively market full of interesting things.
For further information: tel. 055290832.

Mercato nuovo o del Porcellino
Every weekday
The Porcellino (Little Pig) Market is named after the statue by the fountain (actually a wild boar...): leather goods.
For further information: tel. 055290832.

GREVE IN CHIANTI

Mercatino delle cose del passato
Easter Monday and second Sunday in October
Started over twenty years ago, an antique and second-hand market in the town's delightful main piazza: old farming implements, antique embroidery, majolica and porcelain, prints and engravings, crystal glassware, old furniture, paintings and local food products.
For further information: tel. 0558546287.

LASTRA A SIGNA

Oggetti d'uso e botteghe d'arte
April 25th, third Sunday in June, last Sunday in August, December 8th
This market began at the end of the 18th-century as an agricultural and country fair; today, a variety of creative as well as traditional arts and crafts.
For further information: tel. 055290832.

RUFINA

Bacco Artigiano
Last week of September (from Thursday to Sunday)
Held in the old town center, and in Villa Poggio Reale; a fair for Chianti Rufina and Pomino wine, local arts and crafts products, olive oil, and leather goods.
For further information: tel. 0558396528.

SCARPERIA

**Mostra-mercato dei ferri taglienti
e del ferro battuto**
September 8th
Top market fair for wrought iron and knife

enthusiasts: the superb quality goods produced locally are displayed, along with Italian and foreign antique collections.
For further information: tel. 0558468165.

VICCHIO
Mostra dell'artigianato del Mugello Alto, val di Sieve
Last ten days in August
Interesting showcase of the best Mugello arts and crafts: products in wood, marble, wrought iron, gold, embroidery, paper and textiles.
For further information: tel. 0558439244.

VINCI
Fiera di Vinci
Last week in July
A real festival, with traditional procession in costume, tournments, jousts, local arts and crafts, food and a fantastic fireworks display to finish the day.
For further information: tel. 0571567930.

LIVORNO
Effetto Venezia. Spettacoli e mostra dell'artigianato locale nel quartiere Venezia
From the last Sunday in July to the first Sunday in August
A week of concerts, photographic exhibitions, plays, dancing, debates, arts and crafts stalls, and antique stalls, all in the charming 18th-century "Little Venice" area.
For further information: tel. 0586204611.

LUCCA
Arti e Mestieri. Mostra-mercato artigianato
Last Sunday of every month
The Arts and Crafts Association organises this market, where you can buy and be directly involved in making objects in wood, stone, glass, ceramics, metal and fabric.
For further information: tel. 0583491205.

PISA
Mostra mercato nazionale del libro e della stampa antica
Second weekend in November
Italy's second most important antique book fair, held in the area around Leopolda Station, in Piazza Guerrazzi. Exhibitors from all over Italy and from abroad, for real connoisseurs.
For further information: tel. 050554039.

PISTOIA
Mercato dell'antiquariato
Second Saturday and Sunday every month (except July and August)
An important antique market, an event which has attracted enthusiasts and tourists to the city for many years.
For further information: tel. 057321622.

SIENA
Festa di San Giuseppe
March 19th
In the Onda contrada (quarter), throughout the day, local cakes and sweet specialties, as well as creative local arts and crafts (ceramics, terracotta, glass, wood and wrought iron).
For further information: tel. 0577280551.

Festa di Santa Lucia
December 13th
A market in the Chiocciola contrada (quarter), on St Lucy's day: ceramics, terracotta, majolica and local cakes and biscuits.
For further information: tel. 0577280551.

Palio di Siena p. 181

PIENZA
Fiera di settembre
September 21st
Traditional market held in the streets of the old historic town center.
For further information: tel. 0578749071.

SAN GIMIGNANO
Festa e fiera di Santa Fina
March 12th and first Sunday in August
A lively fair in the historic center, on the feast day of the town's patron saint, after the church service in the Basilica di Santa Maria Assunta.
For further information: tel. 0577940008.

SINALUNGA
Mercatino Biancalana
June 2nd
A fair for antiques, arts and crafts, various types of collections, plants and flowers, and organic food products.
For further information: tel. 0577636045.

The Tuscan fashion sector is the third largest in Italy, after Lombardy and the Veneto, in terms of the number of people it employs, and production. In the last decade, significant restructuring has taken place, through partnerships, mergers and initiatives aimed at adding value to the sector and its local production. The region's center of fashion and design is Florence; neighbouring Prato has a long history of textiles manufacturing, while Arezzo is renowned for gold-working activities.

Some important Italian brands are based in the region, and many have at least one sales onlet in the main cities; in Florence, most of the big traditional fashion names are in via Tornabuoni and via della Vigna Nuova.

In the Tuscan capital, as in the main European cities, the idea of the "concept store" is spreading: great places to meet friends, with exhibitions, events, workshops, cultural initiatives and much more besides. Ideal for an evening aperitif, for chilling out, and for browsing among clothes, accessories, books, furnishings and countless interesting things.

There are fashion events all year round in Florence. The internationally-important Pitti shows are held in the Fortezza da Basso: Pitti Immagine Uomo (men's fashions), Pitti Immagine Bimbo (collections for ages 0 – 18), Pitti Immagine Casa (household linen and accessories), and Pitti Immagine Filati (yarns and knits). Twice a year, the Fortezza also houses Pratoexpo, an international fair for garment textiles produced in the Prato area (for information: www.pittimmagine.com).

A large number of Tuscan designer factory outlets stock the main Italian fashion brands at really good prices. They're normally located on the outskirts of the main towns, often near motorway exits, and are generally open on Sundays. Before you go though, it's best to phone to check on opening times.

In the region's main towns there are also many long-established shops which sell goods made by hand using traditional methods; examples are the leather goods shops in the Santa Croce area, and the gold boutiques in the Ponte Vecchio area, in Florence.

Shops in Tuscany are open every weekday in the morning and again in the afternoon; in winter they are closed on Monday mornings. Department stores, malls and some central shops in the bigger cities don't close at lunchtime.

AREZZO

Emporio Armani
Corso Italia 306, www.armani.it
Elegant and easy to wear, a famous brand, known and acclaimed worldwide.

Nannini
Corso Italia 231, www.nannini.it
Large shop windows, clean modern white interior, and great lighting, in this shop which opened in 2003; great display of bags and accessories.

Pelletieri d'Italia
Montevarchi-Levanella, tel. 055978781
40km from Arezzo, in the direction of Florence, a fairly limited range with current models of Miu Miu dresses and Prada bags.

FLORENCE

Artpell Coke
Via dei Neri 25/r, tel. 0552396660
In a beautiful palazzo, traditional suitcase, bag and hat-box maker since

1938; also current collections of the best brands, as well as jackets and hats.

Boutique Giorgio Armani
Via Tornabuoni 48/r, tel. 055219041, www.armani.it
Unsurprisingly in Florence's main fashion street, one of Italy's best-known designers. Very distinctive style for men's and women's wear, and also accessories, perfumes and eyewear.

BP Studio
Via della Vigna Nuova 15/r, tel. 055213243, www.bpstudio.it
Fashion knitwear: garments in fine wool, cashmere and the best yarns from all over the world. Highly creative, men's wear and women's wear.

Brioni
Via de' Rondinelli 7/r, tel. 055210646
One of the pioneers of the Italian Look in the sixties; today elegant men's wear and women's wear, as well as the latest casual and sports lines.

Casa dei Tessuti
Via dei Pecori 20-22-24, tel. 055215961
An outstanding range of colors and fabrics of excellent quality to choose from, in an environment that seems straight out of the Middles Ages and the Renaissance.

Città San Gallo
Via Por Santa Maria 60/r, tel. 0552396249
Founded in 1922 by the current owner's father, with typical Tuscan textile products: shirts, handkerchiefs, doilies, and lace work.

Conte of Florence
Via Por S. Maria 15/r, tel. 0552398611, www.conteofflorence.com
Casual clothing for men and women, in unmistakably Italian style.

Dolce & Gabbana
Rignano sull'Arno-Pian dell'Isola, tel. 0558331300, www.outlet-firenze.com
20km south of Florence. Collections from the previous season, discounted by 50% to 70%.

Echo
Via dell'Oriuolo 37/r, tel. 0552381149
Women's wear by a superbly creative young woman designer; reasonable prices for a chic or casual look.

Ermenegildo Zegna
Piazza Ruccellai 4-7/r, tel. 055283011, www.zegna.com
Everything for men: from smoking jackets to sports clothing, designed and created by one of the best woven garment producers.

Fendi
Rignano sull'Arno, tel. 055834981
20km south of Florence. Discounted prices.

Fendi
Via degli Strozzi 1, tel. 055212305, www.fendi.it
Latest models by the creative Fendi sisters. Clothing, accessories and the bags with the famous "F".

Gazzarrini Giuseppe
Via Porta Rossa 71-73/r, tel. 055212747
In the early 1800s this was a saddlery and suitcase shop; in 1911, it was bought by Gazzarrini, the first Italian to make rigid suitcases. Fine artisan leather goods.

Gherardini
Via della Vigna Nuova 57/r, tel. 055215678, www.gherardini.it
In the same building where Garibaldo Gherardini opened his artisan leather goods factory in 1885. Since then, the famous "G" has become known worldwide, on bags, small leather articles, and raincoats, constantly and carefully improving, experimenting and creating, and always keeping up with the times. Wide choice of bags, leather belts, and small leather goods, from traditional classical models to more recent ones.

Gianni Versace
Via Tornabuoni 13-15/r, tel. 0552396167, www.versace.it
The shop stocks the more classical clothing lines of this international fashion leader. Versus, for young people, is in via della Vigna Nuova 36-37/r.

Gucci
Via Roma 38/r, tel. 055759221, www.gucci.it
Gucci's second sales outlet, specialised in leather goods and accessories. A third shop in via Tornabuoni 81/r has the brand's jewelery line.

Gucci
Via Tornabuoni 73/r, tel. 055264011, www.gucci.it
Historic Florentine fashion house, founded by Guccio Gucci in 1921, to produce artisan suitcases, and horseriding equipment. This is the brand's concept store, with everything made by Gucci: men's wear and women's wear (first floor), footwear, leather goods, eyewear, and accessories (ground floor).

La Perla
Via della Vigna Nuova 17/r, tel. 055217070
Fine lingerie and the latest swimwear.

Laura Mussi
Via Metastasio 1, tel. 0552280642,
www.lauramussi.com
Goods exclusively in cashmere, in every possible color, for every possible occasion.

Liverano
Via dei Fossi 43/r, tel. 0552396436,
www.liverano.com
Going into this shop is like walking into the past: clothes hand-sewn by the two brothers, Luigi and Antonio. Unique garments, perfectly cut, made with superb fabrics.

Loro Piana
Via della Vigna Nuova 37/r,
tel. 0552398688
Complete range of clothing, knitwear, scarves, stoles and household accessories.

Luisa Via Roma
Via Roma 19-21/r, tel. 055217826,
www.luisaviaroma.com
Enormous premises, with the latest in fashion and design: two floors of small boutiques with the trendiest designers, and loads of new ideas to choose from.

Nannini
Via Calzaiuoli 82/r, www.nannini.it
Nannini's second sales outlet, in lively Via Calzaiuoli. Showroom in via Faentina 77.

Nannini
Via Porta Rossa 64/r, www.nannini.it
Another Florentine leather goods brand, well-known both in Italy and abroad. For the cosmopolitan woman, interested in fashion but not in being a fashion slave, bags and accessories for every occasion.

Open
Corso dei Tintori 43/r,
tel. 0552638258
In the Santa Croce area: concerts, events and art exhibitions, along with clothing, design objects, books, furniture and furnishings; many of the articles on sale are only found in Florence, or Italy. A real treasure trove full of unusual, beautiful and interesting things.

Papini Pelletterie
Lungarno degli

Mercato Nuovo o Del Porcellino p. 166

Archibusieri 12/r, tel. 055287879
Founded in 1896 by Ettore Papini: leather goods, book and case bindings, and later bags and suitcases. Wonderful old décor in Slavonia oak decorated with gold leaf, and stucco work dating from 1929.

Prada
Via Tornabuoni 53/r and 67/r,
tel. 055283439, www.prada.it
Bags, clothing, accessories, and shoes for him and her, in two shops. Made using both traditional and ultra-modern techniques and materials, for elegant and informal-chic style.

Roberto Cavalli
Via Tornabuni 83/r,
tel. 05532421,
www.robertocavalli.it
The shop of an innovative and unusual designer, in his home city: clothing, underwear, accessories, eyewear, perfumes, children's clothing and a new line of household objects.

Salvatore Ferragamo
Via Tornabuoni 14, tel. 055292123,
www.ferragamo.it
Historic brand founded in 1927 by Salvatore Ferragamo, a Tuscan by adoption. Shoes, clothing, leather goods, accessories, watches, perfumes: everything for men and women. Classical style, Italian tradition keeping up with the times. The Ferragamo museum is at 2 via Tornabuoni, near Palazzo Spini Ferroni; visits by appointment (tel. 055 29123).

Scuola del Cuoio
Piazza S.Croce 16 (Convent of S. Croce), tel. 055244534
The school was started after the war by the Franciscan friars of the Basilica di Santa Croce, and an important family of Florentine leather goods dealers, to teach the art of making and selling bags, satchels, small leather articles, writing desks and jewel boxes. Exclusive materials and service.

Stefano Bemer
Borgo San Frediano 143/r,
tel. 055211356,
www.stefanobemer.it
The ancient art of making shoes to measure; a small workshop, a favorite with international celebrities.

The place for you if you're after a really stylish but also casual look. In via Stagi 42, Armani Junior, for kids.

Patrizia Pepe
Piazzetta Tonini 17, tel. 058482029, www.patriziapepe.it
Not at all surprising to find this outlet in chic Forte dei Marmi; the brand has become popular in the last few years with women who want minimalist elegance as well as comfort.

Versace
Via Montauti 3, tel. 0584874144, www.versace.it
A selection of the main collections by this great Italian fashion brand known all over the world.

PRATO

Luisa Via Roma
Via Roma 24, tel. 0574401840, www.luisaviaroma.com
The Prato branch of the Florentine shop of the same name. Interesting design, select but smaller range of goods than in the huge main shop in Florence.

Maglificio Denny
Via Zarini 261, tel. 0574592350, www.denny.it
Near the Prato Est motorway toll booth. A well-stocked factory outlet, with quality knitwear garments for men, women and children; great cashmere products.

The Mall
Leccio Repello, via Europa 5, tel. 0558657775, www.outlet-firenze.com
Around 30km from Florence, going towards the south, a shopping mecca with discounts of up to 70%. Brands include: Agnona, Bottega Veneta, Emanuel Ungaro, Ermenegildo Zegna, Giorgio Armani, Gucci, Hogan, La Perla , Loro Piana, Salvadore Ferragamo, Sergio Rossi, Tod's, Valentino.

LUCCA

Camiceria Cerri
Via Fillungo 178, tel. 0583491180
Tailored shirts for a serious, sophisticated style. In the workshop upstairs, exclusive garments made with superb fabrics and great attention to detail. The result: perfectly fitting shirts which are lovely to wear.

Cappellificio Bocci
Via della Formica 94, tel. 0583580278
Hats, scarves, sashes and gloves for all tastes, styles and occasions; a traditional shop, opened in 1870.

FORTE DEI MARMI
Emporio Armani
Via Carducci 29, tel. 058489138, www.emporioarmani.it

SIENA

Abbigliamento Cortecci
Via dei Banchi di Sopra 27, tel. 0577280096
Shop renowned in Siena for its quality men's and women's wear. Collections by Armani, Gucci, Cavalli, Etro, Brioni, Zegna.

Barbara
Via dei Montanini 81, tel. 0577280848
Small shop with best lingerie, underwear and swimwear brands, such as: Roberto Cavalli, Baci Rubati, Prada, Gucci.

Il Bagaglio
Via dei Pellegrini 22, tel. 057744065
Shoes, accessories, bags and leather goods by the best brands (Prada, Gucci, Coccinelle, Miu Miu, Tod's) and in the best Florentine tradition.

SHOPPING

	MUSIC
	FOLKLORE

Traditional events and cultural festivals are held all times of the year with an emphasis on religious themed festivals at Christmas and Easter. Throughout the summer major cities host a variety of historical, musical, and gastronomic celebrations. But some of the most interesting events may be found in the lesser known towns and villages. Festivals devoted to locally grown produce, religious rituals and centuries old costume pageants that often date back to the Middle Ages are not uncommon. Nor is it unusual to happen upon an entire town full swing in festivities for a celebration uniquely of their own creation.

Highlights

- Maggio Musicale fiorentino
- Elba, Isola musicale d'Europa
- Festival Pucciniano di Torre del Lago
- Siena Jazz
- Pistoia Blues
- Florence, Calcio in costume (Football in Costume)
- Viareggio, Carnevale (Carnival)
- Siena, Palio

MUSIC

Musical life in Tuscany moves on a variety of levels. Florence and Siena are fast-moving, boasting institutions and events of national importance.

Florence has some of the region's finest concert halls, theaters and institutions: the Teatro Comunale, the Teatro Verdi, where the ORT (Orchestra of Tuscany) is based, the Teatro Goldoni and the Teatro della Pergola, founded in the 17th century. The Luigi Cherubini Conservatory of Music was created in the mid-19th century, and houses one of Italy's most important music libraries, and the Museum of Musical Instruments. Just outside Florence, the Teatro Romano di Fiesole hosts the well-known Estate Fiesolana festival.

The Accademia Chigiana is Siena's main music school. Founded in the early 1900s, it organises courses and concerts and has a museum and library.

Pisa, Lucca and Livorno are also active, though at a more local level. The main cultural institutions in these provinces have formed CittàLirica, a consortium which co-produces high-quality productions performed in all three provinces. Lucca in particular is renowned for its promotion of both church and secular music.

The other provinces are more marginal to the region's musical culture, in part because of their less central geographical position. Grosseto is an exception, with its sophisticated summer festival, Musica nel Chiostro (Cloister Music), which takes place in the 17th-century convent of Santa Croce in Batignano. In addition to this more classical tradition, Tuscany also offers a series of high-level events and festivals, featuring top performers from a wide range of musical styles, including popular music, jazz, world music, blues, as well as new trends where music is combined with the figurative arts and drama.

AREZZO

Arezzo Wave
Early July
A cultural festival, first started eighteen years ago, covering music, literature, drama, and figurative arts. Its aim is to promote youth culture in all its forms.
For further information: tel. 0575401722, www.arezzowave.com

Europlà
Late June
This party-style festival, in true Renaissance tradition, hosts drama companies from various European countries and showcases the best comic character and street theater productions.
For further information: tel. 0559121421, www.comune.san-giovanni-valdarno.ar.it

Fondazione Toscana Musica e Arte
Via Guido Monaco 32, tel. 0575405166, www.fondazionetoscana.it

I Grandi Appuntamenti della Musica
November - December
Concerts are organised especially for this classical festival, or jointly with other organisations. Concerts take place in Florence and Cortona as well.
For further information: tel. 0575399776, www.entefilarmonicoitaliano.it

Teatro Petrarca
Via Guido Monaco 12, tel. 057523975

ANGHIARI

Teatro dei Ricomposti
Via del Teatro, tel. 0575788659

CORTONA

Accademia degli Arditi
Teatro Signorelli, piazza Signorelli 13, tel. 0575601882-0575630163

Teatro Signorelli
Piazza Signorelli 13, tel. 0575601882

FLORENCE

Auditorium Flog
Via M. Mercati 24/B, tel. 055487145, www.flog.it

Costante Cambiamento
February
International festival of dance, theater and literature, promoting interaction between cultures, with both big, established names and young, new names in the arts.
For further information: tel. 0552340231, www.costantecambiamento.com

Florence Dance Festival
July - December
Wide-ranging dance styles, including contemporary experimentation, traditional folk dance, flamenco, Russian dancing, South Korean Zen choreography, and the best of Italian contemporary dance. Most

performances are in the Fiesole Theater.
For further information: tel. 055289276,
www.florencedance.org

Maggio Musicale Fiorentino
April - June
A long-standing, prestigious festival, with
very original staging and sets for the best-
known works, and particular attention to
visual and theatrical effects.
For further information:
www.maggiofiorentino.com

Museo degli Strumenti Musicali
*Galleria dell'Accademia, via
Ricasoli 60, tel. 0552388609,
www.sbas.firenze.it/accademia*

Music Pool
February - June
A festival of jazz, rock, popular and
ethnic music which started over 20
years ago, on a circuit including both
large and smaller towns in the Province
of Florence; very popular with the
general public.
For further information: tel. 055240397,
www.eventimusicpool.it

Musica dei Popoli
October
The most prestigious international
festival of ethnic and folk music in Italy,
aiming to promote world music.
For further information: tel. 0554220300,
www.flog.it

Sala Vanni
*Santa Maria del Carmine,
piazza del Carmine 14*

Saschall
*Lungarno Aldo Moro 3, tel. 0556504112,
www.saschall.it*

Suoni e Colori in Toscana
August - September
Outstandingly varied festival: medieval
music, jazz, folk and contemporary
music, with internationally famed artists
and musicians performing in villas,
country estates and churches in the area
of Bagno a Ripoli and Rignano sull'Arno.
For further information:
tel. 0558347833, www.rignano.org

Teatro del Maggio Musicale Fiorentino
*Via Solferino 15, tel. 05527791,
www.maggiofiorentino.com*

Teatro della Pergola - ETI
*Via della Pergola 12/32, tel. 05522641,
www.pergola.firenze.it*

Teatro di Rifredi
*Via Vittorio Emanuele 303,
tel. 0554220361,
www.toscanateatro.it*

Teatro Goldoni
Via S. Maria 13/15

Teatro Le Laudi
Via L. da Vinci 2/R, tel. 055572831

Teatro Puccini
*Piazza Puccini,
tel. 0553362067, www.teatropuccini.it*

Teatro Verdi
*Via Ghibellina 99, tel. 055212320,
www.teatroverdifirenze.it*

Capodanno
Fiorentino p. 156

ÉMPOLI

Teatro Excelsior
Via Ridolfi 75, tel. 057172023

Teatro Shalom
Via Busoni 24, tel. 057177528

FIÈSOLE

Teatro Romano
*Museo Archeologico, via Portigiani 1,
tel. 05559477, www.fiesolemusei.it*

SAN CASCIANO IN VAL DI PESA

Teatro Comunale Niccolini
*Via Roma 47, tel. 0558290146,
www.teatroniccolini.it*

GROSSETO

Ex Convento Santa Croce
*Batignano, tel. 0564338096-
0564494770,
www.musicanelchiostro.info*

Teatro degli Industri
*Via Mazzini 99, tel. 056421151,
www.gol.grosseto.it/industri*

Teatro Moderno
Via Tripoli 33/35, tel. 056422429

Teatro Teleme
Via Solferino 24, tel. 056428341

FOLLÒNICA

Grey Cat Festival
July - August
Very prestigious jazz festival. Also
special for its location in the Maremma.
For further information:
tel. 056659374,
www.comune.follonica.gr.it/grey-cat/

MASSA MARITTIMA

Lirica in Piazza
Early August
An important national event; every year
two operas are produced.
For further information: tel. 0566913714,
www.comune.massamarittima.gr.it

EVENTS

Nuovo Teatro delle Commedie
Via G.M. Terreni 1, tel. 0586404121
Teatro di Livorno - C.E.L.
Via Goldoni 83, tel. 0586204211-
0586204205, www.celteatrolivorno.it
Teatro Goldoni
Via E. Mayer 9, tel. 0586204290,
www.celteatrolivorno.it
Teatro I 4 Mori
Via Tacca, tel. 0586896440
Teatro La Goldonetta
Via E. Mayer 9, tel. 0586204211,
www.celteatrolivorno.it
Teatro La Gran Guardia
Via Grande 121, tel. 0586885165

The facade of Teatro Goldoni, Livorno, in an old photo

Teatro Metropolitan
Piazza Cappelletti 2, tel. 056530385

Elba, Isola musicale d'Europa
September
A full program of chamber and symphonic music, with the Elba Festival Orchestra conducted by Yuri Bashmet. Concerts in Marciana and Rio nell'Elba too.
For further information: tel. 0565960157, www.elba-music.com
Teatro dei Vigilanti
Piazza Gramsci 1, tel. 0565915043

Festival Opera Barga
July - August
Festival of Baroque and contemporary music, in medieval Barga and other towns in the Valle del Serchio area. Specialised in reviving rare 17th and 18th century scores; there are also performances of modern and contemporary music.

For further information: tel. 0583723250, www.barganews.com/operabarga
Lunatica
July - August
In villages around Lucca, medieval castles, Renaissance palazzi and loggias, the festival includes jazz, ethnic music, church music, experimental theater, and dance companies.
For further information: tel. 0585816638, www.eventimusicpool.it
Museo di Casa Puccini - Fondazione Giacomo Puccini
Via di Poggio, corte S. Lorenzo 9, tel. 0583584028
Pievi e Castelli in Musica
July - September
Performances blend in with a background of beautiful Romanesque churches, ancient feudal castles and historic piazze in the Casentino.
For further information: tel. 0575507232
Summer Festival Lucca
July
Extremely interesting and well-organised festival in the beautiful city of Lucca.
For further information: tel. 058430335, www.summer-festival.com
Teatro Del Giglio
Piazza del Giglio 13/15, tel. 058346531-
0583467521, www.teatrodelgiglio.it

Festival Pucciniano di Torre del Lago
Torre del Lago Puccini, piazzale Belvedere Puccini 4, tel. 0584359322, www.puccinifestival.it
Villa Puccini
Torre del Lago Puccini, viale Puccini 266, tel. 0584341445, www.giacomopuccini.it

Teatro Guglielmi
Viale Chiesa 1, tel. 058541678

Musica e Suoni dal Mondo
Early August
A kaleidoscope of sound, in this town situated between the sea and the Apuan Alps. Musicians from all over the world, in a colorful and cosmopolitan atmosphere.
For further information: tel. 0585641393, www.toscanamusiche.it

PISA

Concerti della Settimana Santa
April - May
Festival of old music, aimed at
promoting and encouraging music
culture in Pisa and its Province.
For further information: tel. 050580580,
www.concertisettimanasanta.org

Festival Sete Sóis Sete Luas
July
Promoted by a cultural network of 30 cities
from five different countries, the festival
mainly concentrates on popular, ethnic and
traditional music, street theater and the
plastic arts. Performances take place in
Montemurlo and Pontedera.
For further information: tel. 0587476013,
www.7sois7luas.com

Teatro di Pisa - Teatro Verdi
*Via Palestro 40, tel. 050941111,
www.teatrodipisa.pi.it*

VOLTERRA
Teatro Persio Flacco
Via dei Sarti 37, tel. 058888204
Volterrateatro
Late July
The festival develops and transforms
themes related to drama, and presents
them to the public in a number of ways:
performances, workshops, seminars and
talks, which are held in Volterra and its
surroundings.
For further information: tel. 058880392,
www.volterrateatro.it

PISTOIA

Itinerari Musicali - Sentieri Acustici
July - August
This festival focuses on traditional Tuscan
music and its interaction with contemporary
world music in Pistoia and its Province; it
organises concerts, courses and cultural
initiatives related to local traditions.
For further information: tel. 0573974671,
www.provincia.pistoia.it/sentieriacustici

Pistoia Blues
July
Started in 1980 with the intention of
combining the atmosphere of big rock
festivals with performances by
contemporary artists (blues, rock, soul);
the festival invites top international
groups and bands.

For further information: tel. 0573975208,
www.pistoiablues.com
Teatro Manzoni
*Corso Gramsci 127, tel. 0573991609,
www.pistoiateatri.it*

MONTECATINI TERME
Teatro Imperiale
Piazza D'Azeglio 5, tel. 057278510

PRATO

Teatro Fabbricone
Via Targetti 11/12, tel. 0574690962
Teatro Metastasio
*Via Cairoli 59, tel. 05746084,
www.metastasio.it*
Teatro Politeama Pratese
*Via Garibaldi 33/35, tel. 0574603758,
www.politeamapratese.com*

SIENA

Siena Jazz
July - August
The festival organises a variety of musical
events in and around Siena, such as the
Siena Jazz Seminars, the Enoteca Jazz Club,
and the Jazz Festival. For further information:
tel. 0577271401, www.sienajazz.it
Siena Jazz
*Fortezza Medicea 10, tel. 0577271401,
www.sienajazz.it*
Teatro dei Rinnovati
*Piazza del Campo 1, tel. 0577292265-
0577292266*
Teatro dei Rozzi
Piazza Indipendenza 1, tel. 057746960

MONTEPULCIANO
Teatro Poliziano
Via del Teatro 4, tel. 0578757281

PIENZA
Festival della Val d'Orcia
July - August
"Art and culture itineraries" to discover
villages, churches, castles and squares in
the picturesque towns of Val d'Orcia, with
high-quality performances and concerts.
For further information: tel. 0577897211,
www.parcodellavaldorcia.com

POGGIBONSI
Teatro Verdi
Via del Commercio 15, tel. 0577981298

Tuscany's folk traditions have been strongly influenced by the historical importance of both town and country in the region. Many Tuscan festivals and events center around a struggle, a competition or a fight. This applies both to big, important events, such as the Palio in Siena, the Gioco del Ponte in Pisa, and Calcio in Costume, in Florence, as well as to simpler but just as imaginative events, such as the Bravio delle Botti in Montepulciano. All of them echo in some way the factional struggles that stirred Tuscan towns and cities in the days of the city-states. Today, as in the past, folk theater also occupies an important place in Tuscan cultural tradition; it thrives particularly in areas far from the cities. The various versions of this folk tradition (such as the Maggio, the Befanata, the Zingaresca, the Ruscello, and the Segalavecchia) with their well-defined stock characters, cover

an extremely wide range of dramatic or comic-satirical themes, relating to history and society, and drawing on literature, and folk rituals and celebrations (Epiphany, Carnival, Lent, but also Christmas and Easter). Productions are often surprising and sometimes unexpectedly lively. The texts are generally sung, and are in literary Italian, although generally written by farming people or rural artisans. This reflects the region's great literary tradition, whose strength derives from the widespread familiarity people have with the great classics of poetry.

'Calcio in costume', a combination of rugby, wrestling and football

AREZZO

Giostra del Saracino
June/September
On the evening of the second to last Saturday in June, and the afternoon of the last Sunday in September; before the contest there is a large procession in costume. The contest consists in a tournament between the four quarters of the city, which compete for the prize, a golden lance. Each quarter presents two knights who charge full tilt with their lances at the Saracen, an effigy of an oriental sovereign (Buratto, King of the Indies). The left arm of the effigy bears a steel shield, while dangling from the extended right arm is the "mazzafrusto" (three heavy lead balls on ropes). When the knight's lance strikes the shield, the effigy spins around fast, and the knight has to avoid being thumped in the back by the lead balls.

For further information: tel. 0575377462, www.giostradelsaracino.arezzo.it

FOIANO DELLA CHIANA
Carnevale
January/February
A carnival festival which was first started long ago, in 1593; large floats with satirical themes are built in great secret, at special sites. At the end of the last procession, King Carnival (Re Giocondo) reads out his will, in satirical verse.
For further information: tel. 0575642100, www.carnevaledifoiano.it

SANSEPOLCRO
Palio della Balestra
Second Sunday in September
This historic contest between crossbowmen from Sansepolcro and Gubbio has taken place in Piazza Torre di Berta since 1951. Once the challenge has been read to the Gubbio contestants and the weapons have been blessed, the competition begins,

accompanied by drum rolls and clarion calls, and flag-bearers wielding and tossing their colorful flags.

For further information: tel. 0575736360, www.balestrierisansepolcro.it

FLORENCE

Calcio in costume
June

Florence's traditional version of football ("calcio storico") is revived on the feast day of Florence's patron saint, St John the Baptist. Four teams from the city's four quarters compete in the tournament. Before the match, there's a procession with music, flag-throwers, soldiers in costume, artisans and artists, the page bearing the prize or "paliotto", cowherds with the heifer (the prize in the old days), and the "field master", who referees the match. Each team has twenty-seven "kickers", consisting of: "onward passers" (full-backs), "back passers" (goalkeepers), "bunglers" (halfbacks), and "runners" (forwards). The field - in Piazza della Signoria - is covered with a layer of sand; the players try to score by getting the ball past the opposing team's back line, in any possible way. The match lasts 50 minutes, and is very rough-and-tumble, a bit like a mixture of rugby, American football, and Greek and Roman wrestling.

For further information: tel. 0552616051, www.comune.fi.it

Scoppio del carro
Easter Sunday

At Easter, according to Catholic tradition, the "new fire" is lit. In 14th-century Florence it became customary to light this fire with three flint flakes, which, according to legend, came from the Holy Sepulchre in Jerusalem, and were given to a Florentine noble as a prize for being the first to scale the walls of Jerusalem during the First Crusade. The ceremony is still carried out, in symbolic form: on Easter morning a cart drawn by white oxen arrives at Santa Maria del Fiore. A wire attached to the cart leads to a pole placed near the high altar; meanwhile, a procession of priests brings the holy flame in a brazier from the Chiesa dei Santissimi Apostoli. When the archbishop begins to chant the Gloria, the flame is used to light a rocket in the "colombina" (a dove-shaped structure with an olive branch in the beak). The rocket travels along the wire to the cart, setting off skyrockets and crackers hidden there, in a display of fireworks.

For further information: tel. 0552616051, www.comune.fi.it

PALAZZUOLO SUL SENIO

Medioevo alla Corte degli Ubaldini
Last two weekends in July

A unique festival, and an opportunity not to be missed by anyone interested in knowing more about the Middle Ages: a feast of medieval customs, clothing and even food and smells, from that far-off and fascinating time. Each year the festival chooses a different theme (e.g. hunting, women, magic); and the Oste Ghibellina history group succeeds in recreating the medieval world with incredible accuracy and attention to detail. Both local inhabitants and visitors find themselves caught up in a whirl of events, games and shows which are impressive for their historical precision, artistic quality and originality. The Osteria Bruciata and the Osteria del Cavaliere provide refreshment for hungry visitors; and you can even hire costumes and take part in the shows, if you want to be more actively involved.

For further information: tel. 0558046685, www.osteghibellina.net

LUCCA

Luminara di Santa Croce
September 13th

This ceremony honors the "Volto Santo" (Holy Face), a much revered image of Christ on a wood crucifix said to have been carved by St Nicodemus.

According to legend, a monk transported the crucifix from Palestine on a boat sent from heaven; it was then taken to the church of San Frediano in Lucca, and later placed in the Duomo. The streets which the procession moves along are illuminated by thousands of small lights, creating a magical atmosphere.

For further information: tel. 0583442144, www.lucca.turismo.toscana.it

Museo di casa Puccini p. 176

EVENTS

179

VIAREGGIO
Carnevale

January/February

When first started in 1873, this was a simple parade of floats and carts, with groups of people in fancy dress; over time the Viareggio Carnival has transformed itself into one

of Italy's best-known festival events. A special profession has even developed from the festival: the "carristi", or float artists, specialised artisans who create the gigantic floats that the carnival is famed for. Every year there are nine first category floats (maximum height 20m), and six second category floats (maximum height 9m); it takes months of work to make them, as secretly as possible, in specially fitted out warehouses. The figures and parts are made to move by complicated and clever mechanisms inside the float; there are also hundreds of real people on them. Themes range from political and social satire, to current events. The Mardi Gras procession on Shrove Tuesday, led by Re Burlamacco (the local Carnival King), goes along the seafront and ends with a magnificent fireworks display. The processions follow different routes on the three Sundays before, and the Sunday after.
For further information:
tel. 0584962568,
www.viareggio.ilcarnevale.com

PISA

Gioco del ponte

Last Sunday in June

The "gioco del ponte" (bridge game) is a modern sports version of the ritual medieval battles (no less violent for this reason) between Pisans who lived south and north of the Arno, involving thousands of people. The contest still takes place today on the Ponte del Mezzo over the Arno: two teams of twenty members each try to push an iron cart weighing over seven tons along the narrow tracks laid in the middle of the bridge, into the opposing team's area. Before the contest there is a parade, with thousands of costumed participants.
For further information: tel. 050910473, www.comune.pisa.it

Regata delle Repubbliche Marinare

May/June

This boat race takes places every year, each time rotating between Amalfi, Genoa, Pisa (on the Arno) and Venice. There is always a big procession before the contest, with costumed participants representing the four cities.
For further information: tel. 050910473, www.comune.pisa.it

BUTI
Il Maggio

Spring/autumn

One of the most complex forms of traditional Tuscan theater. The texts, often composed by local poets in literary Italian, are sung to repetitive melodies by actors wearing imaginative and impressive costumes. The themes used are dramatic, often taken from history or tales of chivalry. In the end good and justice inevitably triumph. The performance lasts several hours, and is a great opportunity to see traditional Tuscan folk theater. Usually performed in the open, in a piazza, or in the countryside.
For further information: tel. 0587724281

VOLTERRA
L'Astiludio

First Sunday in September

Four processions starting from the four gates of the medieval town end in beautiful Piazza dei Priori, with all the church bells of Volterra ringing out. The tournament begins: flag-bearers from Volterra and other towns compete in a flag-throwing contest, hurling and twirling brightly-colored flags in the air, with drums rolling and trumpets blaring.
For further information: tel. 058885440, www.sbandieratorivolterra.it

PISTOIA

Giostra dell'Orso

July 25th

This contest, originating in the 13th century, is part of the celebrations for the patron saint of Pistoia, St Jacob. The city's four quarters compete for the "Palio" or prize; three knights represent each quarter, and they are all accompanied to the scenic Piazza del Duomo by a traditional procession, with people dressed in medieval costume. For further information: tel. 0573371690, www.comune.pistoia.it

SIENA

Palio
July 2nd and August 16th
Definitely the best-known and most exciting traditional Italian festival, and the only one to have taken place, without interruption, from the 14th century until today. Initially the Palio took place only on July 2nd, in honor of the Madonna di Provenzano, and was run through the city streets without any particular rules. In 1632, it was held for the first time in the amazing setting of Piazza del Campo. In the 18th century, the race began to be held on August 16th as well, in honor of the Madonna of the Assumption, and rules were established which still apply today. The seventeen quarters ("contrade") which Siena is divided into can enter for the Palio, but horses from only ten quarters, drawn by lot, actually race. There is a lengthy run-up to the race when excitement and tension gradually increase to fever-pitch; this involvement is difficult to really understand unless you are Sienese. In the days before the race, the horse and jockey are watched closely to prevent the animal being poisoned or the rider being bribed by rival quarters. Just before the race, horses and riders are blessed inside each quarter's most important church. There is a magnificent procession in costume before the race, commemorating the Republic of Siena at its peak, and featuring the famous flag-throwers from each contrada. An ox-drawn cart carries the "palio", or the banner which is the symbolic prize for the winning contrada. The jockeys ride bareback, and are allowed to use their whips on other horses and riders too. At the starting line, the horses line up behind a rope: when the rope falls, the race begins. Frequent false starts increase the tense, excited atmosphere among the watching crowds. Finally, when there's a good start, the horses gallop wildly three times around the piazza; the race is very dangerous for both horses and riders, especially at the turns. Riders are often thrown off: riderless horses can continue to race, and have even been known to win... All in all it lasts less than a minute and a half. The victory celebrations last for days in the winning contrada, and culminate in a great banquet for thousands of people. The winning horse is there too, occupying the place of honor.
For further information: tel. 057743875, www.ilpaliodisiena.net

MONTEPULCIANO
Bravio delle botti
Last Sunday in August
The town's eight quarters compete in this contest; two representatives from each quarter race to roll a barrel weighing 85 kilos to the finishing line. For further information: tel. 0578757575, www.braviodellebotti.it

Il Bruscello
August 15th
"Il Bruscello" is one of Tuscany's folk theater traditions. "Brusello" means "little tree"; one of the characters carries a little tree decorated with ribbons. The text is in verse, and sung to a particular tune; often written by local authors, on traditional folk themes related to history and legend. The performances were once very simple, but have now become more elaborate, with impressive scenery, lighting, period costumes, solo performers and choirs. For further information: tel. 0578758529, www.bruscello.it

EVENTS

CARNIVAL CITY

Viareggio's *Cittadella del Carnevale* is a completely new area, created to the north of the city to make space for the large workshops used by the carnival float builders; now visitors can do tours of the area, see exhibitions and enjoy events here. Groups are taken on guided tours of the enormous hangars, where the giant papier mâché carnival floats are made; a 'carrista', or float builder, describes how the floats are created and what this fascinating occupation involves. You can also visit the papier mâché museum, which displays models of winning floats in recent years, and many interesting exhibits, all in a carnival-like atmosphere. Info: tel. 058451176, e-mail: cittadella.carnevale@libero.it

Italy's abundance of natural thermal springs and mineral waters, combined with the mild climate and beauty of the land, have made it a leading destination for spa vacations.

The ancients knew the secret to longevity was rest, relaxation and the curative benefits of the spa. Mud baths, herbal wraps, massage, and hydrotherapy are but a few of the treatments recommended for the restoration and purification of mind, body and spirit.

Today ancient methods and modern technology come together to provide a holistic approach to wellness and beauty with state of the art spa facilities across the region.

Wellness

Highlights

- Cascina Terme, an important spa town in the Pisan hills
- Chianciano Terme, the therapeutic properties of its waters were known to the Etruscans and the Romans
- Montecatini Terme, its thermal springs rise from a water table 60-80 meters below ground
- Saturnia, renowned for its waterfalls of sulfurous water which bubble up at 37.5°C

Inside

Today it's common knowledge that a healthy, attractive appearance reflects a state of inner equilibrium, harmony and serenity. For this reason, increasing numbers of tourists are choosing to spend holidays on beauty and health farms.

The sector is flourishing, especially in Tuscany, a region which has always been in the vanguard when it comes to tourism, and which is blessed with exceptional natural resources. In the first place, all corners of the region have thermal springs, which were already well known at the time of the emperor Augustus. Today, thermal centers provide beauty treatments and traditional wellness treatments, as well as specific treatments for a variety of complaints, according to the properties of the different waters.

There are also many beauty farms and spas which provide treatments in the fields of preventive medicine, functional medicine and cosmetic medicine. These centers generally also offer full accommodation and permanent medical staff. In addition, there are numerous hotels, holiday resorts or sports centers which include fully equipped wellness centers.

Many of these places are located in historic residences and villas, in incredibly beautiful natural landscapes. They are outstanding for the professional level of treatments and services that they provide, and for the exclusive hospitality which they ensure their guests.

BAGNI DI LUCCA

Terme di Bagni di Lucca
Bagni Caldi, piazza S. Martino 11,
tel. 058387221, www.termebagnidilucca.it
Open April to December

The thermal baths of Bagni di Lucca, in the province of Lucca, have been public property since medieval times, but they became known to visitors from outside Italy between the 18th and 19th centuries, when new baths, villas and a municipal casino were built in neo-Classical style. The turn of the 19th century and the Belle Epoque lent the baths an exotic, Art Nouveau touch, at a time when thermal resorts were the height of fashion in Europe.

The spa complex consists of nineteen thermal springs, with water (54°C) containing sulfur, bicarbonate and calcium, and two completely renovated buildings: it specialises in the treatment of arthritic and rheumatic conditions, bronchial and

The Bagni di Lucca thermal springs situated in the natural surroundings of the Lima valley

pulmonary conditions, and vascular and gynaecological complaints. There are two superb natural steam grottos: the Paolina, small and very atmospheric, and next to it, the Grotta Grande. Each has its own hot spring with temperatures ranging between 40°C and 47°C.

Antico Albergo Terme
Via del Paretaio 1,
tel. 058386034
www.termebagnidilucca.it
The hotel is situated in the quiet village of Bagni Caldi, by the Lima stream, and is connected by a tunnel to two thermal baths nearby. The twenty-two comfortable rooms all provide lovely views over the Tuscan countryside, and the peaceful surroundings. The thermal center provides guests with every possible kind of

therapeutic and beauty treatment, and also provides specific treatment packages for the convenience of guests.

Villaggio Globale 🖎 ★
Villa Demidoff, tel. 058386404
www.globalvillage-it.com
The Villaggio Globale is set amongst lush vegetation, on the banks of the Lima stream. It was built in the 19th-century by a Russian, Count Demidoff. An extremely relaxing and peaceful place, it also houses the Centro Internazionale di

Medicina Olistica (International Center of Holistic Medicine) and the Academy of the same name. The center does not provide accomodation, but it has agreements with a number of hotels in the area. Visitors can enjoy the private garden, meditation rooms, bar and reading room. The restaurant has organic and vegetarian food, and menus can be tailored to individual requirements on the advice of the doctor and the nutritionist.

🖎 Beach establishment ⚕ Thermal spa ★ Special TCI Rates

BAGNO VIGNONI

Terme di Bagno Vignoni

via Dante 35, tel. 0577887365
Open June to September

Bagno Vignoni is situated a few kilometers away from San Quirico d'Orcia, in the province of Siena, and blends in perfectly with the beauty of the surrounding countryside where stretches of bare earth alternate with expanses of wheat and sunflowers, vines and olives. With its unusually atmospheric main square swathed in rising steam, this place has continued to amaze and fascinate travelers: the sight of the outdoor thermal bath, built in the 15th century by Pope Pius II, and surrounded by beautiful buildings, is absolutely unique.

The sulfurous, slightly radio-active water, which was used for therapeutic purposes as early as Roman times, rises from below ground at a temperature of 51°C and flows into the large pool built in the 16th century, when the whole town was restructured for defence purposes. Today the thermal center offers a limited range of treatments (only mud therapy and balneotherapy), despite the well-known therapeutic qualities of the water.

Adler Thermae Spa&Wellness Resort
Strada di Bagno Vignoni 1, tel. 0577889000
www.adler-thermae.com

Situated in the superb natural surroundings of the Val d'Orcia, the Resort is built in the style of an old country villa and set in peaceful gardens. The rooms and suites, arranged around a central section, are extremely comfortable and well-equipped, and each has a terrace with view. Services and amenities include: beauty center, hair stylist, Vital Bar, car park, private garden, reading room, baby sitting service, gym, fitness trail, children's playground, swimming pools, flowing stream with water effects, mountain bikes, and trekking. The restaurant has vegetarian menus, and personalised diet menus.

CASCIANA TERME

Terme di Casciana

Piazza Garibaldi 9, tel. 0587644608
www.termedicasciana.it

Legend has it that Countess Matilda di Canossa founded the first thermal baths in Casciana Terme, the most important town in the Colline Pisane (Pisan Hills). The site was known way back in the 11th century as Castrum ad Aquas, indicating that its fame as a thermal center originates in ancient times.

The baths were extended by the Grand-Dukes of Tuscany, and renovated in 1870 when the complex was built whose impressive façade today looks onto the treatments center, as well as the interesting Salone delle Feste (Party Hall) and the Gran Caffè. Behind is the modern spa, circular in shape, which draws on the plentiful waters of the Mathelda spring for balneotherapy, and the San Leopoldo spring for hydropinic (water-drinking) cures. On the upper floor, there is a modern and well-equipped rehabilitation department, a wellness center - with various rooms for various types of massage - and a beauty center. The pride of the Terme are two pools with flowing water: one indoor pool with vascular water trails, and another outdoor pool set in magical surroundings, with fountains and mini-waterfalls.

G. H. San Marco
Via Lischi 1, tel. 058764421
www.sanmarcohotels.it

An elegant, modern building, with garden, gym, swimming pools, solarium and water-exercise circuits. Rooms have air conditioning, satellite TV, telephone and mini bar refrigerator, and are tastefully furnished in classical style. Amenities include a wide range of beauty and manipulative treatmenrts, a restaurant, two bars, conference room, and the Gran Classe area for ceremonies.

La Speranza
Via Cavour 46, tel. 0587646215
www.hotel-lasperanza.com

This peaceful, welcoming hotel, with a family atmosphere, is surrounded by a lovely garden, and situated near a number of thermal spas. The rooms have telephone, mini bar refrigerator and TV. Amenities include a terrace-solarium, bar, private garden, reading room, concert room, swimming pool and beauty center. The restaurant specialises in Tuscan and international cuisine, with personalised diet menus on request.

Chianciano Terme (see p. 86) is very close to the border with Umbria, and lies at the center of a vast area in the province of Siena which literally floats on a thermal water table, a real challenge to nature. The Chianciano thermal area has five springs, with waters of differing mineral compositions and temperatures, suited for differing treatments.

Water gym at Chianciano Terme

Terme di Chianciano
Via delle Rose 12, tel. 057868111
www.termechianciano.it
Terme di Chianciano, has a diagnostic center, clinics and an inhalation center, and includes Parco Acquasanta, Parco Fucoli (where the waters are traditionally taken for liver treatments), and the Stabilimento Sillene, with pools, mud therapy and other therapies, as well as a wide range of beauty and wellness treatments. These include an acqua therapy center, a cosmetic and angiological medical center, a relaxation center, as well as a gym and the Sillene cosmetic product line.

Terme Sorgente Sant'Elena
Viale della Libertà 112, tel. 057831141
www.termesantelena.it
Open mid-April to October
Terme Sant'Elena is the other spa in Cianciano, hosted in a beautiful eighteen-century building. Its waters are particularly recommended for kidney and metabolism disorders.

G. H. Terme 🏖 ★
Piazza Italia 8, tel. 057863254
www.medeahotels.com
A modern hotel set in a pine grove, near the historic center of the town. Rooms are elegant and comfortable; some have hydromassage tubs. Amenities include a private car park, garden, bar, reading room, concert room, cinema, disco, babysitting service, gym, fitness trail, tennis court, golf course, and horse-riding. The restaurant provides low-calory personalised menus on request.

Spa' Deus 🏖
Via Le Piane 35, tel. 057863232
www.spadeus.it
Open mid-March to mid-November
In a lovely natural setting in the Sienese hills, this is the only center in Italy designed according to Californian spa criteria. There are many amenities for guests: gym, fitness trail, tennis court, golf course, underwater gym, full pilates studio, indoor and outdoor climbing tower, gyrotonics, cardio-fitness machines, Olympic swimming pool, thalasso pool, spinning studio. The rooms are well-equipped and comfortable, and great attention has been given to detail. The restaurant places great importance on providing healthy food, and also provides diet and maintenance menus.

Grotta Giusti Terme
Via Grotta Giusti 1411, tel. 057290771
www.grottagiustispa.com
A subterranean grotto about 300 meters long, with stalactites and stalagnites and a small hot-water lake: this is the impressive sight that greets visitors when they descend into the complex of the Giusti grottos, pride of the delightful town of Monsummano Terme (see p. 75) lying between Mount Albano and the Padule di Fucecchio, in the province of Pistoia. Discovered only in 1849, this grotto is deep and has a lot of calcium formations. The water gushes out at 34°C; the steam baths are progressively hotter, and are named accordingly Paradiso, Purgatorio and Inferno. Limbo is a delightful little thermal lake, perfect for a relaxing dip.

🏖 Beach establishment ♨ Thermal spa ★ Special TCI Rates

Grotta Parlanti Terme

*Via Grotta Parlanti 41/D,
tel. 0572953096
www.azzolinihotels.it
Open mid-April to October*
The oldest spa in
Monsummano, known
since the 18th century for
the therapeutic
properties of the steam
rising from its thermal
waters. The spa pavillion
- situated at the
beginning of the town - has a temple
pediment, in the neo-Classical taste of

Grotta Giusti Terme Hotel

*Via Grotta Giusti 1411,
tel. 057290771
www.grottagiustispa.com*
The hotel annexed to the
Grotta Giusti spa provides
discreet and attentive
hospitality, in a 19th-century
residence, and the peace of a
centuries-old garden. The
rooms are classy, and have all
amenities and comforts. The
beautiful communal areas are
tastefully furnished, and
decorated with old paintings.
Clients have access to a
private car park, bar, meeting
center, beauty center, reading
room, concert room,
babysitting service on
request, shuttle service to
Montecatini, gym, fitness trail,
tennis court, golf course, and
fresh water swimming pool.
The restaurant specialises in
carefully prepared Tuscan
cuisine; diet and low-calorie
menus are available on
request.

the time. At the moment both hotel and
spa are being renovated and extended.

MONTECATINI TERME

Le Terme di Montecatini

*Viale G. Verdi 41, tel. 0572778487
www.termemontecatini.it*
Montecatini Terme (province of Pistoia)
is situated on the edge of a ring of hills
in the Valdinievole, half an hour by
motorway from Florence along the route
which for centuries has joined Pistoia
and Lucca (see p. 76). Montecatini
boasts great thermal baths, which it
combines with very elegant and
sophisticated surroundings. It also
hosts many high-level shows and
events, in particular concerts, and is
interesting not only as a thermal resort,
but also as a place where there are
many interesting things to do.
At present there are nine spas in
Montecatini Terme, all situated in the
lovely, large park. **Terme Tettuccio** is a
real Montecatini icon, with its grand,
18th-century façade. Most of the spa
buildings date from the twenties, and
are a wonderful concentration of Art
Nouveau spa style. One modern
building, added in 1989, was designed
by the architect Paolo Portoghesi.
Terme Leopoldine is sumptuous, full of
marble and stucco work; the spring
bubbles up from a fountain in the
middle of the inner courtyard. **Nuove
Terme Excelsior** was built in the early
1900s as a leisure spa, with Casino and
Gran Caffe, and the most beautiful
original rooms have been preserved as
they were; today a modern glass
building houses the treatments center,
and there is also a wellness center.
Terme Tamerici is a kind of fairytale
castle, with its mix of architectural
styles: Moorish Venetian, Tuscan
Renaissance, and Art Nouveau. The
spring of **Terme Regina** (with large hall,
multi-colored windows and impressive
portico) gushes from a small circular
temple. **Terme La Salute** consists of
simple pavillions looking on to the
surrounding park, while the **Terme
Torretta** is built like a castle and is
romantically set on the shores of a
small lake with swans. **Nuove Terme
Redi** has more than 100 rooms, used
for mud therapy and
massages. Lastly, **Istituto
Grocco** has
physiotherapy facilities,
including a thermal pool.
A recent, ambitious
project aims to promote
and reorganise the spa
complex, to make
Montecatini Terme the
new European capital of
wellness.

G. H. Tamerici & Principe

*Viale IV Novembre 4,
tel. 057271041
www.hoteltamerici.com
Open May to October*
A large, elegant, renovated
Art Nouveau mansion,
situated in the center of
Montecatini Terme. There are
well-furnished day rooms,
and light and spacious rooms
for reading, writing, sipping a
cup of tea, or having a drink,
and relaxing with pleasant
music in the background. The
rooms are furnished with a
great deal of care, and are
equipped with every comfort.
The two restaurants have à la
carte menus with traditional
Italian and international
dishes, as well as Tuscan
specialities. The center offers
a wide range of manipulative
and therapeutic treatments.

Terme di Montepulciano

*Sant'Albino, via delle
Terme 46, tel. 05787911
www.termemontepulciano.it*
Montepulciano, in the
province of Siena, is
known for the splendour
of its Renaissance palazzi,
the elegant beauty of its
churches and for its Vino
Nobile, one of Tuscany's
most highly recognised
and renowned wines, at

Thermal baths at Montepulciano

an international level (see p. 88).
The first written mention of
Montepulciano's sulfurous waters was
made in 1571; but until the second half of
the 20th century, therapeutic use was
largely limited to locals, who used to bathe
at the Sant'Albino springs, on the road to
Chianciano Terme. The spa
was built in 1966. At the
same time a well was also
sunk, enabling water to be
collected at a depth of 132
m, and brought up to the
surface without coming
into contact with the air,
thus protecting the
therapeutic qualities of the
sulfur and other minerals

dissolved in it. The spa includes an
orthopedic, vascular and rheumatological
rehabilitation center, and three centers
specialising in illnesses of the respiratory
system. Wellness and fitness programs are
also tailored for clients, with thermal
beauty treatments for face and body.

Podere Ortaglia
*S.S. per Pienza 29,
tel. 0578756091
www.ortaglia.it*
Situated on a hilltop,
surrounded by vineyards, and
far from traffic noise. The
center is built in the traditional
Sienese style and proposes
beauty treatments and foot
reflexology, body relaxation,

lymph drainage, shiatsu and
ayurvedic massages; rooms are
furnished with care and
attention to detail, and some
have hydromassage tubs.
Mountain bikes for hire, a mini-
bus for trips and a swimming
pool with hydromassage, a
great view over the countryside
and a green garden complet
the offer.

Terme della Versilia

*Cinquale, viale Marina
corner via Gramsci,
tel. 0585807788
www.termedellaversilia.com*

The area around Montignoso with its
villages and countryside stretches from the
slopes of the Apuan Alps to pine groves by
the sea, tucked between Marina di Massa
and Forte dei Marmi, and acting as a kind

Villa Undulna
*Cinquale, viale Marina ang.
via Gramsci, tel. 0585807788
www.villaundulna.com
Open Easter to October*
The hotel is situated in
spacious gardens, a few
meters from the sea; it
consists of a number of
buildings, like a group of
country houses. Outdoors
there is a garden, fitness
trail, tennis courts and mini
soccer. The rooms are well
equipped and tastefully

decorated with marble fittings
and beautiful furniture.
Clients also have the use of a
garage, reserved parking, and
a beach, where umbrellas and
loungers can be hired under
an agreement with the hotel.
The restaurant provides
international and traditional
cuisine, as well as menus
personalised according to
directions from medical staff

Agriturismo Karma
*Castello Aghinolfi, via
Guadagni 1, tel. 0585821237*

www.agrikarma.it
A farm stay in an old stone
country house on the slopes of
the Apuan Alps, renovated
according to bioarchitectural
criteria. The rooms are cosy and
private, and equipped with TV
and mini bar refrigerator. The
light, sunny veranda and dining
room have wonderful views
over the sea. The restaurant has
an extensive menu, with
traditional Tuscan and
Mediterranean food and the
beauty center provides wellness
and wellbeing treatments.

of border between the Lunigiana and Versilia (province of Massa-Carrara). The Centro Terme della Versilia is located at Cinquale, Montignoso's thermal village. Here, a stone's throw from the sea, is the Undulna spring, dedicated to the nymphs of the water and the dunes, praised by Gabriele D'Annunzio in Alcyones. On its way to the surface, the thermal water passes through strata of salts, and acquires sodium chloride, iodide and bromide. The water is used for balneotherapy and mud therapy, together with peat from the nearby lake of Massaciuccoli. The thermal center, with large glass windows overlooking the pines in the park, has a pool with hydromassage, a children's area, and an active wellness center which provides treatment programs (good for vascular disorders, arthritic and rheumatic disorders; anticellulite treatments, slimming, wellbeing and beauty treatments, face and neckline treatments, and regenerative treatments).

PORTOFERRAIO

Terme San Giovanni

San Giovanni, tel. 0565914680
www.termelbane.com
Open mid-April to October
Portoferraio, in the province of Livorno, is the main town in Elba island (see p. 53). Terme San Giovanni is situated in the innermost part of the gulf of Portoferraio, where the old saltworks were: five hectares of lagoon, now a habitat for herons and sea birds. The spa is set in an enormous park of eucalyptus trees. Thalassotherapy is carried out, using seawater rich in sodium chloride and iodide. Mud treatments use the sludgy silt which forms naturally in the pools in front of the spa, where the sea water is constantly changed; it contains an unusually high concentration of organic iodine and sulfur (from seaweed and algae), as well as iron, from the old iron mines. The combination of these elements is particularly effective in treating painful joints and skin

complaints. The spa also has a physiotherapy room and a wellness center providing beauty treatments and health weeks.

Portoferraio: sports facilities at the Hotel Airone del Parco e delle Terme

Airone del Parco e delle Terme
San Giovanni, tel. 0565929111
www.hotelairone.info
Situated in the greenery and peacefulness of a large park extending to the seashore, this is the perfect place for those who enjoy comfort. The hotel is modern and very spacious, ensuring peace and privacy. Amenities include two tennis courts, a swimming pool for adults and one for children, an outdoor pool with hydromassage, a beauty center, solarium, sauna and Turkish bath. The restaurant provides lavish buffet meals at breakfast and lunch; there are four different menus to choose from at dinner.

RAPOLANO TERME

Rapolano Terme is 27 km from Siena, and marks the point where the green countryside of the Chianti hills gives way to the bare, rolling expanses of the Sienese hills known as the Crete. Rapolano was most prosperous in medieval times when it was famed for its quarries of marble and travertine: some remains of these long-gone times can still be seen in the historic center, which preserves the Tintori gate and part of the old city walls. In the 19th century it became famous again as a spa town: one famous visitor was Giuseppe Garibaldi, who came here to recover after he was wounded in battle on Aspromonte.

Terme Antica Querciolaia

Via Trieste 22, tel. 0577724091
www.termeaq.it

Terme Antica Querciolaia, a modern spa complex located around 1 km north-east of the town, is one of the two main thermal springs in Rapolano Terme. The remains of a large thermal complex dating from imperial Roman times, discovered at Campo Muri, indicate that this place was a favorite with the Romans. Water in the Rapolano thermal area contains sulfur, bicarbonate and calcium, and has a temperature of 39°C.

Terme San Giovanni

Via Terme San Giovanni 52,
tel. 0577724030
www.termesangiovanni.it

Terme San Giovanni is 2 km south-west of the town in a lovely 19th-century building. According to tradition, St Catherine of Siena came here. The thermal bath is set in a large park of 22,000 square meters where guests can enjoy tennis courts and fitness trails, and hire mountain bikes. The thermal pool is fed from the sulfurous hot-water spring (39 °C): the wellness center and the thermal center provide standard treatments as well as personalised packages.

The Antica Querciolaia Thermal Springs at Rapolano Terme

SAN CASCIANO DEI BAGNI

Centro Termale Fonteverde

Via Terme 1, tel. 057857241
www.fonteverdeterme.com

San Casciano is situated on the southern side of Monte Cetona, among the verdant woods of oak, pine and chestnut which are typical of the Siena countryside. The thermal area is. The San Casciano thermal basin - outside the town, with the church of Santa Maria ad balnea, and the 17th-century baths known as the Bagno del Portico - has various thermal springs which bubble up vigorously at a temperature of 42°C, third in Europe in terms of size. The Etruscan king Porsena is credited with founding the thermal baths: and according to Horace, the Emperor Augustus recovered his health and strength here.

The spa became renowned over the centuries, and was modernised in 1607, under the patronage of the Grand-Duke of Tuscany Ferdinand I. Further sumptuous pavilions were established in the early 1900s. More recently, the treatment centers were modernised, beauty and wellness centers were added, and the elegant hotel Terme dei Medici was built. The magnificent outdoor pool, with its waterfalls and fountains, looks out over the countryside.

There are many indoor pools: two on the ground floor - one linked to the outdoor pool and the other with two depths, and a small adjoining pool for children; and three pools on the upper floor, one with a bio-aquam trail (toning with new hydro-massage techniques), the second for aqua-gym, and the third for our four-footed friends. In the newest section, known as the 'Etruscan Baths' there are various rooms for hydro-massage, relaxation, sauna, steam and Turkish baths.

Beach establishment   Thermal spa   ★ Special TCI Rates

SAN GIULIANO TERME

Terme di San Giuliano

Largo Shelley 18, tel. 050818047
www.termesangiuliano.com
San Giuliano and the area around, in
the province of Pisa, enjoy a location
that combines both sea and hills,
extending between the Arno and
Serchio rivers from the tree-cloaked
heights of Monte Pisano to the regional
park of Migliarino, San Rossore and
Massaciuccoli.

**The impressive facade of the San Giuliano Terme
thermal baths**

The waters of Terme di San Giuliano
have been used for centuries for
thermal baths and muds. Already known
in the Roman period and appreciated in
the Middle Ages, they reached their
apex in the XVIII century, when San
Giuliano became an international spa
town and the magnificent hotel was
built, in a wonderful park. Among the
wide choice of health and beauty
treatments also a new hammam and
two swimming pools. The historic
summer residence of Grand-Duke
Francis Stephen of Lorraine, built in
1843, it has recently been restored to its
ancient splendour. Guests can enjoy
beautifully decorated rooms equipped
with all comforts. There is a wellness
trail in the large olive grove.

SATURNIA

A view of the sulfurous waterfalls at Saturnia

Terme di Saturnia

Via della Follonata, tel. 0564600800
www.termedisaturnia.it
In the hills lying between the valleys of
the Albenga and the Fiora rivers, in the
province of Grosseto, Saturnia is
situated on the site of an ancient town
which, according to legend, was the first
settlement in Italy, dedicated to the god
Saturn. It was a Roman colony, and
became prosperous not only because of
its precious and plentiful thermal
waters, but also because
of its location, near the Via
Clodia, which ran through
Etruria, and the Via
Aurelia, which runs along
the coast.
This thermal spa is not far
from Saturnia and about a
dozen kilometers from
Manciano: it's a beautiful
place, with natural
cascades of gushing
sulfurous water at a
temperature of 37.5
degrees celsius. The spa is
annexed to the exclusive
Terme di Saturnia hotel
with its lovely travertine stone work,
period furniture, and the latest treatment
and wellness facilities. It specialises in
diets and special cosmetic techniques,
massages, and very advanced fitness and
wellness programs. A line of cosmetic
products is also available based on
Bioglea, an exclusive thermal plankton
extract. There is an enormous park with
four thermal pools; the main one (directly
fed from the thermal spring) is in front of
the hotel.

WELLNESS

GETTING TO TUSCANY

By plane

FLORENCE "Amerigo Vespucci" international airport.

At Peretola, 4km from Florence.

Information on international flights tel. 0553061702 (24 hours a day).

Information on national flights tel. 0553061700 (24 hours a day)

Information about lost luggage tel. 0553061302

www.aeroporto.firenze.it

Transport from and to airport: airport terminal – Santa Maria Novella railway station, Florence; from 6am to 11.30pm. Departures from city center, from 5.30am to 11pm.

PISA "Galileo Galilei" international airport

Freephone: 800018849

Flight information office: tel. 050500707 (from 8am to 10pm)

Ticket office: tel. 050849404

www.pisa-airport.com

Airport link to Pisa railway station. Check-in also at the Air Terminal, platform 5, Santa Maria Novella railway station, Florence.

Between the airport and downtown Pisa: "City Bus" number 3.

By train

The main trunk line between Milan and Rome passes through Tuscany.

Trenitalia, tel. 892021, every day, from 7am to 9pm, www.trenitalia.com; Telephone Bookings 199166177, every day from 7am to 9pm, from landlines and mobiles.

By car

Milan-Rome-Naples A1 Motorway, (exits for Florence and Arezzo) and Genoa-Rosignano A12 Motorway, (exits for Massa Carrara, Pisa and Livorno); State Road 1, the Aurelia, which runs along the coast of Tuscany.

Motorway information center: tel. 0643632121 24 hours a day, Freephone: 800269269, www.autostrade.it

Radio information: Isoradio, FM 103,3 and Viaradio FM 102,5

By bus

Sena Autolinee: connections from and to Valle d'Aosta, Umbria, Piedmont, Lombardy, Emilia Romagna, Umbria, Lazio, Abruzzo, Calabria, Puglia, Campania.

Freephone: 800930960 (from landlines), 199730760 (from mobiles, it will be a pay call); www.sena.it

Eurolines: Siena-Munich, Siena-Frankfurt (with stops in Ulm, Stuttgart, Karlsruhe and Heidelberg), Rome-Vienna (stop in Florence), Naples-London (stop in Florence) and Siena-London.

Italy headquarters: tel. 055357110, www.eurolines.com

TRANSPORT WITHIN TUSCANY

Train

All the main, capital cities of the Tuscan Provinces are on the national Italian rail network. Discounted tickets can be purchased by some rail travelers:

Carta Verde: for young people up to 26 years of age, the carta verde (green card) is valid for a year. It gives a 10% discount on 1st and 2nd class train tickets (on regional trains as well) and a 25% discount on international trains. Green cards can be bought in all Trenitalia ticket offices and travel agencies.

Carta Argento: for people over 60 years of age, the carta argento (silver card) is valid for a year. It gives a discount of 40% on 1st class travel, and of 30% on 2nd class travel, and can be bought in all Trenitalia ticket offices and travel agencies.

Bus

FLORENCE

Florentia Bus: from Florence to the Mugello, the Valdarno and Arezzo. Tel. 055967024 www.florentiabus.it

Lazzi: from Florence to Prato, Versilia, Pontedera and the Valdarno; from Empoli to Fucecchio and Montecatini; from Viareggio to La Spezia; from Pisa to Lucca and Viareggio; from Lucca to Viareggio, Camaiore and San Marcello Pistoiese. Tel. 055363041, www.lazzi.it

Sita: in the areas of northern Mugello, of Chianti and Val di Pesa, Valdelsa, the Valdarno and Valdambra, the Casentino and the Valtiberina. Tel. 05547821 (Florence branch), 057574361 (Sansepolcro branch). www.sita-on-line.it

AREZZO

La Ferroviaria Italiana: (LFI), both a rail and bus service, from Arezzo to Sinalunga and Stia. Tel. 057539881, www.lfi.it

GROSSETO

Rama: travel all over Grosseto Province, and to Florence and Piombino. Tel. 056425215, www.griforama.it

LIVORNO

ATL: runs the bus network in the province of Livorno, on the island of Elba, and Pisa. Tel. 0586847225, www.atl.livorno.it

MASSA CARRARA

CAT: bus network in the province of Massa Carrara. Tel. 058585211, freephone 800223010, www.catspa.it

PISA

CPT: bus network in the province of Pisa and Livorno. Freephone: 800012773, www.cpt.pisa.it

PISTOIA

Co.pi.t: bus network in the province of Pistoia and services to Florence, Empoli, and Porretta Terme. Tel. 05733630, freephone 800277825, www.copitspa.it

PRATO

CAP Autolinee: from Prato to Florence, Castiglione dei Pepoli, Carmignano; from Florence to Casola Val Senio and Impruneta; from Montemurlo to Siena; from Pistoia to Florence.

CLIMATE

Like all central Italy, Tuscany has a generally mild climate, especially in coastal areas where summers tend to be pleasant and winters temperate. Further inland, the climate becomes more continental, with noticeably lower temperatures in mountainous areas: it can be very hot at times in the summer and winters can be pretty cold in the inland valleys. Temperatures in summer rarely reach 40° C in the cities.

TOURIST INFORMATION

Turismo in Toscana:
www.turismo.toscana.it
Costa di Toscana: specialises in coastal areas.
Call Center: 800883388,
www.costaditoscana.com

USEFUL NUMBERS

EMERGENCY NUMBERS
112 Military Police (Carabinieri)
113 State Police (Polizia)
115 Fire Department
116 Road Assistance
118 Medical Emergencies

Tel. 05746081,
www.capautolinee.it

SIENA
Train: local city transport in Siena, Colle Val d'Elsa, Poggibonsi and Certaldo, and bus links with Florence, Arezzo and Grosseto.
Tel. 0577204111, www.trainspa.it

Ferries

The main companies run ferries between the key tourist islands of the Tuscan Archipelago. The number of ferries and schedules vary according to season.

Moby Lines: ferries between Piombino and Elba (Portoferraio). Bookings at travel agencies.
Tel. 05659361, www.moby.it

Toremar: ferries between Livorno and the islands of Gorgona and Capraia; from Piombino to Elba (Portoferraio) and Pianosa; from Porto Santo Stefano to the island of Giglio.
Call Center 199123199,
www.toremar.it

Maregiglio: ferries between Porto Santo Stefano and the islands of Giglio and Giannutri.
Tel. 0564812920, www.maregiglio.it

Car rental

AVIS
"Amerigo Vespucci" airport – Florence, tel. 055315588
"Galileo Galilei" airport – Pisa, tel. 05049187
Florence (via del Termine 1) tel. 055315588, bookings 199100133,
www.avisautonoleggio.it

HERTZ
"Amerigo Vespucci" airport, tel. 055307370
Florence (via Finiguerra Maso 33/R) tel. 0552398205, bookings 199112211,
www.hertz.it

EUROPCAR
"Amerigo Vespucci" airport – Florence, tel. 055318609
"Galileo Galilei" airport – Pisa, tel. 05041081
Florence (via Borgo Ognissanti 53) tel. 055290437, bookings 800014410,
www.europcar.it

Inside

Hotels and restaurants
Tourist information
Museums and monuments
At night
Golf and other sports

ANGHIARI

ℹ️ **Pro Loco**
*Corso Matteotti 103,
tel. 0575749279,
www.anghiari.it*

How to get there

BY CAR: exit Arezzo, A1
motorway Milano-Roma-
Napoli

BY TRAIN: FS Railway
Station in Arezzo; bus
connection

Hotels

La Meridiana ★★★
*Piazza IV Novembre 8,
tel. 0575788102
www.hotellameridiana.it*
26 rooms. Restaurant, parking
Credit Cards: American Express,
Diner's Club, Mastercard, Visa
In the medieval town, family-
managed for forty years,
comfortable and efficient.
Tuscan cuisine.

Oliver ★★★
*Via della Battaglia 16,
tel. 0575789933
www.oliverhotel.it*
36 rooms. Restaurant, parking,
air conditioned, swimming pool
Credit Cards: American Express,
Diner's Club, Mastercard, Visa
Modern building, with services
and facilities for both tourists
and business meetings.
Restaurant with typical local
cuisine.

Rural Lodgings

Ca' del Viva
*Scheggia, via Ca' del Viva 63,
tel. 0575749171
www.go.to/cadelviva*
Restaurant
Set amongst woods and fields,
complex consisting of country
mansion and two stone
cottages; small lake nearby.

Ca' Faggio ♿
*Toppole 42, tel. 0575749025
www.cafaggio.it*
Swimming pool, availability of
bikes
Countryside with woods, olive
groves and grapevines, an ideal
setting for the organic
agriculture courses held on the
farm.

Restaurants

Da Alighiero 🍴 ★
Via Garibaldi 8, tel. 0575788040
Closed Tuesday
Cuisine: Tuscan
Credit Cards: Mastercard, Visa
Two rooms with 15th-century
stone walls. Traditional but
refined cuisine; wide selection
of oils and wines.

At night

Giardini del Vicario
*Piazza del Popolo 7/A,
tel. 0575788301
www.giardinidelvicario.it*
Fantastic location on the walls
of the old town, with great view;
bruschetta (toasted bread with
tomato), sandwiches and
"piadine" sandwiches, with a
vast assortment of wines.

Museums, Monuments and Churches

Palazzo Taglieschi
*Piazza Mameli 16,
tel. 0575788001*
Opening times: Tuesday-
Saturday 8.30-19.00; Sunday
9.00-13.00. Closed Christmas,
New Year's Day and 1 May.

AREZZO

ℹ️ **Agenzia per il Turismo
di Arezzo**
*Piazza Risorgimento 116,
tel. 057523952-3,
www.apt.arezzo.it*
ℹ️ **Agenzia per il Turismo
di Arezzo**
*Piazza della Repubblica
28, tel. 0575377678,
www.apt.arezzo.it*

How to get there

BY TRAIN: La Ferroviaria
Italiana Railway Station via
G. Monaco 37,
tel. 057539881

BY CAR: exit Arezzo, A1
motorway Milano-Roma-
Napoli

BY TRAIN: FS Railway
Station piazza della
Repubblica 1

Hotels

Piero della Francesca ★★★ ♿
*Via Adrigrat 1, corner via
Romana, tel. 0575901333
www.hotelpierodellafrancesca.it*
40 rooms. Restaurant, parking,
air conditioned
Credit Cards: American Express,
Diner's Club, Mastercard, Visa
In modern five-floor building,
sound-proofed rooms and
several suites; good "129"
restaurant; experienced family
management.

Cavaliere Palace Hotel ★★★ ♿
*Via Madonna del Prato 83,
tel. 0575726836
www.cavalierehotels.com*
27 rooms. Restaurant
Credit Cards: American
Express, Diner's Club,
Mastercard, Visa
In the historic center, former
boarding house converted to
modern hotel, well-furnished
rooms; buffet breakfast.

Etrusco Palace Hotel ★★★ ★
*Via Fleming 39, tel. 0575984067
www.etruscohotel.it*
80 rooms. Restaurant, parking,
air conditioned
Credit Cards: American Express,
Diner's Club, Mastercard, Visa
Modern, five-floor building, air-
conditioning, and well-furnished
rooms; restaurant with Tuscan
cuisine.

Minerva ★★★ ♿ ★
*Via Fiorentina 4,
tel. 0575370390
www.hotel-minerva.it*
132 rooms. Restaurant, parking,
air conditioned
Credit Cards: American Express,
Diner's Club, Visa
Attractive rooms on six floors,
several comfortable suites;
lounges with internet point.
Professional management, polite
staff.

Patio ★★★
*Via Cavour 23, tel. 0575401962
www.hotelpatio.it*
7 rooms. Restaurant, air
conditioned
Credit Cards: American Express,
Diner's Club, Mastercard, Visa
In the historic center, with
attractive rooms and suites
inspired by Bruce Chatwin's
travels, with authentic objects
from China, India, Australia and
Africa.

Rural Lodgings

Badia Ficarolo ★
*Badia Ficarolo, tel. 0575369254
www.badiaficarolo.com*
Swimming pool
On a hill with a view,
surrounded by woods,
independent apartments in
stone farmhouse.

Barone Albergotti ★
*Ceciliano 78, tel. 057520978
www.villaalbergotti.com*
Restaurant
Farm-stay in renovated
farmhouses, around a wonderful
mid 16th-century villa.

Magnanini Massimo ★
*Via Fontebranda 47,
tel. 057527627
www.retetoscana.it*
Restaurant
At the foot of the Poti Alps, old
farmstead, with terracotta floors
and original, wooden beams.

Villa Cilnia
*Bagnoro, via Montoncello 27,
tel. 0575365017*

www.villacilnia.com
Restaurant, swimming pool, availability of bikes
Credit Cards: American Express, Diner's, Visa, Mastercard
In renovated 14th-century villa; comfortable and cosy rooms, breakfast with local specialities, swimming pool, lake for fishing, horse-riding.

Bed & Breakfast
Le Bilodole ★
Cincelli, via di Cincelli 11/A, tel. 0575364655
www.bilodole.it
In 18th-century country house, eight rooms in rural Tuscan style. Swimming pool, dinner available on request, bus to town center nearby.

Restaurants
Antica Trattoria al Principe ⫪ ⌖
Giovi, piazza Giovi 25, tel. 0575362046
Closed Monday
Cuisine: Tuscan
Credit Cards: American Express, Diner's Club, Mastercard, Visa
Charming atmosphere, with lacunar ceilings and period furnishings. Local cuisine, with meat, mushrooms and fresh fish; good wine cellar.

Buca di San Francesco ⫪
Via S. Francesco 1, tel. 057523271
www.bucadisanfrancesco.it
Closed Monday evening and Tuesday
Cuisine: Tuscan
Credit Cards: American Express, Diner's Club, Visa
Interior lined with wood and frescoes with 14th-century motifs; natural, simple, tasty food; specialities include finocchiona and other local salamis.

La Lancia d'Oro ⫪ ⌖
Piazza Grande 18-19, tel. 057521033
www.loggevasari.it
Closed Monday, Sunday evening
Cuisine: Tuscan and traditional
Credit Cards: American Express, Diner's Club, Mastercard, Visa
Historic premises with well-served outdoor tables. Especially good: chicken carpaccio, spelt lasagne, stuffed baby pheasant; excellent wine list.

Logge Vasari ⫪
Via Vasari 19, tel. 0575295894
www.loggevasari.it
Closed Tuesday, Wednesday at lunch

Cuisine: creative Tuscan
Credit Cards: American Express, Diner's Club, Mastercard, Visa
Great ambience, in frescoed rooms of 16th-century palazzo; menu full of surprises and original ideas, based on regional cuisine; good choice of desserts.

Antica Osteria l'Agania ⌖
Via Mazzini 10, tel. 0575295381
www.osteriagania.it
Closed Monday
Cuisine: Tuscan
Credit Cards: American Express, Diner's Club, Mastercard, Visa
Osteria with traditional menu (pasta and desserts by the house) and traditional decor; experienced family management.

Saraceno ⌖
Via Mazzini 6, tel. 057527644
www.ilsaraceno.com
Closed Wednesday
Cuisine: Tuscan
Credit Cards: American Express, Diner's Club, Mastercard, Visa
Family trattoria; good quality traditional dishes at good prices; olive oil produced on the owner's farm and good wine selection.

Torre di Gnicche ⌖
Piaggia S. Martino 8, tel. 0575352035
Closed Wednesday
Cuisine: Tuscan
Credit Cards: Mastercard, Visa
Simple but superb, with excellent choice of local wines, salamis and hams, and cheeses, and menu with natural, tasty dishes; excellent value for money.

Trattoria Bruschetteria Toscana ⌖ ⌖ ★
Via di Tolletta 14-20, tel. 0575299860
Closed Tuesday
Cuisine: Tuscan
Credit Cards: American Express, Diner's Club, Mastercard, Visa
Three dining rooms decorated in country style with internal courtyard in the summer; traditional menu, both fish and meat, good homemade desserts, local cheeses, hams and salamis.

At night
Gli Smarriti
Via Cavour 23, tel. 0575324777
www.glismarriti.com
Music and drinks from Wednesday to Sunday.

Grace
Via Madonna del Prato 125, tel. 0575403669
www.grace.it
Stylish disco with modern décor and excellent restaurant: Mediterranean cuisine at weekends.

Museums, Monuments and Churches
Museo Archeologico Nazionale «Gaio Cilnio Mecenate»
Via Margaritone 10, tel. 057520882
Opening times: Monday-Sunday 8.30-19.30. Closed 1 May, Christmas and 6 January.

Museo Statale d'Arte Medievale e Moderna
Via S. Lorentino 8, tel. 0575409050
Opening times: Tuesday-Sunday 8.30-19.00.

S. Francesco - La leggenda della vera croce
Piazza S. Francesco, tel. 0575352727
www.pierodellafrancesca.it
Opening times: November-March: Monday-Friday 9.00-18.00. Aprile-October: Monday-Friday 9.00-19.00. Saturday 9.00-17.30. Sunday 13.00-17.30.

BARBERINO VAL D'ELSA

☑ **Ufficio informazioni turistiche del Comune**
Via Cassia 32/A, tel. 0558075622, www.barberinovaldelsa.net

How to get there
BY CAR: exit Firenze-Certosa, A1 motorway Milano-Roma-Napoli, then exit Tavernelle, highway Firenze-Siena
BY TRAIN: FS Railway Station in Firenze or Poggibonsi; bus connection

Hotels
Primavera ★★ ★
San Filippo a Ponzano, via della Repubblica 27, tel. 0558059223
www.hotelprimavera-chianti.it
27 rooms. Parking
Credit Cards: Mastercard, Visa
In the hills of Chianti, with its vineyards, farms and interesting towns; spacious rooms, balconies with views.

Rural Lodgings
Fattoria Sant'Appiano
Via S. Appiano 11, tel. 0558075541

www.santappiano.it
Restaurant, swimming pool, tennis, availability of bikes
Credit Cards: Diner's Club, Visa, Mastercard
Small, old, Chianti-producing vineyard and farm; apartments in the farmstead, in the small hamlet, and in a renovated barn near the swimming pool.

La Spinosa &
Via Le Masse 8, tel. 0558075413
www.laspinosa.it
Open mid-March to mid-November
Swimming pool, tennis
Credit Cards: Mastercard
Two 17th-century country houses, with nature trails, small lake and botanic garden; large garden with English lawn and recreational activities.

Bed & Breakfast
Il Paretaio ★
San Filippo, strada delle Ginestre 12, tel. 0558059218
www.ilparetaio.it
Eighteenth-century country house, in garden with swimming pool; grapevines, olive trees and woods. Meals also available on request; riding school.

Restaurants
Il Paese dei Campanelli ¶ &
Petrognano 4, tel. 0558075318
www.ilpaesedeicampanelli.it
Open dinner only and lunch on Sunday (lunch and dinner in Summer), closed Sunday
Cuisine: creative
Credit Cards: American Express, Diner's Club, Visa
Thirteenth-century, simple atmopshere; creative menu, from colorful antipasti to desserts, all carefully made by a young couple.

CAMPO NELL'ELBA

How to get there
BY CAR: from Piombino, ferries to the Isola d'Elba getting to Portoferraio or Porto Azzurro or Rio Marina
BY TRAIN: FS Railway Station in Piombino Marittima; ferry; bus connection from Portoferraio

At night
Giannino
Zuffale, tel. 0565978034
Near Marina di Campo airport, in the hills, with peaceful garden and live music. Very popular, for snacks or a plate of spaghetti, until late at night.

Il Tinello
Casina, tel. 0565976645
At the entrance to Marina di Campo, live music, and kitchen open till late.

CAPOLIVERI

How to get there
BY CAR: from Piombino, ferries to the Isola d'Elba getting to Portoferraio or Porto Azzurro or Rio Marina
BY TRAIN: FS Railway Station in Piombino Marittima; ferry; bus connection from Portoferraio

Hotels
Antares ★★★
Lido di Capoliveri, tel. 0565940131
www.elbahotelantares.it
Open May to mid-October
49 rooms. Restaurant, parking, swimming pool, tennis
Credit Cards: Visa
By the sea, white building, with great view of the Isle of Montecristo; well-furnished rooms, with balcony.

Capo Sud ★★★
Lacona, via del Campo Marinaro 311, tel. 0565964021
www.hotelcaposud.it
Open May to September
42 rooms. Restaurant, parking, air conditioned, swimming pool, tennis
Credit Cards: Mastercard, Visa
Bungalows, surrounded by lush greenery, with communal areas and beach; restaurant with Elban and traditional cuisine.

Dino ★★★ ★
Pareti, tel. 0565939103
www.hoteldino.com
Open April to October
30 rooms. Restaurant, parking
Credit Cards: Mastercard, Visa
In natural environment; every room has a terrace with sea view. Restaurant with typical Elba cuisine; family management.

Le Acacie ★★★ &
Naregno, tel. 0565966111
www.acacie.it
Open May to September
78 rooms. Restaurant, parking, swimming pool, tennis
Credit Cards: American Express, Diner's Club, Visa
Mediterranean-style hotel complex, rooms and apartments ideal for families with children; friendly management.

G.H. Elba International ★★★ &
Naregno, via Baia della Fontanella 1, tel. 0565946111
www.elbainternational.it
Open Easter to October
130 rooms. Restaurant, parking, air conditioned, swimming pool, tennis
Credit Cards: American Express, Diner's Club, Mastercard, Visa
In large garden by the sea; pleasantly-furnished rooms and suites. Piano bar in the evening, restaurant with Tuscan and traditional cuisine; two swimming pools.

Rural Lodgings
Bioelba ★
Via Straccoligno 1, tel. 0565939072
www.bioelba.it
Restaurant, availability of bikes
Credit Cards: Visa
In the Parco dell'Archipelago Toscano, organic farm, with independent apartments in uncrowded area of the Elban coast.

Restaurants
Il Chiasso ¶¶ ★
Vicolo N. Sauro 9, tel. 0565968709
Open mid-April to October, dinner only, closed Tuesday (low season only)
Cuisine: Tuscan and national
Credit Cards: American Express, Diner's Club, Mastercard, Visa
Simple style, thirteenth-century building, family management, very professional; local cuisine with good selection of oils.

At night
Sugar Reef
La Trappola, t.3389179026
www.sugar-reef.com
Live music for all tastes: blues, jazz and rock. Latin American evening Tuesday.

CARRARA

🖅 **Ufficio informazioni turistiche del Comune**
Piazza Farini, tel. 0585779707
How to get there
BY CAR: exit Carrara, A12 motorway Genova-Rosignano and Civitavecchia-Roma
BY TRAIN: FS Railway Station Carrara-Avenza; bus connection

TEXTILES MUSEUM

Since medieval times, the Prato area has been famed for textiles manufacturing and wool cloth production. Today Prato is one of Europe's most important industrial districts for textiles, both in terms of the number of companies operating there and the number of people employed by the industry, which has an annual turnover of over €5bn.

So the Museo del Tessuto (Textiles Museum) in Prato was founded to conserve and nurture the historic and industrial heritage of the city, both past and present. The first nucleus of the museum was established in 1975, thanks to a *corpus* of 14th- to 19th- century textiles donated by a private collector, Loriano Bertini. The collections have increased, and today constitute an extremely important and valuable heritage in international terms. The art of textile manufacture and its various techniques are documented from early-Christian times up to the present day, for a total of around 6000 exhibits. The museum also includes a library; a collection of small, 19th-century, fashion mannequins; textile machinery; exhibits illustrating the chemistry of dyeing; and weaving equipment from various periods.

via S. Chiara 24
Tel. 0574611503
Fax. 0574444585
www.museodeltessuto.it
info@museodeltessuto.it

Hotels

Michelangelo ★★★
Corso F.lli Rosselli 3,
tel. 0585777161
www.rivieratoscana.com
30 rooms.
Credit Cards: American Express, Diner's Club, Visa
In the old town; rooms furnished with period furniture in various styles, very welcoming.

Bed & Breakfast

Mauro e Luisa B&B ★
Avenza, via Cavaiola 29,
tel. 058555975-3388635953
A few kilometers from the renowned marble quarries, small independent cottage with fireplace. Generous breakfast with local products; bicycles available.

Restaurants

Enoteca Ninan ￥￥￥
Via Bartolini 3, tel. 058574741
Closed Sunday
Cuisine: Tuscan
Credit Cards: American Express, Diner's Club, Mastercard, Visa
Small, cosy restaurant, a good idea to book; local cuisine, meat and fish dishes, modern and efficient kitchen.

Venanzio ￥￥
Colonnata, piazza Palestro 3,
tel. 0585758062
Closed Sunday evening and Thursday
Cuisine: Tuscan
Credit Cards: Visa
Absolutely charming, near the quarries, in village famed for its lard; traditional dishes brilliantly modified, courteous service.

Museums, Monuments and Churches

Accademia di Belle Arti
Via Roma 1, tel. 058571658
Opening times: on demand.

Museo Civico del Marmo
Stadio, viale XX Settembre,
tel. 0585845746
www.giove.cnuce.cnr.it/museo.html
Opening times: July-August: Monday-Saturday 10.00-20.00. May, June, September: Monday-Saturday 10.00-18.00. October-April: Monday-Saturday 9.00-17.00. Closed Sunday and holy-days.

CASTELLINA IN CHIANTI

> ✒ **Ufficio turistico comunale**
> *Piazza del Comune 1,*
> *tel. 0577742311*
>
> **How to get there**
> **BY CAR:** exit Poggibonsi, highway Firenze-Siena
> **BY TRAIN:** FS Railway Station in Castellina in Chianti-Monteriggioni; there is no bus connection to the town

Hotels

Belvedere di San Leonino ★★★
San Leonino, tel. 0577740887
www.hotelsanleonino.com
29 rooms. Restaurant, parking, swimming pool
Credit Cards: American Express, Mastercard, Visa
Fifteenth-century country house set among vineyards and olive groves; restaurant with large garden for al fresco dining and swimming pool with a view.

Palazzo Squarcialupi ★★★ ♿
Via Ferruccio 22, tel. 0577741186
www.chiantiandrelax.com
Open mid-March to October
17 rooms. Parking, air conditioned
Credit Cards: Diner's Club
Renovated 15th-century palazzo; rooms equipped with all modern amenities, and excellent family management; buffet breakfast.

Salivolpi ★★★
Via Fiorentina 89,
tel. 0577740484
www.hotelsalivolpi.com
19 rooms. Parking, swimming pool
Credit Cards: American Express, Mastercard, Visa
Traditional 15th-century cottage, rooms with wrought-iron beds; peace and relaxation in very hospitable ambience.

Tenuta di Ricavo ★☆★
Ricavo, tel. 0577740221
www.ricavo.com
Open March to November
22 rooms. Restaurant, parking, air conditioned, swimming pool, gym
Credit Cards: Mastercard, Visa
Attractive and comfortable; carefully-furnished rooms, in elegant country style, and several suites; restaurant with Tuscan as well as other types of cuisine.

Villa Casalecchi ★☆★
Casalecchi 18, tel. 0577740240
www.villacasalecchi.it
19 rooms. Restaurant, parking, air conditioned, swimming pool, tennis

Credit Cards: American Express, Diner's Club, Mastercard, Visa

In park with centuries-old oaks, 19th-century villa with elegant rooms and period furnishings; restaurant with traditional cuisine.

Rural Lodgings

Casavecchia alla Piazza
La Piazza 37, tel. 0577749754
www.buondonno.com
Restaurant

Credit Cards: American Express, Diner's, Visa, Mastercard

In charming village, farmhouse dating from 16th century, when it was owned by Michelangelo's family; excellent Chianti wine and olive oil.

Castello di Fonterutoli
Fonterutoli, via Rossini 5, tel. 0577773571
www.stagionidelchianti.com
Swimming pool

Credit Cards: Visa, Mastercard

Charming hill town in the heart of Chianti; accomodation in tastefully furnished apartments, with loggias and small courtyards.

Restaurants

Al Gallopapa ⚑ &
Via delle Volte 14/16, tel. 0577742939
www.gallopapa.com
Open dinner only, except May to September, closed Thursday
Cuisine: Tuscan

Credit Cards: American Express, Diner's Club, Mastercard, Visa

Attractive premises with charming vaulted stone ceilings; traditional cuisine, creatively prepared.

Albergaccio di Castellina ⚑ &
Via Fiorentina 63, tel. 0577741042
www.albergacciocast.com
Closed Wednesday and Thursday at lunch, Sunday
Cuisine: Tuscan and creative

Credit Cards: Mastercard, Visa

In an old barn, simple, relaxing atmosphere; cuisine with creative touches and seasonal variations; local oils, cheeses, hams and salamis.

Antica Trattoria la Torre ⚑ & ★
Piazza del Comune 15, tel. 0577740236
www.anticatrattorialatorre.com
Closed Friday
Cuisine: Tuscan

Credit Cards: American Express, Diner's Club, Mastercard, Visa

Old trattoria, family managed for over 120 years; local Chianti cuisine, an ancient culinary heritage.

CASTELNUOVO BERARDENGA

☑ **Ufficio turistico comunale**
Via del Chianti 61, tel. 0577355500, www.comune.castelnuovo-berardenga.si.it

How to get there

BY CAR: exit Siena from the highway Firenze-Siena or exit Val di Chiana from the A1 motorway Napoli-Roma-Milano

BY TRAIN: FS Railway Station in Siena; bus connection

Hotels

Posta del Chianti ★★★ & ★
Colonna del Grillo, tel. 0577353000
www.postadelchianti.it
16 rooms. Restaurant, parking

Credit Cards: American Express, Diner's Club, Mastercard, Visa

Old mill; exceptional family management; restaurant with Tuscan cuisine. Guests may use the nearby Rapolano thermal spa, at special prices.

Relais Borgo San Felice ★☆★
San Felice, tel. 05773964
www.borgosanfelice.com
Open April to October
43 rooms. Restaurant, parking, air conditioned, swimming pool, tennis, gym

Credit Cards: American Express, Diner's Club, Mastercard, Visa

Wonderful balance between modern and traditional architecture, in exclusive surroundings; excellent sports facilities for recreation and relaxation.

Villa Arceno ★☆★
San Gusmé, tel. 0577359292
www.relaisvillarceno.com
16 rooms. Restaurant, parking, air conditioned, swimming pool, tennis

Credit Cards: American Express, Diner's Club, Mastercard, Visa

Villa built in 1670 with light, airy rooms, elegant lounges, and swimming pool; buffet breakfast, traditional cuisine.

Rural Lodgings

Casalgallo &
Quercegrossa, via del Chianti Classico 5, tel. 0577328008
www.casalgallo.it
Restaurant, tennis, availability of bikes

Credit Cards: Visa, Mastercard

Farmhouses on two hills either side of the village of Quercegrossa; warm, relaxed atmosphere, vegetable garden and orchard produce available for guests.

Castello di Montalto
Montalto 16, tel. 0577355675
www.montalto.it
Open mid-March to November and Christmas
Restaurant, swimming pool, tennis, availability of bikes

Credit Cards: Visa, Mastercard

Complex including medieval castle and tiny hamlet; refined atmosphere, discrete service attuned to guests' needs.

Fattoria di Selvole
Selvole, tel. 0577322662
www.selvole.com
Open Easter to October
Restaurant, swimming pool, tennis

Credit Cards: Diner's Club

Within the walls of the old castle, the village buildings provide independent and stylish accomodation; small garden equipped with garden furniture.

Podere le Boncie
San Felice, strade delle Boncie 5, tel. 0577359383
Restaurant, swimming pool, tennis

Credit Cards: American Express, Diner's, Visa, Mastercard

Unique accomodation: beautiful and romantic, with relaxed, family atmosphere; excellent Chianti wine; wine-tasting courses organised.

Poderi di Miscianello ★
Ponte a Bozzone, tel. 0577356840
www.miscianello.it
Restaurant, swimming pool, tennis

Comfortable rooms, furnished with style, in a historic home, in the wonderful Chianti countryside.

Bed & Breakfast

Villa di Sotto
Via S. Caterina 30, tel. 0577330220
www.villadisotto.it
Traditional style and modern comfort in the Tuscan countryside. Use of kitchen for most rooms.

Restaurants

Bottega del 30 ⚑
Villa a Sesta, via S. Caterina 2, tel. 0577359226
Open dinner only (in Summer) except Sunday and holydays,

☆☆ ☆☆ ★☆★ ★★★ ★★ ◆ Hotels ⚑⚑⚑ ⚑⚑ ⚑ ⚑ Restaurants & Disabled ★ Special TCI Rates

closed Tuesday and Wednesday

Cuisine: creative Tuscan

Credit Cards: Mastercard, Visa

Charming, with view over the hills and sophisticated Tuscan cuisine; very personal service, excellent pastries, cakes and wine list. Booking recommended.

Poggio Rosso ▦
San Felice, tel. 05773964
www.borgosanfelice.com
Open April to October

Cuisine: Tuscan

Credit Cards: American Express, Diner's Club, Mastercard, Visa

Pleasant restaurant in medieval village; carefully-prepared dishes inspired by regional traditions; good selection of wines.

Castell'in Villa ▦
Castell'in Villa, tel. 0577359356
www.castellinvilla.com
Open dinner only, closed Monday

Cuisine: Tuscan

Credit Cards: Mastercard, Visa

Modern restaurant in charming medieval village; traditional and also creative cuisine, using produce from the restaurant farm.

Del Pellegrino ▦ ♿ ★
Via del Paradiso 1, tel. 0577355282
www.laterradeivini.com
Closed Monday and Tuesday in Winter

Cuisine: modern Tuscan

Credit Cards: American Express, Diner's Club, Mastercard, Visa

Former stables converted into sophisticated country style restaurant; meat and fish dishes, with a large selection of wines; excellent service.

Terre delle Arti ▯ ♿
San Gusmè, piazza dei Rossi 1, tel. 0577358009
Open dinner only, closed Tuesday

Cuisine: Tuscan

Credit Cards: American Express, Mastercard, Visa

Delightful wine bar and restaurant in well-restored palazzo in the historic center; range of hot dishes, and cold dishes, with cheeses, and hams and salamis.

CHIANCIANO TERME

ℹ Agenzia per il Turismo
Piazza Italia 67, tel. 0578671122, www.terresiena.it

How to get there
BY CAR: exit Chiusi-Chianciano T., A1 motorway Milano-Roma-Napoli

BY TRAIN: FS Railway Station in Chiusi; bus connection

Hotels

Ardea ★★★
Via Piave 12, tel. 057863783
Open mid-April to October

28 rooms. Restaurant, parking

Credit Cards: American Express, Diner's Club, Mastercard, Visa

Traditional, close to thermal spas, experienced family management; restaurant with Tuscan and traditional cuisine.

Bellaria ★★★ ★
Via Verdi 57, tel. 057864691
Open Easter to October and New Year's Eve

54 rooms. Restaurant, parking, air conditioned

Credit Cards: American Express, Diner's Club, Visa

Friendly, family hotel; large rooms, many with balconies; restaurant with Tuscan and traditional cuisine.

Irma ★★★ ♿
Viale della Libertà 302, tel. 057863941
Open mid-April to October

72 rooms. Restaurant, parking, air conditioned

Not far from thermal spas, a simple and functional complex; jacuzzi available.

San Paolo ★★★
Via Ingegnoli 22, tel. 057860221
www.evols.it/hsanpaolo
Open March to November

44 rooms. Restaurant, parking

Credit Cards: American Express, Mastercard, Visa

In quiet, central location, recently renovated; lounges, light and airy rooms, freshly redecorated.

Ambasciatori ★★★
Viale della Libertà 512, tel. 057864371
www.barbettihotels.it

115 rooms. Restaurant, parking, air conditioned, swimming pool, tennis, gym

Credit Cards: American Express, Diner's Club, Visa

A few minutes from the thermal spa, rooms with jacuzzi, good sports facilities and three meeting rooms.

G.H. Excelsior ★★★
Via S. Agnese 6, tel. 057864351
www.grandhotelexcelsior.it
Open April to October

75 rooms. Restaurant, parking, air conditioned, swimming pool, sauna, tennis

Credit Cards: American Express, Visa

Excellent facilities and elegant period furnishings; also several suites and a conference center.

G.H. Terme ★★★ ★
Piazza Italia 8, tel. 057863254
www.medeahotels.com

72 rooms. Restaurant, parking, air conditioned, swimming pool, sauna, gym

Credit Cards: American Express, Diner's Club, Mastercard, Visa

Located between the pine grove and main piazza, elegant and comfortable rooms; restaurant with Tuscan cuisine; well-equipped wellness center.

Grand Hotel ★★★ ♿ ★
Piazza Italia 80, tel. 057863333
www.grandhotelchianciano.it

72 rooms. Restaurant, parking, air conditioned, swimming pool, gym

Credit Cards: American Express, Diner's Club, Mastercard, Visa

In centuries-old park, early 20th-century hotel complex, beauty and fitness center, two restaurants and complimentary use of bicycles.

Michelangelo ★★★
Via le Piane 146, tel. 057864004
www.hotel-michelangelo.it
Open Easter, May to mid-October

63 rooms. Restaurant, parking, air conditioned, swimming pool, sauna, tennis

Credit Cards: American Express, Diner's Club, Mastercard, Visa

In a large garden, hotel with renovated rooms, functional bathrooms, goods sports facilities, also for children.

Moderno ★★★
Viale Baccelli 10, tel. 057863754
www.htlmoderno.com

70 rooms. Restaurant, parking, air conditioned, swimming pool, tennis, gym

Credit Cards: American Express, Diner's Club, Mastercard, Visa

Long-established family business, with good standard of hospitality, in renovated premises; restaurant with traditional cuisine.

Rural Lodgings

Palazzo Bandino &
Palazzo Bandino, via Stiglianesi 3,
tel. 057861199
www.valerianigroup.com
Swimming pool
Credit Cards: Visa, Mastercard
Sophisticated accomodation in
17th-century farmhouse; hotel-
standard amenities, for an
extremely comfortable country
holiday.

Museums, Monuments and Churches

Museo Civico delle Acque
Via Dante, tel. 057830471
www.musei.provincia.siena.it
Opening times: April-October:
Tuesday-Sunday 10.00-13.00,
17.00-19.00. November-March:
Saturday, Sunday and holydays
10.00-13.00, 16.00-19.00.

Museo della Collegiata
Via Solferino 38, tel. 057830378
Opening times: April-October:
Tuesday-Sunday 10.00-12.00,
16.00-19.00. November-March:
on demand.

CHIUSI

☑ Pro loco
Piazza Duomo 1,
tel. 0578227667

How to get there
BY CAR: exit Chiusi-
Chianciano T., A1
motorway Milano-Roma-
Napoli
BY TRAIN: FS Railway
Station in Chiusi Stazione;
bus connection

Hotels

La Fattoria ★★★ ★
Paccianese, tel. 057821407
www.la-fattoria.it
8 rooms. Restaurant, parking,
air conditioned
Credit Cards: American
Express, Diner's Club,
Mastercard, Visa
Very old farmhouse with terrace
overlooking lake; comfortable
rooms and restaurant with local
specialities; horse-riding,
mountain bike hire and vintage
car hire.

Villa il Patriarca ★★★ &
Querce al Pino, S.S. 146,
tel. 0578274407
www.ilpatriarca.it
24 rooms. Restaurant, parking,
air conditioned, swimming pool
Credit Cards: American Express,
Diner's Club, Mastercard, Visa
In garden, early 19th-century
villa with rooms differing in type
and style; business meeting
room; buffet breakfast.

Bed & Breakfast

Casa Toscana ★
Via Baldetti 37, tel. 0578222227
www.valerianigroup.com/casat
Elegant, in the center of Chiusi,
in late 18th-century palazzo;
lovely terrace for breakfast.

Restaurants

I Salotti di Villa il Patriarca ﬀﬀﬀ &
Querce al Pino, S.S. 146,
tel. 0578274407
www.ilpatriarca.it
Closed Monday
Cuisine: innovative Tuscan
Credit Cards: American
Express, Diner's Club,
Mastercard, Visa
Elegant, romantic restaurant,
and polite, professional service;
sophisticated menu, both meat
and fish; excellent choice of
wines, spirits and oils.

Zaira ﬀﬀ
Via Arunte 12, tel. 057820260
www.zaira.it
Closed Monday in Winter
(except holydays)
Cuisine: Tuscan
Credit Cards: American
Express, Diner's Club,
Mastercard, Visa
Old traditional restaurant, in
medieval palazzo; good local
menu; well-stocked wine cellar,
dug out of tufa.

Osteria la Solita Zuppa ﬀ
Via Porsenna 21, tel. 057821006
www.lasolitazuppa.it
Closed Tuesday
Cuisine: Tuscan
Credit Cards: American
Express, Diner's Club,
Mastercard, Visa
In 17th-century palazzo, warm
atmosphere with brick vaults;
cuisine inspired by ancient
recipes, and seasonal produce.

Museums, Monuments and Churches

Museo Archeologico Nazionale
Via Porsenna 93, tel. 057820177
Opening times: Monday-Sunday
9.00-20.00.

Museo della Cattedrale
Piazza del Duomo 7,
tel. 0578226490
Opening times: June-15 October:
Monday-Sunday 9.30-12.45,
16.00-19.00. 16 October-May:
Monday-Saturday 9.30-12.45;
Sunday 9.30-12.45, 16.00-19.00.

Necropoli Etrusca
tel. 057820177
Opening times: on demand (for
infomation ask Museo
Archeologico Nazionale).

COLLODI

☑ Ufficio turistico comunale
Via B. Pasquinelli 54,
tel. 0583978205

How to get there
BY CAR: exit Chiesina
Uzzanese, A11 motorway
Firenze-Pisa Nord
BY TRAIN: FS Railway
Station in Pescia Stazione;
bus connection

Museums, Monuments and Churches

Parco di Pinocchio
Via S. Gennaro, tel. 0572429342
www.pinocchio.it
Opening times: Monday-Sunday
8.30 till sunset.

Villa Garzoni
Piazza della Vittoria 1,
tel. 0572429590
Opening times: Villa closed.
Garden every day 8 till sunset.

CORTONA

☑ Agenzia per il Turismo di Arezzo
Via Nazionale 42,
tel. 0575630352

How to get there
BY CAR: exit Cortona,
highway Bettole
Val di Chiana-Perugia
BY TRAIN: FS Railway
Station in Camucia; bus
connection

Hotels

Oasi ★★★ &
Via Contesse 1, tel. 0575630354
www.hoteloasi.org
Open April to October
63 rooms. Restaurant, parking
Credit Cards: American Express,
Mastercard, Visa
Thirteenth-century building in
large garden, good for
conferences and business
meetings. Simple "arte povera"
furnishings, local Aretine cuisine.

Portole ★★★ ★
Pòrtole, via Umbro Cortonese 39,
tel. 0575691008
www.portole.it
Open April to November
20 rooms. Restaurant, parking,
tennis
Credit Cards: American Express,
Diner's Club, Mastercard, Visa
Surrounded by nature, combining
comfort with the charm of Tuscan
country architecture; traditional
home cooking, wide choice of
Italian wines.

Relais la Corte dei Papi ★★★ &
Pergo, via La Dogana 12,
tel. 0575614109

www.lacortedeipapi.com

8 rooms. Restaurant, parking, air conditioned, swimming pool

Credit Cards: American Express, Diner's Club, Mastercard, Visa

Renovated 18th-century farmhouse; comfortable, well-equipped rooms and suites; elegant, simply-furnished restaurant and regional cuisine.

Il Falconiere *⋮* &
San Martino a Bocena, tel. 0575612679

www.ilfalconiere.com

19 rooms. Restaurant, parking, air conditioned, swimming pool

Credit Cards: American Express, Mastercard, Visa

In the hills, elegant hotel with classy atmosphere, frescoed walls, original restored furniture, four-poster beds.

Relais Villa Baldelli *⋮* & ★
San Pietro a Cegliolo, tel. 0575612406

www.villabaldelli.it/villabaldelli

15 rooms. Restaurant, parking, air conditioned, swimming pool

Credit Cards: Diner's Club, Mastercard, Visa

Elegant 18th-century villa, with very comfortable rooms; buffet breakfast, golf practice course and swimming pool.

Relais Villa Petrischio *⋮* &
Farneta, via del Petrischio 25, tel. 0575610316

www.villapetrischio.it

18 rooms. Restaurant, parking, air conditioned, swimming pool

Credit Cards: American Express, Diner's Club, Mastercard, Visa

Eighteenth-century villa, antique furniture in rooms; restaurant with regional specialities, and gazebo for lunches and dinners beside the pool.

Villa Marsili *⋮* & ★
Via C. Battisti 13, tel. 0575605252

www.villamarsili.net

27 rooms. Restaurant, parking, air conditioned

Credit Cards: American Express, Visa

Eighteenth-century villa, elegant, private and comfortable; well-designed décor with period furniture. Restaurant with typical Aretine cuisine.

Rural Lodgings
Borgo Elena ★
Cegliolo, via Manzoni 18, tel. 0575604773

Restaurant, swimming pool, tennis, availability of bikes

Small group of country houses converted to farm-stay accomodation, faithfully respecting local building traditions.

Da Domenico &
Via Teverina c.s. 24, tel. 0575616024

www.agriturismodadomenico.com

Swimming pool, tennis

In the Apennines between Umbria and Tuscany; swimming pool, wood oven for bread-making and barbecues.

Fattoria Fabbri &
San Marco in Villa 2, tel. 0575630502

www.fattoriafabbri.com

Restaurant, tennis, availability of bikes

Farm-stay in comfortable apartments, among green vineyards and olive groves; great for outdoor activities or as a base for cultural excursions.

Fattoria le Giare ★
Fratticciola, via Ronzano 14, tel. 0575638063

www.fattorialegiare.com

Restaurant, swimming pool, tennis, availability of bikes

Old country house in peaceful position with view, a great base for many Tuscan and Umbrian tourist spots.

I Pagliai & ★
Montalla 23, tel. 0575605220

www.ipagliai.it

Restaurant, swimming pool, tennis, availability of bikes

Credit Cards: Visa, Mastercard

Two independent cottages in the green hills of Cortona; whole roasted pig or "bistecca alla fiorentina" on request, with wines produced on the farm.

La Renaia & ★
Case Sparse 760, tel. 057562787

www.larenaia.it

Restaurant, swimming pool, tennis, availability of bikes

Country house with watermill; spacious rooms, lovely atmosphere. Great view and good leisure facilities.

Rosa dei Venti
Creti, via Quaratola 71, tel. 0575638085

www.rosadeiventi.net

Restaurant, swimming pool, tennis, availability of bikes

On a hill in the Valdichiana; apartments in 18th-century farmhouse or in charming independent cottages.

Bed & Breakfast
Casa Bellavista B&B ★
Creti, tel. 0575610311

www.casabellavista.it

In 19th-century country house, surrounded by large garden and olive grove. Swimming pool and

mountain bikes for excursions in the area.

Il Borgo
Camucia, via di Manzano 1001, tel. 0575 601165

www.agriturismoilborgo.com

Four apartments in the countryside, with private garden. Continental breakfast; mountain-bike excursions and wine-cellar visits organised.

Restaurants
Il Falconiere ⅲ
San Martino a Bocena, tel. 0575612679

www.ilfalconiere.com

Closed Monday (in Winter), Tuesday at lunch

Cuisine: Tuscan and creative

Credit Cards: American Express, Mastercard, Visa

In green and peaceful countryside, excellent service; good fish and meat dishes; large choice of wines and spirits.

Agrisalotto ⅲ ★
Santa Caterina, via Burcinella 87, tel. 0575617417

www.agrisalotto.it

Closed Monday

Cuisine: creative Tuscan

Credit Cards: American Express, Diner's Club, Mastercard, Visa

Marvellous country relais, with al fresco dining in the summer; cuisine based on carefully combined seasonal ingredients, range of desserts made by the house; excellent wine list.

Osteria del Teatro ⅱ &
Via Maffei 2, tel. 0575630556

www.osteria_del_teatro.it

Closed Wednesday

Cuisine: modern Tuscan

Credit Cards: American Express, Diner's Club, Mastercard, Visa

Interesting osteria, two dining rooms with walls covered by photos of well-known actors; traditional cuisine, with some excellent innovations.

Preludio ⅱ & ★
Via Guelfa 11, tel. 0575630104

www.ilpreludio.net

Open dinner only, except in Summer, closed Monday (in Winter)

Cuisine: Tuscan

Credit Cards: American Express, Diner's Club, Mastercard, Visa

Charming atmosphere in the old town center, both traditional and creative cuisine; full range of wines and spirits, good selection of oils, hams and salamis, and cheeses.

La Grotta ⅰ
Piazzetta Baldelli 3, tel. 0575630271

Closed Tuesday
Cuisine: Tuscan
Credit Cards: American Express, Diner's Club, Mastercard, Visa
In old 19th-century warehouse, family run, with regional Tuscan cuisine: homemade pasta, grilled steak alla fiorentina, and tagliata.

At night
La Saletta
Via Nazionale 26, tel. 0575603366
Café and wine bar where you can enjoy wine by the glass and local gastronomic specialities.

Museums, Monuments and Churches
Madonna del Calcinaio
Cinque Vie, tel. 0575604830
Opening times: 15.30-19, groups on demand.

Museo dell'Accademia Etrusca
Piazza Signorelli 8, tel. 05756304157
www.accademia-etrusca.org
Opening times: April-October: Tuesday-Sunday 10.00-19.00. (November-March: 10.00-17.00).

Museo Diocesano
Piazza Duomo 1, tel. 057562830-0575603256
www.provincia.arezzo.it/museidentrolemura/diocesano/home.html
Opening times: Summer: 10.00-19.00. Winter: Tuesday-Sunday 10.00-17.00.

Tanella di Pitagora
Cinque Vie, tel. 05756304157
Opening times: On demand (for infomation ask Museo dell'Accademia Etrusca).

ÉMPOLI

🔲 **Associazione turistica Pro Empoli**
Via Giuseppe del Papa 41, tel. 057176115
How to get there
BY CAR: exit Firenze Signa, A1 motorway Milano-Roma-Napoli
BY TRAIN: FS Railway Station via don Minzoni

Hotels
Il Sole ★★★ ★
Piazza Don Minzoni 18, tel. 057173779
12 rooms.
Credit Cards: American Express, Diner's Club, Mastercard, Visa
Attractive early 19th-century building, family management; lovely rooms with terracotta floors and tasteful furnishings.

Restaurants
Cucina Sant'Andrea ⑪ &
Via Salvagnoli 43-47,
tel. 057173657
Closed Monday
Cuisine: Italian
Credit Cards: American Express, Diner's Club, Mastercard, Visa
Variety of fish and meat dishes: everything homemade, from the bread to the chocolates at the end; good wine list.

Café de l'Acadèmia ⑪
Via del Gelsomino 28, tel. 057172185
www.laforesteriadelacademia.it
Closed Sunday
Cuisine: modern Tuscan
Credit Cards: American Express, Diner's Club, Mastercard, Visa
Charming place with inviting menu; good choice of cheeses, and cold cuts.

Museums, Monuments and Churches
Casa di F. Busoni
Piazza della Vittoria 16, tel. 0571711122
www.centrobusoni.org
Opening times: Monday-Friday 10.00-13.00, 16.00-18.00. August closed.

Museo della Collegiata
Piazza della Propositura, tel. 057176284
www.comune.empoli.fi.it/notizie%20home%20page/turismo/ab.html
Opening times: Tuesday-Sunday 9.00-12.00, 16.00-19.00.

FIÈSOLE

🔲 **Agenzia per il Turismo di Firenze**
Via Portigiani 3/5, tel. 055598720-0555978373
How to get there
BY CAR: exit Firenze Sud, A1 motorway Milano-Roma-Napoli
BY TRAIN: FS Railway Station in Florence; bus connection

Hotels
Villa dei Bosconi ★★★ & ★
Via Ferrucci 51, tel. 05559578
www.villadeibosconi.it
21 rooms. Parking, air conditioned
Credit Cards: American Express, Diner's Club, Mastercard, Visa
Villa in the countryside, close to Fiesole; very comfortable rooms (all with internet access). Lovely garden and splendid terrace.

Villa Fiesole ★★★ &
Via Fra' Angelico 35, tel. 055597252
www.villafiesole.it
32 rooms. Restaurant, parking, air conditioned, swimming pool
Credit Cards: American Express,
Diner's Club, Mastercard, Visa
Nineteenth-century villa, with splendid view of Florence; frescoed ceilings and comfortable rooms. Restaurant, large garden, terrace and swimming pool.

Rural Lodgings
Poggio al Sole &
Torre di Buiano, via Torre di Buiano 4, tel. 055548839
www.poggioalsole.net
In the splendid setting of the Florentine hills, interesting farm where saffron is grown; accomodation in two charming country houses.

Bed & Breakfast
Le Cannelle
Via Gramsci 52, tel. 0555978336
www.lecannelle.com
In the heart of Fiesole, completely restructured; five attractive rooms, all furnished differently.

Museums, Monuments and Churches
Area Archeologica
Via Portigiani, tel. 05559477
www.fiesolemusei.it
Opening times: Monday-Sunday 9.30-19.00. (November-march: 9.30-17.00), Tuesday closed.

FLORENCE

🔲 **Agenzia per il Turismo di Firenze**
Amerigo Vespucci Airport, tel. 055315874
Via Cavour 1/r, tel. 055290832-3, www.firenze.turismo.toscana.it
Via Manzoni 16, tel. 05523320, www.firenze.turismo.toscana.it
🔲 **Ufficio informazioni turistiche del Comune**
Borgo S. Croce 29/r, tel. 0552340444
Piazza Stazione 4/A, tel. 055212245
How to get there
BY CAR: exits Firenze Nord, Firenze Signa, Firenze Certosa or Firenze Sud, A1 motorway Milano-Napoli; exits Firenze-Viale Gori, Santa Cristina, Vespucci Airport and Firenze Ovest, A11 motorway Firenze-Pisa
BY TRAIN: FS Railway Station main station: Santa Maria Novella, piazza della Stazione; other stations: Campo di Marte, Rifredi, Cascine
BY AIR: see page 192

★★★ ★★★ ★★★ ★★★ ★★ ★ Hotels   ⑪⑪⑪ ⑪⑪ ⑪ ⑪ Restaurants   & Disabled   ★ Special TCI Rates

Hotels

Casci ** ♿
Via Cavour 13, tel. 055211686
www.hotelcasci.com
25 rooms. Air conditioned
Credit Cards: American Express,
Diner's Club, Mastercard, Visa
In 14th-century building;
recently renovated, air-
conditioned rooms; internet
point, and buffet breakfast.

Centro ** ★
*Via De' Ginori 17,
tel.* 0552302901
www.hotelcentro.net
16 rooms. Air conditioned
Credit Cards: American Express,
Diner's Club, Mastercard, Visa
Restructured Renaissance
building, attractive and
comfortable; buffet breakfast.

Cimabue **
Via B. Lupi 7, tel. 055475601
www.hotelcimabue.it
16 rooms. Air conditioned
Credit Cards: American Express,
Diner's Club, Mastercard, Visa
Late 19th-century palazzo in Art
Nouveau style, well-furnished
rooms, also suited for families;
buffet breakfast and excellent
family management.

Lombardi ** ★
Via Fiume 8, tel. 055283151
www.hotel-lombardi.net
15 rooms. Air conditioned
Credit Cards: American Express,
Diner's Club, Mastercard, Visa
Comfortable, simple and
informal ambience, in early
20th-century renovated building.

Albion *** ★
Via il Prato 22/r, tel. 055214171
www.hotelalbion.it
21 rooms. Air conditioned
Credit Cards: American Express,
Diner's Club, Mastercard, Visa
In early 19th-century palazzo;
comfortable rooms, courteous
management, bicyles for use
free of charge, library and
internet point.

Aprile ***
Via della Scala 6, tel. 055216237
www.hotelaprile.it
35 rooms.
Credit Cards: American Express,
Diner's Club, Mastercard, Visa
Frescoed ceilings, antique
furniture and paintings, peaceful
rooms, and a lovely garden, in an
old, renovated Medici palazzo.

Beacci Tornabuoni ***
*Via Tornabuoni 3,
tel.* 055212645
www.tornabuonihotels.com
28 rooms. Restaurant, air

conditioned
Credit Cards: American Express,
Mastercard, Visa
Elegant Florentine Renaissance
house, rooms furnished with
tapestries and period furniture;
comfortable, with a lovely roof
garden.

Best Western Hotel Capitol ***
★
*Viale Amendola 34,
tel.* 0552343201
www.vivahotels.com
92 rooms. Restaurant, air
conditioned
Credit Cards: American Express,
Diner's Club, Mastercard, Visa
Modern building, with very
spacious rooms particularly
suited to families; internet
point.

Best Western Hotel Fleming ***
♿ ★
*Viale Guidoni 87,
tel.* 0554376773
www.vivahotels.com
118 rooms. Parking, air
conditioned
Credit Cards: American Express,
Diner's Club, Mastercard, Visa
Near the airport, with functional
rooms, and facilities for
business clientèle; buffet
breakfast.

Best Western Hotel Select ***
★
*Via G. Galliano 24,
tel.* 055330342
www.bestwestern.it/select_fi
39 rooms. Parking, air
conditioned
Credit Cards: American Express,
Diner's Club, Mastercard, Visa
In restructured 19th-century
villa; well-furnished rooms,
small room for business
meetings, internet point, elegant
lounges.

Bonifacio *** ♿
*Via Bonifacio Lupi 21,
tel.* 0554627133
www.hotelbonifacio.it
19 rooms. Air conditioned
Credit Cards: American Express,
Diner's Club, Mastercard, Visa
In 19th-century building,
guesthouse with comfortable,
carefully-furnished rooms;
meeting room lined with
bookshelves.

Calzaiuoli ***
Via Calzaiuoli 6, tel. 055212456
www.calzaiuoli.it
45 rooms. Air conditioned
Credit Cards: American
Express, Diner's Club,
Mastercard, Visa
In neo-Classical palazzo,
guesthouse with spacious,

comfortable, carefully-furnished
rooms; buffet breakfast.

Classic ***
*Viale Machiavelli 25,
tel.* 055229351
www.classichotel.it
20 rooms. Parking, air
conditioned
Credit Cards: American Express,
Diner's Club, Mastercard, Visa
Delightful, small, late 19th-
century building, with simple
rooms and period furnishings.

David *** ♿ ★
*Viale Michelangiolo 1,
tel.* 0556811695
www.davidhotel.com
25 rooms. Parking, air
conditioned
Credit Cards: American Express,
Diner's Club, Mastercard, Visa
In late 19th-century villa, with
spacious, indivualised rooms;
pleasant garden with garden
furniture; polite, helpful staff.

Della Signoria ***
*Via delle Terme 1,
tel.* 055214530
www.hoteldellasignoria.com
27 rooms. Air conditioned
Credit Cards: American Express,
Diner's Club, Visa
Long-established hotel between
Piazza della Signoria and Ponte
Vecchio, excellent family
management for over half a
century.

Goldoni ***
*Via Borgo Ognissanti 8,
tel.* 0552284080
www.hotelgoldoni.com
20 rooms. Air conditioned
Credit Cards: American Express,
Diner's Club, Mastercard, Visa
In the antique dealers' street, a
renovated 18th-century palazzo;
peaceful and comfortable; buffet
breakfast.

Hermitage *** ★
*Vicolo Marzio 1, corner piazza
del Pesce, tel.* 055287216
www.hermitagehotel.com
27 rooms. Air conditioned
Credit Cards: Mastercard, Visa
Palazzo in neo-Classical style, with
very comfortable, attractive rooms;
on sixth floor, lovely roof garden
with view of the Ponte Vecchio.

Il Guelfo Bianco *** ♿ ★
Via Cavour 29, tel. 055288330
www.ilguelfobianco.it
29 rooms. Air conditioned
Credit Cards: American Express,
Diner's Club, Mastercard, Visa
Late 16th-century palazzo;
rooms with wood ceilings and
period furniture, small but well-
furnished lounges.

Le Cascine ★★★ ★
Largo F.lli Alinari 15,
tel. 055211066
www.hotellecascine.it
20 rooms. Parking, air conditioned
Credit Cards: American Express,
Diner's Club, Mastercard, Visa
A 19th-century building with
renovated structure and fittings;
attractive, comfortable rooms.

Liana ★★★ ♿
Via Alfieri 18, tel. 055245303
www.hotelliana.com
24 rooms. Parking
Credit Cards: American Express,
Diner's Club, Mastercard, Visa
A good guesthouse, large rooms
with original floors and
functional bathrooms; reserved
parking.

Loggiato dei Serviti ★★★
Piazza della SS. Annunziata 3,
tel. 055289592
www.loggiatodeiservitihotel.it
29 rooms. Air conditioned
Credit Cards: American Express,
Diner's Club, Mastercard, Visa
In 16th-century building; elegant,
classy atmosphere. Rooms
furnished with period furniture,
rugs and four-poster beds.

Malaspina ★★★ ♿ ★
Piazza Indipendenza 24,
tel. 055489869
www.malaspinahotel.it
31 rooms. Air conditioned
Credit Cards: American Express,
Diner's Club, Mastercard, Visa
Old Florentine residence,
modern amenities, areas for
business meetings, internet
point; comfortable rooms, buffet
breakfast.

Morandi alla Crocetta ★★★
Via Laura 50, tel. 0552344747
www.hotelmorandi.it
10 rooms. Air conditioned
Credit Cards: American
Express, Diner's Club,
Mastercard, Visa
Where the 16th-century Crocetta
convent once was; exceptional
atmosphere, and tastefully
furnished rooms.

Orto de' Medici ★★★ ♿
Via S. Gallo 30, tel. 055483427
www.ortodeimedici.it
31 rooms. Air conditioned
Credit Cards: American
Express, Diner's Club,
Mastercard, Visa
Mid 19th-century building,
renovated rooms, spacious
frescoed lounges, and lovely
terrace garden and view.

Palazzo Benci ★★★
Piazza Madonna Aldobrandini 3,
tel. 055213848
www.palazzobenci.com
35 rooms. Air conditioned
Credit Cards: American Express,
Diner's Club, Mastercard, Visa
In Renaissance palazzo,
retaining much of the original
décor and structure; attractive
garden courtyard.

Pitti Palace ★★★
Borgo S. Jacopo 3,
tel. 0552398711
www.vivahotels.com
73 rooms. Air conditioned
Credit Cards: American Express,
Diner's Club, Mastercard, Visa
In the heart of medieval
Florence, modern comfort in
period building, rooms furnished
in modern style and breakfast
room with view.

Porta Faenza ★★★ ♿
Via Faenza 77, tel. 055217975
25 rooms. Air conditioned
Credit Cards: American Express,
Diner's Club, Mastercard, Visa
Eighteenth-century palazzo in
the center, skilfully modernised.
Excellent hospitality.

Relais Uffizi ★★★ ♿
Chiasso de' Baroncelli - chiasso
del Buco 16, tel. 0552676239
www.relaisuffizi.it
10 rooms. Air conditioned
Credit Cards: American Express,
Mastercard, Visa
In 16th-century palazzo,
wonderful atmosphere;
comfortable rooms, delightful
buffet breakfast room with view.

Royal ★★★
Via delle Ruote 52,
tel. 055483287
www.hotelroyalfirenze.it
39 rooms. Parking, air
conditioned
Credit Cards: American Express,
Diner's Club, Mastercard, Visa
In late 18th-century villa,
comfortable, suited both for
business clientèle and tourists
passing through; buffet breakfast.

Villa Liberty ★★★
Viale Michelangiolo 40,
tel. 0556810581
www.hotelvillaliberty.com
18 rooms. Parking, air conditioned
Credit Cards: American Express,
Diner's Club, Mastercard, Visa
Period villa with modern
facilities, retaining the
atmosphere of a lovely home;
buffet breakfast served in the
garden in summer time.

Albani ★★★ ♿
Via Fiume 12, tel. 05526030
www.hotelalbani.it
90 rooms. Restaurant, air
conditioned, sauna, gym
Credit Cards: American Express,
Diner's Club, Mastercard, Visa
Sophisticated, elegant
ambience; rooms furnished in
simple Florentine style; multi-
functional space for meetings,
shows and fashion parades.

Anglo American
Hotel Regina ★★★
Via Garibaldi 9, tel. 055282114
www.framonhotels.com
113 rooms. Restaurant, air
conditioned
Credit Cards: American Express,
Diner's Club, Mastercard, Visa
Nineteenth-century palazzo with
Art Nouveau décor and period
furniture; restaurant with
Mediterranean cuisine and
patio-garden with bar.

Best Western G.H. Adriatico
★★★ ♿ ★
Via M. Finiguerra 9,
tel. 05527931
www.hoteladriatico.it
119 rooms. Restaurant, parking,
air conditioned, gym
Credit Cards: American Express,
Diner's Club, Mastercard, Visa
Near conference centers,
modern; rooms and suites of
various types, comfortable,
quiet, and elegantly-furnished.

Best Western Hotel Rivoli ★★★ ★
Via della Scala 33,
tel. 055278601
www.hotelrivoli.it
65 rooms. Air conditioned,
swimming pool
Credit Cards: American Express,
Diner's Club, Mastercard, Visa
Fifteenth-century, former
Franciscan convent; rooms with
solarium or private terrace,
business meeting rooms, indoor
garden with swimming pool.

Boscolo Hotel Astoria ★★★ ★
Via del Giglio 9,
tel. 0552398095
www.boscolohotels.com
92 rooms. Restaurant, air
conditioned
Credit Cards: American Express,
Diner's Club, Mastercard, Visa
In a 17th-century Baroque
palazzo, efficient hotel with
several luxury suites; restaurant
with Tuscan and Mediterranean
cuisine.

Brunelleschi ★★★ ★
Piazza S. Elisabetta 3,
tel. 05527370
www.hotelbrunelleschi.it
96 rooms. Restaurant, air
conditioned
Credit Cards: American Express,
Diner's Club, Visa
Combining modern amenities
with a unique, historic ambience.

Good rooms, conference hall with internet point.

Croce di Malta *✦*
Via della Scala 7, tel. 055261870
98 rooms. Restaurant, air conditioned, swimming pool
Credit Cards: American Express, Diner's Club, Mastercard, Visa
In an old convent, modern facilities and professional service; buffet breakfast.

G.H. Baglioni *✦*
Piazza Unità Italiana 6,
tel. 05523580
www.hotelbaglioni.it
193 rooms. Restaurant, air conditioned
Credit Cards: American Express, Diner's Club, Mastercard, Visa
In the 19th-century residence of the noble Carrega family, a classical hotel; comfort combined with the charm of bygone days.

G.H. Minerva *✦*
Piazza S. Maria Novella 16,
tel. 05527230
www.grandhotelminerva.com
102 rooms. Restaurant, air conditioned, swimming pool, gym
Credit Cards: American Express, Diner's Club, Mastercard, Visa
Sophisticated and comfortable hotel, excellent facilities and

conference hall; view of Florence from the swimming pool on the terrace.

Gallery Hotel Art *✦*
Vicolo dell'Oro 5, tel. 05527263
www.lungarnohotels.com
74 rooms. Restaurant, air conditioned
Credit Cards: American Express, Diner's Club, Mastercard, Visa
Near the Ponte Vecchio; simple, almost oriental atmosphere. Sushi bar, with Italian, French and Japanese cuisine.

J and J *✦*
Via di Mezzo 20, tel. 05526312
www.jandjhotel.com
20 rooms. Air conditioned
Credit Cards: American Express, Diner's Club, Mastercard, Visa
Former 16th-century convent, peaceful, elegant and comfortable. Air-conditioned rooms, charming suites; buffet breakfast.

Jolly Hotel Carlton *✦* ★
Piazza Vittorio Veneto 4/A,
tel. 0552770
www.jollyhotels.it
152 rooms. Restaurant, air conditioned
Credit Cards: American Express, Diner's Club, Mastercard, Visa

Very special location; completely renovated rooms, internet point, buffet breakfast, restaurant.

Lorenzo il Magnifico *✦* & ★
Via Lorenzo il Magnifico 25,
tel. 0554630878
www.lorenzoilmagnifico.net
29 rooms. Air conditioned
Credit Cards: American Express, Diner's Club, Mastercard, Visa
Nineteenth-century villa in Florence's conference area; comfortable rooms with jacuzzi, meeting rooms and small garden.

Lungarno *✦*
Borgo S. Jacopo 14,
tel. 05527261
www.lungarnohotels.com
73 rooms. Restaurant, air conditioned
Credit Cards: American Express, Diner's Club, Mastercard, Visa
Rooms with views of the Ponte Vecchio, very classy atmosphere and extremely comfortable; also has a contemporary art collection and antique furniture.

Pierre *✦* & ★
Via Lamberti 5, tel. 055216218
www.remarhotels.com
44 rooms. Air conditioned
Credit Cards: American Express, Diner's Club, Mastercard, Visa

RIDE & TREK

Hiking along trails, horseback riding in wild, unspoiled natural scenery, at one with the surrounding environment: these activities enable us to get back to nature and enjoy its beauty. Tuscany has a vast network of signposted trails, which are famed all over Europe: there are both horseback riding and trekking trails, of various lengths, for beginners, enthusiasts and experts.
Trekking and riding trails are found all over the region: you can choose from the wide range of options according to season and your level of fitness.

Riding

Arezzo
Club Ippico Aretino

San Zeno, tel. 057599204
www.gfsarezzo.com

Barberino Val d'Elsa
Il Paretaio
strada delle Ginestre 12,
tel. 0558059218
www.ilparetaio.it

Castelnuovo Berardenga
Centro Ippico della Berardenga
podere Santa Margherita,
tel. 0577355071

Cortona
Centro Ippico Cortonese
Piazzanella 10, tel. 0575601214

Florence
A.C.A La Valle
via dell'Olmatello 25,
tel. 0554250216
www.aca-firenze.it

Grosseto
Associazione Italiana Monte da Lavoro
strada del Pollino 77,
tel. 0564404191
www.meattini.it

Massa
Centro Trekking Monte Brugiana

via Bergiola Maggiore,
tel. 058540840
www.montebrugiana.it

Pisa
Associazione Nazionale Monta Maremmana – ANMM
piazza Martiri della Libertà 23,
tel. 050554039

Pistoia
Centro Equitazione Western Inglese
Spazzavento, via di Groppoli,
tel. 0573913315
www.cewi.it

Sansepolcro
Centro Ippico Violino
Gricignano 99, tel. 0575720174

Siena
Centro di Equitazione Il Ginepreto Trekking
Casciano di Murlo, tel. 0577817779
www.ginepreto.com

Trekking

Prato
Alta Via Trekking
via del Serraglio 90,
tel. 0574606453

A minute's walk from Ponte Vecchio, elegant rooms with parquet floors, and marble in bathrooms, extremely comfortable; buffet breakfast.

Plaza Hotel Lucchesi *‡* ★
Lungarno della Zecca Vecchia 38, tel. 05526236
www.plazalucchesi.it
97 rooms. Restaurant, air conditioned
Credit Cards: American Express, Diner's Club, Mastercard, Visa
Built in 1860 on the banks of the Arno, with attractive, comfortable rooms; restaurant with Tuscan and classical cuisine.

Relais Certosa *‡* ★
Galluzzo, via Colle Ramole 2, tel. 0552047171
www.bettojahotels.it
69 rooms. Restaurant, parking, air conditioned, swimming pool, tennis
Credit Cards: American Express, Diner's Club, Mastercard, Visa
In the old Certosa del Galluzzo (Galluzzo Charterhouse), attractive villa with wonderful garden; charming rooms with great atmosphere, restaurant with classical cuisine.

Sofitel Firenze *‡* ⑂ ★
Via de' Cerretani 10, tel. 0552381301
www.sofitel.com
84 rooms. Restaurant, air conditioned
Credit Cards: American Express, Diner's Club, Mastercard, Visa
Seventeenth-century building, with attractive rooms and comfortable lounges. Tuscan cuisine, and American bar for cocktails or brunch.

Starhotel Michelangelo *‡* ⑂ ★
Viale F.lli Rosselli 2, tel. 0552784
www.starhotels.com
119 rooms. Restaurant, air conditioned
Credit Cards: American Express, Diner's Club, Mastercard, Visa
Modern seven-floor building, wide range of facilities and amenities for business clientèle. Restaurant, wi-fi internet, use of bicycles with no charge.

Starhotel Tuscany *‡* ★
Via di Novoli 59, tel. 055431441
www.starhotels.com
127 rooms. Restaurant, parking, air conditioned
Credit Cards: American Express, Diner's Club, Mastercard, Visa
Not far from the motorway, completely renovated hotel complex.

Torre di Bellosguardo *‡*
Via Roti Michelozzi 2, tel. 0552298145
www.torrebellosguardo.com
16 rooms. Parking, swimming pool
Credit Cards: American Express, Diner's Club, Mastercard, Visa
A 14th-century tower connected to a 16th-century stately home, elegant frescoed reception rooms; rooms and seven suites at prices to be negotiated.

UNA Hotel Vittoria *‡* ⑂ ★
Via Pisana 59, tel. 05522771
www.unahotels.it
84 rooms. Restaurant, air conditioned
Credit Cards: American Express, Diner's Club, Mastercard, Visa
Hotel designed as "theatre of life", creating the perfect atmosphere in all rooms; extremely comfortable.

Villa Carlotta *‡* ⑂ ★
Via Michele di Lando 3, tel. 0552336134
www.hotelvillacarlotta.it
32 rooms. Restaurant, parking, air conditioned
Credit Cards: American Express, Diner's Club, Mastercard, Visa
Late 19th-century Florentine villa, tastefully decorated, with terrace-garden; American bar and restaurant with Tuscan cuisine.

Ville sull'Arno *‡* ⑂ ★
Lungarno C. Colombo 5, tel. 055670971
www.hotelvillesullarno.com
47 rooms. Restaurant, parking, air conditioned, swimming pool
Credit Cards: American Express, Diner's Club, Visa
Eighteenth-century villa, with garden and outdoor swimming pool; modern amenities and facilities; restaurant with Tuscan and classical cuisine.

Rural Lodgings
La Fattoressa
Galluzzo, via Volterrana 58, tel. 0552048418
www.intervos.com/fattoressa
Eighteenth-century country house below the Certosa di Firenze, surrounded by garden, orchard and fields; rooms in renovated barn.

Le Macine
Viuzzo del Pozzetto 1, tel. 0556531089
www.agriturismolemacine.com
Availability of bikes
Seventeenth-century building, tastefully-furnished rooms and independent mini-apartments; landscaped garden, planted with evergreens and flowers.

Bed & Breakfast
Casa Pucci
Via S. Monaca 8, tel. 055216560
www.casapucci.artwork-inform.com
In old 15th-century convent. Large rooms, luxury bed linen, Italian-style breakfast with local cheeses, served in rooms or on patio.

Dei Mori
Via Alighieri 12, tel. 055211438
www.bnb.it/deimori
On second floor of 19th-century building in the historic center; simply-furnished, comfortable rooms.

Quartopiano B&B
Via Panicale 3, tel. 055287975
www.quartopiano.com
In the center of Florence, traditionally furnished in warm colours; breakfast on the terrace with view. Bicycles available.

Relais Grand Tour
Via S. Reparata 21, tel. 055283955
www.florencegrandtour.com
Exceptional 15th-century building, with small private theatre on the ground floor, traditional décor, well-furnished. Breakfast served in rooms, all furnished differently.

Residenza Giulia ★
Via Porte Nuove 19, tel. 055321646
www.residenzagiulia.com
In the center of Florence, on top floor with terrace and view of hills, classically furnished, also some more modern pieces. Breakfast served in rooms.

Soggiorno Michelangelo
Via Frà Bartolomeo 24, tel. 0555048268
www.soggiorno-michelangelo.it
Mid-nineteenth century building with rooms furnished in classical style; wrought-iron beds, telephone, television, and air-conditioning.

Villa le Anatre ★
Via Bolognese 163, tel. 055400777
www.villaleanatre.it
Fifteenth-century villa in beautiful park with centuries-old trees, period furniture in rooms, romantic atmosphere.

Restaurants
Enoteca Pinchiorri ❙❙❙❙❙
Via Ghibellina 87, tel. 055242777
www.enotecapinchiorri.com
Closed Sunday and Monday, Tuesday and Wednesday at lunch
Cuisine: Tuscan and creative
Credit Cards: American Express,

Mastercard, Visa

In beautiful Renaissance palazzo, wine cellar renowned the world over, with many quality and rare wines; international in its organisation, style and clientèle, but thoroughly Italian food.

Relais le Jardin ¶¶¶¶¶
Piazza D'Azeglio 3,
tel. 055245247
www.regency-hotel.com
Cuisine: creative Tuscan
Credit Cards: American Express, Diner's Club, Mastercard, Visa
Elegant restaurant, traditional Tuscan dishes with creative variations.

Alle Murate ¶¶¶
Via Proconsolo 61/r,
tel. 055240618
www.caffeitaliano.it
Open dinner only, closed Monday
Cuisine: creative Tuscan, and Luccan
Credit Cards: American Express, Diner's Club, Mastercard, Visa
Full of charm, with 14th-century frescoes; fresh, Mediterranean menu.

Beccofino ¶¶¶ &
Piazza degli Scarlatti 1/r
(lungarno Guicciardini),
tel. 055290076
Open dinner only, closed Monday
Cuisine: Tuscan and creative
Credit Cards: Mastercard, Visa
Trendy, lively and popular; local, creative cuisine; good choice of cheeses and desserts, and many wines.

Cibreo ¶¶¶ &
Via del Verrocchio 8/r,
tel. 0552341100
Closed Sunday and Monday
Cuisine: Tuscan and traditional
Credit Cards: American Express, Diner's Club, Mastercard, Visa
Not to be missed; simple food with strong, plain tastes and flavours, warm and interesting atmosphere; excellent wine list, good selection of cheeses.

Don Chisciotte ¶¶¶
Via Ridolfi 4/r, tel. 055475430
Closed Sunday, Monday at lunch
Cuisine: creative Tuscan
Credit Cards: American Express, Diner's Club, Mastercard, Visa
Well-known and popular restaurant; elegant ambience and excellent service; good local cuisine, with creative ideas.

Lo Strettoio ¶¶¶ & ★
Serpiolle, via di Serpiolle 7,
tel. 0554250044
www.lostrettoio.com
Open dinner only, closed Sunday and Monday

Cuisine: creative Tuscan
Credit Cards: American Express, Mastercard, Visa
In the hills, in an old 17th-century oil mill, terrace with view over Florence; Tuscan cuisine with imaginative variations, great range of cheeses.

Oliviero ¶¶¶
Via delle Terme 51/r,
tel. 055212421
www.ristorante-oliviero.it
Open dinner only, closed Sunday
Cuisine: creative Tuscan
Credit Cards: American Express, Diner's Club, Mastercard, Visa
Local cuisine, with creative additions, in a classy, historic restaurant; selection of Tuscan goat's cheese and pecorino cheeses; vegetarian menu too.

Onice ¶¶¶ &
Viale Michelangiolo 78,
tel. 055681631
www.villalavedettahotel.com
Closed Monday
Cuisine: creative
Credit Cards: American Express, Diner's Club, Mastercard, Visa
Modern and sophisticated, tables outside with views; creative cuisine, but with an eye on tradition; good choice of wines and cheeses.

Taverna del Bronzino ¶¶¶
Via delle Ruote 25-27/r,
tel. 055495220
Closed Sunday
Cuisine: Italian
Credit Cards: American Express, Diner's Club, Mastercard, Visa
In palazzo dating from the second half of the 16th century, simple and well furnished; menu varies according to season; wide choice of wines, especially Tuscan wines.

Zibibbo ¶¶¶ &
Via del Terzollina 3/r,
tel. 055433383
www.zibibbonline.com
Closed Saturday at lunch and Sunday evening
Cuisine: Italian
Credit Cards: American Express, Diner's Club, Mastercard, Visa
Small dining room for quick lunches, as well as proper restaurant; colorful décor; seasonal dishes, organic vegetables and vegetarian dishes.

Angels Restaurant & Wine Bar ¶¶ ★
Via Proconsolo 29/31,
tel. 0552398762
www.ristoranteangels.it
Cuisine: creative Tuscan
Credit Cards: American Express, Diner's Club, Mastercard, Visa

Traditional wine bar, American bar with background music and excellent drinks, an appealing restaurant with oriental style décor, but local Tuscan cuisine.

Boccanegra ¶¶ &
Via Ghibellina 124/r,
tel. 0552001098
www.boccanegra.com
Closed Sunday
Cuisine: Italian
Credit Cards: American Express, Diner's Club, Mastercard, Visa
In 16th-century building, country style decor; varied cuisine, wide selection of oils and cheeses; new osteria next door with typical Tuscan dishes.

Buca Mario ¶¶
Piazza Ottaviani 16/r,
tel. 055214179
www.bucamario.it
Closed Wednesday at lunch and Thursday
Cuisine: Tuscan
Credit Cards: American Express, Diner's Club, Mastercard, Visa
Typical Florentine "buca" or cellar, in Palazzo Niccolini; don't miss the Tuscan antipasto, ribollita (local soup), grilled meats, and desserts made by the house.

Cammillo ¶¶ ★
Borgo S. Jacopo 57/r,
tel. 055212427
Closed Wednesday
Cuisine: Tuscan and Emilian
Credit Cards: American Express, Diner's Club, Mastercard, Visa
Classical trattoria; tasty, simple traditional dishes (fresh pasta made by the house); mainly Tuscan wine and olive oil produced by the owners.

Coco Lezzone ¶¶
Via Parioncino 26/r,
tel. 055287178
Closed Sunday, Tuesday evening
Cuisine: Tuscan
Dating from the 14th century, with large tables and benches for communal dining; don't miss the local specialities, especially the ribollita, the pappa col pomodoro, and in season, the chestnut cake.

Dino ¶¶ & ★
Via Ghibellina 51/r,
tel. 055241452
www.ristorantedino.it
Closed Monday, Sunday evening
Cuisine: Tuscan
Credit Cards: American Express, Diner's Club, Mastercard, Visa
In a Renaissance building; regional cuisine based on old recipes, such as the "Medici court" salad; good selection of wines.

Enotria ⅋ ⅊ ★
*Via delle Porte Nuove 50,
tel. 055354350*
www.enotriawine.it
Closed Sunday
Cuisine: Tuscan
Credit Cards: American Express,
Diner's Club, Visa
Successful restaurant, with
quick dishes on the lunch menu;
traditional cuisine, sometimes in
diet versions, or with creative
variations; great choice of
wines.

Frescobaldi Wine Bar ⅋ ⅊
*Via de' Magazzini 2-4/r,
tel. 055284724*
www.frescobaldiwinebar.it
Closed Sunday, Monday at lunch
Cuisine: modern Tuscan
Credit Cards: American Express,
Diner's Club, Mastercard, Visa
Wine bar and restaurant for
tasting Frescobaldi wines. In the
restaurant, traditional dishes,
with local ingredients.

I Quattro Amici ⅋ ⅊ ★
*Via degli Orti Oricellari 29,
tel. 055215413*
www.accademiadelgusto.it
Closed Sunday
Cuisine: fish
Credit Cards: American Express,
Diner's Club, Mastercard, Visa
Two beautiful dining rooms in a
period palazzo; many fish
dishes, forest fruits with
yoghurt, wide choice of oils,
wines and spirits.

I' Toscano ⅋ ⅊ ★
Via Guelfa 70/r, tel. 055215475
www.itoscano.it
Closed Tuesday
Cuisine: Tuscan
Credit Cards: American Express,
Diner's Club, Mastercard, Visa
Courteous, relaxed ambience,
newly established, passionate
about Tuscan culinary tradition,
with good wine list.

Il Guscio ⅋ ⅊
Via dell'Orto 49, tel. 055224421
www.il-guscio.it
*Open dinner only, closed
Sunday and Monday*
Cuisine: Tuscan
Credit Cards: American Express,
Diner's Club, Mastercard, Visa
Informal ambience, simple style,
with garden; regional cuisine,
good desserts and excellent
wine selection.

Il Latini ⅋ ⅊
*Via dei Palchetti 6/r,
tel. 055210916*
Closed Monday
Cuisine: Tuscan
Credit Cards: American Express,
Diner's Club, Mastercard, Visa

In Palazzo Rucellai, Tuscan
cuisine by the Latini family,
using produce they have grown
themselves; excellent value for
money.

La Pentola dell'Oro ⅋ ⅊
*Via di Mezzo 24-26/r,
tel. 055241808*
*www.terraditoscana.com/cucina/
alessi*
Closed Sunday
Cuisine: creative Tuscan
Credit Cards: Mastercard, Visa
Decidedly Tuscan décor and
menu, experts on the history of
Tuscan culinary traditions, from
the Etruscans to the Medici.

Mamma Gina ⅋ ★
*Borgo S. Jacopo 37/r,
tel. 0552396009*
www.mammagina.it
Closed Sunday
Cuisine: Tuscan
Credit Cards: American Express,
Diner's Club, Mastercard, Visa
Typical Tuscan trattoria, in 15th-
century palazzo; traditional meat
and fish dishes: ribollita, spelt
soup and zuppa cotta for dessert.

Omero ⅋
*Arcetri, via Pian de' Giullari 11/r,
tel. 0552200053*
www.ristoranteomero.it
Closed Tuesday
Cuisine: Tuscan
Credit Cards: American Express,
Diner's Club, Mastercard, Visa
In the hills, in a very old,
restructured building, verandah
with view; grilled meats and
desserts made by the house,
good choice of wines, cheeses
and cold cuts.

Osteria del Caffè Italiano ⅋
*Via Isola delle Stinche 11-13/r,
tel. 055289368*
www.caffeitaliano.it
Closed Monday
Cuisine: Tuscan
Credit Cards: Mastercard, Visa
In the historic Palazzo Salviati;
traditional cuisine, cold cuts and
food preserved in oil, grilled
meats and good vegetarian
dishes as well.

Posta ⅋ ⅊ ★
*Via de' Lamberti 20/r,
tel. 055212701*
Closed Tuesday (not in Summer)
Cuisine: Tuscan and traditional
Credit Cards: American Express,
Diner's Club, Mastercard, Visa
Central location, traditional, with
covered terrace in summer; fish
and mushroom dishes in
particular.

Skipper ⅋ ⅊
*Via degli Alfani 78/r,
tel. 055284019*

*Closed Saturday at lunch and
Sunday*
Cuisine: Tuscan and traditional
Name, menu and interior
decoration all on the theme of
the sea; try the "pici" with lardo
di Colonnata, and the Chianina
fillet, stuffed with fossa cheese.

Targa Bistrot Fiorentino ⅋ ⅊
*Lungarno Cristoforo Colombo 7,
tel. 055677377*
www.targabistrot.net
Closed Sunday
Cuisine: Tuscan and creative
Credit Cards: American
Express, Diner's Club,
Mastercard, Visa
Trendy and colorful, with wine
bar and romantic verandah
looking on to the Arno; Tuscan
cuisine with creative touches,
wide range of cheeses, wines
and spirits.

Bibe ⅊
*Galluzzo, via delle Bagnese 15,
tel. 0552049085*
www.trattoriabibe.com
*Open dinner only (lunch on
Saturday, Sunday and holydays),
closed Wednesday*
Cuisine: Tuscan
Informal atmosphere, family
managed since the mid 19th-
century; Tuscan home cooking
and strong, decisive flavours; in
summer, tables in the garden.

Boccadama ⅊ ⅋
*Piazza S. Croce 26,
tel. 055243640*
Closed Monday evening
Cuisine: Tuscan and traditional
Credit Cards: American Express,
Diner's Club, Mastercard, Visa
Simple, elegant, country
atmosphere; classical Tuscan
cuisine, with creative variations.
Good choice of wines, oils,
cheeses and local cold cuts.

Del Fagioli ⅊
*Corso dei Tintori 47/r,
tel. 055244285*
Closed Saturday and Sunday
Cuisine: Tuscan
Located between the Arno and
Santa Croce, a typical Tuscan
trattoria with wooden walls and
pictures by local painters; fish
on Friday.

La Carabaccia ⅊
*Via Palazzuolo 190/r,
tel. 055214782*
Closed Sunday, Monday at lunch
Cuisine: Tuscan
Credit Cards: American Express,
Diner's Club, Visa
Near the Orti Oricellari, country
atmosphere, different Tuscan
menu every day; desserts made
by the house.

⌂⌂⌂ ⌂⌂⌂ ⌂⌂ ⌂⌂⌂ ⌂⌂ ★ Hotels   ⅋⅋⅋ ⅋⅋⅋ ⅋⅋ ⅋ ⅊ Restaurants   ⅋ Disabled   ★ Special TCI Rates

Osteria del Cinghiale Bianco †
Borgo S. Jacopo 43/r,
tel. 055215706
www.cinghialebianco.it
Open dinner only (lunch on
Saturday and Sunday), closed
Wednesday
Cuisine: Tuscan
Credit Cards: Mastercard, Visa
In an old tower, country style
décor; family osteria with
traditional range of dishes.

Trattoria del Carmine † &
Piazza del Carmine 18/r,
tel. 055218601
Closed Sunday
Cuisine: Tuscan
Credit Cards: American Express,
Diner's Club, Mastercard, Visa
Typically Tuscan, near the
Brancacci chapel; try the
chicken breast "alla Carmine"
and the hot chocolate custard
cream.

At night

Astor Café
Piazza del Duomo 20r,
tel. 0552399000
The focal point of the café is the
enormous bar under the
skylight; on the lower floor, live
jazz and blues or DJ with latest
music trends. Breakfasts,
aperitifs, and more
sophisticated menus with fish in
the evenings.

Caffè La Torre
Lungarno B. Cellini 65r,
tel. 055680643
www.caffelatorre.it
In the San Niccolò tower, an
icon of Florentine night-life, and
an alternative to a disco
evening; excellent hot baguette
(French bread) sandwiches,
cocktails, and aperitifs, often
with live concerts and music.
Lunch and brunch too.

Caffè Pitti
Piazza Pitti 9, tel. 0552399863
Right in front of Palazzo Pitti,
popular spot with armchairs and
comfortable sofas everywhere.
Live music evenings with blues
singers and jazz pianists. Dinner
à la carte from 7pm to 10pm but
a smaller menu continues till
much later. Fresh pasta dishes
(ravioli with prosciutti and
gorgonzola cheese, gnocchi,
saffron risotto). Also veal
escalopes with lemon sauce or
ceps, fresh fish specialities and
a range of large salads.

Capocaccia
Lungarno Corsini 12-14r,
tel. 055210751
www.capocaccia.com
Close to Ponte Vecchio, colorful,
refined ambience, friendly staff,

and, especially, large buffet with
delicious snacks and creative
cocktails...very popular for
evening aperitifs. Sushimi
Tuesday evening.

Caracol
Via de' Ginori 10/r, tel. 055211427
Mexican specialities and
margarita or tequila based
aperitifs. Latin American
ambience and music.

Dolce Vita
Piazza del Carmine 6/r,
tel. 055284595
Historic and original, the first of
Florence's trendy nightspots. A
successful mixture of disco-bar,
small exhibitions, mini-concerts,
lots of chat and international
cuisine.

Giubbe Rosse
Piazza della Repubblica 13-14/r,
tel. 055212280
Historic literary café where the
Futurist movement began in
1909. Artists and intellectuals
meet here for evening drinks,
talks and seminars. Interesting
exhibitions by contemporary
painters.

Jaragua
Via Erta Canina 12/r,
tel. 0552343600
www.jaragua.it
Latin American music, with free
merengue, chachacha and salsa
courses. No charge for
admission.

Jazz Club
Via Nuova de' Caccini 3,
tel. 0552479700
Important spot for jazz lovers;
special guests Tuesday.

Le Murate
Via dell'Agnolo, tel. 0552399000
In a former women's prison, very
popular for cultural events: jazz,
cinema, and summer shows in
the open air.

Montecarla
Via de' Bardi 62/r,
tel. 0552340259
On Saturday, the city's most
crowded bar. On two levels;
flowers and leopard-skin sofas.

Negroni Florence Bar
Via dei Renai 17/r,
tel. 055243647
www.negronibar.com
Made famous by the film "Amici
miei" (All My Friends), the
premises have been completely
renovated; 60s décor, rooms for
exhibitions and shows. Don't
miss "Aperimundi", happy hour
with a range of international
food and snacks. In summer,
tables outside.

Rex Café
Via Fiesolana 25/r, tel. 0552480331

www.rexcafe.it
Perfect for an aperitif or to
enjoy an after-dinner drink:
impressive décor, especially the
circular bar covered in a large
ocean mosaic, and the gilded
vault. Piped music.

Universale
Via Pisana 77/r, tel. 055221122
www.universalefirenze.it
Multi-functional: one of the
Florence's most popular discos,
a restaurant and two wine bars,
with happy hour and cocktails.
On the stage, at the back,
multimedia entertainment,
cultural events or live concerts.

Museums, Monuments and Churches

Basilica di S. Croce
Piazza S. Croce 16,
tel. 0552466105
www.operadisantacroce.it
Opening times: Working days
9.30-17.30; holy-day 13.00-17.30.

Battistero di S. Giovanni
Piazza del Duomo,
tel. 0552302885
www.operaduomo.firenze.it
Opening times: 12.00-19.00,
Sunday 8.30-14.00.

Biblioteca Medicea Laurenziana
Piazza S. Lorenzo 9,
tel. 055210760-055214443
www.bml.firenze.sbn.it
Opening times: Library: only
researchers with allowance
admitted. Vestibolo and scala di
Michelangelo: Monday-Saturday
8.30-13.30.

Campanile di Giotto
Piazza del Duomo,
tel. 0552302885
www.operaduomo.firenze.it
Opening times: 8.30-19.30.

Cappelle Medicee
Piazza Madonna Aldobrandini 6,
tel. 0552388602
www.sbas.firenze.it/cappellemedicee
Opening times: Tuesday-
Saturday, the 2nd and the 4th
Monday of the month, the 1st,
the 3rd and the 5th Sunday of
the month 8.15-16.50; holy-days
8.15-16.50.

Duomo o Basilica di S. Maria del Fiore
Piazza del Duomo,
tel. 0552302885
www.operaduomo.firenze.it
Opening times: 10.00-17.00,
holidays 13.30-16.45.

Galleria degli Uffizi e Corridoio Vasariano
Piazzale degli Uffizi,
tel. 0552388651-0552388652
www.polomuseale.firenze.it/musei/uffizi

PLAY THE GREEN TUSCANY

Tuscany is a paradise for golfers, with around fifteen certified 18- and 9-hole courses, and numerous promotional and practice courses: the perfect place to try your first shots, train, or compete, on courses set in an extremely wide range of scenery.
Blessed by a temperate climate and rolling countryside, Tuscany is a place where you can play all year round, beside the sea, on hills, even in the mountains, on many different courses suited to the requirements of all kinds of golfers.

Impruneta
Golf Club dell'Ugolino
Grassina, via Chiantigiana 3,
tel. 0552301009
www.golfugolino.it

Lucca
Wine & Golf
via delle Tagliate 124,
tel. 0583490420

Monsummano Terme
Consorzio Golf Toscana
Pievaccia, via dei Brogi,
tel. 0584971002
www.golfing-tuscany.it

Portoferraio
Elba Golf Club dell'Acquabona
Acquabona,
tel. 0565940066

Prato
Golf Club Le Pavoniere
Tavola, via Taverna il Crocifisso,
tel. 0574620855
www.golfclublepavoniere.com

Opening times: Tuesday-Sunday 8.15-18.50. Closed 1 January, 1 May, Christmas. Corridoio Vasariano: May-15 July and September-December: Friday and Saturday guided tours on demand.

Museo dell'Opera di Santa Maria del Fiore
Piazza Duomo 9,
tel. 0552302885
www.operaduomo.firenze.it
Opening times: Monday-Saturday 9.00-19.30 (last admission 18.50); Sunday 9.00-13.40 (last admission 13.00).

Museo di San Marco
Piazza S. Marco 3,
tel. 0552388608
www.sbas.firenze.it/sanmarco/index.html
Opening times: Tuesday-Friday, the 1st, the 3rd and the 5th Monday of the month 8.15-13.50; the 2nd and the 4th Sunday of the month 8.15-19.00; Saturday 8.15-18.50.

Museo Nazionale del Bargello
Via del Proconsolo 4,
tel. 0552388606
www.sbas.firenze.it/bargello/index.html
Opening times: Tuesday-Saturday, the 2nd and the 4th Sunday of every month 8.15-13.50.

Palazzo Pitti - Galleria d'Arte Moderna
Piazza Pitti 1,
tel. 0552388601-0552388616
www.polomuseale.firenze.it/musei/artemoderna/
Opening times: Monday-Saturday 8.15-13.50. Closed the 1st, the 3rd and the 5th Monday of the month; the 2nd and the 4th Sunday of the month; 1 January, 1 May, Christmas.

Palazzo Pitti - Galleria del Costume
Piazza Pitti 1, tel. 0552388617
www.polomuseale.firenze.it/musei/costume/
Opening times: Monday-Sunday 8.15-13.50. Closed the 1st, the 3rd and the 5th Monday of the month; the 2nd and the 4th Sunday of the month, 1 January, 1 May, Christmas.

Palazzo Pitti - Galleria Palatina e Appartamenti Reali
Piazza Pitti 1,
tel. 0552388614-0552388611
www.polomuseale.firenze.it/musei/palatina/
Opening times: Tuesday-Sunday 8.15-18.50. Closed 1 January, 1May, Christmas.

Palazzo Pitti - Giardino di Boboli
Piazza Pitti 1,
tel. 0552298732-0552651838
www.polomuseale.firenze.it/musei/boboli/
Opening times: Monday-Sunday 8.15-16.30. Closed the 1st and the last Monday of the month, 1 January, 1 May, Christmas.

Palazzo Pitti - Museo degli Argenti
Piazza Pitti 1,
tel. 0552388709-0552388761
www.polomuseale.firenze.it/musei/argenti/
Opening times: Monday-Sunday 8.15-16.30.

Palazzo Pitti - Museo delle Carrozze
Piazza Pitti 1, tel. 0552388611
www.polomuseale.firenze.it/musei/carrozze/
Opening times: On demand.

Palazzo Pitti - Museo delle Porcellane
Piazza Pitti 1, tel. 0552388709
www.polomuseale.firenze.it/musei/porcellane/
Opening times: Monday-Sunday 8.15-16.30.

Palazzo Vecchio
Piazza della Signoria,
tel. 0552768465-0552768325
www.comune.firenze.it/servizi_pubblici/arte/musei/a.htm
Opening times: Monday-Sunday 9.00-19.00; Thursday 9.00-14.00. Closed 1 January, Easter, 1 May, 15 August, Christmas.

S. Maria Novella
Piazza S. Maria Novella,
tel. 055215958
Opening times: 9.30-16.30, Friday and Sunday 13.00-16.30.

FOLLÒNICA

ℹ Agenzia per il Turismo della Maremma
Via Roma 51,
tel. 056652012
Pro Follonica
Piazza Sivieri,
tel. 0566263332,
www.prolocofollonica.it

How to get there
BY CAR: exit Rosignano or Civitavecchia Nord, A12 motorway Genova-Rosignano and Civitavecchia-Roma, then S.S. 1
BY TRAIN: FS Railway Station piazza don Minzoni 5

Hotels
Aziza ★★★
Via Italia 142, tel. 056644441
www.hotelaziza.it
Open April to October
20 rooms.
On the seafront; attractive, comfortable rooms; wonderful breakfast served in the garden;

⋕⋕⋖ ⋙⋙ ⋆⋕⋆ ★★★ ★★ ★ Hotels   ▥▥▥ ▥▥ ▥ ▮ ▮ Restaurants   ♿ Disabled   ★ Special TCI Rates

beach and pine grove owned by the hotel.

Parco dei Pini * ★**
Via delle Collacchie 7,
tel. 056653280
www.hotelparcodeipini.it
25 rooms. Restaurant, parking
Credit Cards: American Express, Diner's Club, Mastercard, Visa
In the shade of centuries-old pine trees, a few steps from the sea; lovely rooms, terrace-solarium, restaurant with traditional cuisine.

Parrini * ★**
Lungomare Italia 103,
tel. 056640293
www.hotelparrini.com
Open March to October and Christmas
38 rooms. Restaurant
Credit Cards: American Express, Diner's Club, Mastercard, Visa
On the beach, rooms with balconies; pine grove with games area; restaurant with view, Tuscan cuisine.

Restaurants

Paolino ❙❙ &
Piazza XXV Aprile 34,
tel. 056652342
www.thermopolia.it
Closed Monday
Cuisine: fish
Credit Cards: American Express, Diner's Club, Mastercard, Visa
New, trendy, with sea view; seafood antipasti buffet, fish and seafood menu; also wine bar and caviar house.

Piccolo Mondo ❙❙ ★
Piazza Guerrazzi 2,

tel. 056640361
www.piccolomondoricevimenti.it
Closed Sunday evening and Monday (except July and August)
Cuisine: Italian
Credit Cards: American Express, Diner's Club, Mastercard, Visa
Unusual, built extending over the sea, rooms with sea views; don't miss the antipasti buffet, and house desserts.

Il Veliero ❙
Puntone Vecchio, via delle Collacchie 20, tel. 0566866219
www.ristoranteilveliero.it
Closed Wednesday (low season only)
Cuisine: Tuscan
Credit Cards: American Express, Diner's Club, Mastercard, Visa
Elegant premises, recently renovated; mainly seafood dishes, simple and excellent; good range of wines and spirits.

At night

Chattanooga
Via Litoranea 89, tel. 056643350
Popular American bar with wines and spirits, sandwiches and salads; live music. Saturday happy hour.

Museums, Monuments and Churches

Museo del Ferro e della Ghisa
Ex ILVA factory area, via Bicocchi, tel. 056640762
www.comune.follonica.gr.it/ferro
Opening times: Wednesday, Friday 16.30-19.30; Saturday 10.00-12.30.

FORTE DEI MARMI

> **ℹ Ufficio informazioni turistiche del Comune**
> *Via A. Franceschi 8D,*
> *tel. 058480091*
>
> **How to get there**
> **BY CAR:** exit Versilia, A12 motorway Genova-Rosignano and Civitavecchia-Roma
> **BY TRAIN:** FS Railway Station in Querceta; bus connection

Hotels

Franceschi *
Via XX Settembre 19,
tel. 0584787114
www.hotelfranceschi.com
Open mid-March to October
55 rooms. Restaurant, parking, air conditioned
Credit Cards: American Express, Diner's Club, Visa
Stately home, authentic period furniture; elegant, classy atmosphere, private beach with restaurant, several suites.

Le Pleiadi * ★**
Via M. Civitali 51, tel. 0584881188
www.hotellepleiadi.it
Open April to mid-October
30 rooms. Restaurant, parking, air conditioned
Credit Cards: American Express, Visa
Modern building, with outdoor terrace; light and airy, functional rooms, in large park with pine trees by the sea; classical and Tuscan cuisine.

Mignon * &**
Via Carducci 58, tel. 0584787495

AND OTHER SPORTS

Tuscany provides plenty of opportunities to do other sports, both common and not so common, such as tennis, rafting, and paragliding.

Bike

Gaiole in Chianti
Associazione Parco Ciclistico del Chianti
piazza Ricasoli 50,
www.parcociclisticodelchianti.it

Kayak

Florence
Uisp - Lega Sport d'Acquaviva
via F. Bocchi 32, tel. 0556583501
www.acquaviva.org

Marciana Marina
Sea Kayak Italy
via del Sette 12, t. 3482290711
www.seakayakitaly.com

Paragliding

Capoliveri
Giuseppe Brotto - Residence Itelba
Norsi, tel. 0565940096

Rafting

Florence
Fuorirotta
via A. Corelli 85,
tel. 0554368552

Tennis

Anghiari
Tennis Club Anghiari
via Libbia, tel. 0575788135

Arezzo
Circolo Tennis Arezzo
via Vecchia 15, tel. 0575324838

Forte dei Marmi
Raffaelli Country Club
via Dell'Acqua 78,
tel. 058489167

Grosseto
Circolo Tennis Marina di Grosseto
Marina di Grosseto, via R. Fucini 2, tel. 056435252

Portoferraio
Tennis Club Isola d'Elba
San Giovanni, Strada Provinciale, tel. 0565915366

Prato
Tennis Club Prato
via Firenze 95, tel. 0574591916

www.hotelmignon.it
Open mid-March to October
34 rooms. Restaurant, parking, air conditioned, swimming pool, sauna, gym
Credit Cards: Visa
In a private pine grove, elegant, and with all amenities and comforts. Verandahs for buffet breakfast, restaurant with Tuscan specialities.

Piccolo Hotel ★★★
Viale Morin 24, tel. 0584787433
www.albergopiccolohotel.it
Open Easter to September
32 rooms. Restaurant, parking, air conditioned
Credit Cards: American Express, Mastercard, Visa
By the sea; attractive, renovated hotel, in verdant, residential area; buffet breakfast, restaurant service in summer.

Raffaelli-Villa Angela ★★★ ★
Via Mazzini 64, tel. 0584787472
www.raffaelli.com
44 rooms. Restaurant, parking, swimming pool, tennis, gym
Credit Cards: American Express, Diner's Club, Mastercard, Visa
In 6000 square meters of park and garden, good for families with children; private beach and cottages in the garden; traditional cooking.

Best Western Raffaelli Park Hotel ★★★★ ★
Via Mazzini 37, tel. 0584787294
www.bestwestern.it/raffaelli_lu
28 rooms. Restaurant, parking, swimming pool, tennis, gym
Credit Cards: American Express, Diner's Club, Mastercard, Visa
In large garden, with sports center, private beach and swimming pool. Renovated rooms and lounges looking onto gardens and greenery.

Il Negresco ★★★★ ♿
Lungomare Italico 82, tel. 058478820
www.hotelilnegresco.com
39 rooms. Restaurant, parking, air conditioned, swimming pool
Credit Cards: American Express, Diner's Club, Mastercard, Visa
Small building on the seafront with lovely view and elegant interiors. Rooms with balconies, meeting room, outdoor pool; buffet breakfast.

Ritz Forte dei Marmi ★★★★
Via F. Gioia 2, tel. 0584787531
www.ritzfortedeimarmi.com
32 rooms. Restaurant, parking, swimming pool
Credit Cards: American Express, Diner's Club, Mastercard, Visa
A few steps from the sea, beautiful Art Nouveau villa: good facilities, lovely swimming pool; buffet breakfast.

Restaurants

Barca 🍴🍴🍴 ♿
Viale Italico 3, tel. 058489323
Closed Monday or Tuesday
Cuisine: Tuscan
Credit Cards: American Express, Diner's Club, Mastercard, Visa
Pleasant indoor dining area, and terrace in summer; fish menu with some meat dishes; good range of oils and pecorino cheeses, wines and spirits.

La Magnolia del Byron 🍴🍴🍴
Viale Morin 46, tel. 0584787052
www.hotelbyron.it
Cuisine: Tuscan and traditional
Credit Cards: American Express, Diner's Club, Mastercard, Visa
Two late 19th-century houses with garden, looking onto the sea; sophisticated menu, variety of wines, oils and cheeses.

Lorenzo 🍴🍴🍴 ♿
Via Carducci 61 c/d, tel. 058489671
Closed Monday and at lunch in July and August
Cuisine: creative
Credit Cards: American Express, Diner's Club, Mastercard, Visa
Lively and very popular; superbly delicious food, quality ingredients, fish cooked fresh from the sea.

Gilda 🍴🍴 ♿
Via Arenile 85, tel. 0584752622
Closed Wednesday in Winter
Cuisine: fish
Credit Cards: Mastercard, Visa
By the sea, three extremely pleasant dining rooms, and personalised menus; good range of wines.

At night

La Capannina
Viale Franceschi 12, tel. 058480169
www.lacapanninadifranceschi.it
Historic night-spot in Versilia, popular with show biz and political personalities. Opened 75 years ago, it's still simple and rustic in style, with open wood-beamed ceiling.

Museums, Monuments and Churches

Museo della Satira e della Caricatura
Piazza Garibaldi 1, tel. 0584876277
www.museosatira.it
Opening times: June-September: Tuesday-Sunday 17.00-20.00, 21.00-24.00. October-May: Friday-Sunday and holidays 15.30-19.30.

GAIOLE IN CHIANTI

Ufficio turistico comunale
Via Galilei 11, tel. 0577749411

How to get there

BY CAR: exit Valdarno, A1 motorway Milano-Roma-Napoli
BY TRAIN: FS Railway Station in Montevarchi-Terranuova; bus connection

Hotels

Castello di Spaltenna ★★★★
Pieve di Spaltenna, tel. 0577749483
www.spaltenna.it
37 rooms. Restaurant, parking, swimming pool, sauna, tennis, gym
Credit Cards: American Express, Diner's Club, Visa
Ancient monastery in large garden; sophisticated ambience, comfortable, air-conditioned rooms and suites; meeting room, wine cellar, excellent sports facilities.

L'Ultimo Mulino ★★★★ ♿ ★
La Ripresa dei Vistarenni, tel. 0577738520
www.ultimomulino.it
13 rooms. Restaurant, parking, air conditioned, swimming pool
Credit Cards: American Express, Diner's Club, Mastercard, Visa
Old mill surrounded by nature; charm as well as comfort; buffet breakfast, restaurant with Tuscan cuisine.

Villa la Grotta ★★★★ ♿
Brolio, tel. 0577747125
www.hotelvillalagrotta.it
Open April to November
12 rooms. Restaurant, parking, air conditioned, swimming pool, sauna
Credit Cards: American Express, Diner's Club, Mastercard, Visa
Tenth-century villa with superb view over Chianti; elegant, comfortable rooms, conference room, heated swimming pool, Turkish bath and solarium.

Rural Lodgings

Borgo Casa al Vento ★
Casa al Vento, tel. 0577749068
www.borgocasaalvento.com
Swimming pool, tennis
Credit Cards: American Express, Diner's, Visa, Mastercard
Medieval village, with accomodation in old, original cottages, comfortably furnished; small lake for fishing.

Castello di Tornano ♿
Tornano, tel. 0577746067
www.castelloditornano.it
Swimming pool, tennis

Credit Cards: American Express, Visa, Mastercard

Elegant, romantic rooms and suites, in the castle and the tower; spacious lounges; farm produce.

Restaurants

Della Pieve ⑪
Pieve di Spaltenna,
tel. 0577749483
www.spaltenna.it
Open April to mid-January
Cuisine: Tuscan and traditional
Credit Cards: American Express, Diner's Club, Visa
Elegant restaurant, in the rooms and cloister of an old monastery; traditional menu varying with the seasons.

Badia a Coltibuono ⑪ ⑤ ★
Badia a Coltibuono,
tel. 0577749031
www.coltibuono.com
Closed Monday (except May to October)
Cuisine: Tuscan
Credit Cards: Mastercard, Visa
In a monastery guesthouse, large garden with view, Tuscan recipes with modifications; fresh pasta and house desserts.

La Terrazza ⑪ ⑤
Brolio, tel. 0577747125
www.hotelvillalagrotta.it
Open mid-March to December, closed Monday
Cuisine: Tuscan
Credit Cards: American Express, Diner's Club, Mastercard, Visa
Elegant restaurant, lovely gardens with views; best local wines and fresh fish specialities.

Osteria del Castello ⑪ ⑤
Brolio, tel. 0577747277
www.seamuschef.com
Open March to mid-November, closed Thursday
Cuisine: Tuscan and traditional
Credit Cards: Diner's Club, Mastercard, Visa
Osteria with garden; traditional menu with pasta and desserts made by the house, local fish and meat; good range of wines and spirits.

GREVE IN CHIANTI

🎫 **Ufficio informazioni turistiche**
Via Verrazzano 33, tel. 0558546287-0558546299, www.chiantiechianti.it

How to get there
BY CAR: exit Firenze Sud, A1 motorway Milano-Roma-Napoli
BY TRAIN: FS Railway Station in Firenze Santa Maria Novella; bus connection

Hotels

Villa le Barone ★★★
Panzano, via S. Leolino 19, tel. 055852621
www.villalebarone.it
Open April to October
28 rooms. Restaurant, parking, swimming pool, tennis
Credit Cards: American Express, Mastercard, Visa
Delightful location among vineyards and olive trees; 16th-century stately home, with simple, comfortable, pleasant rooms. Breakfast and typical Tuscan cuisine.

Villa Sangiovese ★★★ ★
Panzano, piazza Bucciarelli 5, tel. 055852461
www.wel.it/Villasangiovese
Open March to mid-December
19 rooms. Restaurant, parking, swimming pool
Credit Cards: Mastercard, Visa
In a country farmhouse, very pleasant accomodation. Tastefully-furnished rooms, restaurant and terrace with view, local cuisine.

Rural Lodgings

Castello di Lamole
Lamole, via di Lamole 82, tel. 055630498
www.castellodilamole.it
Swimming pool, tennis, availability of bikes
Credit Cards: American Express, Diner's Club, Visa, Mastercard
Old-time atmosphere, created with care and attention to detail; walking and mountain bike excursions organised, with expert guide.

Castello Vicchiomaggio
Le Bolle, via Vicchiomaggio 4, tel. 055854078
www.vicchiomaggio.it
Swimming pool, tennis
Credit Cards: Mastercard
Renaissance-style castle; apartments furnished with elegant simplicity; swimming pool with view; wine tasting in wine-cellars.

Fattoria Castello di Verrazzano ★
Greti, tel. 055853211
www.verrazzano.com
Restaurant, tennis
Credit Cards: American Express, Visa, Mastercard
Very special holiday in castle guest rooms, enjoying wonderful Chianti food (wild boar salamis and hams, grills) and great wines.

Fattoria la Sala
La Panca, via di Cintoia Alta 47, tel. 0558547962

www.agriturismolasala.it
Open April to October
Restaurant, swimming pool, tennis
In the Chianti Classico zone, farm-stay where guests can enjoy extremely comfortable apartments, furnished with period furniture, in old building.

Villa Vignamaggio ⑤
Vignamaggio, via Petriolo 5, tel. 055854661
www.vignamaggio.com
Open mid-March to mid-November
Swimming pool, tennis, availability of bikes
Credit Cards: American Express, Diner's Club, Visa, Mastercard
One of the most highly-regarded Chianti Classico wineries; great choice for keeping fit, with two swimming pools, gym, tennis court and billiards room.

Bed & Breakfast

Casale Le Masse
Via Case Sparse 41, tel. 0558547401
www.casalelemasse.it
Country house, in a hamlet dating from 1100, surrounded by vineyards; accomodation in four elegant rooms.

Restaurants

Il Caminetto del Chianti ⑪ ⑤ ★
Strada in Chianti, via delle Montagnola 52, tel. 0558588909
Closed Tuesday, Wednesday at lunch
Cuisine: Tuscan
Credit Cards: Mastercard, Visa
Opened in the sixties; menu varies, and is fairly traditional; good choice of wines, cheeses, and salamis and hams.

Cernacchie ⑪
La Panca, via Cintoia Alta 11, tel. 0558547968
Closed Monday
Cuisine: Tuscan
Credit Cards: American Express, Diner's Club, Mastercard, Visa
Typical out-of-town trattoria, with portico for summer dining; regional dishes and good choice of wines; don't miss the wild boar "in dolce e forte", and Giuliana's desserts.

GROSSETO

🎫 **Agenzia per il Turismo della Maremma**
Viale Monterosa 206, tel. 0564462611, www.lamaremma.info
🎫 **Agenzia per il Turismo della Maremma**
Via Gramsci, tel. 0564462639-0564427858, www.lamaremma.info

Parco Regionale della Maremma
*Alberese, via del Bersagliere 7/9,
tel. 0564407098,
www.parco-maremma.it*

ⓘ **Ufficio informazioni turistiche del Comune**
*Via Colombo 5,
tel. 0564488816-
0564488818,
www.gol.grosseto.it*

How to get there
BY CAR: exit Rosignano or Civitavecchia Nord, A12 motorway Genova-Rosignano and Civitavecchia-Roma, then S.S. 1
BY TRAIN: FS Railway Station piazza Marconi 6

Hotels
Nuova Grosseto ★★★
*Piazza Marconi 26,
tel. 0564414105*
40 rooms. Parking, air conditioned
Credit Cards: American Express, Diner's Club, Visa
Comfortable 1960s guesthouse, just a few minutes from the railway station, with facilities such as internet access.

Sanlorenzo ★★★
Via Piave 22, tel. 056427918
31 rooms.
Credit Cards: American Express, Diner's Club, Mastercard, Visa
Guesthouse in peaceful, quiet area, with comfortable, individualised rooms; internet point; buffet breakfast.

Bastiani Grand Hotel ★★★ ★
*Piazza Gioberti 64,
tel. 056420047
www.hotelbastiani.com*
48 rooms. Air conditioned
Credit Cards: American Express, Diner's Club, Mastercard, Visa
Early 20th-century hotel, a few minutes from historic center; buffet breakfast, roof garden; comfortable; courteous management and staff.

Fattoria la Principina ★★★ ♿ ★
*Principina Terra, via S. Rocco 465,
tel. 056444141
www.italycongress.com*
194 rooms. Restaurant, parking, air conditioned, swimming pool, sauna, tennis, gym
Credit Cards: American Express, Diner's Club, Visa
In the heart of the Maremma, an elegant, comfortable hotel complex with large garden and sports center. Restaurant with Maremma and traditional cuisine.

Rural Lodgings
Giardini di Varrone
*Roselle, strada il Terzo 1,
tel. 0564457422
www.giardinidivarrone.com*
Restaurant, availability of bikes
Twentieth-century farmhouse, converted into two independent dwellings, with garden. The owner is a painter and sculptor.

Il Duchesco
*Alberese, via Vecchia Aurelia 31/A,
tel. 0564407323
www.ilduchesco.it*
Availability of bikes
Typical Maremma farm, well-known for its wines; recreational activities include enjoying beaches and excursions.

La Fata ★
*Alberese, podere Ermada,
tel. 0564407162
www.agriturismolafata.it*
Restaurant, availability of bikes
Modern building, with rooms opening onto porticos or loggias, in the Parco della Maremma, near beaches and the Argentario.

La Pulledraia del Podere Montegrappa ★
*Alberese, via del Molinaccio 10,
tel. 0564407237
www.pulledraia.it*
Open March to October
Availability of bikes
In the Parco della Maremma: enjoy walking in the woods, canoeing on the river, and relaxing on unspoilt beaches.

Lillastro ♿
*Roselle, tel. 0564401171
www.lillastro.com*
Availability of bikes
Ideal for horse-riding enthusiasts, in an area of great natural and archeological interest, near beaches.

Podere Isonzo ♿
*Alberese, via Strada Aurelia Antica 91, tel. 0564405393
www.agriturismo.net/isonzo*
Restaurant, availability of bikes
For the perfect outdoor holiday, cycling on unsealed roads, fishing or canoeing.

Restaurants
Terzo Cerchio ⫪
*Istia d'Ombrone, piazza del Castello 2, tel. 0564409235
Closed Monday (except holydays)*
Cuisine: Tuscan
Credit Cards: American Express, Diner's Club, Mastercard, Visa
In the old Palazzo Pretorio, elegant and simple; local seasonal cuisine; wines

exclusively from the province of Grosseto.

Canapone ⫪
*Piazza Dante 3, tel. 056424546
Closed Sunday*
Cuisine: Tuscan
Credit Cards: American Express, Mastercard, Visa
Long-established, specialised in fish and spit-roast meat; wide selection of oils, cheeses, and hams and salamis; good wine list.

Trattoria Pinzimonio ⫪ ★
*Via Garibaldi 52, tel. 056420625
Open dinner only (October to May; lunch Tuesday-Thursday), closed Sunday*
Cuisine: vegetarian
Credit Cards: Mastercard, Visa
Vegetable menu, varying according to season; private collections of pocket watches and dolls on display; in summer, al fresco dining.

At night
Discoteca Four Roses
*Marina di Grosseto, via Giannutri 3, tel. 056434658
www.fourroses.net*
In an ex-cinema, lively disco with Egyptian décor. Fridays: commercial, house and live music; Saturdays: commercial, hip hop, r'n'b and live music.

Museums, Monuments and Churches
Museo Archeologico e d'Arte della Maremma - Museo d'Arte Sacra della Diocesi di Grosseto
*Piazza Baccarini 3,
tel. 0564488752-0564488750
Opening times: March-April: Tuesday-Sunday 9.30-13.00, 16.30-19.00. May-October: Tuesday-Sunday 10.00-13.00, 17.00-20.00. November-Febbraio: Tuesday-Friday 9.00-13.00; Saturday and Sunday 9.30-13.00, 16.30-19.00. Closed 1 January, 1 May, Christmas.*

Parco della Maremma
*Alberese, via del Bersagliere 7/9,
tel. 0564407098
www.parco-maremma.it*

IMPRUNETA

ⓘ **Ufficio informazioni turistiche Pro Impruneta**
*Piazza Buondelmonti,
tel. 0552313729*

How to get there
BY CAR: exit Firenze-Certosa, A1 motorway Milano-Roma-Napoli
BY TRAIN: FS Railway Station in Firenze; bus connection from Santa Maria Novella

⫪⫪⫪ ⫪⫪⫪ ⫪⫪⫪ ★★★ ★★ ★ Hotels ⫪⫪⫪⫪ ⫪⫪⫪ ⫪⫪ ⫪ ⫪ Restaurants ♿ Disabled ★ Special TCI Rates

Rural Lodgings

Inalbi ♿ ★
Via Terre Bianche 32,
tel. 0552011797
www.inalbi.it
Swimming pool
Credit Cards: American Express,
Visa, Mastercard
Small hamlet converted to farm-
stay: beautiful country house at
the end of an avenue of
cypresses, and various Rural
Lodgings.

Restaurants

Osteria lo Ziro ⊺ ♿
Via Roma 19/21, tel. 0552012232
www.loziro.it
Closed Monday
Cuisine: Tuscan, Luccan and
traditional
Credit Cards: Mastercard, Visa
In nineteenth-century palazzo, a
recently-opened, excellent
osteria; traditional cuisine with
creative and imaginative
variations; good choice of local
wines, oils and cheeses.

Museums, Monuments and Churches

Museo del Tesoro
Piazza Buondelmonti 28,
tel. 0552036408-0552313729
www.chiantimusei.it
*Opening times: April-October:
Wednesday-Friday 10.00-13.00;
Saturday and Sunday 10.00-
13.00, 16.00-19.00. November-
March: Wednesday-Friday 10.00-
13.00; Saturday and Sunday
10.00-13.00, 15.00-18.00.*

ISOLA DEL GIGLIO

ⓘ Pro Loco
Giglio Porto, via Provinciale 9,
tel. 0564809400,
www.isoladelgiglio.biz

How to get there
BY CAR: exit Rosignano or
Civitavecchia Nord, A12
motorway Genova-
Rosignano and
Civitavecchia-Roma, then
S.S. 1 until Orbetello Scalo
then towards Porto S.
Stefano, ferries to the
Isola del Giglio

BY TRAIN: FS Railway
Station in Orbetello Scalo;
bus connection to Porto
Santo Stefano; ferry

BY FERRY: from Porto
Santo Stefano, Maregiglio
and Toremar Ferries

At night

Lombi
Giglio Castello, via Marconi 5,
tel. 0564806001
Disco with outdoor terrace and
sea view. Local wine and food,
in cellar area: simple country
food and Giglio wine.

LA VERNA

Centro visite del Parco Nazionale Delle Foreste Casentinesi
Viale San Francesco 1,
tel. 0575532098,
www.parcoforestecasentine
si.it

How to get there
BY CAR: exit Arezzo, A1
motorway Milano-Roma-
Napoli

BY TRAIN: La Ferroviaria
Italiana Railway Station
in Bibbiena,
tel. 0575593471; bus
connection

LIVORNO

ⓘ Agenzia per il Turismo Costa degli Etruschi
Piazza Cavour 6,
tel. 0586204611,
www.costadeglietruschi.it

ⓘ Agenzia per il Turismo Costa degli Etruschi
Stazione Marittima,
tel. 0586895320,
www.costadeglietruschi.it

ⓘ Agenzia per il Turismo Costa degli Etruschi
Piazza del Municipio,
tel. 0586204611,
www.costadeglietruschi.it

ⓘ Ufficio turistico comunale
Piazza del Municipio 1,
tel. 0586820454-
0586820226,
www.comune.livorno.it

How to get there
BY CAR: exit Livorno, A12
motorway Genova-
Rosignano and
Civitavecchia-Roma

BY TRAIN: FS Railway
Station piazza Dante

Hotels

Boston ★★★
Piazza Mazzini 40,
tel. 0586882333
www.bostonh.it
37 rooms. Parking, air
conditioned
Credit Cards: American Express,
Diner's Club, Mastercard, Visa
Near the ferry terminal;
renovated, comfortable, late-
1960s guesthouse.

Gran Duca ★★★ ♿
Piazza Micheli 16,
tel. 0586891024
www.granduca.it
83 rooms. Restaurant, air
conditioned, swimming pool,
sauna, gym
Credit Cards: American Express,
Diner's Club, Mastercard, Visa
By the sea, with view of the
port; attractive and comfortable;
several suites; restaurant with
Tuscan cuisine.

Il Romito ★★★ ★
Calignaia, via del Litorale 274,
tel. 0586580520
15 rooms. Restaurant, parking
Credit Cards: American Express,
Diner's Club, Mastercard, Visa
On sea cliffs; simply-furnished
rooms, all with sea views.
Friendly.

Rural Lodgings

I Cinque Lecci ★
Montenero, via di
Quercianella 168,
tel. 0586578111
www.i5lecci.it
Restaurant
In the hills around Livorno; trails
through Mediterranean
"macchia" vegetation ideal for
horse-riding; sea less than four
kilometers away.

Bed & Breakfast

Villa Eugenia
Montenero, via di Montenero 442,
tel. 0586579077-3387243893
*In old 19th-century villa, two
double rooms with sea views,
antique furniture. Bus for the
town center 300m away, private
car park.*

Restaurants

Ciglieri ⊺⊺⊺ ♿
Via O. Franchini 38,
tel. 0586508194
www.ristoranteciglieri.it
Closed Wednesday
Cuisine: creative
Credit Cards: American Express,
Diner's Club, Mastercard, Visa
Very well designed and
comfortable; excellent food,
using top quality ingredients;
when choosing your wine, be
guided by Alessandro, a real
connoisseur.

Gennarino ⊺⊺ ★
Via S. Fortunata 11,
tel. 0586888093
Closed Wednesday
Cuisine: Tuscan
Credit Cards: American Express,
Diner's Club, Mastercard, Visa
Two lovely dining rooms, informal
atmosphere, traditional cuisine
with both fish and meat dishes.

Il Romito ⊺⊺
Calignaia, via del Litorale 274,
tel. 0586580520
*Closed Wednesday (except in
Summer)*
Cuisine: Tuscan
Credit Cards: American Express,

Diner's Club, Mastercard, Visa
Tables on the terrace in summer,
delightful setting. Traditional
menu: vegetables, fish and
some meat dishes.

La Barcarola ⁙ ⅋ ★
Viale Carducci 39,
tel. 0586402367
www.labarcarola.it
Closed Sunday
Cuisine: Tuscan
Credit Cards: American
Express, Diner's Club,
Mastercard, Visa
In a number of small, attractive
dining rooms; outstanding local
specialities, based on fresh fish;
good range of wines.

Cantina Nardi ⅋ ⅋
Via Cambini Leonardo 6,
tel. 0586808006
Open lunch only, closed Sunday
Cuisine: Tuscan
Credit Cards: American Express,
Mastercard, Visa
Centrally located, attractive and
inviting, with family
management; Tuscan specialities
and good wine selection;
excellent house desserts.

Da Galileo ⅋
Via della Campana,
tel. 0586889009
Closed Sunday evening and
Wednesday
Cuisine: Tuscan
Credit Cards: American
Express, Diner's Club,
Mastercard, Visa
Try not to miss this chance to
experience authentic Livorno
cuisine, mostly fish, at good
prices; many photos signed by
celebrities who have dined
here.

Osteria del Mare ⅋
Via Borgo dei Cappuccini 5,
tel. 0586881027
Closed Thursday
Cuisine: fish
Credit Cards: American
Express, Diner's Club,
Mastercard, Visa
Charming, attractive, sea theme
interior decoration, delicious
fish and seafood dishes; house
desserts also excellent.

At night
La Baracchina Bianca
Piazza S. Jacopo in Acquaviva 18,
tel. 0586807270
A stone's throw from the center,
great view of sea, about thirty
tables outside, great for
aperitifs, dinner and to enjoy
after-dinner drinks.

Museums, Monuments and Churches
Fortezza Vecchia

Darsena Vecchia,
tel. 0586820523
Opening times: On demand,
guided tour.

LUCCA

> ⓘ **Agenzia per il Turismo di Lucca**
> *Piazza S. Maria 35,*
> *tel. 0583919931,*
> *www.luccaturismo.it*
> ⓘ **Centro di accoglienza turistica**
> *Piazzale San Donato,*
> *tel. 0583583150*
>
> **How to get there**
> **BY CAR:** exit Lucca, A11
> motorway Firenze-Pisa Nord
> **BY TRAIN:** FS Railway
> Station piazza Ricasoli

Hotels
La Luna ★★★ ★
Via Fillungo, corner Corte
Compagni 12,
tel. 0583493634
www.hotellaluna.com
29 rooms. Air conditioned
Credit Cards: American
Express, Diner's Club,
Mastercard, Visa
A few steps from Piazza
dell'Anfiteatro; family
management providing
comfortable, pleasant
hospitality; lovely rooms and
lounges.

Piccolo Hotel Puccini ★★★
Via di Poggio 9, tel. 058355421
www.hotelpuccini.com
14 rooms.
Credit Cards: American
Express, Diner's Club,
Mastercard, Visa
Neo-Classical building in historic
center; modern, functional rooms,
for relaxed and informal stay.

San Martino ★★★ ⅋ ★
Via della Dogana 9,
tel. 0583469181
www.albergosanmartino.it
9 rooms. Air conditioned
Credit Cards: American Express,
Diner's Club, Mastercard, Visa
Only a small number of much
sought-after rooms and two
suites, in renovated 17th-century
palazzo in the historic center;
elegant and comfortable.

Best Western G.H. Guinigi ★★★ ⅋ ★
Via Romana 1247, tel. 05834991
www.bestwestern.it/guinigi_lu
158 rooms. Restaurant, parking,
air conditioned, sauna, gym
Credit Cards: American Express,
Diner's Club, Mastercard, Visa
Excellent amenities and facilities
(e.g. the conference center).

Extremely comfortable rooms
and suites, buffet breakfast.

Ilaria ★★★ ⅋
Via del Fosso 26, tel. 058347615
www.hotelilaria.com
41 rooms. Parking, air conditioned
Credit Cards: American Express,
Diner's Club, Mastercard, Visa
In the old center, in historic
premises; extremely
comfortable, excellent service,
terrace, buffet breakfast.

Villa la Principessa ★★★
Massa Pisana, via Nuova
per Pisa 1616,
tel. 0583370037
www.hotelprincipessa.com
41 rooms. Restaurant, parking,
air conditioned, swimming pool
Credit Cards: American Express,
Diner's Club, Mastercard, Visa
Exclusive hotel combining
traditional elegance and modern
comfort; large, well-furnished
rooms, warm ambience in
lounges.

Villa San Michele ★★★ ★
San Michele in Escheto, via
della Chiesa 462,
tel. 0583370276
www.hotelvillasanmichele.it
Open April to October
22 rooms. Parking, air
conditioned
Credit Cards: American Express,
Diner's Club, Mastercard, Visa
Fourteenth-century villa
converted into luxury hotel,
period architecture, classy and
comfortable rooms; independent
apartments in separate building.

Rural Lodgings
Villa Latmiral ⅋
Cerasomma, via di
Cerasomma 615,
tel. 0583510286
www.lumet.it/aziende/carlottagori/
Restaurant
Stately 18th-century villa in the
Pisan hills, plenty of outdoor
areas with garden furniture;
good starting point for lovely
walks.

Bed & Breakfast
Centro Storico
Corte Portici 16,
tel. 0583490748
www.affittacamerecentrostorico.com
In 16th-century palazzo, rooms
furnished in simple, early 19th-
century style. Breakfast served
in rooms.

Da Elisa alle Sette Arti
Via Elisa 25, tel. 0583494539
www.daelisa.com
In the historic center, elegant
rooms furnished in 19th-century
style. Bicycle hire.

★★⅋ ★★★ ★⅋★ ★★★ ★★ ★ Hotels �𝄚𝄚𝄚 𝄚𝄚𝄚 𝄚𝄚 ⅋ ⅋ Restaurants ⅋ Disabled ★ Special TCI Rates

La Cappella

La Cappella, via per Camaiore, tel. 0583394347

www.lacappellalucca.it

Old convent with view on the ancient Via Francigena; home-made cakes, Tuscan hams, salamis and cheese for breakfast.

Villa Alessandra

Via Arsina 1100/B, tel. 0583395171

www.villa-alessandra.it

Eighteenth-century villa in the hills, views, traditionally furnished, garden with olive and fruit trees, gastronomy courses for guests.

Restaurants

Mora ⁴⁴⁴

Ponte a Moriano, via Sesto di Moriano 1748, tel. 0583406402

www.ristorantelamora.it

Closed Wednesday

Cuisine: Luccan

Credit Cards: American Express, Diner's Club, Mastercard, Visa

Well-designed, inviting premises with both modern and period furniture; local cuisine, dishes made with top quality ingredients; oils and wines produced by the house.

Puccini ⁴⁴⁴ ⚹ ★

Corte S. Lorenzo 1/3, tel. 0583316116

Open March to October, closed Tuesday, Wednesday at lunch in high season

Cuisine: creative

Credit Cards: American Express, Diner's Club, Mastercard, Visa

In 15th-century palazzo, modern and comfortable with charming outside area; also tasty nibbles with a selection of cheeses, and wines by the glass.

All'Olivo ⁴⁴ ⚹

Piazza S. Quirico 1, tel. 0583496264

Closed Wednesday (except August to September)

Cuisine: Luccan

Credit Cards: American Express, Diner's Club, Mastercard, Visa

Old osteria with lovely verandah; menu largely consisting of local recipes, and a good wine selection.

Antica Locanda dell'Angelo ⁴⁴

Via Pescheria 21, tel. 0583467711

www.locandadellangelo.it

Closed Sunday evening and Monday

Cuisine: Luccan

Credit Cards: American Express, Diner's Club, Mastercard, Visa

Elegant ambience, excellent cuisine; don't miss the house

pastries and cakes; set lunch menu at good prices.

Antica Locanda di Sesto ⁴⁴ ★

Ponte a Moriano, via Lodovica 1660, tel. 0583578181

www.anticalocandadisesto.it

Closed Saturday

Cuisine: Luccan

Credit Cards: American Express, Diner's Club, Mastercard, Visa

Pleasant and inviting premises; oil, wine, pasta and desserts produced by the house; wide range of cheeses, and local hams and salamis.

Buca di Sant'Antonio ⁴⁴ ⚹ ★

Via della Cervia 3, tel. 058355881

www.lunet.it/aziende/bucadisant antonio

Closed Sunday evening and Monday

Cuisine: Luccan

Credit Cards: American Express, Diner's Club, Visa

Long-established restaurant in great location; local cuisine: rabbit stuffed with cep mushrooms, and, in winter, chestnut-based specialities; good selection of wines.

Del Teatro ⁴⁴ ★

Piazza Napoleone 25, tel. 0583493740

Closed Tuesday

Cuisine: Tuscan and traditional

Credit Cards: American Express, Diner's Club, Mastercard, Visa

Simple sophistication and excellent management; fresh fish and some local specialities; good wine selection.

Locanda Buatino ⁴ ⚹

Via Borgo Giannotti 508, tel. 0583343207

Closed Sunday

Cuisine: Luccan

Credit Cards: Mastercard, Visa

Real local Lucca cuisine (farinata, rovelline in salsa, torta coi becchi) with an amazing range of wines, in splendid 19th-century building.

At night

Caffè di Simo

Via Filungo 58, tel. 0583496234

Famous intellectuals used to meet here, in the late 19th and early 20th century. The café still has its original Art Deco décor, and the elegant charm of those days has also survived intact.

Gelateria Veneta

Via Vittorio Veneto 74/76, tel. 0583467037

Long-established ice-cream parlour, opened in 1927. Excellent artisan ice-cream made the traditional way, and natural ingredients.

Museums, Monuments and Churches

Case dei Guinigi

Via S. Andrea

Opening times: 10.00-17.00, in the evening in Summer only.

Duomo

Piazza Antelminelli, tel. 0583490530

Opening times: 9.30-16.45, Sunday 13.00-16.45.

LUCIGNANO

🅘 **Ufficio turistico comunale**
Piazza del Tribunale 22, tel. 0575838001, www.comune.lucignano.ar.it

How to get there

BY CAR: exit Monte S. Savino or Val di Chiana, A1 Milano-Roma-Napoli

BY TRAIN: La Ferroviaria Italiana Railway Station Fossatone 13, tel. 0575845436

Restaurants

Il Goccino ⁴⁴ ⚹ ★

Via Matteotti 88/90, tel. 0575836707

www.ilgoccino.it

Open dinner only (lunch on Sunday and holy-days), closed Monday (except in Summer)

Cuisine: modern Tuscan

Credit Cards: American Express

Fourteenth-century palazzo; traditional Tuscan cuisine with creative touches and excellent presentation; wine by the glass, selection of mountain cheeses.

Museums, Monuments and Churches

Museo Comunale

Piazza del Tribunale 22, tel. 0575838001-0575838033

www.retemusealearetina.net/luci gnano/index.htm

Opening times: Tuesday, Thursday-Sunday 10.00-13.00, 15.00-18.30. (in Winter 10.00-13.00, 14.30-17.30). Wednesday on request, for groups only. Monday closed.

MARCIANA

How to get there

BY CAR: from Piombino, ferries to the Isola d'Elba getting to Portoferraio or Porto Azzurro or Rio Marina

BY TRAIN: FS Railway Station in Piombino Marittima; ferry; bus connection from Portoferraio

Hotels

Bel Tramonto ★★★
Patresi, tel. 0565908027
www.valverdehotel.it
Open April to October
20 rooms. Parking, swimming pool
Credit Cards: American Express, Mastercard, Visa
Attractively renovated, warm and welcoming, country house; breakfast room with lovely sea view, restaurant close by.

Cernia Isola Botanica ★★★
Sant'Andrea, via S. Gaetano 23, tel. 0565908210
www.hotelcernia.it
Open April to October
27 rooms. Restaurant, parking, swimming pool, tennis
Credit Cards: Mastercard, Visa
Attractive rooms and lounges, buffet breakfast, excellent cuisine and large selection of wines. Relaxed atmosphere.

Da Giacomino ★★★
Sant'Andrea, tel. 0565908010
www.hoteldagiacomino.it
Open April to October
33 rooms. Restaurant, parking, swimming pool, tennis
Credit Cards: Visa
Warm, relaxed atmosphere, on small promontory, with direct access to beach; rooms with sea views, and swimming pool.

Gallo Nero ★★★
Sant'Andrea, tel. 0565908017
www.elbalink.it/hotel/gallonero
Open April to mid-October
29 rooms. Restaurant, parking, air conditioned, swimming pool, tennis
Lovely and lively: central block, and three small, independent houses with small terraces; large garden with direct access to the sea.

Del Golfo ★‡★
Pròcchio, tel. 05659021
www.hoteldelgolfo.it
Open mid-May to September
117 rooms. Restaurant, parking, air conditioned, swimming pool, tennis
Credit Cards: American Express, Diner's Club, Visa
Beach in front and pine grove behind, excellent amenities and facilities. Restaurant with Tuscan cuisine, jetty for small boats.

Rural Lodgings

Casa Fèlici ⚳ ★
Via Costarella 30/32, tel. 0565901297
www.elba-agriturismo.it/casafelici
Restaurant
Among vineyards, comfortable apartments, terraces with sea views, barbecues and parking.

Bed & Breakfast

Relais Valle dei Mulini
Pozzatello, tel. 0565901130
www.valledeimulini.it
Just outside the historic center; comfortable, well-furnished rooms.

Restaurants

Luigi ❙❙ ★
Pòggio, via Lavacchio, tel. 056599413
Open April to October, closed Tuesday (Monday at lunch in high season)
Cuisine: Tuscan
Credit Cards: American Express, Diner's Club, Mastercard, Visa
Appealing, country-style ambience, tasty home-style cooking; local oils, vegetables from the kitchen garden.

Publius ❙⚳ ★
Pòggio, piazza XX Settembre, tel. 056599208
Open mid-March to mid-November, closed Monday (at lunch only in high season)
Cuisine: Tuscan
Credit Cards: American Express, Diner's Club, Mastercard, Visa
Delightful, family management, traditional dishes, and fish dishes; good homemade cakes.

MARCIANA MARINA

How to get there
BY CAR: from Piombino, ferries to the Isola d'Elba getting to Portoferraio or Porto Azzurro or Rio Marina
BY TRAIN: FS Railway Station in Piombino Marittima; ferry; bus connection from Portoferraio

Hotels

Marinella ★★★
Viale Margherita 38, tel. 056599018
www.elbahotelmarinella.it
Open April to September
57 rooms. Restaurant, parking, air conditioned, swimming pool, tennis
Credit Cards: American Express, Mastercard, Visa
Friendly; buffet breakfast with wide range of sweet and savoury foods, cuisine specialising in fish dishes.

Tamerici ★★★ ⚳
Viale A. Moro 10, tel. 056599445
www.tamerici.it
44 rooms. Restaurant, parking, air conditioned, swimming pool, tennis
Credit Cards: Visa

Not far from the delightful seafront; comfortable, elegantly furnished hotel; buffet breakfast; traditional and Elban cuisine.

Gabbiano Azzurro Due ★‡★ ⚳
Viale Amedeo 94, tel. 0565997035
www.hotelgabbianoazzurrodue.it
Open Easter to mid-October
20 rooms. Parking, air conditioned, swimming pool, gym
Credit Cards: American Express, Mastercard, Visa
A few steps from the sea; comfortable and elegant suites, terraces with views and leisure activities.

Bed & Breakfast

Villa dei Limoni
Sant'Andrea, via del Cotoncello 25, tel. 0565908332
In the lovely area of Capo Sant'Andrea, five comfortable rooms.

Restaurants

Capo Nord ❙❙❙ ⚳ ★
La Fenicia 79, tel. 0565996983
Closed Monday (except mid-June to mid-September)
Cuisine: fish
Credit Cards: American Express, Diner's Club, Visa
Terrace with sea view; seasonal menu with specialities from various Italian regions; large choice of wines and oils; brunch.

La Vecchia Marina ❙❙ ⚳
Piazza Vittorio Emanuele 18, tel. 056599405
Cuisine: Italian
Credit Cards: American Express, Mastercard, Visa
Restaurant with romantic terrace; good meat and fish dishes, with fresh pasta and house desserts; Tuscan cheeses and oils.

MARINA DI MASSA

ℹ️ *Agenzia per il Turismo di Massa Carrara*
Lungomare Vespucci 24, tel. 0585240063,
www.aptmassacarrara.it

How to get there
BY CAR: exit Massa, A12 motorway Genova-Rosignano and Civitavecchia-Roma
BY TRAIN: FS Railway Station in Massa Centro; bus connection

Hotels

Cavalieri del Mare ★★★
Ronchi, via Verdi 23, tel. 0585868010

‡‡‡ ‰ ★‡★ ★★★ ★★ ★ Hotels   ❙❙❙❙❙ ❙❙❙❙ ❙❙❙ ❙❙ ❙ Restaurants   ⚳ Disabled   ★ Special TCI Rates

www.cavalieridelmare.com

25 rooms. Restaurant, parking, air conditioned, swimming pool

Credit Cards: American Express, Diner's Club, Mastercard, Visa

Eighteenth-century villa in large garden; rooms equipped with all amenities; charming verandahs; restaurant with Tuscan cuisine; buffet breakfast.

Maremonti *‡*
Ronchi, lungomare di Levante 51, tel. 0585241008

Open mid-May to September

24 rooms. Restaurant, parking, air conditioned, swimming pool, tennis

Credit Cards: American Express, Diner's Club, Mastercard, Visa

Early 20th-century villa, on sea front, with classy, carefully-furnished rooms, sports facilities and gazebo in the garden.

Restaurants
Da Riccà ¶¶ &
Lungomare di Ponente, tel. 0585241070

www.ristorantedaricca.it

Closed Monday

Cuisine: fish

Credit Cards: American Express, Diner's Club, Mastercard, Visa

Elegant, wonderful large window overlooking the water; fish menu, varying with the seasons, wide choice of wines, oils and cheeses.

At night
Modo
Viale Vespucci 10, tel. 0585241488

Lively disco on the seafront.

MASSA

How to get there
BY CAR: exit Massa, A12 motorway Genova-Rosignano and Civitavecchia-Roma
BY TRAIN: FS Railway Station Massa Centro, piazza IV Novembre 32

Restaurants
La Peniche ¶¶ &
Marina di Massa, via Lungobrugiano 3, tel. 0585240117

www.lapeniche.com

Cuisine: fish

Credit Cards: American Express, Diner's Club, Mastercard, Visa

Charming, in country and Parisian style; fish specialities; interesting wine list; also pizzeria.

Passeggero ¶¶
Via Alberica 1 ang. piazza Aranci, tel. 0585489651

Closed Sunday

Cuisine: Tuscan

Credit Cards: American Express, Diner's Club, Mastercard, Visa

In Palazzo Ducale, beautifully vaulted and frescoed, traditional fish and meat dishes.

Ruota ¶
Bergiola Maggiore, via Bergiola Nuova 2, tel. 058542030

Closed Monday (low season)

Cuisine: Tuscan

Credit Cards: American Express, Diner's Club, Mastercard, Visa

Simple atmosphere, experienced family management, with both meat and fish dishes.

At night
Baraonda
Ronchi, via Stradella 547, tel. 0585807245

Famous for its concerts, ranging from jazz to disco music.

Museums, Monuments and Churches
Museo Diocesano
At Palazzo Vescovile, via Alberica, tel. 0585499241

www.chiesacattolica.it/pls/cci_di oc_new/consultazione.mostra_p agina?id_pagina=6402

Opening times: On demand.

Museo Etnologico delle Apuane «Luigi Bonacoscia»
Via Oliveti 85, tel. 0585251330-0585252644

Opening times: Tuesday-Sunday 16.00-19.00. On demand too.

Rocca
Via del Fortino, tel. 058544774

Opening times: Saturday 9.00-12.00, Sunday 15.00-18.00.

MASSA MARITTIMA

ℹ Agenzia per il Turismo della Maremma
Via Todini 3/5, tel. 0566904756-0566902757, www.lamaremma.info

How to get there
BY CAR: exit Rosignano or Civitavecchia Nord, A12 motorway Genova-Rosignano and Civitavecchia-Roma, then S.S. 1
BY TRAIN: FS Railway Station in Follonica; bus connection

Hotels
Duca del Mare *** &
Piazza Alighieri 1/2, tel. 0566902284

www.ducadelmare.it

28 rooms. Restaurant, parking, air conditioned, swimming pool

Credit Cards: American Express, Mastercard, Visa

Simple décor, well-managed, peaceful, in good position with view; outdoor pool with jacuzzi and night lights.

Il Sole ***
Via della Libertà 43, tel. 0566901971

51 rooms.

Credit Cards: American Express, Visa

Guesthouse in renovated medieval building; family management since 1991.

Villa il Tesoro *‡* &
Valpiana, tel. 056692971

www.villailtesoro.com

19 rooms. Restaurant, parking, air conditioned, swimming pool

Credit Cards: American Express, Mastercard, Visa

Romantic 1750 hamlet converted into wonderful farm-stay, tastefully furnished, buffet breakfast, traditional and Mediterranean cuisine.

Rural Lodgings
Podere Riparbella &
Sopra Pian di Mucini, tel. 0566915557

www.riparbella.com

Open mid-March to October and Christmas

Extremely pleasant, organic farm: house overlooking the countryside, creative, light cuisine.

Restaurants
Bracali ¶¶¶ &
Ghirlanda, via di Perolla 2, tel. 0566902318

Closed Monday and Tuesday

Cuisine: creative

Credit Cards: American Express, Diner's Club, Mastercard, Visa

Excellent, family restaurant; superb, creative food; quality wine cellar and wide range of cheeses.

Il Vecchio Borgo ¶¶
Via Norma Parenti 12, tel. 0566903950

Open dinner only, closed Monday (and Sunday evening in low season)

Cuisine: Tuscan

Credit Cards: American Express, Diner's Club, Mastercard, Visa

Typical 14th-century Tuscan cellar with barrel vaults and fireplace; local specialities, grilled meats, mushrooms in season.

MONASTERIES AND CONVENTS

Abbeys, monasteries, convents and sanctuaries are dotted all over Italy's and Tuscany's beautiful countryside, and are usually built in superb locations. They include ancient Benedictine foundations, Franciscan monasteries and Cistercian abbeys, and they have been fundamental to Italian art and culture for over a thousand years of history. Accommodation is available in many of these spiritual places. They provide the perfect solution if you want silence, and if you want to treat yourself to a time of reflection, as well as psychological and physical regeneration.

Asciano

Abbazia di Monte Oliveto Maggiore
Olivetan Benedictine Monks
Località Chiusure Monte Oliveto, tel. 0577707611 (guest rooms 0577707652)
The Abbey, standing on a rise, among cypresses, overlooking the beautiful, natural landscape of the Sienese hills, is the Mother House of the Olivetan Congregation, and an exceptional monument to art as well as a center of Benedictine spirituality

Camaldoli di Poppi

Monastero ed Eremo di Camaldoli
Camaldolite Benedictine Monks
Località Camaldoli 12, tel. 0575556012, 0575556013 (guest rooms), 0575556143 (old pharmacy), www.camaldoli.it
The monastery was founded by St Romuald in the mountains of the Casentino, and preserves an exceptional religious and cultural tradition; it is surrounded today, as in the past, by an impressive forest of fir trees.

Chiusi della Verna

Convento-Santuario de La Verna
Franciscan Friars Minor
tel. 05755341, www.santuariodellaverna.com
Set in the woods of the Casentino, in a landscape of wild, fascinating beauty, the monastery complex has for centuries been a center of Franciscan spirituality, and a place of worship and pilgrimage for all Christians.

Cortona

Monastero della Santissima Trinità
Cistercian Nuns
Via San Niccolò 2, tel. 0575603345
In the heart of mystical Cortona, a community of nuns devoted to the austere Cistercian order; the large guest quarters are open to all those who seek spirituality.

Cortona

Eremo Le Celle
Capuchin Franciscan Friars
Località Le Celle, tel. 0575603362, www.lecelle.it
This atmospheric and intensely spiritual place, on the slopes of Monte Sant'Egidio (Mt St Giles), looking over nearby Cortona, is where St Francis retreated to pray in 1211 and founded the first monastery.

Fiésole

Convento di San Domenico
Dominican Friars
Piazza S. Domenico 3, tel. 0555923o
Half way up the hill to Fiesole from Florence, there is a group of houses, a church and a monastery; San Domenico is a wonderful place of art and spirituality, where Beato Angelico took orders.

Florence

Monastero di Regina Pacis "Villa Linda"
Olivetan Benedictine Nuns
via Poggio Gherardo 5, tel. 055603913
In the lovely, green hills of Fiesole above Florence, just past Coverciano; a location which inspires visitors to spirituality and meditation, and is also well-placed for visiting churches and museums in Florence.

Livorno

Abbazia-Santuario di Montenero
Vallombrosan Benedictine Monks
Località Montenero, tel. 058657771, www.santuariomontenero.org
The sanctuary of Madonna delle Grazie - with its many votive offerings - is the oldest and most famed in Tuscany; it stands high on the Livorno coast between Antignano and Calafuria, looking over the sea and the port

Montalcino

Abbazia di Sant'Antimo
Canons Regular of Sant'Antimo Abbey
Località Sant'Antimo, tel. 0577835659, www.antimo.it
The sight of the abbey is unforgettable, standing alone on a background of meadows, woods and olive trees, on the road from Montalcino to Mont'Amiata - once part of the ancient Via Francigena between Rome and France.

Montecatini Terme

Monastero di Santa Maria a Ripa
Benedictine Nuns
Via Porta di Borgo 36, tel. 0572911588, www.italway.it/benedettine
In countryside which is peaceful and full of atmosphere, near Montecatini Alto in Val di Nievole, a community of nuns has lived in spirituality for almost five centuries.

Reggello

Abbazia di Vallombrosa
Vallombrosan Benedictine Monks
Località Vallombrosa 115, tel. 055862251; 055862074 (guest rooms, summer only), www.vallombrosa.it
Founded shortly after the year 1000 by San Giovanni Gualberto, the austere buildings of the Abbey of Vallombrosa stand out against green fir, beech and chestnut woods, which are assiduously tended by the monks.

San Gimignano

Convento di Sant'Agostino
Augustinian Friars
Piazza Sant'Agostino 10, tel. 0577907012, info.supereva.it/augustyn1/
The monastery and church (with the magnificent fresco cycle by Benozzo Gozzoli on the life of St Augustine) are reached from Porta San Giovanni, through wonderful, unspoilt medieval surroundings.

San Miniato

Convento di San Francesco
Conventual Franciscan Friars
Piazza San Francesco 11, tel. 057143051
High above the Arno Valley and modern development there, San Miniato draws together memories of past times and events related to politics, religion and art, and which the mendicant orders were an important part of.

Sansepolcro

Convento il Paradiso dei Cappuccini
Capuchin Franciscan Friars
Località Paradiso 66, tel. 0575742032
In the hills of Sansepolcro, in landscapes reminiscent of Piero della Francesca's life and art; a new aspect has been added to life at the monastery, which now offers hospitality.

Siena

Monastero della Madonna della Visitazione
Cistercian Nuns
Via Bologna 3, tel. 0577593534
A convent of Cistercian nuns, situated on the outskirts of Siena; a peaceful and quiet place for those who wish to explore St. Catherine's city, just one of many possible itineraries combining art and religion.

Museums, Monuments and Churches

Museo Archeologico e Pinacoteca
At Palazzo del Podestà, piazza Garibaldi 1, tel. 0566902289
www.coopcollinemetallifere.it/musei/index.html
Opening times: April-October: Tuesday-Sunday 10.00-12.30, 15.30-19.00, November-March:10.00-12.30, 15.00-17.00.

Museo della Miniera
Via Corridoni, tel. 0566902289
www.coopcollinemetallifere.it/musei/musei/miniera.html
Opening times: Guided tours only. January-March and November-December: Tuesday-Sunday 10.15-11.15-12-15.30-16.15. April-October: 10.15-11.15-12-15.30-16.15-17-17.45.

Museo di Storia e Arte delle Miniere
Piazza Matteotti, tel. 0566902289
www.coopcollinemetallifere.it/musei/musei/artestoria.html
Opening times: April-October: Tuesday-Sunday 15.00-17.30. November-March: on demand.

MASSACIUCCOLI

How to get there
BY CAR: exit Lucca, A11 motorway Firenze-Pisa Nord
BY TRAIN: FS Railway Station in Viareggio; bus connection

Museums, Monuments and Churches

Museo di Villa Puccini
Torre del Lago Puccini, via Puccini 266, tel. 0584341445
www.giacomopuccini.it
Opening times: June-October: Tuesday-Sunday 10.00-12.30, 15.00-18.30. November-February: 10.00-12.30, 14.30-17.30. March-May: 10.00-12.30, 15.00-18.00.

MONSUMMANO TERME

☑ Ufficio turistico comunale
Piazza 4 Novembre 75/H, tel. 0572959226

How to get there
BY CAR: exit Montecatini, A11 motorway Firenze-Pisa Nord
BY TRAIN: FS Railway Station a Montecatini Terme; bus connection

Rural Lodgings

Podere Saliciaia
Via dei Poderi 1142, tel. 0572617286

www.agriturismopoderesaliciaia.it
Swimming pool, tennis, availability of bikes
In the hills dotted with old villages and hamlets, very pleasant accomodation in two simple country houses; mountain bike trails in the Fucecchio Nature Reserve.

At night

Bonaventura Club
Viale Martini 11, tel. 0572953347
www.bonaventuraclub.it
Small club with live music of all types, from jazz to disco music.

Museums, Monuments and Churches

Museo Nazionale di Casa Giusti
Viale V. Martini 18, tel. 0572950960
www.ambientefi.arti.beniculturali.it
Opening times: May-October: 8.00-14.00, 16.00-19.00. November-April: 8.00-14.00, 15.00-18.00. Tuesday close.

MONTE OLIVETO MAGGIORE (ABBAZIA DI)

☑ Ufficio Turistico delle Crete Senesi
Monte Oliveto Maggiore, tel. 0577707262

How to get there
BY CAR: exit Siena, highway Firenze-Siena or exit Val di Chiana, A1 motorway Napoli-Roma-Milano
BY TRAIN: FS Railway Station Asciano-Monte Oliveto Maggiore; taxi

Museums, Monuments and Churches

Abbazia
Monteoliveto Maggiore 1, tel. 0577707611
www.ftbcc.it/monteoliveto
Opening times: 9.15-12.00, 15.15-17.00, estivo 18.00.

MONTECATINI TERME

☑ Agenzia per il Turismo
Viale Verdi 66/68, tel. 0572772244

How to get there
BY CAR: exit Montecatini, A11 motorway Firenze-Pisa Nord
BY TRAIN: FS Railway Station piazza Gramsci

Hotels

Iris **
Via Cavallotti 26, tel. 057278213

www.hoteliris.it
Open April to October
34 rooms. Restaurant, parking, air conditioned
Credit Cards: Mastercard, Visa
Near thermal spas, popular with regular clientèle; simple but well-furnished rooms; excellent and courteous family management.

Best Western Hotel Cappelli-Croce di Savoia *** ★
Viale Bicchierai 139, tel. 057271151
www.bestwestern.it/cappelli_pt
Open April to mid-November
70 rooms. Restaurant, parking, air conditioned, swimming pool
Credit Cards: American Express, Diner's Club, Mastercard, Visa
Situated in the thermal spa park; comfortable lounges, modern rooms, garden with jacuzzi, and well-equipped convention hall.

Corallo *** ★
Via Cavallotti 116, tel. 057278288
www.golfhotelcorallo.it
56 rooms. Restaurant, parking, air conditioned, swimming pool
Credit Cards: American Express, Diner's Club, Visa
Small building in neo-Classical style; outdoor swimming pool on terrace with a view, piano bar and restaurant with Tuscan cuisine.

Imperial Garden *** ⅋ ★
Viale Puccini 20, tel. 0572910862
www.imperialgarden.it
Open mid-March to mid-November
80 rooms. Restaurant, air conditioned, swimming pool, sauna
Credit Cards: American Express, Diner's Club, Mastercard, Visa
Art Nouveau building furnished with style, in line with regulation quality standards; restaurant with Tuscan cuisine, swimming pool on roof garden and lovely garden.

Mediterraneo *** ★
Via Baragiola 1, tel. 057271321
www.taddeihotels.it/hm
Open March to November
33 rooms. Restaurant, parking, air conditioned
Credit Cards: American Express, Diner's Club, Mastercard, Visa
In late 19th-century building in the Parco delle Terme; courteous and professional staff.

Parma e Oriente ***
Via Cavallotti 135, tel. 057278313
www.hotelparmaeoriente.it

Open April to October and
Christmas

65 rooms. Restaurant, parking,
air conditioned, swimming pool,
sauna, gym
Credit Cards: American Express,
Mastercard, Visa

Art Nouveau palazzo and villa,
good amenities, modern
hospitality standards; family
management since 1922.

Villa Splendor ★★★ ♿
Viale S. Francesco d'Assisi 15,
tel. 057278630
www.livihotels.com
Open April to October

32 rooms. Restaurant, air
conditioned
Credit Cards: Diner's Club,
Mastercard, Visa

In the center, Art Nouveau villa
with well-equipped rooms and
lovely solarium-terrace;
restaurant with Tuscan cuisine.

**Adua & Regina di Saba Wellness
and Beauty** ★↨★ ★
Viale Manzoni 46,
tel. 057278134
www.hoteladua.it
Open March to November and
New Year's Eve

72 rooms. Restaurant, parking,
air conditioned, swimming pool,
gym
Credit Cards: American Express,
Mastercard, Visa

Near thermal spas, classical
interior dècor and excellent
family management; garden,
American bar, bicycles available
and wellness center.

Restaurants

Enoteca Giovanni ␣␣␣
Via Garibaldi 25-27,
tel. 057271695
Closed Monday
Cuisine: Tuscan and creative
Credit Cards: American Express,
Diner's Club, Mastercard, Visa

In the modern restaurant dining
room, creative cuisine;
traditional cuisine in the wine
bar, country style décor, and
good range of wines and spirits.

Gourmet ␣␣␣
Via Amendola 6, tel. 0572771012
web.tiscali.it/gourmet
Closed Tuesday
Cuisine: Italian
Credit Cards: American Express,
Diner's Club, Visa

Art Nouveau style decor and
elegant ambience. Excellent
food, good range of wines and
spirits.

Merlo Bianco ␣␣␣ ♿
Viale Verdi 43, tel. 057278474
www.lacascinadimontecatini.it
Closed Monday

Cuisine: creative
Credit Cards: American Express,
Diner's Club, Mastercard, Visa

In large garden, excellent
gourmet food, including nettle
ravioli, Chianina tagliata,
chestnut millefeuille.

Il Cucco ␣␣ ♿
Via del Salsero 3, tel. 057272765
Closed Tuesday, Wednesday at
lunch
Cuisine: Tuscan
Credit Cards: American Express,
Diner's Club, Mastercard, Visa

Clean, and modern; good
regional cuisine and excellent
wine list.

Il Salotto di Gea ␣␣
Montecatini Alto, via Talenti 2,
tel. 0572904318
www.salottodigea.it
Open dinner only
Cuisine: Italian
Credit Cards: American Express,
Diner's Club, Mastercard, Visa

Small and cosy, with pleasant
outdoor dining area and dining
rooms overlooking the medieval
square; regional dishes and
good choice of wines; bread and
desserts made by the house.

San Francisco ␣␣
Corso Roma 112, tel. 057279632
www.sanfrancisco.it
Open dinner only, closed
Thursday
Cuisine: Tuscan
Credit Cards: American Express,
Diner's Club, Mastercard, Visa

Classical, elegant ambience;
both meat and fish dishes; large
range of local cheeses, and
hams and cheeses; pizza too.

At night

Panteraie
Via delle Panteraie 26,
tel. 057271958
www.lepanteraie.it

Three rooms, catering to all
tastes in music: dance
orchestra, Latin American music,
and live groups. Outdoor
swimming pool with restaurant
and bar, open all day.

MONTEPULCIANO

☑ **Pro Loco**
Piazza Don Minzoni 1,
tel. 0578757341,
www.prolocomontepulciano.it

How to get there

BY CAR: exit Val di Chiana
or Chiusi-Chianciana
t. A1 motorway Milano-
Roma-Napoli

BY TRAIN: FS Railway
Station in Montepulciano
Stazione

Hotels

Borgo Tre Rose ★★★ ♿ ★
Valiano, via I Palazzi 5,
tel. 057872491
www.borgotrerose.it
Open mid-March to October and
New Year's Eve

42 rooms. Restaurant, parking,
air conditioned, swimming pool,
tennis
Credit Cards: American Express,
Diner's Club, Mastercard, Visa

Old medieval hamlet, overlooking
the countryside; rooms and
apartments with independent
entrances; restaurant with
traditional cuisine.

Il Marzocco ★★★ ★
Piazza Savonarola 18,
tel. 0578757262
www.cretedisiena.com/albergom
arzocco

16 rooms. Restaurant, parking
Credit Cards: American Express,
Diner's Club, Mastercard, Visa

Sixteenth-century palazzo, lovely
terraces with views; well-
decorated with antique
furniture, buffet breakfast.

Rural Lodgings

Il Greppo ♿ ★
Abbadia, via dei Greppi 47,
tel. 0578707112
www.ilgreppo.it
Swimming pool, availability of
bikes

Fifteenth-century masonry
farmhouse, various types of
apartments; furnishing typical of
local tradition, garden with
wood oven and barbecue.

La Falconara ♿
Via delle Badelle 3,
tel. 0578715554
www.lafalconara.it
Restaurant, swimming pool,
availability of bikes
Credit Cards: American Express,
Diner's Club, Visa

Large 18th-century country
house, surrounded by fields,
woods, orchards, vines and a
natural lake for fishing. Simple,
elegant apartments.

Villa Cicolina ♿ ★
Cicolina, S.P. 11,
tel. 0578758620
www.villacicolina.it
Open April to December
Swimming pool

Former lemon-house in typical
Tuscan stone, rooms with
private bathrooms, three
apartments in independent
guesthouse.

Bed & Breakfast

Casale a Poggiano
Poggiano, via di Poggiano 21,
tel. 0578716446

www.poggiano.com
In 19th-century farmhouse with garden; rooms furnished with antiques, living room with fireplace for breakfast. Mountain bikes available.

Montorio
*S.S. 146 per Pienza 2, tel. 0578717442
www.montorio.com
In 15th-century country mansion, suites in classical style, with soft furnishings in fine fabrics. Range of local products for breakfast.*

Relais Ortaglia
*Ortaglia, S.S. 146 per Pienza 29, tel. 0457150893
www.ortaglia.it
Beautiful, restructured farmhouse, surrounded by vineyards; elegant, classical-style furnishings; swimming pool, mountain bikes, wine tasting.*

Restaurants

Le Logge del Vignola ⁏⁏ ★
*Via delle Erbe 6, tel. 0578717290
www.leloggedelvignola.it
Closed Tuesday*
Cuisine: modernTuscan
Credit Cards: American Express, Diner's Club, Mastercard, Visa
Charming, with parquet made using barrel slats; refined cuisine, range of house desserts; good selection of cold cuts and cheeses.

La Grotta ⁏ ♿
*San Biagio, tel. 0578757607
Closed Wednesday*
Cuisine: Tuscan and creative
Credit Cards: Visa
In the home of the famous architect Antonio da Sangallo; traditional cuisine, good choice of cheese, wines and spirits.

At night

Antico Caffè Poliziano
*Via Voltaia nel Corso 25, tel. 0578758615
In the center, a historic café in Art Nouveau style, elegantly furnished, and with a fantastic view over the Valdichiana. Aperitifs, liqueurs and top wines, with cakes and desserts, and some cold dishes.*

MONTERIGGIONI

ⓘ Ufficio turistico comunale
Piazza Roma, tel. 0577304834

How to get there
BY CAR: exit Monteriggioni, highway Firenze-Siena
BY TRAIN: FS Railway Station in Castellina In Chianti-Monteriggioni or in Siena; bus connection

Hotels

Casalta ★★★
*Strove, via Matteotti 3, tel. 0577301002
Open March to October*
10 rooms. Restaurant, swimming pool
Credit Cards: Mastercard, Visa
In old village, well-furnished and comfortable; restaurant under separate management, also open to outside clients.

Borgo San Luigi ★⁏★ ♿
*Cerreta 7, tel. 0577301055
www.relais-borgosanluigi.it*
70 rooms. Restaurant, parking, air conditioned, swimming pool, tennis, gym
Credit Cards: American Express, Diner's Club, Mastercard, Visa
Late 17th-century group of houses, in simple, country style, but elegantly furnished, romantic ambience in rooms and restaurant; two conference rooms and sports facilities.

Castelbigozzi ★⁏★ ♿ ★
*Strove, strada di Bigozzi 13, tel. 0577300000
www.chiantiturismo.it*
16 rooms. Parking, air conditioned, swimming pool
Credit Cards: American Express, Diner's Club, Mastercard, Visa
Thirteenth-century fortress-house, surrounded by olive grove, suites with all amenities; also suited for business meetings; buffet breakfast.

Rural Lodgings

Castel Pietraio
*Strada di Strove 33, tel. 0577300020
www.castelpietraio.it*
Restaurant, swimming pool, availability of bikes
Credit Cards: American Express, Diner's, Visa, Mastercard
Accomodation in extremely comfortable rooms or in well-furnished apartments, with fully-equipped kitchens, in the Sienese countryside.

Fattoria Gavina di Sopra ♿
*Gavina, strada di Casabocci 34, tel. 0577317046
www.lagavina.it
Open April to mid-October*
Swimming pool, availability of bikes
Typical farmhouse on hill, warm hospitality and comfortable, simply-furnished rooms; courses in the summer.

Restaurants

Casalta ⁏⁏
*Strove, via Matteotti 22, tel. 0577301171
Closed Wednesday*

Cuisine: Tuscan
Credit Cards: Mastercard, Visa
Small restaurant in medieval building, with garden; regional meat and fish cuisine, with innovatory touches; booking recommended.

La Leggenda dei Frati ⁏⁏ ♿
*Abbadia Isola, piazza Garfonda 7, tel. 0577301222
www.laleggendadeifrati.it
Closed Monday*
Cuisine: creative Tuscan
Credit Cards: American Express, Mastercard, Visa
Beautiful, in an old building below an abbey; cuisine using products from the kitchen garden.

Pozzo ⁏⁏ ♿
*Piazza Roma 20, tel. 0577304127
www.ilpozzo.net
Closed Sunday evening and Monday*
Cuisine: Tuscan
Credit Cards: American Express, Diner's Club, Mastercard, Visa
Elegant simplicity here, in a 13th century stable; proudly Tuscan cuisine, since 1969.

ORBETELLO

ⓘ Pro Loco Lagunare
*Piazza della Repubblica, tel. 0564860447,
www.proloco-orbetello.it*

How to get there
BY CAR: exit Rosignano or Civitavecchia Nord, A12 motorway Genova-Rosignano and Civitavecchia-Roma, then S.S. 1
BY TRAIN: FS Railway Station in Orbetello Scalo, piazza della Stazione; tel. 0564863076

Hotels

Vecchia Maremma ★★★ ♿ ★
*Orbetello Scalo, via Aurelia at km 146, tel. 0564862147
www.vecchiamaremma.it*
46 rooms. Restaurant, parking, air conditioned, swimming pool, gym
Credit Cards: American Express, Diner's Club, Mastercard, Visa
Appropriate amenities and facilities, family management. Lovely restaurant with views of countryside and sea.

Rural Lodgings

Fattoria il Casalone ♿
*Orbetello Scalo, via Aurelia Sud at km 140,5, tel. 0564862160
www.agriturismocasalone.com*
Restaurant, swimming pool, tennis
In the hills above the Orbetello

lagoon, among wheatfields, sunflowers and pastures; tastefully furnished apartments; sailing, tennis and golf.

Grazia &
Provincaccia 110,
tel. 0564881182
www.agriturismograzia.com
Restaurant, tennis
Nineteenth-century farm a few kilometers from the Orbetello lagoon; portico and old-time atmosphere, horse-riding center.

La Valentina Nuova &
Talamone, tel. 0564885551
www.lavalentinanuova.com
Restaurant, tennis
In the Parco della Maremma, in rolling hills with grazing cattle; apartments with stone walls.

Peretti &
Fonteblanda, via Melosella 124,
tel. 0564885467
www.agriturismoperetti.it
Restaurant, tennis, availability of bikes
Credit Cards: Diner's Club, Visa
Informal atmosphere, simple and comfortable rooms; the farm breeds Maremma horses; many Etruscan remains and sites in the vicinity.

Restaurants

Baldo Vino ¶¶¶ &
Via Dante Alighieri 4,
tel. 0564860387
Closed Wednesday
Cuisine: modern Tuscan
Credit Cards: Diner's Club, Mastercard, Visa
In late 17th-century palazzo, very courteous family management; quite creative Tuscan cuisine and good selection of wines.

Museums, Monuments and Churches

Biblioteca civica - Frontone di Talamone
Piazza della Repubblica,
tel. 0564850016
Opening times: 9.30-13.00, 16.00-19.00.

PIENZA

🛈 *Ufficio turistico*
Corso Rossellino 59,
tel. 0578749071

How to get there
BY CAR: exit Chiusi-Chianciano T., A1 motorway Milano-Roma-Napoli
BY TRAIN: FS Railway Station in Chiusi; bus connection on working days only

Hotels

Corsignano ★★★ &
Via della Madonnina 11,
tel. 0578748501
40 rooms. Restaurant, parking
Credit Cards: American Express, Diner's Club, Mastercard, Visa
A few steps from Piazza del Duomo, simple and peaceful; free internet service available.

Relais il Chiostro di Pienza ★★★ &
Corso Rossellino 26,
tel. 0578748400
www.relaisilchiostrodipienza.com
37 rooms. Restaurant, air conditioned, swimming pool
Credit Cards: American Express, Diner's Club, Mastercard, Visa
Fifteenth-century convent, comfortable, full of charm; restaurant with typical Tuscan and international cuisine.

Rural Lodgings

Barbi
Monticchiello, podere Montello 26, tel. 0578755149
www.agriturismobarbi.it
Restaurant, availability of bikes
Credit Cards: Visa
View of Pienza and the Val d'Orcia; accomodation in country house built in the early 1900s, comfortable well-furnished rooms.

Cretaiole & ★
Via S. Gregorio 14,
tel. 0578748083
www.cretaiole.it
Restaurant, availability of bikes
Fourteenth-century farmhouse, with great view; accomodation in apartments, kitchen garden available for guests' use, garden and hunting reserve.

Le Macchie
Monticchiello, via della Montagna, tel. 0578755182
www.lemacchie.it
Swimming pool, availability of bikes
In the Val d'Orcia countryside, among wheat fields, olive trees, ancient oaks; accomodation in elegant apartments, swimming pool with a view.

Restaurants

Buca delle Fate ¶
Corso Rossellino 38/A,
tel. 0578748272
www.labucadellefate.it
Closed Monday
Cuisine: Tuscan
Credit Cards: American Express, Diner's Club, Mastercard, Visa
In the 15th-century Palazzo dei

Gonzaga; excellent traditional menu with especially good bread soups, mushrooms and wild boar; good wine selection.

Taverna di Moranda ¶
Monticchiello, via di Mezzo 17/13, tel. 0578755050
www.tavernadimoranda.it
Closed Friday
Cuisine: Tuscan
Credit Cards: American Express, Mastercard, Visa
Simply decorated, brick-vaulted restaurant, specialities are pigeon and duck dishes, no fish; good desserts and wine list.

Museums, Monuments and Churches

Museo Diocesano
Corso Rossellino 30,
tel. 0578749905
www.comunedipienza.it
Opening times: Mid-March to October: Monday, Wednesday-Sunday 10.00-13.00, 15.00-18.30. November to mid-March: Friday-Sunday and holidays 10.00-13.00, 15.00-18.00.

Palazzo Piccolomini
Piazza Pio II, tel. 0578748503
www.comunedipienza.it
Opening times: Only guided tours: Tuesday-Sunday 10.00-12.30, 15.00-18.00. Closed Monday, end of November-beginning of December, end of February-beginnig of March.

PIOMBINO

🛈 *Agenzia per il Turismo Costa degli Etruschi*
Via Ferruccio 1,
tel. 0565225639,
www.costadeglietruschi.it
🛈 *Agenzia per il Turismo Costa degli Etruschi*
Stazione Marittima,
tel. 0565225639,
www.costadeglietruschi.it
🛈 *Agenzia per il Turismo Costa degli Etruschi*
Fiorentina,
tel. 0565276478,
www.costadeglietruschi.it
🛈 *Ufficio turistico comunale*
Via Ferruccio 4,
tel. 056563269
🛈 *Ufficio turistico comunale*
Town Hall Tower,
tel. 0565225639

How to get there
BY CAR: exit Rosignano or Civitavecchia Nord, A12 motorway Genova-Rosignano and Civitavecchia-Roma, then S.S. 1
BY TRAIN: FS Railway Station piazza Niccolini

Rural Lodgings

Podere Santa Giulia ♿ ★
Riotorto-Santa Giulia,
tel. 056520830
www.poderesantagiulia.it
Open April to September and December
Restaurant, swimming pool, availability of bikes
Two types of accomodation: a pretty cottage at the edge of the pine wood, and a farmhouse in the open countryside; warm and friendly atmosphere.

Santa Trice ♿
Santa Trice, tel. 056520618
www.agriturismosantatrice.it
Open mid-April to mid-October, Christmas and Easter
Restaurant, swimming pool
Large farm, specialising in raising Chianina cattle, accomodation in two country houses; near to beaches and Etruscan sites.

Tenuta di Vignale ♿ ★
Riotorto-Vignale 5,
tel. 056520846
www.tenutadivignale.it
Swimming pool, availability of bikes
Early 19th-century villa with seven simply decorated apartments; handy for the beach at Follonica and good day trips.

Museums, Monuments and Churches

Museo Archeologico del Territorio di Populonia
Piazza di Cittadella 8,
tel. 0565221646
www.parchivaldicornia.it
Opening times: January-May and October-December: Saturday and Sunday 10.00-13.00, 15.00-19.00; Tuesday-Friday on demand. June-September: Tuesday-Friday 9.00-13.00; Saturday and Sunday 10.00-13.00, 15.00-19.00. July-August: Tuesday-Sunday 17.00-23.00.

PISA

☑ **Agenzia per il Turismo di Pisa**
Piazza Vittorio Emanuele II 16, tel. 050/42291,
www.pisa.turismo.toscana.it
☑ **Agenzia per il Turismo di Pisa**
Galilei Airport,
tel. 050503700,
www.pisa.turismo.toscana.it
☑ **Agenzia per il Turismo di Pisa**
Piazza del Duomo,
tel. 050560464,
www.pisa.turismo.toscana.it

☑ **Ufficio turistico comunale**
Lungarno Galilei corner piazza XX Settembre,
tel. 05026212

How to get there
BY CAR: exit Pisa Nord, A11 motorway Firenze-Pisa Nord, or Pisa Centro, A12 motorway Genova-Rosignano and Civitavecchia-Roma
BY TRAIN: FS Railway Station main station, piazza della Stazione
BY AIR: see page 192

Hotels

Leonardo ★★★ ♿
Via Tavoleria 17, tel. 050579946
www.pisaonline.it/hotelleonardo
27 rooms. Parking, air conditioned
Credit Cards: American Express, Diner's Club, Mastercard, Visa
In the center, 15th-century residence, renovated to respect the original design; comfortable rooms and private parking.

Minerva ★★★ ★
Piazza Toniolo 20,
tel. 050501081
www.pisaonline.it/hotelminerva
19 rooms. Air conditioned
Credit Cards: American Express, Diner's Club, Mastercard, Visa
Centrally located, 18th-century palazzo with exceptionally well-furnished lounges and rooms; buffet breakfast.

Royal Victoria Hotel ★★★ ★
Lungarno Pacinotti 12,
tel. 050940111
www.royalvictoria.it
48 rooms. Parking
Credit Cards: American Express, Diner's Club, Mastercard, Visa
Old inn dating from 1428, with courteous, professional family management; terrace with view, bike and car hire.

Jolly Hotel Cavalieri ★★★ ♿ ★
Piazza Stazione 2, tel. 05043290
www.jollyhotels.it
100 rooms. Restaurant, air conditioned
Credit Cards: American Express, Mastercard, Visa
Opposite the railway station, with excellent rooms and conference facilities; internet point and restaurant.

Bed & Breakfast

Relais all'Ussero
Lungarno Pacinotti 26,
tel. 050575428
www.ussero.com
Two elegant suites in the 15th-century Palazzo Agostini.

Breakfast in the famous Caffè dell'Ussero or in other select cake and pastry shops.

Restaurants

Sergio ♙♙♙ ♿ ★
Madonna dell'Acqua, S.S. 1 Aurelia al km 338,
tel. 050894068
Closed Sunday, Monday at lunch
Cuisine: Tuscan
Credit Cards: American Express, Diner's Club, Mastercard, Visa
Sophisticated restaurant, with experienced family management; meat and fish specialities, good choice of cheeses, salamis, hams, wines and spirits.

Al Ristoro dei Vecchi Macelli ♙♙
Via Volturno 49, tel. 05020424
Closed Wednesday, Sunday at lunch
Cuisine: Tuscan
Credit Cards: American Express, Diner's Club, Visa
Delightful ambience and traditional menu, well served with excellent wines from the cellar and quality oils.

Antica Trattoria da Bruno ♙♙ ♿
Via Bianchi 12, tel. 050560818
www.pisaonline.it
Closed Monday evening and Tuesday
Cuisine: Tuscan
Credit Cards: American Express, Diner's Club, Visa
Traditional trattoria, experienced family management, with simple, tasty dishes; Tuscan oil, mainly local and Piedmont wines.

Artilafo ♙♙
Via S. Martino 33, tel. 05027010
Open dinner only, closed Sunday
Cuisine: creative Tuscan
Credit Cards: American Express, Diner's Club, Mastercard, Visa
With lovely garden, renowned for Pisan cuisine, excellent and very creative; wide selection of cheeses and wines.

La Rota ♙♙
Madonna dell'Acqua, via Aurelia 276, tel. 050804443
Closed Tuesday
Cuisine: Tuscan
Credit Cards: American Express, Diner's Club, Mastercard, Visa
Spacious, inviting, with gazebo in the garden; mainly fish and seafood menu.

Osteria del Porton Rosso ♙♙ ♿
Vicolo del Porton Rosso 11,
tel. 050580566
Closed Sunday, Monday and holydays
Cuisine: Tuscan

Credit Cards: American Express, Diner's Club, Mastercard, Visa

In typical tower-house dating from 1100, simple ambience, fish (excellent grills); interesting sorbets (melon, chilli, pear and ginger).

Pergoletta ¶¶ ★
Via delle Belle Torri 36, tel. 050542458
Closed Monday
Cuisine: innovative Tuscan
Credit Cards: American Express, Diner's Club, Mastercard, Visa
Charming tower-house with garden and verandah; small selection of local cheeses and compotes; Chianina steaks selected and cooked personally by the owner.

Emilio ¶
Via Cammeo 44, tel. 050562141
Open lunch only (dinner on demand), closed Friday
Cuisine: Tuscan and traditional
Credit Cards: American Express, Diner's Club, Mastercard, Visa
Spacious eatery popular with tourists. Meat and fish dishes, mushrooms and house desserts.

Nuraghe ¶ ★
Via Mazzini 58, tel. 05044368
Closed Monday
Cuisine: Sardinian and traditional
Credit Cards: American Express, Diner's Club, Visa
In centrally-located tower house, a corner of Sardinia in Tuscany; booking recommended; good wine selection.

Osteria dei Cavalieri ¶ ⓓ
Via S. Frediano 16, tel. 050580858
www.toscana.net/pisa/odc
Closed Saturday at lunch and Sunday
Cuisine: Tuscan
Credit Cards: American Express, Diner's Club, Mastercard, Visa
Inviting osteria, in medieval tower house; recommended menus, with all kinds of meat, fish and vegetables; special lunch dish, at reasonable price.

Osteria dei Mille ¶ ⓓ ★
Via dei Mille 30/32, tel. 050556263
Closed Friday
Cuisine: Italian
Credit Cards: American Express, Diner's Club, Mastercard, Visa
Particularly romantic and inviting, with courteous family management; menu based on natural products and quality.

At night

Caffè dell'Ussero
Lungarno Pacinotti 27, tel. 050581100

This historic café in 15th-century Palazzo Agostini opened in 1794: on the walls, pictures of the many illustrious habitués of the past.

Nuovo Lo Sfizio
Via Borgo Stretto 54, tel. 050580281
In the center, very popular with students for lunch. Excellent aperitifs and after-dinner cocktails.

Museums, Monuments and Churches

Battistero
Piazza dei Miracoli, tel. 050560547
www.opapisa.it
Opening times: 9.00-16.30, Summer 19.30.

Campanile o "Torre di Pisa"
Piazza dei Miracoli, tel. 050560547
www.opapisa.it
Opening times: 9.00-17.00.

Camposanto
Piazza Duomo 17, tel. 050560547
www.opapisa.it/piazza/
Opening times: Summer: 8.00-19.30; Winter: 9.00-16.30; Spring: 9.00-17.30.

Duomo
Piazza dei Miracoli, tel. 050560547
www.opapisa.it
Opening times: Winter: 10.00-12.45, 15-16.30; holidays 15.00-16.30. Spring and autumn: 10.00-17.30, holidays 13.00-17.30. Summer: 10.00-19.30, holidays: 13.00-19.30.

Museo dell'Opera del Duomo
Piazza Duomo, tel. 050560547
www.opapisa.it/piazza/
Opening times: November-February: Monday-Sunday 9.00-16.00 (March and October 9.00-18.00, April-September 8.00-19.00). Closed 1 January, Christmas.

Museo Nazionale di San Matteo
Piazza S. Matteo in Soarta 1, tel. 050541865
www.ambientepi.arti.beniculturali.it
Opening times: Tuesday-Saturday 8.30-19.30; Sunday and holidays 8.30-13.30.

PISTOIA

🖊 **Agenzia per il Turismo**
Piazza Duomo 4, tel. 057321622,
www.pistoia.turismo.toscana.it

How to get there
BY CAR: exit Pistoia, A11 motorway Firenze-Pisa Nord
BY TRAIN: FS Railway Station piazza Dante Alighieri

Hotels

Il Convento ★★★ ⓓ
Pontenuovo, via S. Quirico 33, tel. 0573452651
32 rooms. Restaurant, parking, air conditioned, swimming pool
Credit Cards: Mastercard, Visa
Former Franciscan convent with charm of bygone days, and modern hospitality standards; modern rooms and restaurant with Tuscan cuisine.

Milano ★★★
Viale Pacinotti 10/12, tel. 0573975700
www.milanohotelpt.it
55 rooms. Parking
Credit Cards: American Express, Diner's Club, Mastercard, Visa
In central area, suited for business, tourist or sports clientèle; buffet breakfast.

Patria ★★★
Via Crispi 6/8, tel. 057325187
www.patriahotel.com
28 rooms. Air conditioned
Credit Cards: American Express, Diner's Club, Mastercard, Visa
Seventeenth-century palazzo, in the historic center; buffet breakfast. Well managed.

Restaurants

La Volpe e l'Uva ¶¶¶
Piteccio, via di Villa 6, tel. 057342031
www.villavannini.it
Open dinner only, except Sunday
Cuisine: creative Tuscan
Credit Cards: American Express, Mastercard, Visa
Sophisticated ambience in 18th-century villa, with lovely garden; good menu, traditional dishes with creative touches.

L'Oca Rossa ¶¶
Via A. Doria 13, tel. 0573545376
Closed Tuesday, Saturday at lunch
Cuisine: creative
Credit Cards: American Express, Diner's Club, Mastercard, Visa
Pleasant, modern; homecooking, everything skilfully made on the premises.

Lo Storno ¶
Via del Lastrone 8, tel. 057326193
Closed Sunday
Cuisine: Tuscan
Credit Cards: Mastercard, Visa
Typical Tuscan trattoria, both fish and meat dishes.

Rafanelli ⅋
*Via S. Agostino 47,
tel. 0573552046
Closed Sunday evening and
Monday*
Cuisine: Tuscan
Credit Cards: American
Express, Diner's Club,
Mastercard, Visa
Spacious premises, experienced
family management; emphasis
on meat, game and mushrooms;
wide range of wines and spirits,
oils, cheeses, and salamis and
hams.

At night
Valiani
*Via Cavour 55, tel. 057323034
In the 14th-century Oratorio di
Sant Antonio Abate, with
exquisite Giotto-style Pisan-
school frescoes. Soon to
change hands, but the
wonderful atmosphere will
remain.*

Museums, Monuments and Churches
Fortezza di S. Barbara
*Piazza della Resistenza,
tel. 057324212
Opening times: martedì-
domenica 9.00-13.30.*

Museo Civico
*Piazza del Duomo 1,
tel. 05733711-0573371214
Opening times: Martedì-sabato
10.00-19.00; domenica e festivi
9.00-12.30.*

POGGIBONSI

🛈 **Pro Loco**
*Via Borgaccio, tel. 0577987017,
www.comune.poggibonsi.si.it*
How to get there
BY CAR: exit Poggibonsi,
highway Firenze-Siena
BY TRAIN: FS Railway
Station piazza Mazzini

Hotels
Villa San Lucchese *⅋* ★
*San Lucchese, tel. 0577937119
www.villasanlucchese.com*
38 rooms. Restaurant, parking,
air conditioned, swimming pool,
tennis
Credit Cards: American Express,
Diner's Club, Mastercard, Visa
Old country residence in hills with
view, lovely atmosphere; breakfast
in garden pavillion, restaurant in
the old lemon house.

Rural Lodgings
Fattoria di Piecorto
Piecorto, tel. 0558072915

Open April to mid-October
Restaurant, swimming pool,
availability of bikes
Wonderful farm producing
Chianti Classico; five, skilfully-
renovated apartments, with
wonderful views.

Restaurants
Galleria ⅋
*Galleria Cav. Vittorio Veneto 20,
tel. 0577982356
Closed Sunday*
Cuisine: Tuscan
Credit Cards: American Express,
Diner's Club, Mastercard, Visa
The best restaurant in town with
good wine list, and good, varied
meat and especially fish menu.

Antica Posta ⅋ ⅊ ★
*Fosci 23/24, tel. 0577933887
www.ristoranteanticaposta.it
Closed Monday*
Cuisine: Tuscan
Credit Cards: American Express,
Mastercard, Visa
Traditional eatery for travellers,
quick dishes, with traditional
Tuscan bruschette and crostini;
local oils and pecorino cheeses.

POGGIO A CAIANO

🛈 **Pro Loco**
*Piazza Medici 1,
tel. 0558798779*
How to get there
BY CAR: exit Prato Est, A11
motorway Firenze-Pisa Nord
BY TRAIN: FS Railway
Station in Prato; bus
connection

Hotels
Hermitage ★★★ ⅊
*Bonistallo, via Ginepraia 112,
tel. 055877040
www.hotelhermitageprato.it*
61 rooms. Restaurant, parking,
air conditioned, swimming pool
Credit Cards: American Express,
Diner's Club, Mastercard, Visa
In peaceful hills, furnished in
modern style, several suites at
prices to be agreed; ideal for
business tourism.

Museums, Monuments and Churches
Villa Medicea
*Piazza dei Medici 14,
tel. 055877012
www.comune.poggio-a-
caiano.po.it/villa/home.htm
Opening times: Monday-Sunday
8.15-16.30. June-August: 8.15-
19.30. Closed 2nd and 3rd
Monday of the month, 1 January,
Christmas. In the villa only
guided tours.*

PONTREMOLI

🛈 **Pro Loco**
*Piazzetta della Pace,
tel. 0187833309*
How to get there
BY CAR: exit Pontremoli,
A15 motorway Parma-La
Spezia
BY TRAIN: FS Railway
Station piazza Bruno Raschi,
tel. 0187830006

Rural Lodgings
Costa d'Orsola
*Orsola, tel. 0187833332
www.costadorsola.it*
Swimming pool, tennis,
availability of bikes
Credit Cards: Visa, Eurocard,
Mastercard
Entire hamlet with stone houses
on grassy slopes of a hill,
among woods, rocks and
streams; courses and trips
organised.

Podere Rottigliana
*Rottigliana, tel. 0187833480
www.podererottigliana.com
Open on demand*
Restaurant, swimming pool,
tennis, availability of bikes
In the unique Lunigiana
countryside, between the hills
and the sea, strategically placed
for trips to key tourist
destinations.

Bed & Breakfast
Villa Emilia
*Versola, via Versola 4,
tel. 0187836455
www.villaemilia.com*
Beautiful 1920s house, with
large garden. Cosy rooms in
warm colours; period furniture;
breakfast room with fireplace.

Restaurants
Ca' del Moro ⅋
*Via Casa Corvi, tel. 0187830588
www.cadelmoro.it
Closed Sunday evening and
Monday*
Cuisine: creative Tuscan
Credit Cards: American Express,
Diner's Club, Mastercard, Visa
Attractive premises, in what was
once the stable of a country
house; mushrooms and other
traditional dishes; but also an
unusual bison tagliata.

Museums, Monuments and Churches
**Museo delle Statue-Stele
Lunigianesi**
*Via del Piagnaro, tel. 0187831439
www.massacarrara-live.it*

Opening times: Summer: 9.00-12.00, 15.00-18.00. Winter: 9.00-12.00, 14.00-17.00.

PORTO AZZURRO

How to get there
BY CAR: from Piombino, ferries to the Isola d'Elba getting to Portoferraio or Porto Azzurro or Rio Marina

BY TRAIN: FS Railway Station in Piombino Marittima; ferry; bus connection from Portoferraio

BY FERRY: from Piombino with Toremar ferries

Hotels
Belmare ★★★
Quay IV Novembre 21, tel. 056595012
www.elba-hotelbelmare.it
25 rooms. Parking, air conditioned
Credit Cards: American Express, Diner's Club, Mastercard, Visa
In fantastic location overlooking the bay; comfortable rooms, solarium with view, and meeting room; buffet breakfast.

Rural Lodgings
Sapere Italo &
Mola, via Provinciale Ovest 75, tel. 056595033
www.sapereonline.it
Restaurant, swimming pool, tennis
Credit Cards: American Express, Diner's, Visa, Mastercard
Set among olive trees and palms; pleasant farm-stay in country house; garden surrounded by vineyards; swimming pool, tennis court and bar.

PORTOFERRAIO

Agenzia per il Turismo dell'Arcipelago Toscano
Calata Italia 43, tel. 0565914671, www.aptelba.it

How to get there
BY CAR: from Piombino, ferries to the Isola d'Elba getting to Portoferraio or Porto Azzurro or Rio Marina

BY TRAIN: FS Railway Station in Piombino Marittima; ferry

BY FERRY: from Piombino, Toremar or Moby Lines ferries

Hotels
Paradiso ★★★ ★
Vitìccio, tel. 0565939034
www.elbaturistica.it
Open Easter to mid-October
46 rooms. Restaurant, parking, air conditioned, swimming pool, tennis
Credit Cards: Mastercard, Visa
Good location with views; well-equipped rooms in houses set amongst greenery and vegetation; internet point, restaurant with local cuisine.

Viticcio ★★★ & ★
Viticcio, tel. 0565939058
www.hotelviticcio.it
Open April to October
32 rooms. Restaurant, parking, air conditioned
Credit Cards: Mastercard, Visa
By breathtakingly beautiful bay, in delightful garden, with comfortable rooms and suites; local cuisine, often fish dishes, and terrace with view.

Airone del Parco e delle Terme ★★★ &
San Giovanni, tel. 0565929111
www.hotelairone.info
85 rooms. Restaurant, parking, air conditioned, swimming pool, sauna, tennis
Credit Cards: American Express, Diner's Club, Mastercard, Visa
Good views, close to thermal spa, with wide range of leisure activities; some apartments available.

Biodola ★★★ &
La Biòdola, tel. 0565974812
www.biodola.it
Open April to mid-October
89 rooms. Restaurant, parking, air conditioned, swimming pool, tennis
Credit Cards: American Express, Diner's Club, Visa
Charming building in delightful bay, some rooms with terraces, good amenities, comfortable.

Hermitage ★★★
La Biòdola, tel. 0565974811
www.hotelhermitage.it
Open April to mid-October
130 rooms. Restaurant, parking, air conditioned, swimming pool, tennis, gym
Credit Cards: American Express, Mastercard, Visa
Complex by the sea, very comfortable, excellent amenities; accomodation also in attractive bungalows, rooms and suites of good standard.

Villa Ottone ★★★ &
Ottone, tel. 0565933042
www.villaottone.com
Open May to October
80 rooms. Restaurant, parking, air conditioned, swimming pool, tennis, gym
Credit Cards: American Express, Diner's Club, Visa
Nineteenth-century villa in lovely garden by the beach; comfortable, classy rooms, and a number of elegant bungalows.

Rural Lodgings
Casa Marisa & ★
Schiopparello 12, tel. 0565933074
www.casamarisa.it
Restaurant, tennis
Comfortable apartments with terraces looking over the countryside; beaches not far away, bike and boat hire, horse-riding and tennis court.

Monte Fabbrello &
Schiopparello 30, tel. 0565933324
www.montefabbrello.it
Restaurant, tennis, availability of bikes
In the plain by the bay; accomodation in country-style garrets; wood inlay courses organised.

Tenuta il Fortino ★
Buraccio 6, tel. 0565940245
Restaurant, tennis
Apartments with terraces and views over olive trees and Mediterranean "macchia" vegetation. Sunny and sheltered, 5km from the sea.

Restaurants
Emanuel ❚ &
Enfola, tel. 0565939003
Open Easter to mid-October, closed Wednesday (low season only)
Cuisine: Tuscan
Credit Cards: American Express, Diner's Club, Mastercard, Visa
Terrace on the water and two cool gardens; traditional menu with some creative variations.

Stella Marina ❚
Via Vittorio Emanuele II, tel. 0565915983
Closed Monday
Cuisine: Tuscan
Credit Cards: American Express, Diner's Club, Mastercard, Visa
Excellent, imaginative seafood menu, and excellent choice of wines and spirits.

★★★ ★★★ ★★★ ★★★ ★★ ★ Hotels ❚❚❚❚ ❚❚❚ ❚❚ ❚ ❚ Restaurants & Disabled ★ Special TCI Rates

At night

Caffè Roma
Piazza Cavour, tel. 0565914278
Ice-cream parlour and bar; piano
bar in summer.

Club 64
Strada Capannone Biodola,
tel. 0565969988
www.club64.net
On the hill overlooking the Bay
of Biodola and Scaglieri, historic
disco (opened in 1964) with two
dance floors, surrounded by
nature.

Museums, Monuments and Churches

**Casa di Napoleone - Palazzina
dei Mulini**
Piazzale Napoleone,
tel. 0565915846
www.ambientepi.arti.beniculturali.it
Opening times: Monday-
Saturday 9.00-20.00; Sunday
and holidays 9.00-13.30.
Tuesday closed.

PRATO

> ℹ️ **Agenzia per il Turismo
> di Prato**
> Piazza S. Maria delle Carceri 15,
> tel. 057424112,
> www.prato.turismo.toscana.it
>
> **How to get there**
>
> **BY CAR:** exit Prato
> Calenzano, A1 motorway
> Milano-Roma-Napoli, Prato
> Ovest or Prato Est, A11
> motorway Firenze-Pisa Nord
>
> **BY TRAIN:** FS Railway
> Station main station and
> Porta al Serraglio station,
> piazzale della Stazione

Hotels

Art Hotel Milano ★★★ ♿
Via Tiziano 15, tel. 057423371
www.arthotel.it
70 rooms. Restaurant, air
conditioned
Credit Cards: American Express,
Diner's Club, Mastercard, Visa
A few steps from the old town
center, modern and functional;
buffet breakfast and restaurant
with local cuisine.

Giardino ★★★ ★
Via Magnolfi 4, tel. 0574606588
www.giardinohotel.com
28 rooms. Parking, air
conditioned
Credit Cards: American
Express, Diner's Club,
Mastercard, Visa
Palazzo built in the second half
of the 19th century, looking onto

Piazza del Duomo, air-
conditioned and sound-proofed;
buffet breakfast.

Best Western Hotel President
★★★ ♿ ★
Via Simintendi, corner via
Baldinucci, tel. 057430251
www.bestwestern.it/president_po
78 rooms. Restaurant, air
conditioned
Credit Cards: American Express,
Diner's Club, Mastercard, Visa
Modern glass and concrete
building; internet point, modem
socket in rooms, conference
facilities, restaurant with
traditional menu.

Restaurants

Il Piraña 🍴🍴🍴
Via G. Valentini 110 ang. via
Bertini, tel. 057425746
Closed Saturday at lunch and
Sunday
Cuisine: fish
Credit Cards: American Express,
Diner's Club, Visa
Elegant and comfortable;
specialises in fish and seafood
dishes, but several meat dishes
too.

Baghino 🍴🍴 ★
Via Accademia 9,
tel. 057427920
Closed Sunday and Monday at
lunch
Cuisine: Tuscan
Credit Cards: American Express,
Diner's Club, Mastercard, Visa
Pleasant, simple atmosphere,
period furnishings, with garden;
don't miss the special stuffed
celery "alla pratese".

Enoteca Barni 🍴🍴
Via Ferrucci 22, tel. 0574607845
Closed Saturday at lunch and
Sunday
Cuisine: creative Tuscan
Credit Cards: American Express,
Diner's Club, Mastercard, Visa
Sophisticated, minimalist wine
bar and restaurant; quick,
informal meals possible at
lunchtime; interesting fish and
meat dishes.

La Fontana 🍴🍴
Filettole, via di Canneto 1,
tel. 057427282
www.lafontanatrattoria.it
Closed Sunday evening and
Monday
Cuisine: Tuscan
Credit Cards: American Express,
Mastercard, Visa
Small and cosy, with verandah

closed in, in winter; traditional
dishes, with desserts made by
the house and an excellent
choice of Tuscan hams and
salamis.

Tonio 🍴
Piazza Mercatale 161,
tel. 057421266
Closed Sunday and Monday
Cuisine: fish
Credit Cards: American Express,
Diner's Club, Mastercard, Visa
Classical restaurant, in piazza
decked out with plants and
greenery; mainly fish on the
menu, but also some traditional
Florentine dishes.

Osteria Cibbè 🍴 ♿ ★
Piazza Mercatale 49,
tel. 0574607509
Closed Sunday (except
December)
Cuisine: Tuscan
Credit Cards: Mastercard, Visa
In medieval building, small,
pleasant osteria with outside
area for dining too, family
management; excellent,
traditional Tuscan cuisine,
interesting wine list.

At night

Baraka
Piazza Mercatale 133,
tel. 0574442226
www.baraka.tv
Modern cocktail bar: clean lines,
soft lights and white armchairs.
Closed Saturday.

Museums, Monuments and Churches

Castello dell'Imperatore
Piazza S.Maria delle Carceri,
tel. 057438207
Opening times: Monday-Sunday
9.00-13.00, 16.00-19.00, Tuesday
closed. Winter: morning only.

Museo Civico
Piazza del Comune, tel. 05746161
www.comune.prato.it/civico/hom
e.htm
Opening times: Temporary
closed. For information call
05746161.

Museo dell'Opera del Duomo
Piazza Duomo 48,
tel. 057429339-0574433494
www.po-net.prato.it/musei/opera
/home.htm
Opening times: Monday,
Wednesday-Saturday 9.30-12.30,
15.00-18.30; Sunday and
holidays 9.30-12.30. Tuesday
closed.

RADDA IN CHIANTI

ℹ️ Pro Loco
Piazza del Castello,
tel. 0577738494,
www.chiantinet.it

How to get there
BY CAR: exit Valdarno,
A1motorway Milano-Roma-
Napoli
BY TRAIN: FS Railway
Station in Siena; bus
connection

Hotels
La Locanda ★★★ ⅙ ★
Montanino, tel. 0577738833
www.lalocanda.it
Open mid-March to November
7 rooms. Restaurant, parking,
swimming pool
Credit Cards: American Express,
Diner's Club, Mastercard, Visa
Two nineteenth-century
farmhouses among olive trees
and grapevines; comfortable
rooms, bar, library, swimming
pool with view over countryside;
buffet breakfast.

Relais Fattoria Vignale ★⁑★ ★
Via Pianigiani 8, tel. 0577738300
www.vignale.it
40 rooms. Restaurant, parking,
air conditioned, swimming pool
Credit Cards: American Express,
Diner's Club, Mastercard, Visa
Old stately home, attractive and
refined interiors, restaurant with
Tuscan specialities, library,
heated swimming pool, wine bar
and meeting room.

Rural Lodgings
Castello di Volpaia
Volpaia, tel. 0577738066
www.volpaia.com
Swimming pool, tennis
Credit Cards: American Express,
CartaSi, Visa, Mastercard
In a charming 13th-century
village, full of old alleyways and
piazze; farmhouse combining
technology and tradition.

Fattoria Castelvecchi
Castelvecchi 17, tel. 0577738050
www.castelvecchi.it
Swimming pool, tennis
Rooms in 19th-century villa,
apartments in 15th-16th century
cottages; large garden with two
swimming pools and garden
furniture.

**Podere Terreno alla Via della
Volpaia** ★
Volpaia, tel. 0577738312
www.podereterreno.it

Tennis, availability of bikes
Credit Cards: American Express,
CartaSi, Visa, Mastercard
In the heart of the Chianti
Classico area, a uniquely warm
and cosmopolitan atmosphere;
massages and wine therapy on
request.

Restaurants
Al Chiasso dei Portici 🍴🍴🍴 ⅙
Chiasso dei Portici 10,
tel. 0577738774
www.alchiassodeiportici.it
Closed Tuesday
Cuisine: creative Tuscan
Credit Cards: American Express,
Diner's Club, Mastercard, Visa
Pleasant, inviting atmosphere,
with small garden; traditional
dishes with rabbit, lamb and
wild boar.

Vignale 🍴🍴🍴
Via XX Settembre 23,
tel. 0577738094
www.vignale.it
Closed Thursday
Cuisine: creative Tuscan
Credit Cards: American Express,
Diner's Club, Mastercard, Visa
Old seventeenth-century oil mill;
traditional Tuscan dishes made
with imaginative variations;
house-produced bread, pasta
and desserts, and large range of
wines.

RIO MARINA

ℹ️ Pro Loco
*Lungomare Guglielmo
Marconi 2,*
tel. 0565962004,
*www.proloco-
riomarinaecavo.it*

How to get there
BY CAR: from Piombino,
ferries to the Isola d'Elba
getting to Portoferraio or
Porto Azzurro or Rio
Marina
BY TRAIN: FS Railway
Station in Piombino
Marittima; ferry; bus
connection from
Portoferraio
BY FERRY: from Piombino
with Toremar ferries;
Toremar hydrofoil from
Piombino to Cavo

Hotels
Marelba ★★★ ★
Cavo, via Pietri,
tel. 0565949920
www.hotelmarelba.it
Open May to September
52 rooms. Restaurant, parking

Set among olive trees and pines,
a few steps from the beach, in
Mediterranean style, pleasant
interiors, and a reading room.

Maristella ★★★
Cavo, via Kennedy,
tel. 0565931109
www.hotelmaristella.com
*Open mid-May to mid-
September*
24 rooms. Restaurant, parking
Credit Cards: American Express,
Mastercard, Visa
In a large garden by the sea;
rooms in two lovely houses;
water sports. Excellent fish
dishes.

Rio ★★★
Via Palestro 31, tel. 0565924225
www.hotelriomarina.it
32 rooms. Restaurant
Credit Cards: American Express,
Mastercard, Visa
In the small port a few steps
from the beach, attractive décor,
rooms with sea view; buffet
breakfast, restaurant with
traditional cuisine.

Restaurants
Canocchia 🍴
Via Palestro 1, tel. 0565962432
Open February to October,
*closed Monday (except in
Summer)*
Cuisine: Tuscan and traditional
Credit Cards: Mastercard, Visa
Simple, elegant charm, and
excellent seafood; local island
wines and Tuscan wines.

RIO NELL'ELBA

How to get there
BY CAR: from Piombino,
ferries to the Isola d'Elba
getting to Portoferraio or
Porto Azzurro or Rio
Marina
BY TRAIN: FS Railway
Station in Piombino
Marittima; ferry; bus
connection from
Portoferraio

ROSELLE (TERME DI)

How to get there
BY CAR: exit Rosignano or
Civitavecchia Nord, A12
motorway Genova-
Rosignano and
Civitavecchia-Roma, then
S.S. 1 until Grosseto, then
S.S. 223
BY TRAIN: FS Railway
Station in Grosseto

⁑⁑⁑ ⁂⁂ ⁑⁑ ★★★ ★★ ★ Hotels 🍴🍴🍴🍴 🍴🍴🍴 🍴🍴 🍴 🍴 Restaurants ⅙ Disabled ★ Special TCI Rates

Museums, Monuments and Churches

Rovine di Roselle
Area archeologica di Roselle
Scavi, tel. 0564402403
Opening times: every day from 9 to sunset, closed Christmas, 1 January, 1 May.

SAN CASCIANO IN VAL DI PESA

☑ **Pro Loco**
Piazza della Repubblica,
tel. 0558229558

How to get there
BY CAR: exit San Casciano, highway Firenze-Siena
BY TRAIN: FS Railway Station in Firenze; bus connection

Rural Lodgings

Castello di Bibbione
Montefiridolfi, via Collina 66, tel. 0558249231
www.castellodibibbione.com
Restaurant, swimming pool, availability of bikes
Credit Cards: Visa, Mastercard
In Florentine Chianti, among olive groves and grapevines; accomodation in country cottages, blending tradition with modern comfort.

Fattoria le Corti
Via S. Piero di Sotto 1, tel. 055829301
www.principecorsini.com
Restaurant, swimming pool
Credit Cards: Visa
One independent apartment in a wing of the farmhouse, various other rooms with views over the countryside, and private garden.

La Ginestra ⬧
San Pancrazio, via Pergolato 3, tel. 0558248196
www.laginestra.toscana.it
Swimming pool
Credit Cards: American Express, CartaSi, Visa, Mastercard
Model pig-breeding farm; accomodation in two country houses, with great views.

Tenuta il Corno ⬧
San Pancrazio, via Malafrasca 64, tel. 0558248009
Swimming pool
Credit Cards: American Express, CartaSi, Visa, Mastercard
Farm-stay in country houses; photography courses, wine and olive oil tasting, mountain bikes, tennis court and horse-riding.

Villa Branca ⬧
Mercatale Val di Pesa, via Novoli 10, tel. 055821033
www.villabranca.it
Restaurant, swimming pool, availability of bikes
Credit Cards: American Express, Diner's, Visa, Mastercard
In the hills near Florence, 14th-century farm; simple but sophisticated apartments; large English-style garden with solarium.

Restaurants

La Tenda Rossa ⵜⵜⵜⵜ
Cerbàia, piazza del Monumento 9/14, tel. 055826132
www.latendarossa.it
Closed Sunday, Monday at lunch
Cuisine: creative Tuscan
Credit Cards: American Express, Diner's Club, Mastercard, Visa
Attractive modern premises, family management; Tuscan cuisine with excellent fresh ingredients and good selection of wines and cheeses.

Locanda Barbarossa ⵜⵜ ⬧
Via Sorripa 2, tel. 0558290109
www.locandabarbarossa.it
Open dinner only, closed Tuesday
Cuisine: Tuscan
Credit Cards: American Express, Diner's Club, Mastercard, Visa
Garden with swimming pool; local cuisine, using olive oil, fruit, vegetables and poultry produced by the owner.

SAN GALGANO (ABBAZIA)

How to get there
BY CAR: exit Colle Val d'Elsa, highway Firenze-Siena
BY TRAIN: FS Railway Station in Siena; bus connection

SAN GIMIGNANO

☑ **Pro Loco**
Piazza Duomo 1,
tel. 0577940008,
www.sangimignano.com

How to get there
BY CAR: exit Poggibonsi, highway Firenze-Siena
BY TRAIN: FS Railway Station in Poggibonsi-S. Gimignano; bus connection

Hotels

Bel Soggiorno ★★★
Via S. Giovanni 91, tel. 0577940375
www.hotelbelsoggiorno.it
22 rooms. Restaurant, air conditioned
Credit Cards: American Express, Diner's Club, Mastercard, Visa
Two 14th-century buildings, with classical furnishings and modern amenities; restaurant with view, and creative cuisine.

Casolare le Terre Rosse ★★★
San Donato, tel. 05779021
www.hotelterrerosse.com
Open March to October
42 rooms. Restaurant, parking, air conditioned, swimming pool
Credit Cards: American Express, Diner's Club, Mastercard, Visa
Typical country house, lovely lines, spacious rooms, internal courtyards; large swimming pool and restaurant.

La Cisterna ★★★ ★
Piazza della Cisterna 24, tel. 0577940328
www.hotelcisterna.it
49 rooms. Restaurant, air conditioned
Credit Cards: American Express, Diner's Club, Mastercard, Visa
Old 14th-century palazzo overlooking the main piazza, Florentine-style furnishings and modern amenities; discounted parking.

L'Antico Pozzo ★★★ ⬧
Via S. Matteo 87, tel. 0577942014
www.anticopozzo.com
18 rooms. Air conditioned
Credit Cards: American Express, Diner's Club, Mastercard, Visa
Right in the center, in 15th-century palazzo with original frescoes and period furnishings; all amenities, and buffet breakfast.

Le Renaie ★★★ ★
Pancole 10/B, tel. 0577955044
www.hotellerenaie.com
25 rooms. Restaurant, parking, swimming pool, tennis
Credit Cards: American Express, Diner's Club, Mastercard, Visa
On a hilltop, in picturesque hamlet, old country house, tastefully furnished; restaurant with Tuscan cuisine.

Leon Bianco ★★★
Piazza della Cisterna 13, tel. 0577941294
www.leonbianco.com
26 rooms. Parking, air conditioned
Credit Cards: American Express, Diner's Club, Visa
Efficient management, charming

interiors, in the old Palazzo del Podestà.

Relais Chateaux la Collegiata *⁂*
Strada 27, tel. 0577943201
www.lacollegiata.it
21 rooms. Restaurant, parking, air conditioned, swimming pool
Credit Cards: American Express, Diner's Club, Mastercard, Visa
Sixteenth-century, former Franciscan convent, in centuries-old park and gardens, with great view of countryside, and towers of San Gimignano.

Relais Santa Chiara *⁂* & ★
Via Matteotti 15, tel. 0577940701
www.rsc.it
41 rooms. Parking, air conditioned, swimming pool
Credit Cards: American Express, Diner's Club, Mastercard, Visa
Classical, elegant hotel complex, a few minutes from the center of San Gimignano; buffet breakfast.

Villa San Paolo *⁂* & ★
Strada per Certaldo, km 4, tel. 0577955100
www.villasanpaolo.com
18 rooms. Parking, air conditioned, swimming pool, tennis, gym
Credit Cards: American Express, Diner's Club, Visa
Modern rooms, several with patio or balcony, restaurant, wellness center and conference facilities.

Rural Lodgings

Casanova di Pescille
Pescille, tel. 0577941902
www.casanovadipescille.com
Restaurant, swimming pool, availability of bikes
Credit Cards: Visa, Mastercard
In a nature reserve between Volterra, Siena and Florence, 19th-century farmhouse with large farmyard to enjoy; period furnishings, in simple country style.

Fattoria di Pietrafitta ★
Cortennano 54, tel. 0577943200
www.pietrafitta.com
Restaurant, swimming pool
Credit Cards: American Express, Diner's, Visa, Mastercard
Rural community of ancient origin, which has become over time a model farm; accomodation in early 18th-century farmhouses.

Fattoria Poggio Alloro
Sant'Andrea 23, tel. 0577950276
www.fattoriapoggioalloro.com
Swimming pool
Credit Cards: Visa, Mastercard
San Gimignano can be reached by foot from here, through beautiful countryside, both cultivated and uncultivated; organic farm, raising Chianina cattle.

Fattoria San Donato & ★
San Donato 6, tel. 0577941616
www.sandonato.it
Swimming pool
Credit Cards: Visa, Mastercard
Farm-stay accomodation in the heart of a hamlet, around a small church, furnished with antique furniture.

Fattoria Voltrona ★
San Donato, tel. 0577943152
www.voltrona.com
Swimming pool, availability of bikes
Credit Cards: Visa, Mastercard
Country mansion 4 km from village, with large terrace and garden, swimming pool and lake for fishing; organic farm.

Podere Arcangelo &
Capezzano 26, via S. Benedetto 26, tel. 0577944404
www.poderiarcangelo.it
Swimming pool
Accomodation in an ex-convent, which has kept its fascinating atmosphere, in the superb Tuscan countryside.

Podere Cappella &
Lignite 20, tel. 0577941615
Restaurant
Farm in a protected fauna area, with hares, pheasants, and squirrels; accomodation in tastefully renovated country houses.

Podere Villuzza
Strada 25/26, tel. 0577940585
www.poderevilluzza.it
Restaurant, swimming pool
Attractive farmhouse, with young, professional management; well-designed interiors, charming countryside; the village can be reached on foot through the vineyards.

Tenuta Torciano
Ulignano, via Crocetta 18, tel. 0577950055
www.torciano.com
Restaurant, swimming pool,

availability of bikes
Credit Cards: Diner's, Visa, Mastercard
Historic country house, with rooms and independent apartments, comfortable and furnished with style; large garden, solarium and picnic area.

Restaurants

La Collegiata ¶¶¶
Strada 27, tel. 0577943201
www.lacollegiata.it
Cuisine: creative Tuscan
Credit Cards: American Express, Diner's Club, Mastercard, Visa
In the church of a former Franciscan convent, charming, with terrace and picturesque cellar; traditional specialities skilfully modified, and some fish dishes.

Da Pode ¶¶ &
Sovestro 62, tel. 0577943153
www.hotelsovestro.com
Closed Monday
Cuisine: Tuscan
Credit Cards: American Express, Diner's Club, Mastercard, Visa
Surrounded by countryside, simple decor; tasty, traditional, varied Tuscan cuisine, made with top quality ingredients: oil, fresh pecorino, and hams and salamis.

Dorandò ¶¶
Vicolo dell'Oro 2, tel. 0577941862
www.ristorantedorando.it
Closed Monday (low season only)
Cuisine: creative Tuscan
Credit Cards: American Express, Diner's Club, Mastercard, Visa
Cosy restaurant in 15th-century building; imaginative menu items and presentation; excellent range of desserts and Tuscan cheeses.

Le Terrazze ¶¶
Piazza della Cisterna 24, tel. 0577940328
www.hotelcisterna.it
Closed Tuesday, Wednesday at lunch
Cuisine: Tuscan
Credit Cards: American Express, Diner's Club, Mastercard, Visa
Great view; family management, traditional cuisine with strong country flavours (don't miss the tagliata al Chianti with potatoes cooked with rosemary).

Osteria delle Catene ¶ ★
Via Mainardi 18,

tel. 0577941966

Open March to December, closed Wednesday

Cuisine: Tuscan

Credit Cards: American Express, Diner's Club, Mastercard, Visa

Lovely vaulted dining room with brick walls; traditional cuisine with original variations; house desserts.

At night

Caffè Combattenti
Via S. Giovanni 124,
tel. 0577940391

At Porta San Giovanni, a favorite meeting-place since 1924. Excellent artisan ice-cream: don't miss the ricciarello (almond biscuit) ice-cream, or the saffron ice-cream.

Museums, Monuments and Churches

Collegiata
Piazza Duomo, tel. 0577940316

Opening times: Marzo, November-January: Monday-Saturday 9.30-17.00, holidays 12.30-17.00. April-October: Monday-Friday 9.30-19.00, Saturday 9.30-17.00, holidays 12.30-17.00. From 21 January to 28 February openig times changing according to church services.

Museo Civico
Piazza del Duomo,
tel. 0577990312

Opening times: March-October: Monday-Sunday 9.30-19.00. (November-February 10.00-17.30). Closed Christmas, 1 January.

Palazzo del Popolo
Piazza Duomo 2, tel. 0577990312

Opening times: March-October: 9.30-19.00. November-February: 10.00-17.00.

SAN MINIATO

🅘 **Ufficio turistico**
Piazza del Popolo 3,
tel. 057142745,
www.sanminiatotartufo.it

How to get there

BY CAR: exit Firenze Signa, A1motorway Milano-Roma-Napoli

BY TRAIN: FS Railway Station in S. Miniato-Fucecchio; bus connection

Hotels

Villa Sonnino *≛* 🔥
Catena, via Castelvecchio 9/11,
tel. 0571484033

www.villasonnino.com

13 rooms. Restaurant, parking, air conditioned

Credit Cards: American Express, Diner's Club, Mastercard, Visa

Sixteenth-century villa, set in centuries-old woods; well-furnished and comfortable rooms; restaurant with Tuscan cuisine, business meeting rooms.

Rural Lodgings

Fattoria di Scaletta 🔥
Scaletta, via Asmara 37,
tel. 055574410

www.bartolinibaldelli.it

Restaurant, swimming pool

Farm of around 180 hectares, partly vineyards and partly cultivated fields, accomodation in 19th-century farmhouse with two swimming pools, and gardens.

Podere Canova
Corazzano, via Zara 186,
tel. 0571460120

www.agriturismocanova.com

Swimming pool, availability of bikes

With great view, very comfortable 17th-century farmhouse; well-equipped, independent rooms.

Restaurants

Il Convio-San Maiano ⅖ 🔥 ★
Via S. Maiano 2, tel. 0571408114

www.sanminiatoonline.it

Closed Wednesday

Cuisine: Tuscan

Credit Cards: American Express, Diner's Club, Mastercard, Visa

Country style decor, good traditional cuisine; house desserts and oil from the house farm; adjoining pizzeria.

Museums, Monuments and Churches

Museo Diocesano di Arte Sacra
Piazza del Duomo 2,
tel. 0571400458-0571406233

www.comune.san-miniato.pi.it

Opening times: Tuesday-Sunday 10.00-13.00.

SAN ROSSORE

How to get there

BY CAR: exit Pisa Centro, A12 motorway Genova-Rosignano and Civitavecchia-Roma

BY TRAIN: FS Railway Station Pisa-San Rossore, via Padre Fedi

Museums, Monuments and Churches

Tenuta
Centro Visite Tenuta di San Rossore - Parco Regionale Migliarino, San Rossore, Massaciuccoli,
tel. 050530101
www.parcosanrossore.it

SANSEPOLCRO

🅘 **Ufficio turistico comprensoriale Val Tiberina**
Via Matteotti 8,
tel. 0575740536,
www.apt.arezzo.it

How to get there

BY CAR: exit Arezzo, A1 motorway Milano-Roma-Napoli

BY TRAIN: Ferrovia Centrale Umbra Railway Station piazza Battisti 1,
tel. 0575742094

Hotels

Fiorentino ★★★
Via Pacioli 56, tel. 0575740350
www.albergofiorentino.com

16 rooms. Air conditioned

Credit Cards: Mastercard, Visa

Established as a hotel in the early 19th century, situated in picturesque historic center, with old-time atmosphere. Restaurant with Tuscan and traditional cuisine.

Borgo Palace Hotel *≛* 🔥 ★
Via Senese Aretina 80,
tel. 0575736050

www.borgopalace.it

75 rooms. Restaurant, parking, air conditioned

Credit Cards: American Express, Diner's Club, Mastercard, Visa

Elegant, modern building, excellent conference rooms and facilities; restaurant with Tuscan and traditional cuisine. Very welcoming staff.

Rural Lodgings

Calcinaia sul Lago 🔥 ★
Calcinaia, tel. 0575742777
www.wel.it/calcinaia

Restaurant, swimming pool, availability of bikes

Farm-stay in the green Tiber valley; great views, plenty of outdoor space, well-furnished apartments.

La Conca 🔥 ★
Paradiso 16, tel. 0575733301
www.laconca.it

Restaurant, swimming pool

Credit Cards: Visa, Mastercard

In the Tiber valley, old stone houses, simply furnished in country style; organic kitchen garden and 290-hectare farm; leisure activities and courses.

Podere Violino &
Gricignano 99, tel. 0575720174
www.podereviolino.it
Swimming pool, availability of bikes
Credit Cards: Visa, Mastercard
Classy accomodation and local food specialities for riding enthusiasts, in the green Tiber valley; riding courses for children.

Restaurants

Oroscopo di Paola e Marco ⑪
Pieve Vecchia, via Togliatti 68, tel. 0575734875
www.relaisoroscopo.com
Open dinner only, closed Sunday
Cuisine: Tuscan
Credit Cards: Diner's Club, Mastercard, Visa
Early 19th-century villa; light cuisine with traditional Tuscan tastes and flavours; excellent choice of wines.

La Balestra ⑪ & ★
Via dei Montefeltro 29, tel. 0575735151
www.labalestra.it
Closed Monday, Sunday evening
Cuisine: Tuscan
Credit Cards: American Express, Diner's Club, Mastercard, Visa
Classical style; traditional cuisine using select ingredients, good wine list, excellent percorino di fossa.

Da Beppino ⑪ ★
Viale Diaz 12, tel. 0575742287
Closed Monday
Cuisine: Tuscan
Credit Cards: Mastercard, Visa
Three dining rooms and a cool garden for summer dining; traditional meat dishes, but also fish dishes and tasty pizzas.

Ventura ⑪
Via N. Aggiunti 30, tel. 0575742560
Closed Monday and Sunday evening
Cuisine: Tuscan
Credit Cards: American Express, Diner's Club, Mastercard, Visa
In the old town center, three dining rooms furnished in country style; on the menu, local hams and salamis, handmade pasta, mushrooms

and white truffles; good cantucci made by the house.

At night

Enoteca Tirar Tardi
Via S. Antonio 5, tel. 0575741525
www.tirartardi.it
In the old center, wine bar with a great selection of wines, as well as salamis, hams, cheeses and pasta dishes.

Lo Scorpione
Via Vittorio Veneto 1/E, tel. 0575742132
Disco, with restaurant Fridays and Saturdays.

Museums, Monuments and Churches

Museo Civico
Via Aggiunti 65, tel. 0575732218
www.sansepolcro.net
Opening times: June-September: Monday-Sunday, holidays 9.00-13.30, 14.30-19.30. (October-May: 9.30-13.00, 14.30-18.00).

SIENA

> ☑ **Agenzia per il Turismo Terre di Siena**
> Piazza del Campo 56, tel. 0577280551, www.terresiena.it
>
> **How to get there**
> **BY CAR:** exit Siena, highway Firenze-Siena
> **BY TRAIN:** FS Railway Station piazza Rosselli 7

Hotels

Piccolo Hotel il Palio ★★ & ★
Piazza del Sale 19, tel. 0577281131
www.piccolohotelilpalio.it
26 rooms.
Credit Cards: American Express, Diner's Club, Mastercard, Visa
Terracotta vaults in several reception rooms revealing the building's 15th-century origins; small rooms, with lovely period furniture.

Chiusarelli ★★★ ★
Via Curtatone 15, tel. 0577280562
www.chiusarelli.com
49 rooms. Restaurant, parking, air conditioned
Credit Cards: American Express, Mastercard, Visa
Neo-Classical villa with some frescoed rooms and simple "arte povera" furnishings; verandah for buffet breakfast, restaurant with Tuscan cuisine.

Italia ★★★ ★
Via Cavour 67, tel. 057741177
www.hotelitalia-siena.it
66 rooms. Parking
Credit Cards: American Express, Diner's Club, Mastercard, Visa
Simple, traditional guesthouse, in convenient central location; facilities for business meetings, internet point.

Minerva ★★★ & ★
Via G. Garibaldi 72, tel. 0577284474
www.albergominerva.it
59 rooms. Air conditioned
Credit Cards: American Express, Diner's Club, Mastercard, Visa
In central location, with spacious, comfortable rooms; business meeting room, internet point, buffet breakfast.

Piccolo Hotel Oliveta ★★★
Via E.S. Piccolomini 35, tel. 0577283930
www.oliveta.com
15 rooms. Parking, air conditioned
Credit Cards: American Express, Diner's Club, Mastercard, Visa
Nineteenth-century stone house, full of charm, with well-furnished rooms. Large garden with garden furniture, superb cellar and wine bar.

Sangallo Park Hotel ★★★ & ★
Strada di Vico Alto 2, tel. 0577334149
www.sangalloparkhotel.it
50 rooms. Parking, air conditioned, swimming pool
Credit Cards: American Express, Diner's Club, Mastercard, Visa
In the hills, with view of Siena, for business and tourist clientèle; well-equipped rooms, buffet breakfast, swimming-pool in garden.

Santa Caterina ★★★ ★
Via Piccolomini 7, tel. 0577221105
www.hscsiena.it
22 rooms. Parking, air conditioned
Credit Cards: American Express, Diner's Club, Mastercard, Visa
Eighteenth-century residence with rooms furnished in Tuscan style; lovely garden with verandah for buffet breakfast.

Best Western Palazzo dei Priori ★★★ & ★
Via Montalbuccio 31, tel. 0577398909
www.palazzodeipriori.it
75 rooms. Restaurant, parking,

TRENO NATURA

Treno Natura, a project financed by Siena Province, has enabled some disused Tuscan railway lines to be brought back to life as tourist lines: so you can enjoy the Tuscan countryside from lovely old trains, often with steam engines.

The Asciano-Monte line is particularly scenic: it travels through the 'Crete' area and the Asso Valley, past vineyards where the excellent Brunello di Montalcino wine is produced; and then into the Valle d'Orcia, below Monte Amiata, where the *Parco Artistico Naturale e Culturale della Val d'Orcia* is situated. The Park is actively involved in running the railway line. Trains run on certain holidays, especially in autumn and spring. Tickets cost 10 euros (25 on steam trains) and booking is compulsory.

BOOKINGS:
Ferrovia della Val d'Orcia - tel. 0577207413, www.ferrovieturistiche.it
INFORMATION:
APT Siena, tel. 0577280551, www.siena.turismo.toscana.it
APT Amiata, tel. 0577775811, www.amiata.turismo.toscana.it
APT Chianciano Terme Val di Chiana, tel. 0578 671122, www.chianciano.turismo.toscana.it www.parco dellavaldorcia.com

---

air conditioned
Credit Cards: American Express, Diner's Club, Mastercard, Visa
Comfortable rooms and mini apartments with terrace; internet point, business meeting room, internet.

Certosa di Maggiano *‡*
Via Certosa 82, tel. 0577288180
www.certosadimaggiano.com
17 rooms. Restaurant, parking, air conditioned, swimming pool, tennis, gym
Credit Cards: American Express, Mastercard, Visa
In old charterhouse, combining beauty, elegance and comfort; frescoed lounges, well-furnished rooms and restaurant with great atmosphere.

G.H. Villa Patrizia *‡*
Via Fiorentina 58, tel. 057750431
www.villapatrizia.it
38 rooms. Restaurant, parking, air conditioned, swimming pool, tennis, gym
Credit Cards: American Express, Diner's Club, Mastercard, Visa
Lovely villa in garden, attractive and elegant rooms; buffet breakfast, restaurant with regional specialities.

Garden *‡* ★
Via Custoza 2, tel. 057747056
www.gardenhotel.it
125 rooms. Restaurant, parking, air conditioned, swimming pool, tennis
Credit Cards: American Express, Diner's Club, Mastercard, Visa
Eighteenth-century villa in large garden; sumptuously furnished, facilities for business meetings, restaurant and terrace with view over the city.

Jolly Hotel *‡* ★
Piazza La Lizza, tel. 0577288448
www.jollyhotels.it
111 rooms. Restaurant, air conditioned
Credit Cards: American Express, Mastercard, Visa
Modern, efficient and functional hotel complex, with restaurant and several suites.

Villa Scacciapensieri *‡*
Via di Scacciapensieri 10, tel. 057741441
www.villascacciapensieri.it
31 rooms. Restaurant, parking, air conditioned, swimming pool, tennis
Credit Cards: American Express, Diner's Club, Mastercard, Visa
Nineteenth-century villa, with view of Siena and the Chianti hills, large garden; comfortable rooms and suites, good sports facilities, restaurant.

Rural Lodgings
Bagno a Sorra
Strada degli Agostoli 65, tel. 0577393252
www.bagnassorra.com
Restaurant, availability of bikes
Top oil producer, since the 14th century; in superb countryside near Siena; information about prices on booking.

Bed & Breakfast
Villa Corazzesi
Strada del Petriccio e Belriguardo 81, tel. 0577595137
www.villacorazzesi.com
On the top floor of a large 18th-century renovated villa, rooms with wooden beams, furnished in country style.

Restaurants
Il Canto ▯▯▯▯
Via Certosa 82, tel. 0577288180
www.ilcanto.it
Closed Tuesday, Wednesday at lunch
Cuisine: Italian
Credit Cards: American Express, Mastercard, Visa
Charming; excellent food, great taste experiences and wonderful presentation; good selection of local cheeses, and hams and salamis.

Antica Trattoria Botteganova ▯▯▯
Via Chiantigiana 29, tel. 0577284230
www.anticatrattoriabotteganuova.it
Closed Sunday
Cuisine: Tuscan and creative
Credit Cards: American Express, Diner's Club, Mastercard, Visa
Elegant atmosphere, excellent cellar, wide range of dishes; good choice of desserts, such as pear cake with must sauce.

Al Mangia ▯▯ ♿
Piazza del Campo 42, tel. 0577281121
www.almangia.it
Closed Wednesday (low season only)
Cuisine: Tuscan
Credit Cards: American Express, Diner's Club, Mastercard, Visa

On the "Palio" piazza, inviting eatery with stone ceiling; all dishes of proven local tradition, from ribollita to panforte.

Enzo ❙❙
Via Camollia 49,
tel. 0577281277
Closed Sunday
Cuisine: creative
Credit Cards: American Express, Diner's Club, Mastercard, Visa
Classical, family run restaurant. Both meat and fish on the menu, and mushrooms and truffles in season; good choice of wines and spirits.

La Compagnia dei Vinattieri ❙❙ &
Via delle Terme 79,
tel. 0577236568
www.vinattieri.net
Cuisine: Tuscan and traditional
Credit Cards: American Express, Diner's Club, Mastercard, Visa
Charming wine bar with food; great selection of wines, also by the glass, as well as cheeses, and hams and salamis; some interesting hot meals too.

Marsili ❙❙ ★
Via del Castoro 3,
tel. 057747154
www.ristorantealmarsili.it
Closed Monday
Cuisine: Tuscan
Credit Cards: American Express, Diner's Club, Mastercard, Visa
Delightful medieval premises with brick vaulted ceilings; local quality cuisine, excellent cheeses and Cinta Sienese hams and salamis.

Medio Evo ❙❙
Via dei Rossi 40,
tel. 0577280315
www.medioevosiena.com
Closed Thursday
Cuisine: Tuscan
Credit Cards: American Express, Diner's Club, Visa
In medieval building, traditional Sienese dishes: wild boar ham, pappardelle, pappa al pomodoro, and panforte.

La Sosta di Violante ❙
Via di Pantaneto 115,
tel. 057743774
www.lasostadiviolante.com
Closed Sunday
Cuisine: modern Tuscan
Credit Cards: American Express, Diner's Club, Mastercard, Visa

Two inviting rooms with vaulted arches; traditional menu with imaginative touches.

La Taverna del Capitano ❙
Via del Capitano 6/8,
tel. 0577288094
Closed Tuesday
Cuisine: Tuscan
Credit Cards: American Express, Diner's Club, Mastercard, Visa
Charming place to eat, with good service and local menu.

Osteria le Logge ❙
Via del Porrione 33,
tel. 057748013
Closed Sunday
Cuisine: Tuscan
Credit Cards: American Express, Diner's Club, Mastercard, Visa
Period furniture, tables outside in summer; traditional and non-traditional dishes; wine and oil produced by the restaurant farm.

At night

Enoteca Italiana
At the Fortezza Medicea, via Camollia 72, tel. 0577288497
www.enoteca-italiana.it
Wine bar in the 16th-century fortress ramparts, with winding passageways and barrel vaults: top Italian wines. Wine tasting and wine by the glass, with snacks and cold dishes. Closed Sunday.

Museums, Monuments and Churches

Piazza del Duomo
Opening times: 10.30-19.30, holidays 13.30-18.30 (November-February 10.30-18.30, holidays 13.30-17.30).

Museo Civico - Palazzo del Popolo
Piazza del Campo 1,
tel. 0577292226
www.comune.siena.it/museocivico/
Opening times: November to mid-March: Monday-Sunday 10.00-17.00. (Mid-March to October 10.00-19.00). Closed 2 July, 16 August, Christmas.

Pinacoteca Nazionale
Via S. Pietro 29,
tel. 0577281161-0577286143
Opening times: Monday 8.30-13.30; Tuesday-Saturday 8.15-19.15; Sunday and holidays 8.15-13.15.

TAVARNELLE VAL DI PESA

> ☑ **Ufficio informazioni turistiche del Comune**
> Piazza Matteotti,
> tel. 0558077832,
> www.prolocotavarnelle.it
>
> **How to get there**
> **BY CAR:** exit San Donato, highway Firenze-Siena
> **BY TRAIN:** FS Railway Station in Poggibonsi; bus connection

Hotels

Park Hotel Chianti ★★★
Pontenuovo, via Cassia,
tel. 0558070106
www.parkhotelchianti.com
43 rooms. Parking, air conditioned, swimming pool
Credit Cards: American Express, Mastercard, Visa
In Tuscan countryside, good amenities and facilities, for leisure activities too (mountain bikes available).

Rural Lodgings

Fattoria Villa Spoiano
Spoiano, tel. 0558077313
www.toscanaholidays.com
Open mid-March to mid-November and Christmas
Restaurant
Credit Cards: Visa
On the Via Francigena, in countryside with old churches, hamlets and villages, a farm producing organic wine and oil.

Il Bacio ★
Bonazza 35, tel. 0558076437
www.ilbacio.net
Restaurant, swimming pool, availability of bikes
Between Florence, Siena and San Gimignano, family enterprise producing excellent organic Chianti, Vin Santo and grappa.

Sovigliano
Via Magliano 9, tel. 0558076217
www.sovigliano.com
Swimming pool, availability of bikes
Credit Cards: Visa
In countryside dotted with castles, churches and hamlets, a large renovated country house, providing traditional country hospitality and comfort.

‡‡‡ ‡‡‡ ‡‡‡ ★★★ ★★ ★ Hotels ❙❙❙❙❙ ❙❙❙❙ ❙❙❙ ❙❙ ❙ Restaurants & Disabled ★ Special TCI Rates

Restaurants

Macereto ¶
Strada del Canaglia 10/A,
tel. 0558071111
www.ristorantealmacereto.com
Open dinner only (lunch on
Saturday and Sunday), closed
Wednesday
Cuisine: Tuscan
Credit Cards: American
Express, Diner's Club,
Mastercard, Visa
In a beautiful wood, large
premises; strongly regional
cuisine: homemade pasta with
cep mushrooms, with truffles
and with wild boar.

Osteria di Passignano ¶ &
Badia di Passignano, via
Passignano 33,
tel. 0558071278
www.osteriadipassignano.com
Closed Sunday
Cuisine: creative Tuscan
Credit Cards: American
Express, Diner's Club,
Mastercard, Visa
Classy and full of charm;
traditional meat dishes with
modern variations; good
selection of oils, cheeses, and
hams and salamis; small
adjoining wine bar.

La Gramola ¶ & ★
Via delle Fonti 1,
tel. 0558050321
www.gramola.it
Open dinner only, except
Sunday and holydays, closed
Tuesday
Cuisine: Tuscan
Credit Cards: American
Express, Diner's Club,
Mastercard, Visa
Osteria in former stables with
brick vaults; country-style
cuisine, varying according to
season; good selection of
Tuscan oils and pecorino
cheeses.

La Toppa ¶
San Donato in Pòggio, via del
Giglio 43, tel. 0558072900
Closed Monday
Cuisine: Tuscan
Credit Cards: American Express,
Mastercard, Visa
Three pleasant dining rooms
in the old cellars of Palazzo
Malaspina, with garden and
terrace; local cuisine, fresh
pasta, and house desserts.

VETULONIA

☑ **Pro Loco**
Piazza E. Stefani 5,
tel. 0564948116,
www.dunia.it/vetulonia/

How to get there
BY CAR: exit Rosignano or
Civitavecchia Nord, A12
motorway Genova-
Rosignano and
Civitavecchia-Roma, then
S.S. 1
BY TRAIN: FS Railway
Station in Grosseto; bus
connection

Museums, Monuments and Churches

**Museo Civico Archeologico
«Isidoro Falchi»**
Piazza Vetulonia,
tel. 0564948058
www.comune.castiglione-della-
pescaia.gr.it
Opening times: June-September:
Monday-Sunday 10.00-13.00,
16.00-21.00 October-February:
Tuesday-Sunday 10.00-13.00,
14.00-17.00. March-May:
Tuesday-Sunday 10.00-13.00,
15.00-18.00.

VIAREGGIO

☑ **Agenzia per il Turismo
della Versilia**
Viale Carducci 10,
tel. 0584962233,
www.versilia.turismo.
toscana.it
**Agenzia per il Turismo
della Versilia**
F.S. Station, piazza Dante,
tel. 058446382,
www.versilia.turismo.
toscana.it

How to get there
BY CAR: exit Viareggio-
Camaiore, A12 motorway
Genova-Rosignano and
Civitavecchia-Roma
BY TRAIN: FS Railway
Station piazza Dante

Hotels
Lupori ★★
Via Galvani 9, tel. 0584962266
www.luporihotel.it
19 rooms. Air conditioned
Credit Cards: American Express,
Diner's Club, Mastercard, Visa
In the heart of the old town;
simple, renovated, 1960s
guesthouse; completely air-
conditioned.

Miramare ★★★
Viale Carducci 27,
tel. 058448441
www.miramarehotel.net
26 rooms. Restaurant, air
conditioned
Credit Cards: American Express,
Diner's Club, Mastercard, Visa
Near the beach, Art Nouveau
building converted to modern,
comfortable hotel, restaurant
with typical Tuscan cuisine.

San Francisco ★★★
Viale Carducci 68,
tel. 058452666
www.sanfranciscoviareggio.it
31 rooms. Air conditioned
Credit Cards: American Express,
Diner's Club, Mastercard, Visa
Completely renovated
guesthouse, near the sea,
simple furnishings, buffet
breakfast, roof garden with view.

Villa Tina ★★★
Via Saffi 2, tel. 058444450
Open Easter to October
14 rooms. Restaurant, air
conditioned
Credit Cards: Mastercard, Visa
Art Nouveau villa with sea in
front and pine grove behind;
some rooms with period
furniture and with blown-glass
chandeliers; restaurant with
local cuisine.

Astor Hotel ★★★ ★
Lungomare Carducci 54,
tel. 058450301
www.astorviareggio.com
68 rooms. Restaurant, air
conditioned, swimming pool, gym
Credit Cards: American Express,
Diner's Club, Mastercard, Visa
On the elegant seafront
promenade; simply-furnished
rooms with sea views, solarium,
indoor swimming pool and gym;
restaurant renowned for its
seafood specialities.

Excelsior ★★★ ★
Viale Carducci 88,
tel. 058450726
www.excelsiorviareggio.it
Open April to October
83 rooms. Restaurant, air
conditioned, gym
Credit Cards: American Express,
Diner's Club, Mastercard, Visa
Historic hotel complex in Art
Nouveau style; relaxed
atmosphere, several luxury
suites, restaurant with Tuscan
and classical cuisine.

**Grand Hotel Principe
di Piemonte** ★★★ &
Piazza G. Puccini, tel. 05844011

www.principedipiemonte.com

106 rooms. Restaurant, parking, air conditioned, swimming pool, sauna

Credit Cards: American Express, Diner's Club, Mastercard, Visa

Historic hotel in the center, in elegant Art Nouveau building; many rooms furnished in a variety of styles; buffet breakfast and two restaurants.

Palace Hotel *✦* & ★
Via Gioia 2, tel. 058446134
www.palaceviareggio.com

75 rooms. Restaurant, air conditioned

Credit Cards: American Express, Diner's Club, Mastercard, Visa

Art Nouveau style building, modern amenities and facilities, suites with views; restaurant with Tuscan cuisine, American bar, and bicycles.

Plaza e De Russie *✦*
Piazza D'Azeglio 1, tel. 058444449
www.plazaederussie.com

52 rooms. Restaurant, air conditioned

Credit Cards: American Express, Diner's Club, Mastercard, Visa

Viareggio's first hotel; excellent, individualised rooms furnished with period furniture; roof garden restaurant with view.

Restaurants

Romano ❚❚❚❚ &
Via Mazzini 122, tel. 058431382
www.romanoristorante.it
Closed Monday (and Tuesday at lunch in July and August)
Cuisine: Tuscan
Credit Cards: American Express, Diner's Club, Mastercard, Visa

Well known to gourmets and gastronomes; the secret is the extremely fresh, locally caught fish; new, pleasant and lively atmosphere; good choice of desserts, large selection of wines and spirits.

Oca Bianca ❚❚❚
Via Coppino 409, tel. 0584388477
Open dinner only
Cuisine: Italian
Credit Cards: Visa

Elegant, charming, overlooking boats moored in the port; good food and outstanding selection of wines and spirits.

Cabreo ❚❚ &
Via Firenze 14, tel. 058454643
Closed Monday
Cuisine: Tuscan and traditional
Credit Cards: American Express, Mastercard, Visa

Beautiful, elegant restaurant; dishes are new, light versions of local seafood and fish recipes.

Il Porto ❚❚
Via M. Coppino 118, tel. 0584383878
Closed Sunday, Monday at lunch
Cuisine: Tuscan
Credit Cards: American Express, Diner's Club, Visa

Inviting ambience, with terrace; fish and seafood cuisine.

L'Imbuto ❚❚ &
Via Fratti int.308, tel. 058448906
Closed Monday, Tuesday at lunch
Cuisine: Tuscan
Credit Cards: American Express, Mastercard, Visa

In ex-carpentry factory, interesting, new, with mainly fish and seafood dishes, good presentation.

Mirage ❚❚
Via Zanardelli 12/14, tel. 058432222
www.hotelmirageviareggio.it
Closed Tuesday (except July and August)
Cuisine: Tuscan and traditional
Credit Cards: American Express, Diner's Club, Mastercard, Visa

Modern in style; excellent menu inspired by regional traditions, mostly using extremely fresh fish.

Pino ❚❚
Via Matteotti 18, tel. 0584961356
Closed Wednesday, Thursday at lunch
Cuisine: Sardinian
Credit Cards: American Express, Diner's Club, Mastercard, Visa

In central location, two dining rooms in contemporary style; fish menu changes daily according to what's in the market, house desserts.

Vecchio Casale ai Pioppi ❚❚ &
Via Fosso Legname 22, tel. 0584963251
Open June to September dinner

only, closed Wednesday, Thursday at lunch
Cuisine: Tuscan
Credit Cards: American Express, Diner's Club, Mastercard, Visa

Simple but excellent, country style decor; mostly fish and seafood dishes, but also meat and game.

Il Punto Divino ❚
Via Mazzini 229, tel. 058431046
Closed Monday and July to September at lunch
Cuisine: Tuscan and traditional
Credit Cards: American Express, Diner's Club, Mastercard, Visa

Wine bar with kitchen open until midnight; menu inspired by regional tradition, quality oils and good assortment of salamis, hams and cheeses.

At night

Enoclub
Viale Marconi 105, tel. 0584407476
On the seafront, with live music.

Macondo Café
Viale Europa, tel. 0584393961
www.macondocafe.it
Opposite the Vittorio Veneto baths, with a wonderful terrace and live music five evenings a week.

VOLTERRA

🛈 **Ufficio turistico comunale**
Piazza dei Priori 19/20, tel. 058887257

How to get there

BY CAR: exit Rosignano or Civitavecchia Nord, A12 motorway Genova-Rosignano and Civitavecchia-Roma, then S.S. 1 until Cecina Nord, then S.S. 68

BY TRAIN: FS Railway Station in Saline di Volterra; bus connection

Hotels

Sole ★★★ ★
Via dei Cappuccini 10, tel. 058884005
www.volterra-toscana.net /hotelsole

10 rooms. Parking
Credit Cards: American Express, Mastercard, Visa

Family-managed hotel with

large, attractive rooms, and lovely, light, airy room for buffet breakfast.

Villa Nencini ★★★ &
Borgo S. Stefano 55,
tel. 058886386
www.villanencini.it
36 rooms. Restaurant, parking, swimming pool
Credit Cards: American Express, Diner's Club, Mastercard, Visa
Above the town's Etruscan walls, late 17th-century villa; delightfully attractive interiors and rooms, restaurant and indoor swimming pool.

San Lino ★★★ & ★
Via S. Lino 26,
tel. 058885250
www.hotelsanlino.com
43 rooms. Restaurant, swimming pool
Credit Cards: American Express, Diner's Club, Mastercard, Visa
Former convent, equipped with all amentities; rooms with simple "arte povera" furniture, roof garden and terrace with swimming pool.

Rural Lodgings

Fattoria Lischeto & ★
San Giusto, tel. 058830403
www.agrilischeto.com
Swimming pool, tennis, availability of bikes
Credit Cards: American Express, Diner's, Visa, Mastercard
Lovely stone farmhouse with view of the "balze" (impressive ravine near Volterra); excellent organic cheese produced on the farm, guests invited to participate in making it.

Mirandola
Villamagna, S.P. 15 at km 10,
tel. 058833058
www.lamirandola.it
Restaurant, swimming pool, tennis, availability of bikes
In Etruscan territory, country house at the top of rolling hills, great for cycling or riding, and animal-watching in the woods.

Tenuta Orgiaglia &
Ponsano,
tel. 058835029
www.orgiaglia.it
Swimming pool, tennis

Credit Cards: American Express, Diner's, Visa, Mastercard
Between Volterra, San Gimignano and Siena, old country house belonging to Luppiano Castle; Chianti wine and good cuisine in a wonderful atmosphere.

Villa Montaperti & ★
Montaperti, S.R. 439dir at km 11,
tel. 058842038
www.montaperti.com
Open Easter to October
Swimming pool, tennis, availability of bikes
Superb villa with very spacious rooms, furnished very tastefully, with the houses of the old hamlet around the villa, view of Volterra, olive trees and cypresses.

Bed & Breakfast

Holiday San Giusto
Via Pisana 35,
tel. 058886328
www.holidaysangiusto.net
Typical Tuscan stone house, period furniture in rooms, garden with swimming pool.

Restaurants

Del Duca ¶ &
Via di Castello 2,
tel. 058881510
Closed Tuesday (except July to September)
Cuisine: creative Tuscan
Credit Cards: American Express, Diner's Club, Mastercard, Visa
Beautiful, classy restaurant, with charming cellar and outside area; simple traditional menu; good choice of local cheeses and excellent wine list.

Trattoria del Sacco Fiorentino ¶
Piazza XX Settembre 18,
tel. 058888537
Closed Wednesday
Cuisine: Tuscan
Credit Cards: American Express, Diner's Club, Mastercard, Visa
Cleverly restored, seventeenth-century palazzo; menu which varies according to season; good choice of cheeses, and hams and salamis.

Vecchia Osteria dei Poeti ¶ ★
Via Matteotti 55,
tel. 058886029
Closed Thursday
Cuisine: Tuscan

Credit Cards: American Express, Diner's Club, Mastercard, Visa
Sophisticated simplicity in this osteria with stone walls; traditional menu; delicious cheeses, hams and salamis.

Beppino ¶ & ★
Via delle Prigioni 13/21,
tel. 058886051
Closed Thursday
Cuisine: Tuscan
Credit Cards: American Express, Mastercard, Visa
Simple, family-managed eatery; house-made pasta and local specialities; pizzas too.

At night

Web&Wine
Via Porta all'Arco 11/13,
tel. 058881531
www.webandwine.com
The first room has a glass floor, and handcrafted wrought iron tables and chairs; the second is the cellar, in a small space below street level, with antique wooden furniture.

Museums, Monuments and Churches

Museo dell'Opera del Duomo
Via Roma 13, tel. 058886290
www.comune.volterra.pi.it/ museiit/musart.html
Opening times: Mid-March to October: 9.00-13.00, 15.00-18.00. 5 November to Mid-March: 9.00-13.00.

Museo Etrusco Guarnacci
Via Don Minzoni 15,
tel. 058886347
www.comune.volterra.pi.it/ museiit/metru.html
Opening times: November-15 March: Monday-Sunday 9.00-14.00 (16 marzo-October 9.00-19.00). Closed 1 January, Christmas.

Pinacoteca e Museo Civico
Via dei Sarti 1, tel. 058887580
www.comune.volterra.pi.it
Opening times: Mid-March to October: Monday-Sunday 9.00-19.00. (November to Mid-March 9.00-13.30).

Teatro Romano
Vallebona
Opening times: 15 March-October: 10.30-17.30. November-14 March: Saturday, Sunday, holidays 11.00-16.00.

METRIC CONVERTIONS

Kilometres/Miles

km to mi	mi to km
1 = 0.62	1 = 1.6
2 = 1.2	2 = 3.2
3 = 1.9	3 = 4.8
4 = 2.5	4 = 6.4
5 = 3.1	5 = 8.1
6 = 3.7	6 = 9.7
7 = 4.3	7 = 11.3
8 = 5.0	8 = 12.9

Meters/Feet

m to ft	ft to m
1 = 3.3	1 = 0.30
2 = 6.6	2 = 0.61
3 = 9.8	3 = 0.91
4 = 13.1	4 = 1.2
5 = 16.4	5 = 1.5
6 = 19.7	6 = 1.8
7 = 23.0	7 = 2.1
8 = 26.2	8 = 2.4

TEMPERATURE

Fahrenheit/Celsius

F	C
0	-17.8
5	-15.0
10	-12.2
15	-9.4
20	-6.7
25	-3.9
30	-1.1
32	0
35	1.7
40	4.4
45	7.2
50	10.0
55	12.8
60	15.5
65	18.3
70	21.1
75	23.9
80	26.7
85	29.4
90	32.2
95	35.0
100	37.8

WEIGHT

Kilograms/Pounds

kg to lb	lb to kg
1 = 2.2	1 = 0.45
2 = 4.4	2 = 0.91
3 = 6.6	3 = 1.4
4 = 8.8	4 = 1.8
5 = 11.0	5 = 2.3
6 = 13.2	6 = 2.7
7 = 15.4	7 = 3.2
8 = 17.6	8 = 3.6

Grams/Ounces

g to oz	oz to g
1 = 0.04	1 = 28
2 = 0.07	2 = 57
3 = 0.11	3 = 85
4 = 0.14	4 = 114
5 = 0.18	5 = 142
6 = 0.21	6 = 170
7 = 0.25	7 = 199
8 = 0.28	8 = 227

LIQUID VOLUME

Liters/U.S. Gallons

L to gal	gal to L
1 = 0.26	1 = 3.8
2 = 0.53	2 = 7.6
3 = 0.79	3 = 11.4
4 = 1.1	4 = 15.1

Liters/U.S. Gallons

L to gal	gal to L
5 = 1.3	5 = 18.9
6 = 1.6	6 = 22.7
7 = 1.8	7 = 26.5
8 = 2.1	8 = 30.3

GLOSSARY

Aedicule
Small, classical structure, containing a sacred image, either inside a church or building or standing on its own.

Altar-frontal
Decorative panel covering the front, lower part of an altar.

Altar-piece
Painting or sculpture, placed behind or above an altar

Ambulatory
Open-air walkway flanked by columns or trees; also corridor or passageway in theater, amphitheatre, or catacombs.

Apse
Part of a church at the end of the nave; generally semi-cylindrical in shape, with a semi-spherical roof.

Architrave
Horizontal frame above a door or opening.

Archivolt
Molded architrave carried round an arch

Ashlar
Type of external wall covering, made of protruding, roughly-hewn stones

Barrel vault
Vault which has a rectangular ground-plan and semicircular cross-section.

Bas relief
Type of sculpture (in marble, ivory, bronze or other material) where the carved figures stand out on a flat background to a lesser extent than in a high-relief

Candelabra
Bas relief or painting consisting of fruit, flowers, leaves, or other decorative motifs, used to ornament columns, vaults, walls, etc.

Capital
Part which links a column to the structure above. In classical architecture, capitals were Doric, Ionian, or Corinthian.

Cartoon
Full-size, preparatory drawing for a painting, fresco or tapestry

Choir
Area for choir members, either in front of or behind the high altar in a church presbytery.

Ciborium
Square structure with four columns supporting an overhead cover; usually containing an altar or tomb; or

casket or tabernacle containing the host.

Comacine masters
Skilled Lombard stone-masons

Counter-facade
Internal wall of the facade of a building

Cross vault
Vault consisting of two intersecting barrel vaults, with a square ground-plan

Depressed Arch
Arch where the curved part consists of a short segment of a circumference

Drum
Part of a cupola, with vertical walls, which the dome extends from.

Greek cross
Cross with arms of equal length

High relief
Type of sculpture where the carved figures protrude substantially from the flat background

Hypogeum
Subterranean excavation for burial of the dead (usually Etruscan)

Krater
Ancient Greek and Roman mixing bowl, conical in shape with rounded base.

Lacunar ceiling
Ceiling decorated with symmetrically-arranged, embedded panels, usually made of richly-ornamented stucco or wood.

Lantern
Topmost part of a cupola, either open or with windows, to allow light inside. It generally resembles a circular temple.

Latin cross
Cross with a long vertical arm

Lavabo
Hand-basin usually outside a refectory or sacristy.

Lunette
Semi-circular space on a wall, vault or ceiling, often decorated with a painting or relief.

Oeil-de-boeuf
Small, round or oval window

Oratory
Place of worship, reserved for certain people or communities

Pediment
Structure crowning the facade of a building, usually triangular in shape.

Pendentive
Concave surface between arches beneath a dome

Polyptych
Altar-piece consisting of a number of panels. A diptych has two panels; a triptych has three.

Predella
Small painting or panel, usually in sections, attached below a large altar-piece Presbytery
Part of a church where the main altar is situated; generally raised or separated from the rest of the nave by a balustrade or such like.

Pronaos
Front part or entrance area to a building, with columns.

Putto
Figure of a child sculpted or painted; usually nude

Sacristy
Part of church where furnishings and vestments are kept, and where clergy prepare for services.

Splayed portal
Portal set into diagonally-sloped wall facings

Stall
Wide, wooden seat with arm-rests and back, placed in a row with others.

Stoup
Vessel for holy water, generally placed near church entrance

Tabernacle
Aedicule or niche containing sacred image, inside or outside a church, or standing on its own; also a small, enclosed aedicule placed on the altar, containing the host.

Tondo
Round painting or bas relief

Transept
Area perpendicular to the nave, often extending out at the sides and giving the building a cross-shaped ground-plan.

Tribune
Area including the presbytery, choir and apse, in early-Christian basilicas; in churches generally, any loggia set into or protruding from the walls.

Triptych
see Polyptych

PICTURE CREDITS

Aboca Museum, p. 107
S. Amantini p. 54a
G. Andreini p. 39, 43, 50a, 54b, 121
Archivio Alinari p. 6, 31, 33, 34a, 34b, 39a
Archivio Fotografico della Soprintendenza ai Beni Archeologici della Toscana p. 50b, 98
Archivio Fotografico Touring Club Italiano p. 4, 5
Archivio Teatro e Enti Musicali p. 176
E. Caracciolo p. 112, 113, 114, 116b
G. Carfagna p. 38, 51, 53
E. Carli p. 42, 178, 184, 190

O. Chiaradia p. 161
Foto Sprint p. 89
M. Fraschetti p. 71
D. Grimoldi p. 63
S. Galeotti p. 173
G. Ielardi p. 49
M. Mairani p. 44
Museo di storia della fotografia Fratelli Alinari p. 108
Museo Doccia Richard Ginori p. 110
Museo Ferragamo, 109
Museo Piaggio Giovanni Alberto p. 111
R. Palese p. 103
G. Rodante p. 191

Sole di Vetro p. 151, 155
F. Soletti p. 101, 130
G. Sosio p. 7, 8, 12, 15, 21, 25, 26, 35, 40, 48, 55, 56, 59, 62, 81, 92, 104, 106, 115, 116a, 122, 125, 131, 134, 135, 137, 143, 147, 149, 159, 162, 165, 171, 180, 193

Drawings by Antonello and Chiara Vincenti

Illustrations on pages 18-19, 36-37 and 77 by Giorgio Pomella

Some owners of photographic copyright have been impossible to trace; they are invited to contact the publisher

PODERE MASSA VECCHIA

A vacationing paradise in Tuscany, for people who look for a welcoming and informal atmosphere, for a personalized vacation, away from mass tourism. Peaceful and well-kept Podere Massa Vecchia is the perfect setting and the ideal starting point for a well-planned vacation. We'll be glad to have you as our guests and pamper you.

Albergo Podere
Massa Vecchia - Località Massa Vecchia - 58024 Massa Marittima (GR)
Tel. 0566.903885 - Fax 0566.901838 - E-mail: info@massavecchia.it

---

The hotel is situated in the historic centre of Siena, approximately 500 metres from the Duomo and Piazza del Campo, in a quiet area with a wonderful panorama easily reached by way of the city gate, Porta S. Marco. There is ample private parking space (also for coaches) and garage accomodation; which enables clients to leave their car behind and explore the city on foot.

HOTEL SERVICES

- 100 Rooms (90 doubles, 9 singles, 1 suite)
- Safe Deposit Box
- TV - Sat
- Room Service
- Bar
- Hair-Dryer
- Restaurant

- Direct Dial Telephone
- Laundry Service
- Conference Rooms
- Frigo - Bar
- Air Conditioning
- Suitable for Disable People
- Panoramic Terrace

Via P.Mascagni 55 - 53100 Siena
Tel. 0577 286313 - Fax 0577 48153
www.hotelathena.com / www.hotelathena.net
email@hotelathena.com
For informations: e-mail: info@hotelathena.com

ANTICA TORRE
di Via TORNABUONI n. 1

Via Tornabuoni,1 - 50123 - Firenze
Tel. +39 055 2658161 / Fax +39 055 218841
E-mail address: info@tornabuoni1.com
Web site: www.tornabuoni1.com

The Antica Torre di Via Tornabuoni is located in a historical building, in Via Tornabuoni, close to Ponte Vecchio and only a few steps away from all major historic sites of the city center. At the top floor of the medieval Tower (where our b&b is located) there is a very large terrace offering a breathtaking 360° view all around Florence and its surrounding hills. Breakfast is served in this terrace during spring and summer. Antica Torre di Via Tornabuoni has 12 beautiful, spacious and elegantly furnished rooms with all facilities (like tv, telephone, minibar, safe, hairdryer in the private bathroom, air conditioning or heating) and all with a lovely view, some of them with a private balcony. Our rates range from 180 to 350 euro per room per night, (depending on the season and on the kind of the room, standard or superior); breakfast and all taxes are included. Anyway, we can offer different rates on a particular request, depending on the season and on the number of rooms. The reception is open from 8.30 a.m. to 8 p.m. Please do not hesitate to contact us for any additional information you may need.

HOTEL CASCI ★ ★

This small hotel is very centrally located in a fifteenth century palace and boasts some original fresco ceilings. Its location is one of its main features, only 150 yards from Florence Cathedral and 500 yards from the main Railway station, close to all museum and monuments. However, it can easily be reached by car, too, and the garage is only 200 yards away. All rooms are quiet and have private facilities, direct dialling telephone, radio, color TV (CNN and BBC World), hair-dryer, air conditioning, refrigerator and individual safety box. Buffet-breakfast is served in a fre-scoed room. Free internet access in the hotel's coffee-shop and same day laundry service are at guests' disposal.

member of
family hotels and restaurants

Via Cavour, 13 - 50129 Firenze - Tel. +39 055 211686 - Fax +39 055 2396461
E-mail: info@hotelcasci.com - www.hotelcasci.com

Taking the narrow streets of the historic centre, you can easily reach the piazzetta at the back of the hotel and admire the elegant proportions of the sixteenth century town hall building which is situated next to the hotel, it is pleasantly interrupted by the sounds of this ancient village.
The main entrance of the hotel invites you to plunge into the comfort and relaxation it offers.

HOTEL LOGGE DEI MERCANTI
Corso Sangallo, 40/42 - Monte San Savino (AR) Italy
Tel. +39 0575 810710 - Fax +39 0575 849657
E-mail: info@loggedeimercanti.it
Sito: www.loggedeimercanti.it

Terme Salute e Ambiente S.p.A.

The first informations about "Bagni di Petriolo" go back to the XIII century. In 1404 was built the boundary wall of the Petriolo spa: The only one exemple of it, that it is possible to see today also, is the Tower of the Sienese Republic. In 1907 Petriolo was alredy in the official list of the Italy' mineral waters that it was published by the Ministry of Internal Affairs. Today the old and narrow building is replaced by a modern thermal factory.

**Località Bagni di Petriolo - 53015 Monticiano (Siena)
Tel: (+39) 0577/757104 - Fax : (+39) 0577/757092
info@termesaluteambiente.com
www.termesaluteambiente.com**

— Bagni di Lucca —

*An alternative to the usual holiday,
with Nature playing the leading role in a
land rich in history and culture.
Enjoy the mountains, the forests, the plants
and wildlife, the unique colours of Tuscany's landscapes.
Terme di Bagni di Lucca,
where holidays are lived to the full*

tel. 0583 - 86034/87221 - fax. 0583 - 808700/808224
www.termebagnidilucca.it
e-mail: anticoalbergo@termebagnidilucca.it

ANTICO ALBERGO TERME
★ ★ ★

𝓕attoria 𝓜ontalbano

**Loc. Montalbano, 112, I - 50060 Donnini - Reggello (Firenze)
Tel. 055 8652158 - Fax 055 8652285 - GSM 335 6678844
E-mail: info@montalbano.it - www.montalbano.it**

*The Fattoria Montalbano is located in the municipality of Reggello, just 27 km from Florence and convenient to the beautiful artistic cities of Tuscany and is open all the year round. Three great vineyards combine their resources to make the superb "Chianti D.O.C.G. Fattoria Montalbano" and "Il Buio": a great red, pure Sangiovese aged in barriques and produced only in the best vintages. The GRAPPA: full-bodied and silky, obtained by distilling our own fermented marc of Chianti grapes. The VIN SANTO: the quintessential sweet wine from the Tuscan countryside. The surrounding landscape is characterised by the "ledges" (ancient terraces, hand-carved into the land and sustained by stone walls) planted with olives groves, which give us our exquisite EXTRA VIRGIN OLIVE OIL. We can provide comfortable accommodation to our guests in apartments sleeping 2 to 6. Although recently renovated, our flats have maintained the charming feel of the old Tuscan country homes. All of our apartments have a kitchen, television, independent entrance, and terrace or garden furnished with a table, chairs, and chaise lounges for sunbathing. The flats each have an individual thermostat for winter comfort. Swimmingpool.
All of our guests at the Fattoria can take part in cooking courses in Tuscan and vegetarian cuisine, held in the spacious kitchen of the main house.*